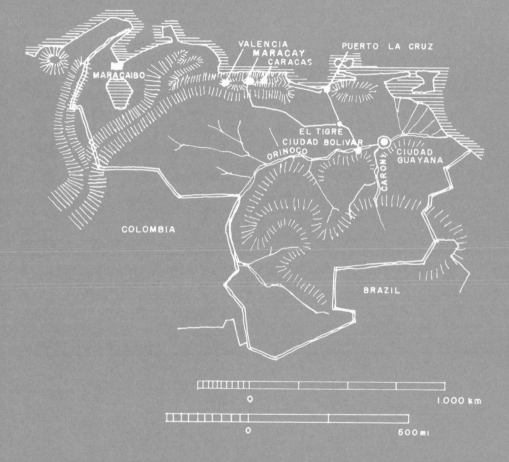

VENEZUELA

VALENCIA
MARACAY
CARACAS

PUERTO LA CRUZ

MARACAIBO

EL TIGRE
CIUDAD BOLIVAR
ORINOCO

CIUDAD
GUAYANA

CARONI

COLOMBIA

BRAZIL

0   1.000 km

0   500 mi

Planning Urban Growth and Regional Development: The Experience of the Guayana Program of Venezuela

A Publication of the Joint Center for Urban Studies of
the Massachusetts Institute of Technology and Harvard University

This book is one of a series published under the auspices of the Joint Center for Urban Studies, a cooperative venture of the Massachusetts Institute of Technology and Harvard University. The Joint Center was founded in 1959 to organize and encourage research on urban and regional problems. Participants have included scholars from the fields of anthropology, architecture, business, city planning, economics, education, engineering, history, law, philosophy, political science, and sociology.

The findings and conclusions of this book are, as with all Joint Center publications, solely the responsibility of the author.

Other books published in the Joint Center series include:

Harvard University Press

The Intellectual Versus the City: From Thomas Jefferson to Frank Lloyd Wright, Morton and Lucia White, 1962.

Streetcar Suburbs, Sam B. Warner, Jr., 1962.

City Politics, Edward C. Banfield and James Q. Wilson, 1963.

Law and Land: Anglo-American Planning Practice, Charles Haar, 1964.

Location and Land Use, William Alonso, 1964.

Poverty and Progress, Stephan Thernstrom, 1964.

Boston: The Job Ahead, Martin Meyerson and Edward C. Banfield, 1966.

The Myth and Reality of Our Urban Problems, Raymond Vernon, 1966.

Muslim Cities in the Later Middle Ages, Ira Marvin Lapidus, 1967.

The Fragmented Metropolis: Los Angeles, 1850–1930, Robert M. Fogelson, 1967.

Law and Equal Opportunity: A Study of the Massachusetts Commission Against Discrimination, Leon H. Mayhew, 1968.

Varieties of Police Behavior: The Management of Law and Order in Eight Communities, James Q. Wilson, 1968.

The Metropolitan Enigma: Inquiries into the Nature and Dimensions of America's "Urban Crisis," James Q. Wilson, 1968.

The MIT Press

The Image of the City, Kevin Lynch, 1960.

Housing and Economic Progress: A Study of the Housing Experiences of Boston's Middle-Income Families, Lloyd Rodwin, 1961.

The Historian and the City, John E. Burchard and Oscar Handlin, editors, 1963.

Beyond the Melting Pot: The Negroes, Puerto Ricans, Jews, Italians, and Irish of New York City, Nathan Glazer and Daniel P. Moynihan, 1963.

The Future of Old Neighborhoods: Rebuilding for a Changing Population, Bernard J. Frieden, 1964.

Man's Struggle for Shelter in an Urbanizing World, Charles Abrams, 1964.

The Federal Bulldozer: A Critical Analysis of Urban Renewal, 1949–1962, Martin Anderson, 1964.

The View from the Road, Donald Appleyard, Kevin Lynch, and John R. Meyer, 1964.

The Public Library and the City, Ralph W. Conant, 1965.

Urban Renewal: The Record and the Controversy, James Q. Wilson, editor, 1966.

Regional Development Policy: A Case Study of Venezuela, John Friedmann, 1966.

Transport Technology for Developing Regions: A Study of Road Transportation in Venezuela, Richard M. Soberman, 1966.

Computer Methods in the Analysis of Large-Scale Social Systems, James M. Beshers, editor, 1968.

Planning Urban Growth and Regional Development: The Experience of the Guayana Program of Venezuela, Lloyd Rodwin and Associates, 1969.

Planning Urban Growth and Regional Development: The Experience of the Guayana Program of Venezuela

by Lloyd Rodwin and Associates

The MIT Press
Massachusetts Institute of Technology
Cambridge, Massachusetts, and London, England

To the people of Venezuela.

Foreword

In 1961 the Joint Center for Urban Studies of M.I.T. and Harvard was given a unique opportunity to participate in the planning of a new city in the interior of Venezuela at the confluence of the Orinoco and Caroní rivers. The city, Ciudad Guayana, was being developed by the Corporación Venezolana de Guayana (CVG), a semiautonomous Venezuelan government agency charged with exploiting the great natural resources of the region—principally hydroelectric power and iron ore. The administration of President Rómulo Betancourt decided not only to take advantage of these resources but in addition to provide coordinated development for the entire region around the new city so as to ensure balanced industrial growth and, above all, the creation of a metropolis that would preserve the natural beauties of the site, supply the facilities for sound community life, and minimize the hardships that inevitably attend rapid population growth in a developing country.

For five years a group of physical planners, economists, urban designers, lawyers, anthropologists, and others recruited by the Joint Center worked as colleagues of the CVG's professional staff in meeting emergencies, assessing alternative strategies, and formulating goals and priorities. The Guayana project staff of the Joint Center was supplemented during the summers and at other times with faculty and students from M.I.T., Harvard, and elsewhere. These scholars had the task of providing advice and assistance to the project on matters of special importance and were also expected to carry out studies that would contribute to our understanding of the fundamental problems of urban and regional growth, and of the ways in which planners can and cannot cope with those problems and assist persons undertaking regional development programs elsewhere. The hope was that the Joint Center could serve not only its client but the teaching and research interests of its two parent universities as well.

Whatever success we had in meeting these dual—and occasionally conflicting—objectives was due in no small part to the imagination, competence, and forbearance of the CVG and especially of its President, General Rafael Alfonzo Ravard. The work of the Joint Center in the Guayana was paid for entirely by funds of the Venezuelan government. The CVG allowed the Joint Center to set aside, out of its budget for this project, a special budget to finance scholarly studies of the project, even though some of these studies were primarily of intellectual interest to the Joint Center rather than of practical value to the CVG. We wish to record our gratitude to the CVG and to the Venezuelan government for not only permitting, but also encouraging, this experiment in combining the functions of adviser and scholar.

This book is one of a series written by men and women who participated in the Guayana project. The series is not intended to be a history of the project or a record of the decisions made there. Each volume is a separate monograph on a subject of intrinsic intellectual interest, written for other scholars and practitioners working in similar fields, and published because it meets the normal requirements of scholarship by which the Joint Center and the M.I.T. Press judge all their manuscripts. What these books have in common is that, whatever their subject, the data were drawn in whole or in part from the Venezuela project. The first volume in this series was *Regional Development Policy: A Case Study of Venezuela*, by John Friedmann. The second was *Transport Technology for Developing Regions: A Study of Road Transportation in Venezuela*, by Richard M. Soberman.

This volume, edited by Lloyd Rodwin (who had general responsibility for the direction of the Guayana project, as well as serving as Chairman of the Faculty Committee of the Joint Center), is intended to give the general reader a critical overview of all aspects of the project. However, it examines a number of problems, ideas, and experiences that are not dealt with in the other volumes. It places special emphasis on the problems and on what was learned from the enterprise. The book has been reviewed by both the CVG and the Joint Center, but the contents are entirely the responsiblity of the authors, who were free to accept or reject any of the suggestions made to them by the CVG or the Joint Center.

Subsequent books in this series will include studies of migration to the region, urban design, economic planning and programming, education in a developing country, and other subjects.

DANIEL P. MOYNIHAN
Director, Joint Center for Urban Studies

LLOYD RODWIN
Chairman of the Faculty Committee
Joint Center for Urban Studies

Contents

Tables

Illustrations

Introduction

Lloyd Rodwin

I first met Colonel Rafael Alfonzo Ravard—later to become General Alfonzo Ravard—President of the Corporación Venezolana de Guayana (CVG), while working on a consulting assignment with Dirección d'Urbanismo in Venezuela in 1959. We got off somehow on a discussion of the nature of planning, and our half-hour meeting lasted more than three hours. Colonel Alfonzo mentioned the possibility of developing some more extended professional association—and then pressed me to visit the Guayana region. He emphasized that the occasion was unique. The CVG had a private plane. Adlai Stevenson and his party were visiting the region; so were some key members of President Betancourt's cabinet. This, plus my somewhat romantic association of Guayana with *Green Mansions* and Eldorado, overcame my distaste for flying and tempted me to look around a bit and see what the Colonel and his associates were up to.

It is still easy for me to drift into a reverie—absorbed by those vivid first impressions of the vast expanses of savanna and forest, the fabulous iron-ore mountain (Cerro Bolívar), the Caroní Falls, almost terrifying at floodtime, the motorboat trip on the Orinoco at sunset, the noisy good-natured hustle and activity at the makeshift port, the teeming squatter settlements, and the discomfort and fatigue as well as the gusto and lure of the frontier. There was also something more: the handsome hydro-electric facilities and the elegant, still unfinished steel plant, conventional but still powerful symbols of big dreams. I felt then and there that this was really the sort of enterprise to which the Joint Center could and ought to make a major contribution. I shared these thoughts with Colonel

1

Alfonzo and some members of the cabinet whom I knew. They were more than interested: this, after all, was their intent.

I suggested that the Joint Center might organize a team that—together with a group of Venezuelan associates—might work out some strategies for attacking the problems of urban and regional development in the Guayana. The team could be backed up by specialists in planning, architecture, law, economics, sociology, public administration, civil engineering, and other relevant disciplines at both universities. But I knew that this proposal was not likely to pass muster in Cambridge unless the Joint Center could also carry out a program of research on many aspects of these activities. I asked whether the Colonel and his associates would support such a research effort. The answer was: Yes!

I reported these discussions to my colleagues in Cambridge. At the outset they were frankly skeptical. They doubted whether the Colonel fully appreciated the implications. The only way to find out, of course, was to frame a specific proposal incorporating all of the relevant terms. I then returned to Venezuela with my colleague Martin Meyerson (then Director of the Joint Center) for more detailed discussions. There were modifications of details, but the essential principles were not altered in the slightest. Both of us returned to Cambridge enthusiastic about this challenging enterprise. But now that agreement appeared so imminent, there were new objections. The Venezuelan government seemed shaky. Acts of terrorism occurred fairly frequently. Some university officials feared that our two institutions might be accused of practicing a new and insidious form of "Yankee imperialism." The task of recruitment and administration was apt to be formidable. Was this operation perhaps more appropriate for a consulting firm than for a university? Why divert resources abroad when they were needed so much at home?

The questions were not unreasonable. The venture would be a major step in the career of the Joint Center, and a decision of this nature had to be weighed carefully. But the arguments in favor of undertaking the assignment were persuasive. The Joint Center was being invited to participate on exceptional terms. This collaborative effort offered opportunities for conducting useful and woefully neglected research on problems that were relevant to the needs of many other developing countries. No one doubted that risks were involved in working in Venezuela at this time, but surely the Joint Center and similar organizations were not going to restrict their operations to "safe" areas. What better or more effective contribution could the Joint Center make in its international activities than to take on this challenge? It was true that an effort abroad entailed some diversion of resources, but such an effort would be only part of the total program of the Joint Center. Besides, no equally imaginative client had appeared on the American scene to take advantage of the Joint Center's resources, so that at the moment we were not slighting Peter to help Paul.

There were some strong reasons for both parties to want this agreement. The Venezuelans needed technical assistance. They valued the technical skills and prestige of the American specialists at both universities. The effort was clearly experimental and would not be conducted on a profit-making basis. They knew a little about the individuals with whom they would be dealing. They got along easily with them.

The Joint Center was equally self-interested. The directors sought a theater for their activities. There were opportunities elsewhere, but the limited resources meant that only one major operation could be mounted. True, it was bruited about that Venezuelans suffered from xenophobia. Certainly the political situation there left much to be desired, and the breakdown of relationships between the government and the Universidad Central de Venezuela aroused concern. So did the terrorism. There were bound to be other serious problems, gulfs in understanding, and differences in basic views. But one could exaggerate these difficulties. After all, "If hopes are dupes, fears may be liars." There were also positive elements in the ledger. Most important perhaps was the fact that the Venezuelans in charge appeared capable and interested in an ambitious effort. The Joint Center representatives were able to speak easily and frankly to them about what the Center could and could not do. Information gleaned from contacts among a wide range of political groups assured the Joint Center representatives that the effort was a significant one and might even succeed. Eventually, therefore—and after much soul searching—the Joint Center and the administrative authorities at both universities endorsed the proposed agreement, albeit not without some misgivings. The Venezuelans, too, however much they may have quailed at some of the prospects, also decided to follow through on the arrangements.

In general, the association turned out to be a successful one on the most important matters. The first contract, which was for a period of three years, provided for renegotiation of the financial terms, if this proved necessary. Changes were necessary, and the terms were rewritten after the first year or so, without difficulty. At the end of the three-year period the contract was extended for another two years, with the understanding that the general contract would be terminated at the end of this period, although arrangements might be worked out for the extension of certain special services. At the end of the fifth year, the Joint Center ended its participation in the program, but special arrangements were worked out for assistance on the educational program with the Center for Studies in Education and Development of Harvard University.

During this five-year period, there were on occasion serious disagreements between the Venezuelans and the Joint Center staff. That such disagreements should arise was hardly surprising, given the differences in the backgrounds, interests, and aims of the participants. Some of these differences are touched on in this volume.[1] Despite the differences, however, the group did manage to collaborate successfully for the entire period; and this accomplishment perhaps ought to be considered as important as any of the technical achievements of the two staffs.

The chapters that follow telescope from many vantage points the experiences of the Guayana project. In these pages the reader can glimpse at what happened there over a period of five years. He can also get a sense of the subject matter and the methods that form the substance of contemporary regional planning and of the diverse professional skills needed to come to grips with these problems.

The book has four parts. The first starts with a brief perspective of the entire Guayana experience. Subsequent chapters in this section deal with the regional, economic, social, and design aspects of this enterprise. They sum up the initial diagnoses, the general policies, the major problems encountered, and some suggestions, based on hindsight, on how performance could have been improved. Part 2 explores the main issues that arose in the process of carrying out the urban development program in different sectors. These chapters focus on the promotion of economic activity, urban transportation, and strategies for the development of land, the business center, housing, and education and for the resolution of legal issues. They show how confrontation with the problems in the field modified the views of the staff of the CVG and the Joint Center. Part 3 scrutinizes some of the methods and goals: for example, the effectiveness of the administrative style, the role of models to gain the help of the computer in making the plans more consistent and flexible, and the leads furnished by surveys and other techniques to evaluate the way Ciudad Guayana was used and viewed by its inhabitants. Still other chapters discuss some unresolved problems that worried the staff and the leadership of the CVG or the Joint Center. The main issues examined are how to measure and improve the efficiency of resource allocation, particularly for urban development; the goals, the priorities, and the incidence of benefits and costs of various investment choices; the special requirements of the poorer families, especially the households without male heads; and the varying attitudes and points of view found in Caracas and Ciudad Guayana. The final chapter (Part 4) reviews some of the problems associated with collaborative planning as practiced by the CVG and the Joint Center. It also draws some inferences about styles of planning based on the methods and goals that guided the development of the Guayana region.

Even though this book is rather long, some topics are dealt with summarily, and there are some gaps and a few differences of opinion that I have chosen deliberately not to edit away. The constraints are inescapable, and the differences of opinion are an essential part of this experience. No complex set of activities extending over a period of five years can be described fully or even consistently in a single volume, even—or especially—if many of the writers were also participants.

Another problem inherent in the preparation of this book was to achieve some focus or common denominator. No collection of papers can have the cohesive, synoptic perspective of a book written by a single author. This volume is no exception. Nonetheless certain features compensate for some of the usual deficiencies. All of the writers deal with the problems of making plans for a resource development region by a public development agency with which the writers were associated either as participants or as research specialists. Each author focuses on the aspect of the program with which he was personally concerned. Almost all of the papers have one other common denominator. Each writer was asked to describe not only what was done and why but also the problems and the errors as they appeared to him or her and the lessons drawn from this experience. This is not easy to do, especially for participants, and we have probably not been altogether successful in our efforts. It might have been wiser—certainly safer—not to testify against ourselves. But we felt it was important to assess these experiences as honestly as we could if all of us were to do our jobs better in the future.

Part I
General
Perspectives,
Diagnosis,
and Policies

Chapter 1

Planning Guayana: A General Perspective

Lloyd Rodwin

The opportunity to make plans for a region and to build a city from the ground up may seem the answer to a planner's dream. It appears to offer a chance for maximum freedom and scope in design without the necessity of having to cope with outmoded existing development, entrenched property interests, and recalcitrant attitudes of the inhabitants. Actually, as experienced planners know, such an enterprise begins with severe handicaps. It lacks at the outset the basic foundations needed for urban and regional development: a trained force of technicians and workers, established community relations and loyalties, consumer and business services, community facilities—in short, the germinal conditions for the support and growth of the urban organism. To prepare sound plans takes time. If, as sometimes happens, work is already under way or must begin immediately, skilled specialists must be imported, housing and schools built, water and electricity supplied, and transportation provided long before the plans are completed. Attracted by the prospects of jobs, poor migrants invade the area, put up makeshift shelters, and complicate the problem of organizing land uses and public services. Most costs tend to be high, almost no amenities exist, and living conditions are bleak. Understandably enough, the inhabitants become impatient with "fancy" long-range plans and delays; they grumble about the neglect of their immediate needs; and they care little if those needs do not fit the priorities or the plans. Up to a point their views can be slighted or ignored, but this is always dangerous. It is hardly surprising that the new city rarely measures up to the the original dreams of its planners.

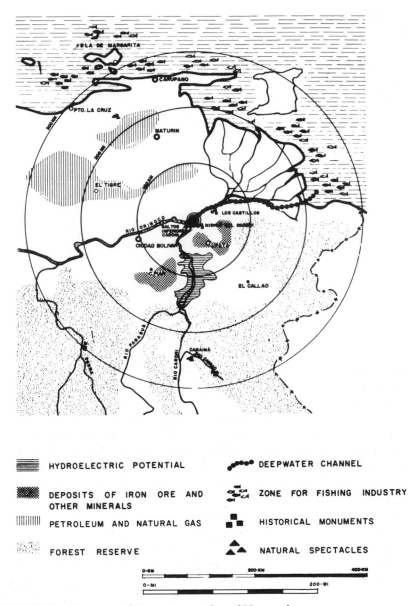

FIGURE 1.1 Resources of the eastern region of Venezuela.

Nevertheless, there are several reasons why planning in these circumstances is still an exciting challenge. It can reinforce national policies for economic growth, help transform backward regions, and relieve the pressures on other cities. It may even—under special and very limited circumstances—afford opportunities for boldness, imagination, and innovation in urban design on a scale rarely possible elsewhere. Ciudad Guayana well exemplifies these problems and opportunities.

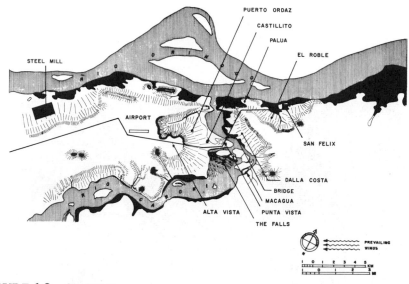

FIGURE 1.2   Ciudad Guayana.

At first blush, the lower Orinoco Valley of southeastern Venezuela would hardly appear to be an inviting place for urban and regional development. Isolated (it is 300 miles from Caracas, the capital city), tropical in climate, and generally poor in agricultural potential, the region is dominated by vast expanses of savanna and tropical forest broken only by treacherous rivers and low mountain ranges. Sporadic discoveries of diamonds, however, combined with memories of gold mining in the nineteenth century, have created the myth of fabulous riches awaiting the adventurous that the "Guayana" still suggests to most Venezuelans. As a result of the myth the region has the allure of Eldorado for those within it as well as those outside.

The region does have extraordinary resources. (See Figure 1.1.) There are rich deposits of high-grade iron ore and promising possibilities for the mining of manganese, nickel, chromium, gold, industrial diamonds, and perhaps bauxite and aluminum laterite; and within sixty miles of Ciudad Guayana there are large fields of petroleum and natural gas. The settlement is on the banks of the Orinoco River, which provides direct access to the ocean. Running through the heart of the city is a branch of the Orinoco, the Caroní River, which has a hydroelectric potential of about ten million kilowatts. With an abundance of potential power, water, timber, and iron ore, Ciudad Guayana is admirably equipped to be a center of industry.

As recently as 1950 the population of the area was only 4,000. Then two U.S.-owned organizations, the Orinoco Mining Company and the Iron Mines Company, built plants in the Guayana for iron-ore processing and created small settlements for their staffs. Later the Venezuelan government

FIGURE 1.3   Aerial view of Ciudad Guayana, 1965.

began the construction of a large steel mill on the Orinoco a few miles west of these centers. In 1960 President Betancourt's administration, recognizing the potential of the Guayana region, created a public corporation to develop it. This agency, the Corporación Venezolana de Guayana (CVG), was entrusted with the job of devising a strategy for the development of the region. The Corporation took over the steel mill, which was still under construction, and the Macagua Dam at the Caroní River Falls. (There are photographs of these facilities at the end of this chapter, as well as views of some of the major areas of the city.) The Corporation also took on the job of planning the growth of the city. It acquired much of the land within the prospective city area, through purchase from private owners and through transfer of public lands from other government agencies. The powers of the Corporation, however, were limited by the activities and jurisdiction of other agencies. Its capacity to act was also handicapped by shortages of skilled staff. To help overcome this limitation the CVG in 1961 engaged the assistance of the Joint Center for Urban Studies of the Massachusetts Institute of Technology and Harvard University.

The site confronting the planners was an area some fifteen miles long on the south side of the Orinoco. (See Figure 1.2.) The terrain was vast and in some respects spectacular. It was dominated by the broad Orinoco, the falls of the Caroní, and the heights above both rivers. Scattered over this area were several disconnected settlements. At the western end was the steel mill, at the eastern end a community called San Félix. Between them were a mining town called Puerto Ordaz, built by the Orinoco Mining Company for its staff, another mining settlement called Palúa, and various smaller developments that sprawled along connecting highways. The Caroní River, running north to south, cut the area in two; a bridge across it was under construction. (See Figure 1.3.)

Logically the first task was to study the economic development potential of the city and region and formulate plans that would encourage the appropriate economic activities and related functions. Before this could be done, however, there were pressing immediate problems. Workers looking for jobs in this promising new industrial center were already arriving in large numbers. By 1961 the population in the Guayana area had mushroomed from 4,000 to 42,000; by 1962 it was 50,000. New shantytowns were springing up overnight. There was a clamor for housing, water, sewers, electricity, roads, and schools. Without waiting for the completion of studies or long-range plans the planners had to find and prepare sites for the temporary settlement of newcomers, for low-rent housing, and for industrial plants and had to redesign site plans that had been made earlier and public works that were already under way in order to avoid damage to the long-range interests of the community.

For example, one immediate issue was the new bridge across the Caroní, on which work was already well advanced. It was too late to enlarge the capacity of the bridge, which should have been twice what it was, but the planners won a short delay in construction that enabled them to design separate lanes for bicycles and pedestrians so that they would not be endangered by automobile traffic across the bridge. The local population ardently desired the Caroní Bridge. Since it was destined to be a critical visual element and an important symbol of the future city, the planning staff wanted to make it as meaningful for the residents of Ciudad Guayana as the Ponte Vecchio is for the people of Florence.

The studies for a long-range plan for the city began with a detailed assessment of the role the region would play in the development of the Venezuelan economy. Over the past twenty-five years the country's economy has grown at the impressive rate of 7 per cent a year, thanks largely to the exploitation of its oil resources. To maintain this growth rate and take care of the needs of the expanding population, which is increasing at the rate of 3 per cent a year, it was estimated that Venezuela would probably have to raise its output of goods and services fourfold in the next twenty years. It would be unsound to depend mainly on petroleum, particularly because this resource is bound to decline in the long run. Examination of the country's needs, potentialities, and existing industries led to the conclusion that its industrial development should focus strongly on the production of metals, petrochemicals, and machinery. Existing Venezuelan industries, which are largely final-assembly activities, require these basic and intermediate products. Their production would not only fill gaps in the domestic economy but also provide Venezuela with export goods for trade with other Latin American countries and the rest of the world. The studies suggested that the country should give high priority specifically to the production of iron and steel, sponge iron, aluminum, other metals and metal products, heavy machinery, electrochemicals, and forest products such as pulp and paper.

Analysis of location, cost, and other factors indicated that if these activities were located in the Guayana region they would enjoy a comparative advantage and could compete successfully in foreign markets. On the basis of the many factors involved, including projections of the future demand and markets for the various products, a comprehensive program for investment in production facilities was worked out. It had two phases:

a program for the period 1963 through 1966 and a follow-up plan for 1967 through 1975. Since Ciudad Guayana is in a food-deficit area, the program included proposals for increasing the production of food, particularly in the area of the Orinoco Delta.

Venezuela incorporated this program in its national plan. It projected a total investment of some $3.8 billion in the Guayana region between 1965 and 1975. Of this the Venezuelan national government itself will provide more than $500 million during the 1965–1968 period and about $1.5 billion during 1969–1975. (This amounts to roughly 10 per cent of the total Venezuelan public investment in both periods.) The rest is expected to come from private capital (domestic and foreign) and from loans by international agencies. As a result of these investments it is hoped that by 1975 the Guayana region will provide about a fifth of Venezuela's total manufacturing and export products.

The economic analysis yielded the first approximations of the prospects for Ciudad Guayana. Corrections will of course be necessary when better data become available and if some of the assumptions turn out to be erroneous. This is an inescapable hazard of planning for the future; fortunately the high-speed computer will at least speed up the chores of calculation. Meanwhile, on the basis of these projections, the planning staff worked out the implications for employment and population characteristics. The indications were that the city would have a population of 115,000 by 1966 and of 415,000 by 1975. (These estimates were later changed to 90,000 by 1966 and 221,000 by 1975.) A rapidly growing city of this size would present social problems of major dimensions. Aware of this, the planners had already instituted several studies of the human side of the equation.

One study, conducted by a social anthropologist, collected basic information about the composition of the population moving into the city, their ways of life, and their responses to the changes going on around them. Another social project was a pilot program to help the inmigrants build their own housing. Other investigations looked into the questions of health, nutrition, and family spending patterns. Still others surveyed migration characteristics, the attitudes of the people toward authority and change, and the relative importance they attached to various public services and physical improvements. One of these inquiries, made for the first time in such a situation, was a survey of how people of different backgrounds perceived and rated the importance of particular features of the physical environment.

These investigations proved helpful in several ways. They indicated the need for communication and for a full explanation of the development program to the people of the community; they highlighted apparent conflicts between the immediate concerns of the residents and the long-range aims of the planners; they pointed up the importance of community participation in planning decisions; above all, they sensitized the planning staff to the extraordinary problems and needs of the lowest income group in the population. For this group it was necessary to work out stable family patterns, find jobs and housing sites, and develop skills and educational opportunities.

While these studies were under way, plans were made for the layout of the city. These had to be versatile enough to ensure the orderly future integration of the scattered settlements and at the same time guide decisions on meeting the immediate needs of the citizens. The primary objective was to create conditions that would foster economic growth. While holding to this main aim, the planners also wished to minimize investment expense, recapture the increments in value resulting from the massive investments of the government, make economical, accessible, and flexible arrangements suited to different stages of the city's growth, maintain a high standard of design that would serve as a model for developments elsewhere and attract enterprising organizations to the Guayana, provide variety and interest in the community's living and social facilities, and take advantage of the normal forces of the market rather than run counter to them.

After much discussion it was decided that first consideration had to be given to housing, education, and the establishments required by the local government. The location of the facilities had to be related, of course, to the principal industrial and business activities of the city. Here four main considerations were involved: the site was large; the location of the steel mill at the western end made that area the principal center for industrial development; a large proportion of the population was already living on the eastern side of the site; and the most beautiful part of the site was in between the industrial area and the population center toward the south along the Caroní River. A basic question was whether the new city should be built around the steel mill. The planners finally decided that for several reasons it would be preferable to form the city by uniting the existing elements. This not only would be less expensive but also would conform to existing growth patterns, provide greater flexibility and security if the projections proved optimistic, and encounter less political opposition.

The spread-out character of the city affected the location of various centers (see Figure 1.4) and presented difficult transportation issues. It

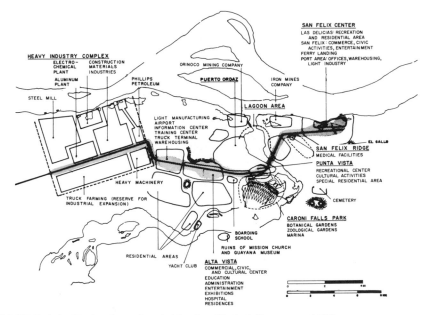

FIGURE 1.4   Early plan of activities for Ciudad Guayana: 1970.

was imperative to reduce the cost and time of travel to the central business district, the civic center, and other areas frequented by most of the population. Because a rapid-transit system would prove too expensive an investment for the postulated size of the city and the travel distances, most of the travel would be by automobile: private cars, taxis, buses, and *por puestos* (jitneys). With the help of a high-speed computer the staff tested a number of possible arrangements. The alternatives included various combinations of possible locations for jobs, homes, and other centers and the different modes of transportation.

For the layout of the city that was selected as optimal from various points of view, it turned out that when the city's population reached 250,000 its people would be spending about 12 to 16 per cent of their disposable income on transportation in the city. This figure is not far from those in relatively comparable cities in the United States: in Los Angeles the average cost is 16 per cent, in Cleveland 14 per cent, and in Chicago 13 per cent. Because incomes in Venezuela are considerably lower than in the United States, however, the travel cost will be a greater burden to the residents of Ciudad Guayana. This burden is inherent in the present low-density settlements and the considerable distance between the industrial areas in the west and the main residential areas in the east. In addition, the facilities will not be used efficiently because of the tidal traffic flows. In view of the constraints, there was probably no feasible or less expensive alternative, but as the residential areas grow

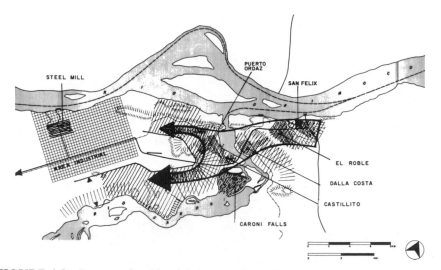

FIGURE 1.5   Pattern of residential growth. To unify development and to take advantage of the existing stock of services and facilities, new residential growth will be encouraged adjacent to existing settlements and in the areas between them. To reduce the distances between residential areas and workplaces, the greatest part of the new growth will be encouraged at the western extreme, or as near to the locations for heavy industry as contiguous development will permit. The new commerical center, located in the west, will help to form a new community there. Residential growth can continue to extend in a westerly direction over time.

westward toward the industrial center in the future (see Figure 1.5) the journey to work and the cost should decline.

When it came to planning the location of industry in Ciudad Guayana, the western part of the site was found to be clearly the best area. The steel mill was already there; there is plenty of suitable land around it for building a large complex of heavy industry; and the site is usually downwind from the rest of the city so that its smoke and odors will be blown away from the residential sections. It also has good access to land and water transportation, and truck traffic generated by the industries can reach domestic markets without passing through the city.

The plan developed for this industrial area contemplated ore-reduction plants, foundries and forges as satellites of the steel mill, and also chemical industries, an aluminum plant, construction materials industries, factories for the manufacture of heavy machinery, and a reserve area that would be used for truck farming until other industries came in. Moreover, the planners made provision for light industries, to be located elsewhere in the city. An area east of the heavy industry complex was reserved for the manufacture of consumer goods; for warehousing, trucking, and transportation; and for commercial facilities around the city's airport. Two other areas destined for light industry are on the eastern side of the Caroní River, close to the old residential settlements.

For the main city center, where the principal business offices and retail establishments will be located, the site selected is an area called Alta Vista. Eventually this area will have maximum accessibility from all parts of the city; its level terrain allows for inexpensive expansion of the business area, and it is bordered on three sides by still undeveloped land that is admirably suited for residential use. If the projected growth and commercial development occur, the Alta Vista center will become an important revenue producer for the city, helping to finance the heavy investment that must be made in the community. To ensure more rapid development in the early stages, however, the planners decided to detach the civic center from the cultural center, with which it had been combined, and to locate it instead at the eastern end of the Alta Vista plateau. This decision was also justified on the grounds that there are important functional ties between government offices, the courts, and the principal business services and establishments. Moreover, at this location the civic center would be visible from a great distance in all directions as a symbol of civic activity.

No less important for the future of the city, in the planners' view, was the building of an attractive cultural center. This is particularly crucial in a new city as an inducement to bring in the enterprising managers, professionals, educators, and other specialists on whom the creation of a vital community depends so heavily. An excellent site for such a center was available. It is an area, called Punta Vista, at an elbow of the Caroní River near its confluence with the Orinoco. Overlooking the Caroní Falls, the site is one of varied terrain and great natural beauty. Within this area space has been assigned for educational and recreational activities. Although some educational facilities may initially be located at Alta Vista, Punta Vista will eventually contain a technical college, a research establishment, a hotel, clubs, a library, a museum, and other institutions. Around the Falls there are to be a large public park, which will contain a boat basin and landing, a botanical garden, a zoological garden, an aviary, and a variety of other facilities. There is also room for an attractive residential settlement to be built next to the park.

Finally, rounding out the list of specialized areas, a medical center is planned at a site on the eastern side of the Caroní near the San Félix settlement. It will include a major hospital, clinics, and allied health services.

Up to this point the plan for Ciudad Guayana consisted of a set of separate centers devoted to specialized land uses. The problem now was to tie them all together—in particular to join up the largest existing settlement, San Félix, with the planned new city centers. (See Figure 1.6.) The element in the plan designed to accomplish this is a major highway

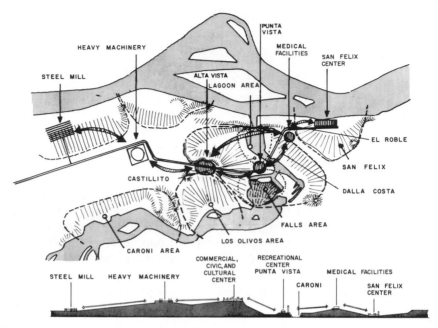

FIGURE 1.6   The linkage of old and new centers.

running from the steel mill at the western end to San Félix in the east. Passing through or close to the other centers along its route, this highway, Avenida Guayana, will link together all the main elements of the city: the area of heavy industry, the airport, the centers of light industry and warehousing, the commercial and civic center, the cultural center, the residential areas, the medical center, and the established San Félix community. It will serve as an artery and a backbone, making the city a unified organism.

The highway provides a special opportunity to give the city character and physical distinction. Starting as a heavy-duty road in the industrial area, it will change into a boulevard as it passes through the business and civic center; then it will sweep down the hill into the cultural center, proceed across the Caroní Bridge, and, as a limited-access highway, go on past residential areas and the medical center and finally enter San Félix as a boulevard. (See Figure 1.7.) To a driver along the highway the trip will present a succession of different experiences composed of the city's natural sights and varied activities. Probably no other physical element will show the city's features as effectively as this highway, and the planners have given special attention to the avenue's physical and visual aspects. In the design of the road they are considering aesthetics as well as efficiency in the location of the activities it will pass, the handling of road alignments, grades and lighting, the landscaping, and the visual impressions and behavior of the people now in Ciudad Guayana.

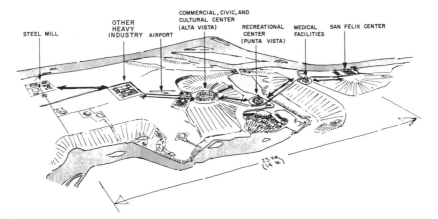

FIGURE 1.7   Avenida Guayana.

Unfortunately shortages of staff precluded the detailed evaluations and revisions that ought to accompany such efforts. Another major problem faced by the designers was how to provide for a pattern of land uses now while simultaneously planning for new uses that will be possible and appropriate in the future. Partly for this reason the staff attempted to develop criteria and methods for handling "high" and "low" control zones, which would allow concentration on visually and functionally significant areas. Design competitions, the awarding of prizes for well-designed areas, the setting up of architectural review committees, and other positive incentives may be established, ranging from general zoning and building regulations to more specific restrictions for key points in the city. In spite of these efforts the odds are that the final results will be far different from the original intent. This is understood by the designers, although they hope that the process will not get out of hand.

The Corporación Venezolana de Guayana was charged with the responsibility not only of planning the city but also of seeing that it was built. First, the general plans had to be translated into specific projects, each with a financial budget and a definite time schedule. In addition to housing, for which there was an immediate need, three projects obviously required high priority. One was the main highway, needed both to establish communication between the developing centers of the city and to encourage the start of new enterprises, particularly in the commercial areas. Another pressing project was the provision of space and facilities for industry. The third, which soon had to be given temporary precedence over the second, was the development of the commercial center. The strategy decided on was to bring in a large department store and a supermarket and to build the headquarters of the Corporation itself, so that these strategic establishments would generate other substantial high-level developments in the area. The original program of building the commercial facilities by 1967 proved to be too leisurely; when it began to look as if key firms would not wait that long but would seek locations elsewhere in the city, the staff recommended that the program for the business center should be speeded up. For many reasons, however, this speedup did not occur, and the prospects for the commercial center have been jeopardized.

Housing became the thorniest of all the problems. The Corporation did not want to get into the housing business; for reasons of protocol and because of its own heavy obligations in many areas, it sought to avoid any tasks that might be handled more effectively by other agencies. The Venezuelan government has a special agency, Banco Obrero, for building low-income housing. In the early years of the program, Banco Obrero could not provide all of the housing needed in Ciudad Guayana, nor could the job be done in time by any other organization. As time went on, however, the capabilities of the organization improved substantially. Meanwhile, the Corporation had to resort to a variety of strategies to get housing built.

To provide mortgage funds the Corporation started a savings and loan association (Asociación Guayanesa de Ahorro y Préstamo—AGAP). It also made arrangements with a private nonprofit organization, the Fundación de la Vivienda Popular (Foundation for Popular Housing), to build 854 houses for middle-income families. The Corporation, in collaboration with the U.S. Agency for International Development (AID), also offered special guarantees to the International Housing Associates, a private building organization, to induce it to build 800 housing units with less expensive foreign capital; unfortunately it took two years to negotiate the final agreement and clear it through the various government agencies, and in the end only 200 units were built. In addition, the Corporation has made land available to private builders at reduced prices, adjusted to the income levels of the people for whom the houses are to be built, and has discussed and is still negotiating various other possible arrangements with builders and industrialists. Notwithstanding all these efforts, the Corporation has found it necessary to build some houses itself, because it had made an agreement with the steelworkers' union to provide a certain number of houses at stipulated price levels by the end of 1965.

In the experimental project of helping low-income families to build their own homes the Corporation provided land, public utilities, schools, loans for construction materials, and technical assistance. Interestingly, it has turned out that the most important factor in inducing these families to build houses to replace their shanties is the construction of streets; so far

FIGURE 1.8   Guri Dam.

the existence of streets has proved a greater inducement than water, sewage facilities, electricity, or schools, apparently because it distinguishes city living from country living.

The Corporation has established the Municipal Housing Foundation (Fundación de la Vivienda del Caroní—Funvica) in Ciudad Guayana to supervise the self-help house-building programs, and it will mount an independent low-income housing program with funds provided by various sources. The Corporation is also studying the use of local building materials and may look into the possibility of financing a plant to produce basic elements for prefabricated houses.

The Corporación Venezolana de Guayana has found it necessary to take an active part in many other phases of the area's physical, economic, and social development. In addition to managing and planning the expansion of the steelworks (through a subsidiary), it is building a new dam at Guri. (See Figure 1.8.) The first stage was to be completed in 1968 and add a capacity of 575,000 kilowatts to the 350,000 kilowatts available from the present Macagua Dam. The Corporation is promoting efforts to attract business enterprises to the city, providing inexpensive sites, conducting preliminary feasibility studies, and helping on occasion to obtain investment capital, tax benefits, customs exemptions, leaseback arrangements for plant and equipment, and in some cases even equity capital. It is assisting the Venezuelan Ministry of Education to set up facilities to train a skilled labor force for the new industries and high-level educational facilities for professional personnel. It is helping the city government to draft a code of ordinances and to train administrators. By 1980, some $400 million will have been invested in the city's structure of public services. This activity is expected to engage nearly 10,000 persons.

A circumstance that calls for special comment is that most of the land on which Ciudad Guayana is being developed is publicly owned—a most unusual situation. To begin with, the Corporation acquired nearly all the land in the area of the future city proper, except for the properties of the Orinoco Mining Company and some other small private holdings in the vicinity of the company's settlement. Altogether it owned about 40 per cent of the land in the Caroní district as a whole. The planners figuratively rubbed their hands with pleasure at the advantages this offered. The Corporation appeared able to shape and control the use of the land for a considerable period into the future: it could reserve areas needed for public purposes, and it could capture for its financing needs a reasonable share of the gains from rising land values as the city developed. The latter benefit is important because in Venezuela, as in most developing countries, local communities do not levy taxes of any consequence on real estate.

These factors did indeed prove to be useful, but they also had some drawbacks. The job of managing the publicly owned land presented a heavy burden to the Corporation, which had its hands full with a host of other problems. The private enterprises coming into the city needed outright ownership of their sites in order to use the land as mortgage security for financing improvements. Moreover, the Corporation realized that the image of Ciudad Guayana as a government-owned city might discourage private investment in the building of housing, commercial enterprises, and industries.

The Corporation decided on a flexible policy. The preponderance of the commercial land and the highly desirable residential and industrial land, which was likely to be most profitable, would be held by the Corporation and made available to the users under leases. Other land, including some commercial sites, would be sold, subject to restrictions on its use and perhaps even on the transfer of title until the completion of the developments. In general, land would be sold only when it was necessary to speed up development, and the Corporation would try to ensure itself a share of the gains in land value by being a partner in the enterprises or by witholding strategically located parcels from sale.

Ciudad Guayana has become a lusty, booming town whose future is still in the balance. Certainly as it grows it will modify the script written by its planners. All in all it is a unique situation: a new city planted by a tour de force in an isolated frontier region by a comparatively wealthy government (thanks to its oil riches) that has donated the land for the enterprise and called in expert assistance from universities in an advanced country. For all its uniqueness, however, the Ciudad Guayana project has some useful lessons to offer on the strategy of urban planning in developing countries.

The Ciudad Guayana enterprise has demonstrated, first of all, the importance of popular and political support for any such project. By remarkable acumen and leadership the Corporación Venezolana de Guayana managed to maintain an impressive reputation and political backing even during the beginning years when there was little to show for the heavy investment and effort. The project itself brought many problems into sharp relief. For example, we do not yet know how to build simple, expandable, and genuinely inexpensive housing quickly, and we still must rely on clumsy, primitive techniques for the analysis and control of land use. The research thus far undertaken on these and similar matters is woefully inadequate. The persistent shortages of staff also made it clear that one of the hardest tasks is to determine not only what must be done but also what problems the policymaker must live with, given the constraints and opportunities. For the same reason it has proved even more difficult to innovate than appeared possible at first. Experiments must be few and critical, and adequate means must be devised for getting feedback from them. On the other hand, the university connections established by the Corporation make it likely that several significant studies will emerge describing what was done.

The unusual collaboration between the Venezuelan corporation and the Joint Center for Urban Studies of M.I.T. and Harvard has itself been an instructive experience. In the approach to the problems of Ciudad Guayana there were not only individual variations in point of view but also more deep-rooted differences in outlook between the Venezuelan experts and their consultants from the United States. Inescapably, conflicts arose in the course of the work. Such conflicts involve more than personalities. Groups of human beings working together develop styles of acting and valuing and conceptions of reality that suit the situations they confront, and these situations vary. The foreign technical expert not only has a different native language and different past experience but also is subject to the pulls of a career line different from those of his resident counterpart. They have different professional audiences and different personal futures to build. There are no simple rules on how to deal with this problem beyond emphasis on the obvious: in the choice of a staff, ability and common objectives are necessary, not sufficient, conditions; sincere respect for different views and sympathy for failings are also essential qualities.

One of the general benefits that may emerge from the Ciudad Guayana project is the demonstration that the political leaders and builders of cities can profit from formal enlistment of the skills and resources of knowledge available in universities. The universities, too, have gained much from this remarkable venture. Perhaps the outstanding lesson of the Venezuelan experience will be a demonstration of the value of creating appropriate mechanisms with which to assess and link the growth potentials of the city and region with the national goals for development. Economic, social, and physical plans—jointly prepared within this framework—help to maintain consistency, to guide the policymaker in the process of making critical decisions, and to promote more effective urban, regional, and national development.

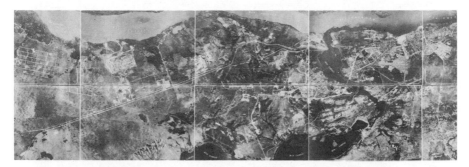

FIGURE 1.9   Aerial photograph of Ciudad Guayana, 1968.

FIGURE 1.10   Macagua Hydroelectric Plant. In the background, the Cachamay Falls and the bridge over the Caroní River.

FIGURE 1.11 The Orinoco Steel Mill.

FIGURE 1.12 Caroní Falls.

FIGURE 1.13 Aerial view of San Félix and Puerto Ordaz, 1968.

FIGURE 1.14 The old town of San Félix. In the background, the new port on the Orinoco River.

FIGURE 1.15   Rancho area in Dalla Costa along the Caroní.

FIGURE 1.16   A street in San Félix.

FIGURE 1.17 A market in San Félix.

FIGURE 1.18 Zone of the old market in San Félix's port on the Orinoco River.

FIGURE 1.19   Scene at Dalla Costa along the Caroní.

FIGURE 1.20   Houses in "reception area" in San Félix. These are the areas to accommodate inmigrants who were formerly settled in rancho areas in other parts of the city. Some ranchos are also visible.

FIGURE 1.21 Self-help housing in El Gallo, near San Félix.

FIGURE 1.22 San Félix, Avenida Centurión, La Salle Artisans School, Avenida Guayana (under construction), and the Iron Mines Company port on the Orinoco.

FIGURE 1.23 Old and new housing in Puerto Ordaz. In the foreground, Castillito and Urbanización Cachamay. On the left side, Avenida Guayana; on the right side, Avenida los Américas, which converges toward the background to Centro Alta Vista.

FIGURE 1.24 Ciudad Guayana from west to east. In the foreground, Puerto Ordaz; in the background, the bridge over the Caroní River, and San Félix.

FIGURE 1.25   Puerto Ordaz from east to west. In the foreground, part of the construction in Alta Vista.

FIGURE 1.26   A street view of apartment houses of the CVG in Puerto Ordaz.

FIGURE 1.27 Interior court of CVG apartments in Puerto Ordaz.

FIGURE 1.28 Detail of the CVG apartments.

FIGURE 1.29   Puerto Ordaz: Villa Alianza.

FIGURE 1.30   Modern chapel in Puerto Ordaz.

FIGURE 1.31   A hospital in San Félix.

FIGURE 1.32   Public primary school in San Félix.

FIGURE 1.33 Cachamay Park, Ciudad Guayana.

Chapter 2

The Changing Pattern of Urbanization in Venezuela[1]

John Friedmann

What is happening in the Guayana today happened, though with less forethought and planning, in the Caracas metropolitan region during the three preceding decades and is now being duplicated, on a reduced scale, in the Valencia Basin. In oversimplified terms, Venezuela has adopted an implicit "core-region" strategy. This means that over a sustained period Venezuela is investing large sums in the expansion of a few metropolitan regions that have great potentialities for economic growth and is guiding the spread effects of these investments to areas that are functionally linked with the core region.

Such a strategy is not new; it is an adaptation to the historical pattern of growth in the industrially advanced economies. The strategic or policy aspects enter chiefly with the decision to shift the concentration of investments from one core region to another; they are concerned with timing and location.

This chapter is concerned with the impact that the development of the Guayana can be expected to have as an element in a national core-region strategy on the distribution of the urban population in Venezuela. To trace this impact we shall follow a historical approach that will seek to identify the evolution of the country's settlement pattern within recent decades.

Shifts in the Pattern of Settlement

In discussing the changes that have occurred in the structure of Venezuela's space economy,[2] I shall confine myself to the quarter century from 1936 to 1961. Three national censuses were taken during this period;

40

TABLE 2.1

Urbanization in Venezuela, 1936, 1950, and 1961
(thousands and per cent)

	1936	1950	1961
Total population	3,364	5,035	7,524
Population in cities of 5,000 or more	743	2,121	4,333
Per cent	22.1	42.1	57.6
Nonurban population	2,621	2,914	3,191
Per cent	77.9	57.9	42.4
Per cent of total population in cities of			
25,000 or more	12.7	32.6	44.3
100,000 or more	9.3	20.6	25.4

Reprinted from John Friedmann, *Regional Development Policy* (Cambridge, Mass.: The M.I.T. Press, 1966), Table 6.2, p. 132.

the census of 1926, unfortunately, does not contain sufficient data for a full-scale comparison.

This was the period of Venezuela's great urban revolution, a revolution that swept over much of South America at the same time. In 1926 Venezuela's urban population was about 400,000. During the following thirty-five years it leaped forward by a factor of ten, while total population, though growing at one of the highest rates in the world, increased only two and a half times. Dozens of settlements, both new and old, grew to urban size, while the rural population experienced a sharp relative, though not an absolute, decline. (See Table 2.1.)

By 1961, 4.3 million Venezuelans, nearly 60 per cent of the total population, were living in 128 cities with a population of 5,000 or more. Most of them resided in small cities, but the long-term trend was toward a gradual convergence of the country's population upon the larger urban centers. (See Map 2.1.)

This trend had been barely visible a generation earlier. At that time the East Central States had just begun to assert themselves as the dominant center of urban population. (The regional division adopted for this study is shown in Map 2.2.) Maracaibo, a distant provincial capital with fewer than 100,000 inhabitants, was several days' journey away from this center. In the Andean region, a number of middle-sized cities had been able to maintain themselves over the centuries as local trade centers: chief among them was the border city of San Cristóbal. In the East, only Cumaná and Ciudad Bolívar were of more than local importance. In sum, except for a certain cohesiveness of structure at the center, Venezuela at the beginning of the 1920's consisted of a number of town-centered regional economies that had little commerce with each other and could be governed from the center only with difficulty.

By mid-century, however, four dramatic changes in the pattern of settlement could be observed:

Emergence of Caracas as the national metropolis. The population of Caracas

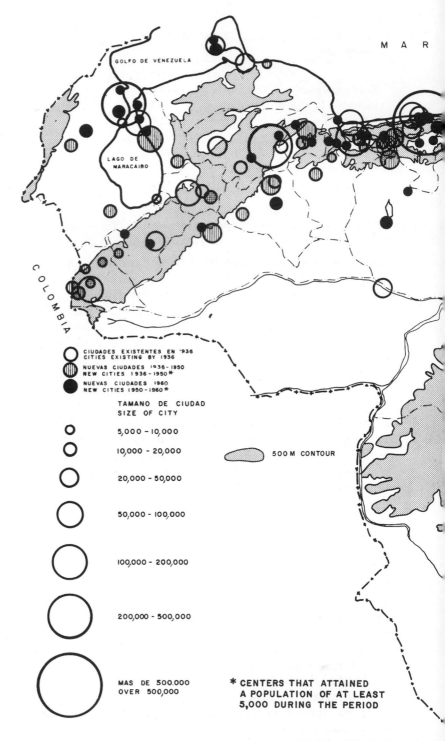

MAR

GOLFO DE VENEZUELA

LAGO DE
MARACAIBO

C O L O M B I A

○ CIUDADES EXISTENTES EN '936
CITIES EXISTING BY 1936
◐ NUEVAS CIUDADES 1936-1950
NEW CITIES 1936-1950 *
● NUEVAS CIUDADES 1960
NEW CITIES 1950-1960 *

TAMANO DE CIUDAD
SIZE OF CITY

○ 5,000 - 10,000

○ 10,000 - 20,000

○ 20,000 - 50,000

○ 50,000 - 100,000

○ 100,000 - 200,000

○ 200,000 - 500,000

○ MAS DE 500.000
OVER 500,000

▨ 500 M CONTOUR

*** CENTERS THAT ATTAINED
A POPULATION OF AT LEAST
5,000 DURING THE PERIOD**

MAP 2.1 Distribution of

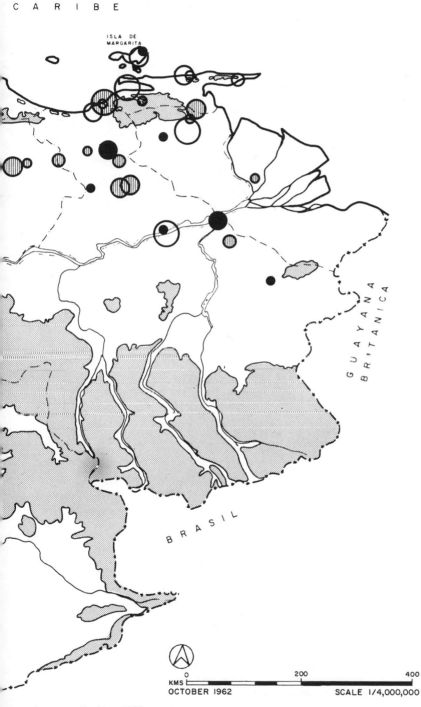

urban population, 1961.

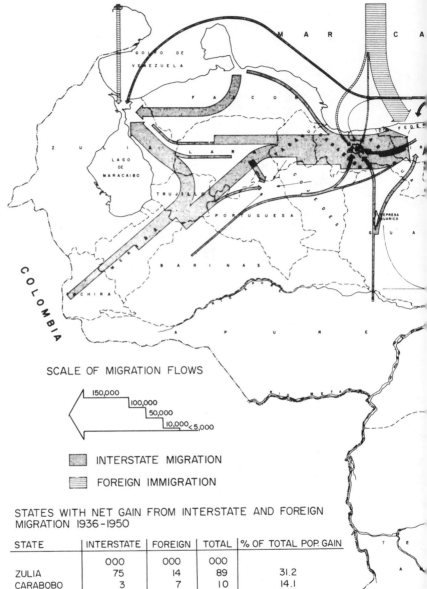

SCALE OF MIGRATION FLOWS

150,000
100,000
50,000
10,000 < 5,000

▨ INTERSTATE MIGRATION

☰ FOREIGN IMMIGRATION

STATES WITH NET GAIN FROM INTERSTATE AND FOREIGN
MIGRATION 1936-1950

STATE	INTERSTATE	FOREIGN	TOTAL	% OF TOTAL POP. GAIN
	000	000	000	
ZULIA	75	14	89	31.2
CARABOBO	3	7	10	14.1
ARAGUA	10	5	15	25.0
DTO. FEDERAL	163	77	240	56.2
PORTUGUESA	20	2	22	44.0
ANZOATEGUI	38	7	45	40.2
MONAGAS	12	1	13	15.7

SOURCE: POPULATION CENSUS, 1950

NOTE: MIGRANTS REPRESENT NUMBER OF NONLOCAL POPULATION
CLASSIFIED BY PLACE OF BIRTH, RESIDENT IN PRINCIPAL
RECEPTION AREAS IN 1950

MAP 2.2   Apparent migratory movements

to principal reception areas up to 1950.

rose phenomenally from 92,000 in 1920 to 495,000 in 1950, with the total population of the metropolitan area reaching 700,000 during the latter year. The principal reasons for this were the concentration of the oil wealth in the form of government revenues at the capital and the eagerness of the central government to make splendid improvements in the city's physical appearance. In the short span of a single generation Caracas was transformed from a sleepy colonial town into a modern metropolis.

Movement to the new oil regions. The oil-producing regions failed to share in the wealth extracted from them. Nevertheless, there were jobs to be had, and intensive exploration activity resulted in fairly large local expenditures by the oil corporations. As a result the states of Zulia and Anzoátegui (to a lesser extent also Guárico and Monagas) received a large migration from adjoining regions, most of it concentrated in a few cities. Maracaibo had attained a size of 325,000 by 1950, and a string of nondescript oil towns had grown up along the eastern shore of the lake. To the east, oil explorations led to the founding of new cities at Puerto la Cruz, Cantaura, and El Tigre, as well as to the expansion of older centers such as Maturín.

Descent from the mountains to the plains. The country's new wealth brought many farm people to the principal metropolitan centers. Population pressure relative to arable land was so great, however, that other outlets had to be found. Between 1936 and 1950 the southeastern piedmont was being rapidly colonized, and a number of earlier settlements grew to urban size in serving the expanding farm population in their surroundings.

Intensification of agriculture in existing farm areas. The simultaneous increase in total and urban populations created a great demand for agricultural products. This led to intensification of farming in the central states, where several new towns sprang up as rural service centers.

Barquisimeto benefited most from these developments. Its almost fivefold expansion from 23,000 in 1926 to 105,000 in 1950 can be ascribed to its central location in a relatively prosperous and growing farming area (Yaracuy Valley, Portuguesa), its midway position on the increasingly traveled route between Caracas and Maracaibo, its function as a traffic distributor to some of the principal regions of the country, and its proximity to the Andean region, an area of heavy emigration.

The national territory was not yet fully integrated by 1950, but a beginning had been made. The several regions of the country were coming to be linked with each other and especially with the nation's capital. At the same time, as the interurban grid of highways took shape, the basic east-west structure of the country became accentuated; with the passing

TABLE 2.2

Typical City Expansions, 1950–1961
(thousands)

	1950	1961	Percentage Gain
Maracaibo	235	421	79.1
Cabimas	42	93	121.4
San Carlos del Zulia	7	14	100.0
San Cristóbal	54	99	83.3
Barquisimeto	105	200	90.5
Valencia	89	164	84.3
Maracay	64	135	110.9
Caracas metropolitan area	694	1,336	92.5
Acarigua	16	31	93.7
San Juan de los Morros	14	37	164.2
Puerto la Cruz	28	59	110.7
Maturín	25	54	116.0
Ciudad Bolívar	31	64	106.4

Reprinted from John Friedmann, *Regional Development Policy* (Cambridge, Mass.: The M.I.T. Press, 1966), Table 6.4, p. 136.

of time, this structure would become even more firmly ingrained. Caracas' central location in this structure should be noted: once the basic road grid had been laid down, the city was the logical choice for the seat of government as well as cultural and business leadership. Eventually all roads converged upon the national metropolis and contributed to its splendor.

The period of incipient industrialization after 1950 came about partly in response to the external stimulus of World War II, but even more as a consequence of the dynamics of growth within the country itself. The first point to be noted in analyzing the spatial impact of this period of rapid economic change is that the structural pattern of urban growth that had begun to emerge by 1950 continued; most of the older cities, with some significant exceptions, about doubled in size between 1950 and 1961, maintaining annual growth rates of 7 to 9 per cent. (See Table 2.2.)

Caracas' gain does not especially stand out in comparison with other cities. Its increase, equivalent to nearly 30 per cent of the national increase in population between 1950 and 1961, was no more than proportional to its size. In fact, the remarkable thing about urban growth during this period is its ubiquity: nearly all parts of the country shared in it to some extent, the principal exceptions being the East Coastal States of Sucre and Nueva Esparta.

Examination of the data for 1936 and 1961 shows that even states with heavy outmigration experienced high urban growth rates. The center clearly gained at the expense of the Mountain, West Central, and East Coastal States, with the oil regions barely maintaining their relative positions. Over the eleven years under study, the four East Central States alone accounted for over 40 per cent of the total population increase in the country.

But this tendency for demographic concentration in the center was balanced by high rates of urban growth elsewhere, as the excess of rural population streamed to the cities everywhere.

During the decade of the 1950's, forty-six places attained "urban" status, if size alone is the criterion. One important clustering of these "new" cities appeared in the vicinity of Maracaibo as a direct consequence of continued oil explorations there. The two "new" cities on the Paraguaná Peninsula (state of Falcón) were also related to the expanding oil industry, which had important refining facilities there. A second cluster of cities developed in the vicinity of Caracas, as a sign of the physical expansion of this great metropolis. And finally, some 300 miles to the southeast, the country's third major industrial center was under construction at Ciudad Guayana. By 1965 this dynamic urban nucleus had more than 70,000 inhabitants and was growing at an annual rate of 20 per cent.

The dramatic urbanization of the central regions, 84 per cent of whose population was classified as urban at the time of the last census, resulted from a conjunction of several circumstances:

Central position. The region from Caracas to Valencia is centrally located: any part of Venezuela lies within 500 miles as measured over the existing road system from any point along the Caracas-Valencia axis. From this it follows, given the high concentration of population and income in the region, that a national market can be served most efficiently out of this central location. During the late forties and fifties the bulk of the country's manufacturing industry did, in fact, choose this location.

Seat of the national government. Venezuela's unitary form of government proved to be of exceptional advantage for the further growth of the central regions. Not only did public investments almost continuously favor the central area, particularly Caracas, but many private entrepreneurs found proximity to government offices a decisive element in location decisions. A cumulative growth cycle was thus set in motion. Government expenditures, location of commercial and industrial enterprise, foreign immigration, and expansion of the banking system created a pattern of economic and social linkages that was increasingly attractive to potential investors. A start was made with the creation of a mass market for the tastes of a metropolitan society. More than one half of the national consumer market was, in fact, developed at the center: outlying provinces shared to only a limited degree in national progress.

Traditional entrepreneurship in Valencia. The industrial expansion of Caracas—physically constrained as it was by the topography of the city's site—eventually spilled over into adjacent regions. When industrial land in Caracas became scarce, the cities of the Valencia Basin began to compete effectively with the nation's capital. They had not only the land but also a tradition of enterprise and the necessary surplus wealth and family connections to take the lead in bringing manufacturing industries to their areas. Today the Valencia Basin, together with its adjacent coastal areas, has become a serious industrial rival to Caracas and has one of the best organized promotional programs in the country. A toll road connecting the basin with Caracas is forging linkages among all the cities in the East Central States, none of which is now farther than two hours' driving distance (four hours by truck) from the hub of national power.

Patterns of Structural Persistence

The changes in the pattern of settlement just described took place within underlying patterns of stability that change only gradually and over relatively long periods of time. The basic scaffolding of Venezuela's pattern of settlement consists of ecological and topographical determinants:

Ecological complexes. The present order of ecological complexes—a series of five roughly parallel bands extending from east to west—was laid down during the sixteenth and seventeenth centuries. In a general way these complexes correspond to the outstanding physiographic features of the country. (See Map 2.3.)

Each complex may be identified by its dominant activity: (1) offshore fisheries, (2) intensive agriculture, (3) forest products, and (4) cattle raising. A final complex (5) includes the largely uninhabited and arid regions of Falcón and the tropical forests of Zulia and Guayana. Soil, climate, topography, and relative location contributed to determining the characteristic activity of each complex. These natural conditions were sufficiently strong to imprint a pattern on the landscape that would survive five centuries of colonization and development.

Topographical structure. Two major patterns of city location are discernible: locations in intermontane valleys and "gateway" locations. It may be argued that the topographical structure of the country has made these patterns unavoidable, has contributed to the emergence of a stable hierarchy of cities, and has inhibited the development of major centers that fail to conform to this general structure. Exceptions to this rule are few. (See Map 2.4.)

The principal intermontane cities are Caracas, Valencia, and Maracay

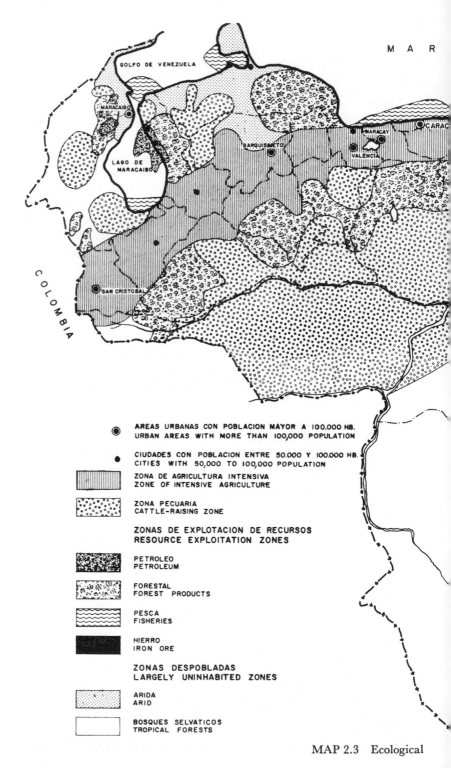

MAP 2.3 Ecological

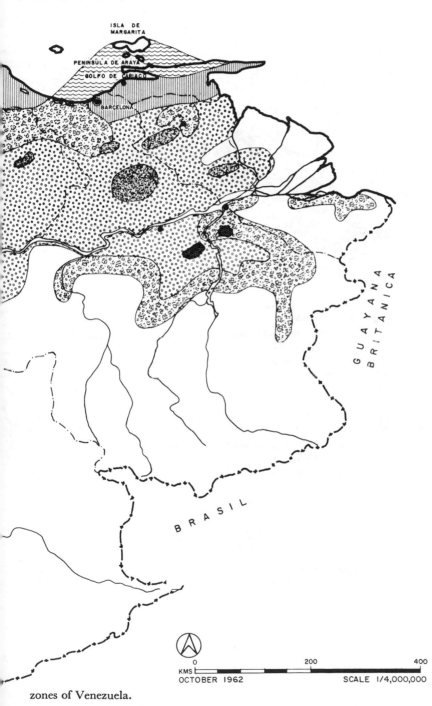

zones of Venezuela.

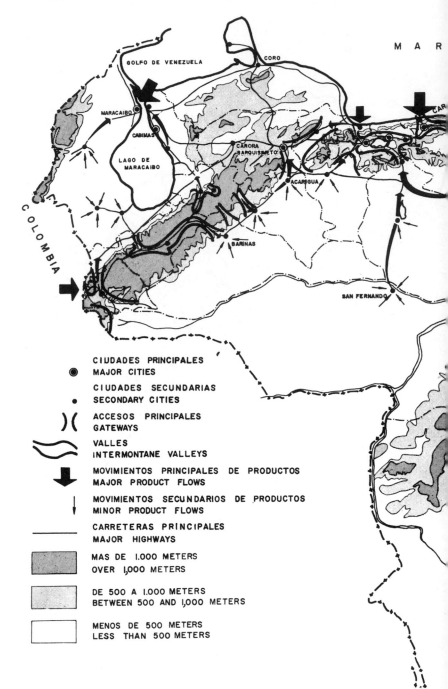

MAR

CAR

GOLFO DE VENEZUELA

CORO

MARACAIBO

CABIMAS

LAGO DE
MARACAIBO

CARORA
BARQUISIMETO

ACARIGUA

C O L O M B I A

BARINAS

SAN FERNANDO

CIUDADES PRINCIPALES
MAJOR CITIES

CIUDADES SECUNDARIAS
SECONDARY CITIES

ACCESOS PRINCIPALES
GATEWAYS

VALLES
INTERMONTANE VALLEYS

MOVIMIENTOS PRINCIPALES DE PRODUCTOS
MAJOR PRODUCT FLOWS

MOVIMIENTOS SECUNDARIOS DE PRODUCTOS
MINOR PRODUCT FLOWS

CARRETERAS PRINCIPALES
MAJOR HIGHWAYS

MAS DE 1.000 METERS
OVER 1,000 METERS

DE 500 A 1.000 METERS
BETWEEN 500 AND 1,000 METERS

MENOS DE 500 METERS
LESS THAN 500 METERS

MAP 2.4   Topographical

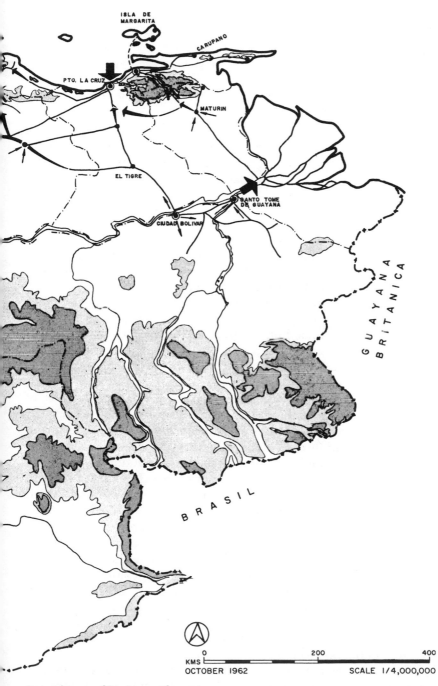

CARIBE

ISLA DE MARGARITA

CARUPANO

PTO. LA CRUZ

MATURIN

EL TIGRE

SANTO TOME DE GUAYANA

CIUDAD BOLIVAR

GUAYANA BRITANICA

BRASIL

0   200   400
KMS
OCTOBER 1962   SCALE 1/4,000,000

determinants of human settlements.

TABLE 2.3
Rank Order of Cities, 1926, 1936, 1950, and 1961

	1926	1936	1950	1961
1	Caracas[a]	Caracas[a]	Caracas[a]	Caracas[a]
2	Maracaibo	Maracaibo	Maracaibo	Maracaibo
3	Valencia	Valencia	Barquisimeto	Barquisimeto
4	Barquisimeto	Barquisimeto	Valencia	Valencia
5	Ciudad Bolívar	Maracay	Maracay	Maracay
6	Cumaná	San Cristóbal	San Cristóbal	San Cristóbal
7	San Cristóbal	Cumaná	Cumaná	Cabimas
8	Maiquetía	Ciudad Bolívar	Cabimas	Maiquetía
9	Coro	Puerto Cabello	Maiquetía	Cumaná
10	Maracay	Cabimas	Puerto Cabello	Ciudad Bolívar

Reprinted from John Friedmann, *Regional Development Policy* (Cambridge, Mass.: The M.I.T. Press, 1966), Table 6.9, p. 147.
[a] Metropolitan area.

in the central range, and Mérida and San Cristóbal in the Andean range. These valleys were preferred by the early settlers because of their fertile soil and their salubrious climates. Moreover, the central location of the Caracas and Valencia basins gave a natural advantage to the cities that grew up in them, particularly during the recent industrial phase.

"Gateway" locations include both seaports and entries to mountain passes. In contrast to the intermontane valley cities, the country's major seaports were all built in a hot, humid, and malarial climate. They achieved their early eminence because the country's economy was fundamentally oriented toward export, and all external trade had to be channeled through them. However, only ports with a productive hinterland, responsive to changes in the international marketplace, attained a size of any consequence (Maracaibo, Puerto Cabello, La Guaira, Puerto la Cruz). Cities in the southeastern piedmont and along the central range in the llanos (plains) are invariably situated at the point of entry to a major pass leading into the main population centers in the mountains and, beyond them, to the coast. Barinas, Acarigua, San Carlos, San Juan de los Morros, and Altagracia de Orituco are the cities of principal access through which traffic to and from the llanos has to pass.

A comparison of the ranking of Venezuela's ten largest cities in 1926, 1936, 1950, and 1961 shows a remarkable stability in the general order of relative dominance of cities. (See Table 2.3.) The four top cities of the hierarchy have remained dominant despite the many changes that have occurred. With somewhat more qualification—because of shifts in rank order—one can point to the fact that of the first ten cities in 1926, nine were still on the list by 1961. Greater mobility can be observed in the lower ranks, but in view of the large number of cities of middling to small size, this is well within the range of normal expectation.

This stability of the urban hierarchy should not be construed as a statistical oddity, a somehow curious but irrelevant phenomenon. Among the major reasons for its relative invariance is the influence of physiographic features on the location, functional role, and expansion of urban settlements in Venezuela.

The urban pattern that has emerged in Venezuela thus has a double rationale in the stratification of major ecological complexes and the topographical advantages of city location. This pattern may be considered basic and, with the passing of years, has been reinforced by a secondary pattern of trade linkages, including roads between the major centers and their respective tributary areas. This secondary pattern has rarely departed from the fundamental structure suggested by the country's physiographic features; every instance of significant departure has produced centers of only local significance. These patterns will continue to exert an influence over the evolution of Venezuela's space economy during the coming decades.

Implications of a Core-Region Strategy

The three core regions of national significance are Caracas, of course, the Valencia Basin, and Ciudad Guayana. Caracas already has a high rate of spontaneous economic growth that is spilling over into adjacent Valencia. Here the main problems are those of ordering and facilitating further growth through selective investments in infrastructure and improved spatial arrangements within the region. Caracas and Valencia are jointly emerging as the country's first bipolar "megalopolis." In the Guayana the task is primarily that of activating a new core region through the development of its resources base; the main problem is not to adapt to spontaneously occurring growth but to generate new productive forces.

Second-order core regions are Maracaibo and the Barcelona–Puerto la Cruz conurbation, while Barquisimeto, San Cristóbal, and Maturín rank as the centers of potential third-order core regions.

Given this pattern of present and future development areas, with investments shifting from higher- to lower-order regions as the growth process becomes more or less autonomous in the former, what will be the pattern of Venezuela's space economy a generation hence? My projections of the distribution of population and employment in the decade 1985–1995 may be summarized as follows:

For *population*, the projections indicate:
There will be no major structural shifts from the present interregional distribution of total population. No change in the percentage of national population located in any group of states will exceed five percentage points.

Although the East Central States will remain nationally dominant, their share of the total urban population will gradually decline, from 47 per cent in 1961 to 45 per cent, a relatively small change over a single generation but significant in view of the long-term objective of decentralizing the economy.

Since only 20 per cent of the total population and 17 per cent of the urban population will be residing in the eastern states (Eastern Oil, East Coastal, and the Guayana) by about 1990, the national market will continue to lie predominantly in the west, with its center of gravity along the Caracas-Valencia axis.

Approximately two million nonurban people will have to be settled over a period of three decades in the promising agricultural regions of Zulia, the llanos, and eastern Monagas. They will either be engaged in farming or be tied to the rural economy through local service activities. The scale of this dramatic new development can be appreciated by comparing it to the growth of nonurban populations in these three regions during the past twenty-five years. The earlier growth rate was only one fourth of the projected rate.

Notwithstanding the very considerable effort that this implies for reducing population pressure in the overcrowded and impoverished regions, the Mountain and East Coastal States will still experience an absolute rise of nearly one million in total population, of whom one third will be residing in rural areas.

Results for *employment* must be distinguished separately for the urban and rural sectors:

Urban employment includes all economic sectors except agriculture, forestry, and fishing. A total increase of 3.7 million urban jobs is projected for the country as a whole. Their regional distribution will not depart in a major way from the existing pattern. The principal projected change in urban employment is a relative decline in the participation of the Mountain and East Coastal States. Despite the multimillion dollar investments contemplated for the Guayana, urban employment in that region may rise to only 5 per cent of the national total over the next generation.

The absolute gains projected are nonetheless impressive. The Western Oil States, for instance, comprising Zulia and Falcón, will need to develop 670,000 new job opportunities. This is nearly three times the amount of manufacturing employment in the whole country in 1963. Anzoátegui and Monagas, together comprising the Eastern Oil States, will need to add 340,000 jobs; the Guayana an additional 240,000; and the East Central States will top all other areas with a projected increase of nearly 2,000,000 urban jobs.

The employment projections are based on an explicit policy of regional decentralization and the strengthening of a series of potential core regions throughout the country. The relative stability of the interregional structure of employment is therefore surprising. Should the core-region strategy turn out to be unsuccessful in its implementation phase, a slippage of employment toward the East Central group of states can be expected. In other words, the natural tendency of development would be for the periphery to "collapse" upon the center.

In the rural areas the shifting pattern in agricultural employment may be readily discerned. The total projected increase of 760,000 workers will be "absorbed" primarily in three regions: the llanos, the Western Oil States (chiefly Zulia), and the Eastern Oil States (especially Monagas). However, despite sharp relative declines in rural employment, the overpopulated, downward-transitional areas of the Mountain and East Coastal States will continue to gain. This suggests that farming in these areas is likely to be in a depressed condition for at least another generation, despite extensive outmigration.

The Guayana, which includes the Orinoco Delta, is projected to have a rather sizable increase of 70,000 farm jobs over those existing in 1961, a greater increment than that projected for the Mountain States. Whether this gain will in fact be realized will depend to a large extent on the outcome of current investigations into the feasibility of large-scale agricultural development in the delta.

The principal projections (summarized in Table 2.4) suggest a pattern of population and employment that, organized around a small number of metropolitan centers, seems reasonable for an economy that has achieved a high degree of industrial development, and most of whose twenty million inhabitants will be living in relative comfort as members of a thoroughly urban society. The proportional measures indicate rather minor shifts in the demographic and employment structure in Venezuela, in particular in the relative importance of the central region.

One becomes aware of the real significance of the projection only by studying the *absolute* numbers involved: the emergence of multimillion metropolitan regions, the gradual shift to predominance in urban service occupations, the great drift of population from the mountains into the plain states, and the revitalization of the economy in the eastern third of the country. The emerging new pattern gives its proper due to history, in that the existing spatial structure, as it has evolved over the centuries, will continue to be expressed in the relative distribution of population and employment over the major regions of the country, in the hierarchy of the

TABLE 2.4

Some Regional Economic Projections to 1990±5[a]

Group of States	Total Population 1990±5 (thousands)	Principal Core Region	Total Population 1990±5 (thousands)	Employment, 1990±5 Manu-facturing (thousands)	Other Urban (thousands)	Non-urban (thousands)
Western Oil	3,400	Maracaibo	1,800	160	750	250
		Specialization: food products, textiles, machinery, transport equipment, chemicals and chemical products				
Mountain	1,600	San Cristóbal	500	20	180	250
		Specialization: food products, forest products, furniture, ceramics, textiles, especially woolens				
West Central	1,600	Barquisimeto	1,000	60	330	140
		Specialization: food products, farm-related industries, construction materials, apparel, shoes, furniture				
East Central	6,800	Caracas Valencia– Maracay	4,400 2,400	610	1,890	110
		Specialization: consumer goods of all types, chemicals and chemical products, transport equipment, especially automobiles and shipbuilding				
Llanos (plains)	2,600	San Juan de los Morros[b]	200	20	240	420
		Specialization: food products and farm-related industries, lumber and wood products, paper pulp				
Eastern Oil	2,000	Barcelona– Puerto la Cruz	900	100	340	230
		Specialization: food products, textiles, shoes, apparel, machinery, chemicals and chemical products, metal fabrications, transport equipment				
East Coastal	800	Cumaná[b]	200	10	110	110
		Specialization: marine products, textiles, other labor-intensive industries				
Guayana	1,200	Ciudad Guayana	600	120	160	90
		Specialization: heavy metals, machinery, industrial chemicals, ferroalloys, paper pulp, electric energy				
Venezuela	20,000			1,100	4,000	1,600

a. Population estimates were made by assuming the continuation of a 3 per cent growth rate for the country as a whole, so that total population would reach twenty million sometime during the decade 1985–1995. This total was then allocated among groups of states on the basis of the existing distribution pattern and of foreseeable changes based on internal migration to previously identified core regions.

To obtain city populations, total regional population was first divided into urban and nonurban. The resulting figure for urban population provided a guideline for estimating the share attributable to the largest urban center in each region. The resulting estimate is very approximate but may be taken as a significant order of magnitude reliable to two digits.

Employment estimates were derived by applying assumed labor force participation rates to total urban and nonurban populations. Given an estimated over-all 35 per cent participation rate nationally, the more urbanized a group of states appeared to be, the higher its labor force participation rate was assumed to be. Actual ratios run from a low of 28 per cent to a high of 42 per cent of the urban population. The nonurban labor force participation was taken to be a uniform 28 per cent.

Manufacturing employment was first estimated nationally on the basis of a sectoral employment model in which the share of manufacturing employment is permitted to rise, because of automation, from 10 per cent in 1960 to 16 per cent between 1985 and 1995. The resulting national total was then allocated to regions according to the predetermined structure of core regions and the estimated potential for industrial development.

A more detailed explanation of projection methods is given in John Friedmann, *Regional Development Policy* (Cambridge, Mass.: The M.I.T. Press, 1966), pp. 235–242.

b. Taken as a representative center.

core regions, and in the broad east-west orientation of the settlement pattern. Yet, although the old may be recognized in the new features, the projected pattern represents a major expansion of Venezuela's space economy in heretofore unexplored directions. New core regions, such as the Guayana, will be drawn into its orbit as permanent integral elements; urban areas confronted with incipient economic decline will be given an important new role as major foci in the nation's life; and the rural economy will be more closely related to the basic urban structure of the country. Older regions, such as the Mountain and East Coastal States, will continue to pose problems of equity and internal adjustment, but their relative importance will have substantially declined (in demographic terms, from 29 per cent of the national total in 1936 to only 12 per cent by about 1990). In short, the regional problem, seemingly so urgent in the 1960's, will have shrunk to vestigial proportions, while policy will come to focus increasingly on internal problems of metropolitan organization.

Chapter 3

Economic Diagnosis and Plans

Roberto Alamo Blanco and Alexander Ganz

Latin America is the somewhat more affluent area of the developing world, with its $400 per capita gross domestic product. It is bent on achieving a per capita level one fourth that of the United States in ten years' time, through the Alliance for Progress program. To attain this goal, all principal Latin American countries have established national plans. These generally combine a public sector investment program with private sector "indicative" goals to be achieved through market incentives and other inducements. Venezuela's *Plan de la Nación*[1] is said to be one of the best and most ambitious planning efforts in Latin America.[2]

In this context of a major planning effort in a developing country, the Guayana region offered two unusual opportunities: the possibility of creating a regional heavy industry complex, with detailed individual projects, as a prime instrument for implementing a key part of the national plan; and the challenge to undertake a more comprehensive regional planning effort than could be found in most countries. This involved economic development and industrial programming as the basis for urban design in the broadest sense, including education and social welfare as well as public and private urban infrastructure services and facilities.

The Guayana program differs fundamentally from other types of regional programs. It is neither a scheme for upgrading a depressed area (such as the Tennessee Valley Authority or the program for Appalachia in the United States, or the Northeast Development Program in Brazil) nor a simple river basin development operation in a purely regional context (such as the Cauca Valley program in Colombia or the Columbia River

TABLE 3.1

Venezuela: Gross Domestic Product, 1936–1980, Total and Per Capita

	Gross Domestic Product, Total (Bs. millions at 1957 prices)	Population (thousands)	Gross Domestic Product, Per Capita (Bs. at 1957 prices)
1936	5,166	3,364	1,536
1950	12,728	5,035	2,528
1959	26,065	7,089	3,677
1964	32,135	8,427	3,813
1965	34,224	8,722	3,924
1968	42,504	9,686	4,388
1970	48,663	10,400	4,679
1975	68,252	12,434	5,489
1980	95,727	14,490	6,606
	Annual Rate of Change (per cent)		
1936–1965	6.7	3.3	3.3
1965–1980	7.0	3.4	3.5

Sources: Gross domestic product for *1936–1950:* unpublished estimates of real gross product by economic sector prepared by Bernardo Ferran, Banco Central de Venezuela, Caracas; for *1950–1964:* Banco Central de Venezuela, *La Economia Venezolana en los Ultimos Veinti-Cinco Anos, Hechos y Cifras Relevantes* (Caracas, 1966), and its *Memorias y Informes Económicas* for 1959–1964 (Caracas); for *1965:* preliminary estimate by Banco Central de Venezuela; for *1965–1968:* targets of the Oficina Central de Coordinación y Planificación, *Plan de la Nación, 1965–1968* (Caracas, 1965); and *1968–1980:* based on long-term (1963–1975) targets of the Oficina Central de Coordinación y Planificación, *Plan de la Nación, 1963–1966* (Caracas, 1963), and detailed projections of consumer investment and export demand, production and import supply, labor force and productivity, prepared by the Corporación Venezolana de Guayana, Departamento de Planificación, Sector Económico.
Population figures for *1936–1961* are from Ministerio de Fomento, Oficina Central del Censo, *Noveno Censo General de Población, Febrero 1961*, *Resumen General de la República,* Part A (Caracas, 1966); and for *1961–1980*, based on Ministerio de Fomento, Dirección General de Estadística y Censos Nacionales, *Proyección de la Población de Venezuela,* prepared by Julio Paez Celis (Caracas, 1963; publication No. DGE–OAD/1).
Note: In 1965 prices, which are about 10 per cent above 1957 prices, one bolívar is equivalent to U.S. $0.22.

project in the United States). Rather, the whole program is an integral part of the Venezuelan national plan, created to help achieve national goals through the development of industry, power, and a new city in what was virtually an empty space. The perspectives of the program range from the global, national, and regional levels to the details of the principal individual projects. An analysis of the Guayana program, then, must take place within the framework of a diagnosis of Venezuela's development needs and plans.

In addition to describing the Guayana program in the context of the national plan, this chapter will review the planning effort, the problems encountered, and some of the conclusions drawn from the experience.

The National Plan for Economic Development

For three decades Venezuela has had one of the highest, long-sustained rates of economic growth of any nation in modern times, with total and per capita annual growth rates in real gross domestic product of 7 per cent and more than 3 per cent, respectively, over the 1936–1965 period. (See Table 3.1.) Although this outstanding rate of growth was based principally on the dynamic expansion of petroleum investment, production, and exports, Venezuela shows evidence of the successful transformation of its economic structure and growth base to offset the relative decline in the role of petroleum since 1959. (See Table 3.2.) The national development plan calls for a continuation of this historical rate of growth, to be achieved through industrial development and diversification and through substantial new exports.

The *Plan de la Nación, 1963–1966* (completed in 1962) and the *Plan de la Nación, 1965–1968* (a biennial extension and updating of the plan and a review of the 1963–1964 performance) set ambitious over-all four-year targets for economic growth, with fundamental changes in the structure of production and employment. (See Table 3.3.) In addition to the targets for the four-year plan period, the current plan sets down a long-term perspective. Production of goods and services is to rise at an annual rate of 7 per cent, which would mean a fundamental change in Venezuelan living standards. With output almost tripling, by 1980 per capita gross product would attain a level comparable with that of Western Europe.

An ambitious investment rate (well within Venezuela's past performance) would be achieved almost wholly through the mobilization of domestic savings, including a modest increase in the national tax burden. Industrialization is counted on to provide the main elements for growth in production, productive employment opportunities, and net new savings for investment. Public investment is expected to continue to play a strong role (about two fifths of the total investment program) in support of industrial development by the private sector.

Although over-all foreign exchange earnings are not expected to match their former growth rate, petroleum exports are expected to continue to expand. These export earnings would be complemented by a range of new industrial export products (principally from the Guayana region); enriched, prereduced iron ore, metals, chemicals, and metal fabrications are expected to make up one fourth of an expanding level of foreign exchange earnings by 1980.

The need for new productive employment opportunities is urgent, for, with petroleum accounting for 25 per cent of the gross product but only 2 per cent of the nation's employment, Venezuela is experiencing the paradox of high unemployment in the midst of a booming economy. Nor

TABLE 3.2
Venezuela: Composition of Gross Domestic Product, 1936–1980, by Economic Sector
(per cent)

	Total	Agriculture	Mining and Petroleum[a]	Manufacturing[b]	Construction, Power, Commerce, and Services
1936	100.0	21.0	20.8	11.7	46.4
1959	100.0	6.3	30.6	11.6	51.5
1965	100.0	7.0	29.0	12.9	51.1
1980	100.0	7.0	18.1	21.5	53.4
		Annual Rate of Increase			
1936–1958	7.3	1.8	9.1	7.2	7.8
1959–1965	4.7	6.5	3.7	6.6	4.5
1965–1980	7.0	7.0	3.7	10.8	7.4

Sources: See Table 3.1.
Note: Components may not add up to total due to rounding.
a. Includes petroleum refining.
b. Excludes petroleum refining.

TABLE 3.3
Venezuela: Employment, 1951–1980, by Economic Sector

	Total	Agriculture	Petroleum and Mining	Manufacturing	Other
		Thousands of Workers			
1951	1,750	789	43	227	691
1959	2,151	777	49	304	1,021
1964	2,456	793	44	363	1,256
1968	2,892	813	47	445	1,587
1970	3,120	820	50	495	1,755
1975	3,730	901	58	679	2,092
1980	4,347	990	67	931	2,359
		Annual Rate of Change (per cent)			
1951–1964	2.6	0.1	0.2	3.7	4.7
1964–1980	3.6	1.4	2.7	6.1	4.0
		Percentage Composition			
1951	100.0	45.0	2.5	13.0	39.5
1964	100.0	32.3	1.8	14.8	51.1
1980	100.0	22.8	1.5	21.4	54.3

Sources: See Table 3.1.

can agriculture be counted on to provide significant new employment opportunities. Relatively ambitious targets for the expansion of agricultural output, in substitution of imports and in line with the anticipated moderate growth in domestic demand, can be achieved, it is hoped, principally by raising agricultural productivity from the present unacceptably low levels. (See Tables 3.2 and 3.3.)

The expansion of industrial production, on the other hand, based on a high elasticity of domestic and export demand, is counted on to provide substantial new employment opportunities. The higher levels of productivity are calculated to yield higher wages and salaries. However, fundamental changes in Venezuela's industrial structure are needed. Manufacturing, which has been expanding recently at a rate of 12 per cent a year, is characterized by the final assembly of materials and components, largely imported. Since this growth will soon strike against the limitations on import capacity, the production of basic metals, chemicals, metal fabrications, and industrial components is urgently needed if industrial expansion is to continue within the framework of a moderately expanding level of foreign exchange earnings.

Another need is to channel a significant share of public investment resources into industrial development. The Venezuelan government has long played an important role in total investment; it receives a large revenue and is determined to utilize this income to expand the productive capacity of the economy. Part of this public revenue is used to finance private investment through instruments such as the Corporación Venezolana de Fomento; part is for traditional public works, such as roads, schools, waterworks, sewage disposal, irrigation schemes, and public

TABLE 3.4
Guayana Region:[a] Growth and Development Targets, 1961–1980, as Per Cent of Venezuelan Total

	Guayana as Per Cent of Venezuela				
	Actual		Potential		
	1961	1965	1970	1975	1980
Population	0.6	0.8	1.4	1.9	2.3
Employment	0.5	0.9	1.4	1.9	2.3
Gross product, total	1.0	2.8	4.0	5.0	7.6
Gross product, manufacturing	0.4	7.5	9.0	15.3	21.0
Exports	6.4	5.8	6.6	15.8	23.5

Source: Corporación Venezolana de Guayana, The Guayana Program, Key to the Development of Venezuela (Caracas, July 1966).
a. Refers to the development area of the Guayana region.

buildings; and part is directly invested in electric power and in those industrial enterprises that are either too large for the financial capacity of the domestic private sector or imbued with a public interest due to their key role in the national economy. With the government accounting for some 40 per cent of total domestic saving, the problem of productive investment opportunities becomes increasingly important.

The Guayana region, which in 1965 already accounted for 7.5 per cent of Venezuela's manufacturing production (value added), is counted on to provide by 1980 one fifth of Venezuela's manufacturing output and almost one fourth of an expanded level of exports. (See Table 3.4.) The *Plan de la Nación* established targets calling for 10 per cent of the nation's investment, public and private, to be devoted to the Guayana region program in the period 1963–1966. (See Table 3.5.) The Guayana's share of the national investment effort is substantially greater than 10 per cent in certain priority areas: 14 per cent of the investment in mining and petroleum, 21 per cent in manufacturing, and 34 per cent in electric power. Thus the Guayana program has a substantial part to play in Venezuela's national plan and the over-all needs of the economy.

The Heart of the Guayana Program: Heavy Industry and Power

In the framework of the need to transform the national economy, the formulation of the Guayana region development program began with the

TABLE 3.5

Venezuela: *Plan de la Nación* Investment Targets and the Role of the Guayana Program, 1963–1966

	Investment (Bs. millions at 1960 prices)		Percentage Composition		Guayana as Per Cent of Venezuelan
	Venezuela	Guayana	Venezuela	Guayana	Total
Agriculture	2,681	40	10.2	1.5	1.5
Petroleum and mining	3,000	411	11.4	15.2	13.7
Manufacturing	5,134	1,061	19.5	39.2	20.7
Electricity, gas, and water	1,373	472	5.2	17.4	34.4
Transport and communications	2,802	313	10.6	11.5	11.2
Commerce	2,187	22	8.3	0.8	1.0
Housing and urban development	5,414	273	20.6	10.1	5.0
Government and other services	3,757	117	14.2	4.3	3.1
Total	26,348	2,709	100.0	100.0	10.3

Source: Oficina Central de Coordinación y Planificación, *Plan de la Nación, 1963–1966* (Caracas, 1963), Tables III.2 and XVIV.3.

postulation of targets for heavy industry and power. From the earliest days of the planning (in 1961 and 1962), there were some fundamental uncertainties about the heavy industry and power program. Would the production programs prove to be feasible when full-blown engineering and financial feasibility studies had been made? Could a well-ordered regional program for a new city be carried out with frequent changes and the occasional elimination of important projects and the introduction of new projects in the early critical years of the development program? Would fluctuations in world markets for basic Guayana products make planning or plants obsolescent? Would the preliminary conclusions on the optimum location of projects in the Guayana, in relation to other sites in Venezuela and Latin America, be confirmed? Were the technology and scale appropriate for production and export at competitive prices? Could private investors be attracted to bring their know-how and capital to the Guayana? Since the Guri Dam's electric power, the gas pipeline from Eastern Venezuela, and the flat steel products mill were essential building blocks on which other industrial projects rested, what would be the effect of delay or postponement of these projects? The new industrial city and the Guayana region program would be made or broken, shaped or misshaped, by the the outcome of these crucial tests.

The heavy industry complex. In the context of the resources available in the Guayana region, and taking the specific needs of and targets for the Venezuelan economy set down in the national plan, the planners designed a heavy industry complex with specific targets and programs for the production of steel, enriched iron ore, sponge iron, aluminum, chemicals, pulp and paper, metal fabrications, and electric power. The short-term (1965–1968) and long-term (to 1980) regional development program was formulated around this heavy industry complex. From the beginning the major considerations in project selection included (1) modern technology that was related to the Guayana's unique resources, (2) domestic and export demand, (3) economic scale to achieve competitive output and pricing, (4) integration and complementarity with the Venezuelan economy as a whole, and (5) linkages, external economies, and transportation factors.

The principal production targets center on the upgrading of iron ore to enriched iron ore, sponge iron, and steel. Targets for aluminum and pulp involve the industrial processing of electric power and forest reserves, respectively. The production of ammonia takes advantage of nearby natural gas. The metal fabricating industry would be linked to the iron and steel development. Venezuela has recently entered into the Latin American Free Trade Association and the region's common market movement; Venezuela would be at a decided disadvantage if it did not have an expanding, competitive export capacity. Venezuela's principal possibilities for developing substantial new exports lie in the Guayana's export potential of enriched iron ore, prereduced iron ore, steel sheet, plate and pipe, other metals, and chemicals. For this reason the Guayana's heavy industry must be technologically advanced and competitive.

Because of the long lead time that precedes actual investment, as well as the long-term nature, complexity, and large size of the kinds of projects involved, it was necessary to plan for the period beyond 1968. Large projects may require five or more years of planning plus five or more years of construction and installation. For the period beyond 1970, "firm" and "potential" targets were established, and these reflect the best current assessment of the range of alternatives. The "firm" targets are based on projects already in an advanced stage of development. The "potential" targets include those projects that reflect the needs of the nation for more ambitious goals, projects that have been seriously studied and considered to be feasible and desirable but are presently at a preliminary stage of promotion and development.

The "firm" targets for 1980 are geared to domestic and export markets, modern technology, and the Guayana resources; they call for the

TABLE 3.6

Guayana Region: Principal Production and Export Goals for 1980, "Firm" and "Potential"[a]

	"Firm"		"Potential"	
	Production	Exports	Production	Exports
	Thousands of Metric Tons			
Iron ore	27,000	2,300	40,000	9,000
Enriched iron ore	10,000	10,000	12,000	12,000
Sponge iron	4,100	4,100	4,100	4,100
Steel	4,000	—	6,600	2,500
Aluminum	21	—	86	25
Pulp and paper	50	—	130	—
Ammonia	—	—	330	330
	Millions of Bolívars			
Metal fabrications	52	—	420	50

Source: Corporación Venezolana de Guayana, *The Guayana Economic Program, Key to the Development of Venezuela* (Caracas, July 1966), Chart V–5, p. 19.
a. For definition of "firm" and "potential," see text.

production of ten million tons of enriched iron ore, four million tons of sponge iron, and four million tons of steel. (See Table 3.6.) Also included in the "firm" targets for 1980 are projects for 21,000 tons of aluminum, 50,000 tons of pulp, and Bs. 50 million of metal fabrications. With the exception of enriched iron ore and sponge iron, most of the "firm" targets are based mainly on supplying domestic markets.

The "potential" targets, for the most part, add a margin of domestic supply—for example, pulp and paper and metal fabrications—or an ambitious though feasible margin of exports—steel, aluminum, and ammonia. Serious export capabilities, apart from enriched iron ore and sponge iron, are not expected to be developed and available before 1975.

Modifications of the plans in the formative years. In the course of the five-year planning effort, the main focus of the heavy industry and power program was sustained, but there were some important amendments.

TABLE 3.7
Modification of Guayana Region Heavy Industry and Power Goals, "Before" and "After"

	Production Targets				
	"Before"	"After"			
		"Firm"		"Potential"	
Projects	1975	1975	1980	1975	1980
	Thousands of Metric Tons				
Iron ore	45,000	27,000	27,000	32,000	40,000
Prereduced enriched ore	—	5,000	10,000	5,000	12,000
Sponge iron	10,000	2,100	4,100	2,100	4,100
Steel	4,760[a]	2,080	4,000	3,000	6,600
Aluminum	200	16	21	30	86
Pulp	—	33	50	60	130
Ammonia	200	—	—	330	330
Phosphorus	50	—	—	—	—
	Millions of Bolívars				
Heavy machinery	1,800	160	230	300	420
	Megawatts of Power Capacity				
Guri and Macagua dams	1,945	1,770	2,120	1,770	2,120

Sources: For "before" targets see Oficina Central de Coordinación y Planificación, *Plan de la Nación, 1963–1966* (Caracas, May 1963), Table XVII.5, p. 433; for "after" targets see Corporación Venezolana de Guayana, *The Guayana Economic Program, Key to the Development of Venezuela* (Caracas, July 1966), Charts V–5 and V–15, pp. 19 and 27.
a. This target, set in 1962, was modified in 1963; see Table 3.8.

Details of the program, demand analyses, feasibility studies, and the promotion and implementation of projects are reported on elsewhere in this book[3] and in reports of the Guayana development authority (the Corporación Venezolana de Guayana—CVG).[4] What follows here is a review of the factors involved in the modification of the early focus.

Table 3.7 compares two sets of targets for heavy industry and power: the first set ("before") was prepared in 1963, the second ("after") in 1966. The two sets are similar, but there are important additions, subtractions, modifications, and time lags. This comparison reflects the time lags experienced between feasibility study completion and project implementation: the targets for 1975 in the earlier version are similar to the "potential" targets for 1980 in the later version. The program as a whole (1980 "potential" targets) has grown larger in the course of the evolution of the plans. The changes within the program reflect new technological developments, the completion of feasibility studies, and revised evaluations of foreign markets.

Iron-ore targets were adjusted to accommodate an expanding Venezuelan utilization of ore for steel, sponge iron, and prereduced enriched iron ore and a reduced prognosis for the export of ore as ore.[5] Important new projects included a new process for the prereduction and enrichment of iron ore, a new process for fluidized iron-ore reduction (sponge iron), and a relatively new process for the production of pulp from tropical hardwood. One potentially important project that was eliminated when detailed feasibility studies showed only marginal profit possibilities was the electric reduction of elemental phosphorus. Because of the longer time required to reach the target levels of efficiency and production for the steel mill, and the delay in the installation of the flat steel products plant, steel production goals were set back. While the potential market for heavy machinery is large, feasibility studies and project development thus far cover only a portion of it.

The demand for steel in Venezuela is expected to continue to grow substantially, which is of fundamental importance since targets for steel expansion are geared mainly to the domestic market. (See Table 3.8.)[6] However, world steel capacity has expanded at a much more rapid rate than was predicted. In 1962 a United Nations study foresaw a doubling of steel capacity in fifteen years' time, from 300 million tons in 1960 to 600 million in 1975.[7] By 1966, however, capacity had reached 450 million tons, foreshadowing an early overshooting of the 1975 projection, a more than matching of world steel capacity with demand and thus a smaller margin for potential Venezuelan steel exports. This development suggested positing somewhat smaller finished steel exports for Venezuela in 1975, though Venezuela's role would be marginal in any case.

On the other hand, this expanding world steel capacity means an even bigger market for enriched prereduced iron ore, sponge iron, and other preprocessed iron and steel products for the world's steel industry. Almost all developed countries have limited domestic sources of high-grade iron ore and low-cost energy and are increasingly dependent on imports. At the moment Venezuela's Guayana is in a good competitive position with respect to Africa, Australia, and Brazil because of its unique combination of high-grade ore, low-cost energy, and easy ocean transport. Recent independent studies fully confirm the competitiveness of the Guayana location, especially for the production of steel.[8]

TABLE 3.8

Guayana Region: Targets for the Production and Export of Steel, "Before" and "After" (thousands of metric tons)

	"Before"	"After"			
		"Firm"		"Potential"	
	1975	1975	1980	1975	1980
Demand	4,400	2,870	4,440	3,870	6,940
Domestic	3,080	2,870	4,440	2,870	4,440
Export	1,320	—	—	1,000	2,500
Supply	4,440	2,870	4,440	3,870	6,940
Production	3,860	2,080	4,000	3,000	6,600
Import	540	790	440	870	340

Sources: For "before" targets see Corporación Venezolana de Guayana, *Guayana, Cornerstone of the Development of Venezuela* (Caracas, July 1963), p. 18; for "after" targets see Corporación Venezolana de Guayana, *The Guayana Economic Program, Key to the Development of Venezuela* (Caracas, July 1966), Charts V–5, V–6, V–8, V–9, and V–10, pp. 19–22.

The "before" and "after" comparison shown in Table 3.8 confirms the initial over-all strategy but points up both the need for a continuous review of markets, technology, and feasibility analyses and the gap between project study and groundbreaking.

Plans for Supporting Activities

Based on the heavy industry and power program, requirements for supporting activities were studied and plans developed. These included programs for agriculture, light industry, construction, housing, trade, transport, education, health, and other urban services. Although patterns in other Venezuelan industrial cities provided some guide to the relationship between manufactures for regional export and manufactures and services for local market needs, there were special problems in projecting and programming the economic structure of a rapidly growing new city based on modern, large-scale, capital-intensive technology.

From the beginning Ciudad Guayana had a dual economy: the modern regional export industry had a high level of investment and capital per worker, high labor productivity, and high wages; local market-orientated manufactures and services, on the other hand, had traditional, lower-scale, and older technologies and more limited levels of productivity and wages. The pressure of productivity and the wage levels of the modern sector would minimize the job opportunities at artisan-scale levels and would accelerate the adaptation of modern techniques to traditional activities.

In addition, local manufacturing would supply an expanding share of local market consumption as the growth of the city's population and income made feasible the attainment of an economic scale of production in a rising proportion of manufactures. Moreover, future increases in employment in service activities would respond not only to the growth in population and income levels but also to the correction of shortages: in 1961 there was virtually no telephone service, and there were scarcities in housing, water supply, schools, roads, health services, wholesale and retail trade, storage and warehouse capacity, and recreational facilities.

Furthermore, the nature of the development program implied a substantial construction employment phase, to be followed by the production employment phase. Variations in timing of both aspects could mean serious fluctuations in employment levels, which might threaten the viability of the city's economy. Another problem was how to convert construction workers into production workers. Finally, employment in Ciudad Guayana might not mean residence in the city because of the severe shortage of housing. Even as late as early 1965, one third of the steel mill workers were commuting from outside Ciudad Guayana, traveling from as far as Ciudad Bolívar (the nearest city of any size), sixty miles away.

There were other problems, too. The Guayana was already a food-deficit area; high food costs could mean high wage costs, thereby offsetting the unique competitive potential of the heavy industry. Shortages in housing, urban services, and amenities, especially in the first years of the program, proved to be a serious obstacle to attracting urgently needed technicians, professionals, and businessmen. To transform a newly migrated traditional society into a modern industrial society needed a proper environmental setting. To provide the economic attractions of choice, linkages, complementarities, and external economies, a cosmopolitan city was needed. Yet all of this had to be done without placing an undue burden on the city's economy.

In effect, programming for the production of goods and services to supply the development area and its central focus, Ciudad Guayana, required systematic, detailed studies. Modern sector and traditional sector employment, productivity, and wages and salaries were analyzed and projected and checked as the program advanced. Surveys were conducted to throw light on family income levels, employment, unemployment, characteristics of inmigrants, occupational composition of the labor force, and the structure of the consumption of goods and services.Consumer demand, including housing, was projected in line with future expected

TABLE 3.9
Guayana Region: Investment Targets, 1965–1980, by Economic Sector

	"Potential" 1965–1980	
	Millions of Bolívars	Percentage Composition
Investment, total	13,000	100.0
Heavy industry and power activities	8,800	67.7
Mining	1,600	12.3
Energy	1,500	11.5
Heavy manufacturing	5,700	43.9
Supporting activities	4,200	32.3
Agriculture	700	5.3
Light manufacturing	250	1.9
Construction	250	1.9
Housing	1,580	12.2
Retail and wholesale trade[a]	400	3.1
Communications	20	0.2
Transport	200	1.5
Government	35	0.3
Education	140	1.1
Medical services	65	0.5
Sewage, water, and sanitation	175	1.3
Recreation, cultural, religious, and other	385	3.0

Source: Corporación Venezolana de Guayana, The Guayana Economic Program, Key to the Development of Venezuela (Caracas, July 1966), Charts VI–1 and VI–2, pp. 26, 27, and 28.
a. Includes finance, insurance, and real estate.

TABLE 3.10

Guayana Region: Employment Targets, 1980, by Economic Sector

	"Potential" 1980
Employment, total	100,000
Heavy industry and power activities	33,800
Mining	6,900
Energy	900
Heavy industry	26,000
Supporting activities	66,200
Agriculture	5,500
Light industry	14,000
Construction	7,600
Retail and wholesale trade	10,000
Finance, insurance, and real estate	1,300
Communications	400
Passenger transport (bus, taxi, air)	3,750
Freight transport (road, sea)	1,450
Government	3,900
Educational services	3,700
Medical services	2,000
Sewage, water, and sanitation services	1,100
Business services	1,200
Recreational services	1,000
Domestic services	5,000
Other services	4,300

Source: Corporación Venezolana de Guayana, *The Guayana Economic Program, Key to the Development of Venezuela* (Caracas, July 1966), Chart V–2, p. 17.

population and income levels. Systematic hypotheses were set forth about the pattern of development of local manufactures to substitute for imports. The needs for retail trade facilities were examined in line with expected population and income levels and the evolution of the Venezuelan urban economy from the open-air trade market to the modern shopping center. Transport facility needs were estimated on the basis of the expected demand for goods transport and the origin and destination of the journey to work. Requirements for public service facilities were analyzed as a function of expected population levels; the targets for service standards were slightly higher than existing Venezuelan patterns. Special studies of construction activity and construction employment were made.

The resulting program for production and service activities to support the economic base may be expected to absorb two thirds of the region's labor force but only one third of the long-term investment needs. (See Tables 3.9 and 3.10.) These proportions in supporting activities are a smaller share of total activities than in the Venezuelan economy as a whole. This is true even with an urban plan that is considered both attractive and adequate. Consequently the ambitious urban plan complements the highly productive features of the industry and power program in terms of resource-use efficiency and optimization.

The Emerging Picture of the Guayana Region's Economy

After the programming of heavy industry and power and local market-oriented activities, it was possible to envisage the structure of the whole economy of the development area.[9] The Guayana region development program could be fully defined in terms of the production of goods and services; productivity, employment, wages and salaries; family income levels and income distribution; and the consumption of goods and services, including the demand for housing by income group. But these estimates implied enough changes within a short period of time to make the planners skeptical of the answers of their slide rules; acceptance came with a lag, confirmed by the force of events. The January 1965 family income and expenditure survey, for example, showed a significant upgrading of family income levels since the August 1962 survey.[10] The surveys revealed a reduction in the *number* of families in the lowest of five income groups over a period in which the city's population had grown by 40 per cent. Even in the earliest days, wage and productivity levels were above those in the rest of Venezuela, due to the role of heavy industry; analyses showed that this trend could be expected to continue as new industrial projects came into the picture. But the implications for the structure of the demand for goods, services, and housing were hard to swallow in 1962, when inmigration outpaced new jobs, and unemployment rose temporarily to a rate of 20 per cent of the labor force. Projections of the demand for consumer goods and services (based on demand-elasticity studies) showed that levels of demand by 1970 would be large enough to justify the local production of two fifths of the area's food requirements and one fourth of its other manufactures.

Because it has a larger share of large-scale, technologically modern capital-intensive industry and power projects, the Guayana region may be expected to grow more rapidly and at higher levels of manpower productivity than the Venezuelan economy as a whole. This was the experience from 1961 to 1965; gross product per worker, an over-all measure of productivity, in 1965 was already more than three times that in the Venezuelan economy as a whole. This margin is expected to continue though 1968 and 1980. (See Table 3.11.) And as the Guayana's share of the national economy grows, the higher levels of manpower productivity there will help lift the level for the nation as a whole. In comparison with a possible threefold expansion of Venezuelan production of goods and services by 1980, the Guayana perspective suggests a

TABLE 3.11

Production, Employment, and Productivity, Guayana and Venezuela, 1961, 1965, and 1980

	Gross Domestic Product (Bs. millions at 1957 prices)	Employment (thousands)	Gross Product Per Worker (Bs. thousands at 1957 prices)
Guayana			
1961	416	11.4	36
1965	1,080	21.4	50
1980 (potential)	7,240	100.0	72
Venezuela			
1961	26,881	2,191	12
1965	34,224	2,572	13
1980 (target)	95,727	4,347	22

Sources: For the Guayana region see Corporación Venezolana de Guayana, *The Guayana Economic Program, Key to the Development of Venezuela* (Caracas, July 1966); and for Venezuela see Table 3.1.

possible fivefold to sevenfold growth by that year. Of note also is the possibility that the Guayana region, with a 1965 employment of 21,000, may provide some 80,000 to 100,000 jobs by 1980.

In terms of production, heavy industry has already matched iron-ore preparation and shipping as the main activity of the Guayana region, and it has displaced them in levels of employment. The long-term development program, to 1980, carries the relative importance of heavy industry output even further. Substantial, but lower, rates of growth in output and employment in agriculture, mining, energy, and light manufacturing industry are foreseen. (See Table 3.12.)

Urban services represent a modest share of the total regional economy. Present and projected employment in urban services for the Guayana region barely absorbs 40 per cent of total employment. Output and investment shares are even smaller, in comparison with the more than 50 per cent absorbed in urban infrastructure in the Venezuelan economy as a whole. In effect the Guayana plan, by limiting the absorption of resources in urban services to a modest share without sacrificing needs and standards, enhances the optimization of manpower and capital resource use.

Even if the very ambitious targets are achieved by 1980, however, development will not have been sufficient to eliminate the dual-economy characteristic. Heavy industry and power activities are expected to account for two thirds of the region's output, with one third of the labor force; the reverse is anticipated for the supporting activity sectors. Significant differences in productivity levels, by economic sector, are expected to continue.

By 1965 the Guayana region development area was already a going

TABLE 3.12

Guayana Region: Production, Employment, and Productivity by Sector, 1961, 1965, and 1980[a]

	Gross Product (Value Added)			Employment			Productivity (Gross Product Per Worker)		
	1961	1965	1980	1961	1965	1980	1961	1965	1980
	(Bs. millions)			(number of workers)			(Bs. thousands)		
All activities	416	1,080	7,240	11,400	21,420	100,000	36	50	72
Heavy industry and power	306	668	4,920	2,930	8,050	33,800	104	83	146
Mining	290	350	1,000	2,280	2,530	6,900	127	138	145
Energy	3[b]	23	170	100	170	900	30[b]	135	190
Heavy manufacturing	13[b]	295	3,750	550	5,350	26,000	24[b]	55	144
Supporting activities	110	412	2,320	8,470	13,370	66,200	13	31	35
Agriculture	2	9	100	890	1,500	5,500	2	6	18
Light manufacturing	13	37	450	960	1,700	14,000	13	22	32
Construction	29	116	300	1,900	3,170	7,600	15	37	39
Trade	21	73	400	1,360	2,010	10,000	15	36	40
Housing and other urban services	45	177	1,070	3,360	4,990	29,100	14	35	37

	Percentage Composition			Percentage Composition			Index Total = 100		
All activities	100	100	100	100	100	100	100	100	100
Heavy industry and power	73	61	68	26	38	34	289	166	203
Mining	70	32	14	20	12	7	354	276	201
Energy	1	2	2	1	1	1	83	270	264
Heavy manufacturing	3	27	52	5	25	26	67	110	200
Supporting activities	27	39	32	74	62	66	36	62	49
Agriculture	1	1	1	8	7	5	6	12	25
Light manufacturing	3	3	6	8	8	14	36	44	44
Construction	7	11	4	17	15	8	42	74	54
Trade	5	7	6	12	9	10	42	72	56
Housing and other urban services	11	16	15	29	23	29	39[b]	70	51

Source: Corporación Venezolana de Guayana, The Guayana Economic Program, Key to the Development of Venezuela (Caracas, July 1966).
Note: Components may not add up to total due to rounding.
a. 1961 and 1965 figures are actual; 1980 figures are the "potential" targets (see text).
b. In 1961 the Orinoco Steel Mill had not yet been completed, the steel furnaces were not fully installed, and pig-iron production was just beginning. The Macagua Electric Power Plant was just beginning to produce.

concern. Over the five-year span 1960–1965, the production of goods and services increased almost threefold.

The growth and change in the production structure have had an extensive impact on the level and composition of employment in Ciudad Guayana. Employment has risen spectacularly, from 1,100 in 1950 to 11,400 in 1961 and 21,420 in 1965. More striking than the growth in employment has been the change in its composition. In 1961, iron-ore processing made up one fifth of total employment and was the largest single category of production activity. In 1965, iron and steel production accounted for one fourth of total employment, which was twice that in ore processing. Employment levels attained in 1965 were nevertheless lower than those programmed earlier. Unforeseen time lags between completion of the feasibility study and groundbreaking were the principal factors slowing down the tempo of the program as envisioned in the early years.[11]

TABLE 3.13

Final Demand, Guayana and Venezuela, 1965 and 1980

	Gross Domestic Product, Total	Consumption	Investment	Exports	(Less) Imports
	Millions of Bolívars (1957 prices)				
Guayana					
1965 actual	1,080	430	320	830[a]	−500
1980 potential	7,240	2,040	1,700	6,700[a]	−3,200
Venezuela					
1965 actual	34,224	25,454	7,110	8,958	−7,298
1980 potential	95,727	67,925	22,017	18,708	−12,923
	Percentage Composition				
Guayana					
1965 actual	100.0	39.8	29.6	76.8[a]	−46.2
1980 potential	100.0	28.2	23.5	92.5[a]	−44.2
Venezuela					
1965 actual	100.0	74.4	20.8	26.2	−21.4
1980 potential	100.0	71.0	23.0	19.5	−13.5

Sources: For the Guayana region see Corporación Venezolana de Guayana, *The Guayana Economic Program, Key to the Development of Venezuela* (Caracas, July 1966); and for Venezuela see Table 3.1.

a. Exports to the rest of Venezuela and to the world.

If broad-brush characterizations may be made, Venezuela is a "consumption" economy, and the Guayana development area is a "regional export economy." In 1965, the export share of the Guayana economy (77 per cent) was three times the relative size of that for the Venezuelan economy as a whole; the investment share was 50 per cent larger. (See Table 3.13.) In contrast, even with a higher level of per capita income, the consumption share of the Guayana economy was less than half that of the nation as a whole. Over time these proportions will change, but the main characteristics will remain.

The evolution of the city's population from a traditional society to an industrial society is perhaps best reflected in the expected improvement in family income levels. A significant improvement has already occurred since 1960 as a consequence of the change in the production and employment structure and in the occupational composition of the labor force. Reinforcing these continuing factors in the future will be (1) the programmed improvement in levels of education, health, and welfare and (2) the effect of external economies of the developing industrial complex, and the wider range of job and investment choice. As a consequence, the proportion of families with annual incomes of less than Bs. 12,000 may be expected to decline from close to 60 per cent in 1965 to less than 20 per cent by 1980. At the same time the share of families in the Bs. 12,000–24,000 class may be expected to rise from 30 per cent in 1965 to over 50 per cent by 1980.

Investment Needs and Financing Strategy

To plan the regional development program comprehensively, it was urgent to obtain at an early date a systematic estimate of medium- and long-term investment requirements, covering the whole program. Feasibility studies of the key heavy industry projects had already been made, so reliable estimates of their investment needs were available. For other heavy industry projects and supporting activities, however, there was no other recourse in 1962 than to use capital coefficients, based on Venezuelan, Latin American, and U.S. experience and the rough approximations made for certain sectors in the Guayana program. Thus there was uncertainty about whether these estimates would hold up over time, as more feasibility studies were conducted. The first comprehensive estimate of long-term net investment requirements, made in 1962, totaled Bs. 13,100 million (equivalent to $2,880 million) for the twelve-year period 1963–1975. This figure is identical to the July 1966 evaluation of net investment requirements for the fifteen-year period 1965–1980 (see Table 3.14), but this identity is largely coincidental.

TABLE 3.14

Comparison of Guayana Region Investment Targets, 1963–1975 "Before" and 1965–1980 "After"

(Bs. millions)

	1963–1975 "Before"	1965–1980 "After"
Investment, total	13,100	13,000
Resource development	2,700	3,800
Agriculture	100	700
Mining	1,500	1,600
Energy	1,100	1,500
Heavy manufacturing	6,000	5,700
Light manufacturing and construction	900	500
Urban services	3,500	3,000
Housing	1,400	1,580
Trade	400	400
Public and private services	1,700	1,020

Sources: For "before" targets see Joseph D. Phillips, *Estimates of Investment Requirements for the Guayana Region, 1963–66 and 1963–75* (Caracas: Corporación Venezolana de Guayana, November 1962; working paper B–33), summary of the Guayana region investment program presented in Oficina Central de Coordinación y Planificación, *Plan de la Nación, 1963–1966* (Caracas, 1963); for "after" targets see Corporación Venezolana de Guayana, *The Guayana Economic Program, Key to the Development of Venezuela* (Caracas, July 1966).

In the interim, many new elements and changes entered the picture, apart from the transition from an estimate based largely on capital coefficients to one derived largely from feasibility studies and actual project development. There were significant changes in the heavy industry program, as discussed earlier, and lags in implementation. The programming effort was extended to new areas and pulled back in others. The completion of feasibility studies showed lower investment requirements in some industries and higher ones in others. Most important, in a time span of less than four years, new technology had brought forth major new projects.

A brief review of some of the major elements of change highlights the need for continuous study and review of project development. Agricultural investment estimates of 1962 dealt largely with a handful of experimental and field study programs; those of 1966 reflected some substantive development programs, especially in the Amacuro Delta, which hardly figured in the earlier assessment. As the agricultural program is further defined and extended in the course of the next few years, investment requirements may be expected to expand significantly. Iron mining experienced substantial unforeseen disinvestment (export of capital equipment) in 1962 and 1963, requiring replacement as well as expansion for marginally lower output targets for 1980. For electric power, the larger investment program for 1965–1980 is related to the planned continued expansion of power capacity after 1975. Iron and steel investment needs, as currently evaluated, reflect a lag in implementation, larger requirements for 1980 for an expanding Venezuelan economy, and a reduction in investment requirements per unit of output as a consequence of new technology (oxygen furnaces, improved blast furnaces, and continuous casting). Prereduction and enrichment of iron ore and fluidized iron-ore reduction are large new projects developed after 1962 as a result of technological breakthroughs; the evolution of these projects may change the export strategy of the Guayana complex. The lagged implementation of the first aluminum projects suggested more cautious goals (than earlier) despite a larger market prospect; for the future, new projects are likely to develop in pursuit of outstanding market prospects. Elemental phosphorus production has been eliminated, as only marginally profitable, while a project for the production of liquefied anhydrous refrigerated ammonia has been substantially expanded. Heavy machinery feasibility studies have been completed for only a fraction of the product lines suggested by market studies (used for earlier targets), and current programs have been limited to those; when steel plate becomes available, and further feasibility studies are carried out, goals in this area are likely to expand.

As the investment program planning moved from market studies and capital coefficients to substantive projects based on feasibility studies, targets for light manufacturing suffered from the dearth of promotional and developmental activities. Apart from the development of industrial parks (prepared sites for light manufacturing industry) and the promotion and development of several construction materials enterprises, little developmental activity was carried out in manufactures for the local market, and the current investment program reflects this.

Housing, education, health, water, sanitation, recreation, and cultural facilities received substantive attention early in the development program, and both early and current investment programs reflect similar orders of magnitude in these areas. Current estimates of investment needs for warehousing and transport activities, however, reflect a narrower scope as well as very limited developmental activity. Whereas the 1962 estimate, relying on projections of the demand for goods and passenger transport, set forth investment requirements for road, rail, water, and air transport (including bridges, rolling stock, and other investments), current investment estimates are based mainly on road construction needs.

Viewed in retrospect, the 1962 evaluation of investment requirements provided a broad vision of the whole investment program at an early date. Such a vision was urgently needed as a guide to private enterprise, the national planning agency, public international financing organizations, and the Guayana development authority itself. The subsequent implementation of that program experienced changes and lags, and the uncovering of new technology and new projects, but the substance and focus of the early vision remain valid and fully support the technique of bold-sketching the whole potential program at an early date. Experience has revealed, nevertheless, the need for continuous follow-through, the substitution of thorough-going feasibility studies for rough designs, and the implementation of the studies through promotional and developmental activities.

Investment programs and targets. As we have seen (Table 3.14), an estimated Bs. 13,000 million of net investment over the long-term period 1965–1980 is needed in resource, industry, and urban service facilities to achieve the targets of the Guayana program. This fifteen-year investment effort represents about three times the current annual level of total net investment in Venezuela and will make up somewhat less than 10 per cent of total Venezuelan net investment in the 1965–1980 period. Manufacturing takes the lion's share, 44 per cent, about twice the proportion of manufacturing investment in the national economy.

The public and private investment installed in the Guayana, in excess of Bs. 3,000 million ($660 million) by 1965, will have nearly doubled by the end of 1968, in line with the expectations of the 1965–1968 *Plan de la Nación.* The Guayana program will account for about 10 per cent of total investment in Venezuela in this period also.

Investment in manufacturing activities is expected to grow rapidly during the plan period, through the establishment of new manufacturing plants and the expansion of existing facilities. Investment to 1970 is geared to establish a range of heavy industry enterprises across a broad front of industry lines. After 1970 the main task will be the consolidation and substantial expansion of scale in industries and enterprises previously established—enriched iron ore, sponge iron, steel, foundry products, metal fabrications, aluminum, chemicals, and pulp and paper.

The CVG's role in this process is primarily that of catalyst, developing the base for attractive private investment opportunities as well as indicating the need for supporting public investment and urban services. The public investment share, while initially higher than that of private investment, is expected to decline in the 1970's.

Financing viability. Analyses and projections of the income and expenditure cash flow for all of the principal projects of the program, and for the program as a whole, indicate that a high rate of return is in prospect. A net investment of Bs. 16,000 million (Bs. 3,000 million prior to 1965 and

Bs. 13,000 million during 1965–1980) is expected to yield an annual value added of Bs. 7,240 million by 1980, representing a value added per unit of investment of Bs. 0.45 for the Guayana program, some 12 per cent greater than the recent level for the Venezuelan economy as a whole.[12] Annual export earnings by 1980 are expected to exceed Bs. 3,600 million (equivalent to one half of total value added) and surpass import saving.[13] While absorbing less than 10 per cent of national investment the development program will provide one fifth of an expanding level of manufactures and almost one fourth of a rising flow of exports.

Substantial net earnings are expected at an early date, even while major aspects of the program are in a start-up stage. By 1970, annual net earnings of the program as a whole may reach Bs. 300–500 million, equivalent to a return of 5 to 8 per cent on investment. The rate of return for heavy industry and power is expected to be substantially greater. By 1980, annual net earnings may rise to Bs. 1,500 million, with a rate of return of 10 per cent. Most of these earnings will be accounted for by heavy industry and power, whose annual rate of return is expected to be more than 15 per cent.[14] Up to the present, however, the program as a whole has had operating deficits, characteristic of the early start-up stage of major industrial enterprises. The rosy medium- and long-term financial prospects of the program are based on the relatively major role of large-scale modern enterprises, which are expected to have a high and rapid rate of return.

Over the long term (to 1980), roughly two fifths of the program could be financed through the reinvestment of earnings. (See Table 3.15.) Reinvestment may reach one third of annual financing needs by 1970 and is expected to surpass three fourths of annual needs by 1980.[15] The high return to the economy, the early payoff, and the prospect for internal generation of financing for investment needs all signify an outstanding financial viability—for the economy and for the program.

High and rapid rates of return are expected to attract private investment and to facilitate the mobilization of loan capital. While public investment currently exceeds private investment, the latter is expected to grow more rapidly after 1970. This is in line with the structure of the investment program, whereby basic public investment in steel, power, and urban infrastructure makes possible a range of private enterprises in heavy industry, light manufacturing, and services.

Public investment is counted on to provide one fourth of the total long-term investment needs for the Guayana program. Of this, two thirds would come from the CVG itself—mainly for heavy industry and power. Other Venezuelan public agencies are called on to provide the remaining

TABLE 3.15

Guayana Region: Potential Financing of Investment and Sources of Funds by Investment Sector, 1965–1980

	Investment Uses (Percentage Composition)				
	Total Program	Resource Development	Industrial Projects	Housing	Urban Infrastructure
Total sources	100	100	100	100	100
Reinvestment of earnings	42	59	47	28	6
Long-term loans	17	6	17	60	—
Private direct investment	15	9	17	13	24
CVG investment	17	17	19	—	19
Other public investment	8	9	—	—	50
Total program	100	29	48	12	11
Reinvestment of earnings	100	29	61	7	2
Long-term loans	100	8	55	37	—
Private direct investment	100	12	60	9	19
CVG investment	100	22	64	—	14
Other public investment	100	25	—	—	75

Sources: George Kalmanoff, "Financing Strategy for the Guayana Region Development Program, 1965–1975" (unpublished working paper, Corporación Venezolana de Guayana, Departamento de Planificación, Sector Económico, Caracas, June 1965); and Corporación Venezolana de Guayana, *The Guayana Economic Program, Key to the Development of Venezuela* (Caracas, July 1966), Chart VI–4, pp. 28 and 29.
Note: Components may not add up to totals due to rounding.

one third of public investment needs, including two thirds of the total needs for urban public services. (See Table 3.15.)

Herein lies the classic problem of a regional development authority. While one unit of public investment is expected to mobilize four units of total investment, a large share of the urban public service investment needs lies in the domain of specialized national public agencies. In the early years of the program these agencies lagged in the provision of the much-needed urban facilities, and the CVG had then to engage in the business of building roads, bridges, ports, water supply and sewage systems, schools, and health centers. By 1966, however, other public agencies were fulfilling their roles, and the Guayana development authority was gradually relinquishing to them the task of maintaining and expanding the facilities it had constructed.

The problem of investment phasing. The problem of timing and phasing a complex group of resource, industry, and urban infrastructure projects is perhaps the most difficult aspect of launching an ambitious regional development program in a virtual *tabula rasa* situation, and one in which the lags and gaps have serious consequences. Idle urban infrastructure is an important and ill-afforded capital cost, but industrial plant efficiency may be adversely affected if key technical personnel cannot be recruited and labor turnover is high as a consequence of shortages of housing, schools, water supply, hospitals, and other urban amenities.

In broad terms, the Guayana program was favored by a roughly optimal sequence of installation of resource, industry, and urban infrastructure facilities and by an almost compatible phasing of construction and production employment. Electric power was developed earliest, followed by the steel mill and by housing and urban facilities, in roughly that order. Thus power was available when needed for steel production; and demand for urban facilities was on tap, as housing and schools were built. In addition, as employment in steel mill construction tapered off, that in production expanded, and construction of the Guri Dam was begun. While some distress and dislocation occurred, it was short lived.

Gaps and lags occurred, nevertheless, with serious threats to the viability of the program. The lag in housing and urban infrastructure threatened the operations of the steel mill and the financial returns on this large government enterprise. The development and installation of industrial enterprises took substantially longer than was indicated by the painstaking studies and plans. Fortunately by 1966 substantial strides had been made in housing and other vital aspects of urban infrastructure, and the power and industry complex was in an active stage of development and implementation.

The Size of the New City

By 1961, when substantive planning for the heavy industry and power complex was under way, Ciudad Guayana had already had one of the most spectacular rates of growth of any city in the history of Venezuela. The city's population, which had been 1,000 in 1936 and 4,000 in 1950, measured 42,000 in the February 1961 census.

As may readily be appreciated, the question of what size city to plan for was one of the earliest concerns of the CVG. At the end of 1961, before systematic estimates were prepared, a report spoke of "a city . . . capable of accommodating 100,000 people in the first stage, and 250,000 in the next 20 years."[16] But these were rough figures, based on a comparison of the growth curve of Ciudad Guayana with that of other Venezuelan cities that had experienced rapid growth.

At first, interest centered on the concept of an ideal size. This was quickly dismissed on the grounds that neither Venezuelan nor international experience points to an "ideal" size limitation. The city must be large enough to provide external economies; and its size would be a function of the growth of its heavy industry and power activities.

There remained, nevertheless, important considerations affecting planning. How rapidly would the city grow? How could adequate account be taken of possible leads and lags in migration of the population to the city in relation to population "requirements," in line with actual job expansion, and in terms of the provision of urban facilities and amenities, education, and technical training facilities? Was the pool of potential inmigrants from depressed eastern Venezuela (the main source of the bulk of free-flowing inmigrants) sufficient for medium- and long-term targets? Would the inmigrants' skills match the job requirements?

The population reached an estimated 73,000 in February 1965, according to a Central Bank survey, and was approaching 90,000 toward the end of 1966. Present plans and expectations foresee populations of 200,000 in the mid-1970's and 300,000 around 1980. (See Table 3.16.)

TABLE 3.16
Ciudad Guayana: Population, 1936–1980

Year	Population (thousands)
	Actual
1936	1
1941	1
1950	4
1961	42
1965	73
	Projected
1970	150
1975	221[a]
1980	326[a]

Sources: For 1936–1961 see Ministerio de Fomento, Oficina Central del Censo, Novena Censo General de Población, Febrero 1961 (Caracas, 1965), and population censuses for 1936, 1941, and 1950 (Caracas); for 1965 see Encuesta sobre Características Demográficas en Santo Tomé de Guayana, Febrero 1965, published by the Banco Central de Venezuela for the Corporación Venezolana de Guayana; and for 1965–1980 see Corporación Venezolana de Guayana, The Guayana Region Economic Program, Key to the Development of Venezuela (Caracas, July 1966).
a. Potential.

The more moderate rate of unemployment in 1965 (13 per cent) indicated a rough balance between the inmigration flow and jobs. The make-up of migrants' skills, however, reflected an excess of unskilled workers and a shortage of qualified workers and technicians. The demographic and economic outlook for eastern Venezuela pointed to an adequate pool of migrants far into the future.

Revison of population targets. Earlier analyses had foreseen an even more rapid population build-up, but the shortage of housing, lags in the industrial program, and changes in the employment implications of a key industrial project combined to make for a lower rate of growth. In mid-1963, for example, estimates based on analyses and projections of heavy industry and power activities and requirements for supporting production of goods and services yielded population projections of 115,000 by 1966; 250,000 by 1970; and 415,000 by 1975.[17] In February 1965, however, when Ciudad Guayana's population was only 73,000, a reported one third of the steel mill's 5,000 workers were forced to commute from urban areas as far as Ciudad Bolívar due to the lack of housing in Ciudad Guayana. More important in the stretchout of population growth expectations were the unforeseen time lags in the implementation of industrial projects. Added to this was a tendency for the private industrial projects and joint ventures to start out at a level below that called for by criteria of market potential and economic scale—presumably to minimize risk and financial commitment in an industrial complex at a pioneer venture stage.

Another element involved in the modification of the population estimates was a substantial reduction in projected employment in the heavy machinery project. This industry had traditionally been characterized by small-scale, custom-manufacture, job-shop operations, according to the U.S. Census of Manufacturers in 1958; in such an industry economic scale could be achieved at relatively low levels of output. This factor, together with the outstanding Venezuelan market for certain types of machinery and metal fabrications and the possibilities of linkages and external economies, indicated that this industry would be a natural one for the Guayana. A preliminary project study was prepared, modeled on the characteristics of the U.S. industry. A subsequent feasibility study, however, showed that modern technology suggested a higher scale of capacity with a much lower requirement for employment per unit of output.

Consequences of the modified population estimates. What were the consequences of the stretchout in population estimates? Overestimating population growth could have resulted, conceivably, in an overbuilding of urban infrastructure facilities; also, failure to achieve growth expectations could have disheartened the planners and might have discredited the planning operation. There were, fortunately, two saving graces in the situation. Partly as a consequence of the lag in construction of housing and urban infrastructure, the population projections were modified long before there was any possibility of overtaking urban infrastructure needs. More important perhaps was the fact that the heavy industry complex would develop along the general lines foreseen but would take several more years than estimated to attain the specified stages of growth.

In what alternative ways might the population projections have been handled? In retrospect, it would seem that systematic alternatives should have been used from the beginning to analyze the sensitivity of the planning effort to changes in some of its basic elements. The urgent need to study program alternatives had been emphasized by the program directors at an early date. With so much to be done by a small staff just to complete the full preparation of *one* plan, however, the systematic study of alternatives was bypassed in the early years. The need to formulate alternatives was also highlighted by an independent review group in April 1964.[18] These recommendations were implemented in 1965.

Conclusions

In a sense, the problems of programming for the Guayana covered the whole range of urban development issues, but perhaps in a more accentuated form.

Regional export activities are the key to planning the development of a new industrial city. Fluctuations in national and international markets can easily outmode planning and plans at a sensitive stage; the planners must be aware of market developments at all times. The Guayana program has been hampered from the very beginning by a steel mill designed for the market of the 1950's—large diameter pipe and construction steel—and inappropriate for the market of the 1960's and 1970's, which favors steel plate and sheet. Although intensive analyses of domestic, Latin American, and world markets were carried out in the early years, these studies have been updated on a hit-and-miss basis only, and the present program may be seriously deficient in this important respect.

To achieve growth targets in any urban area requires a commensurate effort in supporting production and service activities, especially education, health, welfare, transportation, housing, and public services. Shortcomings in urban infrastructure can hamper the efficiency and productivity of an industrial program. There was clear evidence between 1962 and 1964 that the shortage of these facilities was adversely affecting production at the steel mill—and consequently the return to the economy on a $350-million investment. The mill was seriously short of engineers, technicians, and skilled workers in that period; it was frequent for recruits to fly in on a Thursday and leave the following Tuesday, after they had seen the shortage of urban amenities. This contributed to the disappointing performance of the mill and slowed down expansion plans. Delay in urban infrastructure planning and implementation, while the best design was sought, was understandable, but it bore with it very serious economic consequences.

The provision of adequate urban services requires a major role on the part of other public agencies in addition to the CVG. The problem of mobilizing the participation of other public agencies is part of the general problem of the relationship of a regional authority to a national government agency. In the circumstances, nevertheless, a larger effort might have been undertaken to involve other government agencies in the work of the CVG.

Private enterprise responded early and strongly to the attractive investment opportunities offered by the unique resource and location characteristics of the Guayana, but to move from project conception to feasibility study completion, plant construction, and installation proved to be more tortuous and time consuming than originally anticipated, upsetting program timetables. (The aluminum enterprise, for example, was planned in 1961 but did not break ground until 1966.) There should have been greater flexibility in the programming effort to provide for the possibility of these delays.

The population of Ciudad Guayana was expanding at a very rapid rate (15 per cent a year) from 1961 to 1965 in response to the industrial development, but earlier prognoses had foreseen an even more rapid growth rate, 18 per cent a year for the period 1961–1975. Such an overstatement of growth prospects might have had serious consequences. Although it was natural to concentrate on the pursuit of an ambitious development target, the planning effort should have focused on a range of alternatives at an early date. This would have enabled the planners to test the program's sensitivity to changes in key areas and would have minimized their self-questioning about the credibility of the program.

By the time the program became fully defined it was cumbersome and not readily susceptible to the systematic modification and adjustment required by the frequent changes in project size, characteristics, and timing that are to be expected in a developing program. To correct this problem and to provide systematic, consistent estimates of requirements for supporting production and service activities, the planners began in 1965 to adapt the economic program for automatic data processing. The computer analysis model that was developed looks promising, but it had several inherent model problems and in its way was also unwieldy. The model made no adequate provision for growth in productivity and real wages over time. Family income levels remained constant over a fifteen-year period, which made pointless the analysis of income elasticity of demand. The over-all effect was to understate employment and investment requirements for local market-oriented commerce and services. From a strategy viewpoint, the model was designed primarily to derive the direct and indirect requirements for local market-oriented manufactures, an aspect of regional production that is less important than the requirements for urban services. Nevertheless, the model proved to be eminently useful in its capacity to manipulate data inputs, express relationships, and provide orders of magnitude on program elements, even though its results were not directly utilizable; certainly the use of computer analyses will lead to improved programming in the future.[19]

While heavy industry was relatively well studied and programmed, with feasibility studies in every important field, a number of key areas have been relatively neglected. These include agriculture and light industry. Tropical agriculture in an arid region with a granite shield dating from the pre-Azoic era (before the beginning of life on earth and therefore lacking in organic matter) is an extremely chancy thing. For this reason, economists of the CVG Planning Department were reluctant to encourage ventures in agriculture. But this reluctance went so far as to minimize the need for an over-all systematic study of agricultural demand and the potential for agricultural development in the region. Such a study, including the implications of land reclamation and flood control in the Amacuro Delta in terms of production, employment, investment, and yields, is still urgently needed. Potential development of light industry in the Guayana was a matter of tertiary importance—following heavy industry and power, housing, and urban infrastructure. Partly on this account, partly because of lack of staff, and partly because it was felt that market forces alone ought to be relied on to bring forth ventures in this area, no effort has been launched to promote and develop light industry. This may be a serious oversight. Ciudad Guayana needs productive employment opportunities for unskilled workers and for women, as well as a competitive source of supply of light manufactures.

Perhaps most serious of all, the economic planners developed no adequate continuous system for measuring and reporting economic activity. The only information on production, employment, and investment comes from occasional ad hoc surveys and rough quantitative assessments. Thus we have the paradox of a modern, highly respected, large-scale enterprise, the CVG, whose fixed assets are approaching $600 million, without current economic information on key aspects of growth in the development area for which it is responsible. In a way the programming effort was operating blind due to this information deficiency. How seriously this has limited the effectiveness of the programming effort would be difficult to say.

In a sense, most of the shortcomings cited derive from one final shortcoming: for the magnitude of the task at hand, the staff of the Economic Section of the Planning Department has proved to be extremely inadequate in size, so that it has been impossible to maintain programming continuity, with staff shifted from one high-priority task to another from day to day. At its largest, the staff of the Economic Section included ten full-time professionals, four full-time consultants, and six part-time consultants.

An ambitious, meaningful, and significant planning effort, with deep involvement and commitment, is not a neat, tidy affair. In the last analysis, this effort must be judged by its accomplishments. The planning method was bold, to match the needs of the Venezuelan economy and its accustomed rate of growth. The planning operation complemented and assisted the vision of Venezuelan leaders. Will and determination, perhaps the most important ingredients, were on hand to carry out an ambitious, large-scale program. In the framework of expansive national targets, a comprehensive urban and regional program was designed and is being carried out. Regional planning has been demonstrated as an effective instrument for implementing national goals and for giving national plans a concrete, specific project and location reality. Despite the limited size of the planning staff, the full range of programming and project studies and surveys dictated by accepted economic programming techniques was made, though perhaps at the expense of attention to flexibility and alternatives. Effective regional planning must relate to the economic and social needs of the nation and the region, embrace all aspects of the economy from goods production to urban services, combine a global view with specific project development, look ahead to the medium term and long term, involve a partnership of the public and private sectors, and be flexible to accommodate new technology and change. Regional planning in this style can pay off handsomely, as it is doing in the Guayana.

Chapter 4

Regional
Transportation
Issues

Richard M. Soberman

Planning a complete system of regional transportation involves specification of both the types of transport facilities required and the time at
which they will be needed. In particular, a regional plan for transportation should specify

1. the location of transport routes in space
2. the physical description of these routes in terms of their type and
   standards
3. the scheduling of future investments in the transportation system
4. methods of financing construction of the transportation system
5. methods of operating and maintaining the completed system
6. the pricing policy to be employed in charging for transport services
   provided by the system.

Three steps are usually involved in this procedure. First, the demand for
transportation—the magnitude and character of commodity flows and
of passenger movements—must be determined. Traffic variation over
time, average shipment size, and the nature of the cargo involved are of
primary concern in describing the characteristics of commodity movements. The nature and magnitude of these anticipated commodity flows
will be the major determinants of the transport plan, although some basic
network of transportation facilities will be dictated by the minimum
administrative, social, and military functions required of any responsible
government. Second, the supply side of transportation must be investigated. Estimates of cost characteristics and quality of service must be

compared for alternative modes of transportation and for alternative technologies within a particular mode. The final step involves evaluating alternative transport solutions, taking into account the availability of factor inputs needed for the supply of transportation, differences in service quality, and the indirect consequences associated with each alternative. These steps, of course, are not entirely independent, since there may be considerable interaction between the conditions of transport supply, such as costs and quality of service, and the level of transport demand that eventually materializes.

This chapter attempts to illustrate the application of some of these procedures by evaluating the transport needs of the newly developing Guayana region of Venezuela. A detailed discussion of all the procedures and calculations involved is outside the scope of this volume.[1] However, the following analyses of estimated demand for transportation (primarily interregional commodity flows) and the alternative methods of meeting that demand should enable us to draw conclusions about whether the transportation system in the Guayana region will be adequate during the development period.

The Demand for Transportation

Predicting the demand for transportation in underdeveloped regions characteristically is complicated by the fact that data upon which to base predictions of transportation demand are usually lacking—either because the transport link under consideration is a completely new one for which no history exists or because no attempts have been made to collect data in the past. Moreover, future developments are clouded with a great deal more uncertainty than usually exists in more advanced economies. The first road constructed in an area may generate traffic beyond the planner's wildest expectations, or it may generate a one-way, one-time flow of traffic out of the area into the existing centers of population. In other words, induced traffic (new traffic generated by the facility) is generally more significant in developing regions, and the element of uncertainty is always greater for induced traffic than for diverted traffic (existing traffic transferred from an old facility to a new or improved one). Uncertainty also exists because many underdeveloped countries have specialized or "one-crop" economies, with the result that small changes in the world markets for these goods can produce far-reaching effects on the total economy of the country.

As with any other good offered in the market, more transportation will be demanded as its price is reduced. Because the demand for transportation is a derived demand, however, its price sensitivity depends largely upon the magnitude of transportation costs relative to the total value of the commodity moved. Transport costs also affect demand in a more indirect manner. In the Guayana region, for example, the cost of transporting foods and other consumer goods leads to high costs of living and correspondingly high wage rates that in turn lead to higher costs of production. Even though for many final goods the costs of transporting them may not loom large in terms of their total value, transport costs may be reflected indirectly in higher costs of production—and thus in reduced demand for the products of the region.

Because of timing considerations and the lack of the relevant demand function data, the demand for final goods that could be produced competitively in the Guayana region was determined on the basis of historical trends, notably, the effects of rising per capita income on the consumption of various goods and services that had been experienced in the past. These estimates of domestic demand were coupled with projections of the demand for exports, based on an analysis of future Latin American and world markets.[2] On the basis of the demand estimates, a list of potential industrial projects for the Guayana region was drawn up, taking into account the resource endowments that would give this region particular competitive advantage. These resources included the availability of very high-grade iron ore, relatively cheap hydroelectric potential, access to nearby deposits of natural gas and petroleum, and the existence of deep-water shipping facilities.

The targets for the production of various goods and services developed by the economic planning staff of the Corporación Venezolana de Guayana (CVG) were translated into estimates of employment and income that were subsequently used to estimate the future population of Ciudad Guayana and the region. Given these estimates of production and population, the total demand for transportation can be separated into the following categories:

1. transportation of the primary input materials necessary for production
2. transportation of final goods produced to other locations in the region, country, and world
3. transportation of consumer and agricultural goods not produced locally that are necessary to sustain populations of the indicated magnitudes
4. passenger transportation.

Because it is of relatively minor importance in terms of new transportation

TABLE 4.1
Summary of Total Estimated Commodity Flows to and from Ciudad Guayana, 1966, 1970, 1975, and 1980

Annual Commodity Flows (thousand metric tons)

Origin or Destination	1966		1970		1975		1980	
	In	Out	In	Out	In	Out	In	Out
Iron ore								
Cerro Bolívar	14,000	—	14,000	—	14,000	—	14,000	—
El Pao	6,000	—	6,000	—	6,000	—	6,000	—
San Isidro	2,100	—	12,900	—	28,000	—	31,000	—
Export	—	20,300	—	24,600	—	33,000	—	37,800
Total	22,100	20,300	32,900	24,600	48,000	33,000	51,000	37,800
Other								
Amacuro Delta	200	—	400	—	800	—	2,000	—
Eastern Guayana	—	—	—	—	290	—	550	—
Guacuripa	320	—	720	—	1,340	—	2,390	—
Apure	4	—	6	—	11	—	17	—
Barinas	—	19	—	45	—	101	—	185
Barquisimeto	—	4	—	10	—	21	—	39
Caracas	65	131	104	319	172	698	246	1,270
Coro	140	—	140	—	350	—	700	—
El Tigre	—	24	—	58	—	124	—	227
Guárico	5	—	8	—	14	—	22	—
Maracaibo	12	77	25	192	47	416	79	755
Maracay	29	23	42	55	68	120	89	219
Margarita	—	—	—	—	100	—	100	—
Maturín	6	27	10	64	19	139	30	253
Naricual	420	—	840	—	1,580	—	2,720	—
Pertigalete	281	—	631	—	1,130	—	2,080	—
Puerto Cabello	14	2	21	5	34	10	44	19
Puerto la Cruz	27	8	45	23	109	50	194	88
Valencia	51	113	83	298	138	622	201	1,120
West of Valencia	25	—	40	—	68	—	103	—
Valera	—	16	—	38	—	86	—	158
Export	549	640	1,095	1,020	2,074	1,800	3,588	3,040
Total (excluding iron ore)	2,148	1,084	4,210	2,127	8,344	4,187	15,153	7,373

Reprinted from Richard M. Soberman, *Transport Technology for Developing Regions* (Cambridge, Mass.: The M.I.T. Press, 1967), Table 4.4, pp. 90–91.

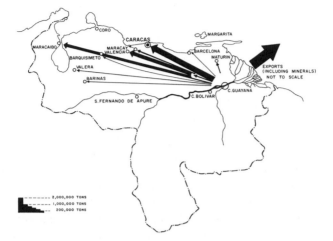

FIGURE 4.1   Destination of commodity flows originating in Bolívar State in 1975.

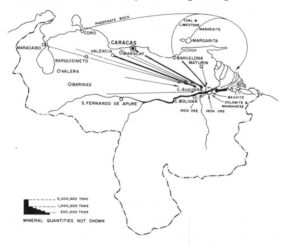

FIGURE 4.2   Origin of commodity flows entering Bolívar State in 1975.

facilities, passenger transportation is not considered here. Demand estimates for the first three items are included in the summary figures shown
in Table 4.1. Flow diagrams based on Table 4.1 are shown in Figures
4.1 and 4.2. Such diagrams are useful to show the origins and destinations
that can be grouped along principal transportation routes. They also
highlight the imbalance of incoming and outgoing flows for the region.

   There is, of course, some uncertainty in these commodity flow estimates,
stemming in part from national or world conditions that are outside the
control of regional planners. Uncertainty about estimates of the growth
rates of the Venezuelan population and economy causes uncertainty about
both the type and the level of production that can be achieved in the
Guayana region.

   Another uncertainty is whether or not *all* the planned industrial activities will in fact materialize. A proposed iron-ore reduction plant is an example: the economics of the plant are based on the feasibility of a gas-reduction process that could use the natural gas available nearby. Whether or not this plant is built thus depends on the technical feasibility of the natural gas process, aside from any consideration of the market for the ore. If this process should not prove feasible it would be safe to assume that no reduced iron ore would be produced for export.

There is also uncertainty about the level of demand in some industries. For many of the industries being planned, a certain minimum level of demand is almost guaranteed, particularly if government controls are introduced. A large part of the anticipated production of the Guayana industrial complex is planned to replace basic commodities that are now being imported. Moreover, for some time to come the Guayana region will be the only domestic producer of many of these commodities (for example, structural steel shapes, reinforcing bars, rails, and sheet metal). Thus a government decision to reduce or prohibit further imports of these products will immediately create a demand for domestic producers, although the extent of this demand (as well as export demand) will still depend upon prices, quality, and national population and economic growth rates. Precedent has already been set for this sort of government action in a well-defined program for reducing imports of automobiles.

The major effects of these uncertainties on transportation planning relate to the capacity and quality of the transport network that must be provided (and hence to the investment requirements of the transport sector). In addition, as shown in the following section, the decision about what *modes* of transportation ought to be provided hinges to a great extent on the levels of transport demand that materialize. In view of these uncertainties, it should be emphasized that the estimates of transport demand summarized in Table 4.1 represent estimates of what the transportation needs of the region will be if production achieves the projected levels.

A Comparison of Alternative Systems

Commodity flow estimates for the Guayana region indicate the need for both water and overland transportation systems. Water transportation is particularly suited to the Guayana industrial complex, since water routes are available to practically all major urban and industrial areas along the northern coast of Venezuela. At the present time, however, domestic water transportation is discouraged by inefficient port administration, excessive port handling charges, and high shipping costs for Venezuelan flag vessels. In view of the bulk nature of the commodity flows expected to originate

FIGURE 4.3   Map of the Guayana region.

from this region, however, the relative importance of shipping as a mode of transportation can be expected to increase in the future.

Within overland transportation systems the question of road versus rail becomes an important consideration. The principal population centers of the region are presently connected by good all-weather roads. The major link to the rest of the country is the road along the south bank of the Orinoco between Puerto Ordaz and Ciudad Bolívar that then continues north to El Tigre. In 1967 the completion of a bridge across the Orinoco at Ciudad Bolívar greatly improved highway transport to the rest of the country. A bridge across the Caroní connecting Puerto Ordaz and San Félix was completed in 1964. Railroading is limited to the modern, highly efficient line connecting the Orinoco Mining Company's mine at Cerro Bolívar to its port at Puerto Ordaz and the Iron Mines Company line between its mine at El Pao and port facilities at Palúa, just west of San Félix on the southern bank of the Orinoco. Both lines are used exclusively for the carriage of iron ore and are privately operated. (These locations are indicated on the map of the region shown in Figure 4.3.)

Railroads are currently a controversial issue in Venezuela. Although at one time railroad lines were to be found throughout the country, many of these were abandoned as highways were improved and trucking became more competitive. The competitive disadvantage of railroad transportation was in no small part caused by the fact that it was composed of separate lines operating on different gauge tracks. Today railroading in Venezuela is limited to four separate lines (excluding the privately owned lines of the Orinoco Mining Company and the Iron Mines Company), one of which will undoubtedly be abandoned following completion of a highway around the western side of Lake Maracaibo.[3]

Despite the present state of railroad development in the country, there are pressures for further railroad construction. A national commission has strongly urged the construction of an extensive system of railroads running from east to west across Venezuela, with branches to San Cristóbal and San Félix in the south. Although attempts have been made to demonstrate the economic viability of such a system, the basic arguments really rest on the belief that any nation undergoing rapid industrialization should equip itself with an adequate system of railroads. Separate proposals have also been made for the construction of a railroad between Guanta on the northern coast and the steel mill at Matanzas for the purpose of transporting coal and limestone to the steel mill. A new line has recently been completed from the coal mines at Naricual to the port of Guanta.

However, a World Bank mission to Venezuela strongly recommended that no further railroad construction be undertaken anywhere in Venezuela. The mission argued that railroad construction would constitute an unnecessary duplication of transport facilities, particularly in view of the high construction costs and low revenues of the line recently constructed between Puerto Cabello and Barquisimeto.[4]

Nevertheless, the construction of the Naricual-Matanzas railroad might look economically feasible now in light of the plans for increased industrial development in the Guayana region. For this reason we will need to analyze and compare the costs for the alternative transportation systems, one using the existing modes (truck, ship, and truck-ship combination) and the other using the railroad.

Truck, ship, and truck-ship combination. The distribution of commodity flows between truck and ship modes of transport depends to a great extent on the relative costs for each.

A comparison of the estimated costs of transporting finished steel products by truck and by ship from Ciudad Guayana to various destinations in the country is shown in Table 4.2.[5] Trucking costs include only fully distributed operating costs (both fixed and variable), without any allowance for road construction or maintenance costs. For destinations that are not ports, shipping costs were estimated to the nearest port and

TABLE 4.2

A Comparison of Estimated Shipping and Trucking Costs for General Cargo Originating in Ciudad Guayana[a]

Destination	Nearest Port	Ship-Truck Combination[b]				Truck Only[b]		Difference (Bs. per ton)
		Shipping Costs (Bs. per ton)	Remaining Road Distance (km.)	Trucking Costs (Bs. per ton)	Total Costs (Bs. per ton)	Road Distance (Bs. per ton)	Total Costs[c] (Bs. per ton)	
Caracas	La Guaira	59.4	20	9.6	69.0	745	96.5	27.5
Maracay	Puerto Cabello	61.6	107	20.0	81.6	754	98.0	16.4
Valencia	Puerto Cabello	61.6	57	14.0	75.6	796	102.7	27.1
Puerto Cabello	Puerto Cabello	61.6	—	7.2	68.8	853	109.7	40.9
Barquisimeto	Puerto Cabello	61.6	173	28.0	89.6	984	125.2	35.6
Barinas	Puerto Cabello	61.6	417	57.2	118.8	1,156	146.7	27.9
Valera	Maracaibo	70.5	216	33.1	103.6	1,229	154.7	51.1
Maracaibo	Maracaibo	70.5	—	7.2	77.7	1,304	164.2	86.5

Reprinted from Richard M. Soberman, *Transport Technology for Developing Regions* (Cambridge, Mass.: The M.I.T. Press, 1966), Table 4.5, p. 100.

a. 1959 prices.

b. Trucking costs do not include road construction or maintenance costs.

c. Includes Bs. 7.2 per ton for loading and unloading and line-haul costs of Bs. 0.12 per ton-kilometer.

allowances made for transporting goods by truck for the remaining distance. In allocating shipping costs to general cargo, only incremental costs and not fully distributed average costs were considered. In other words, if a ship carrying limestone from Guanta is also used to carry structural steel to La Guaira, the only costs charged against the general cargo are those over and above the costs that would have been incurred had the ship returned directly to Guanta. These incremental costs include:

1. terminal charges for loading the general cargo in Matanzas and unloading it in La Guaira
2. daily operating charges for the additional time spent in port (both Mantanzas and La Guaira)
3. daily operating charges for the difference in trip time between returning directly to Guanta and returning via La Guaira.

Table 4.2 shows that despite very heavy terminal charges for general cargo, ship and ship-truck combinations of transport cost less than highway transportation alone for all destinations shown. For many finished steel products, lead time in ordering will be sufficient to compensate for the additional time for ship transport. This is particularly true for such commodities as seamless steel pipe and structural steel, which will represent a large proportion of total steel production in the Guayana.[6]

Despite the cost advantage of water transportation, however, there is still likely to be a substantial demand for truck transportation. For many high-value commodities, the savings in using water transportation may

TABLE 4.3
Estimated Distribution of Commodity Flows Between Truck and Ship for Traffic Between Ciudad Guayana and Selected Points, 1966, 1970, 1975, and 1980

Traffic Between	Commodity Flows (thousand metric tons)							
	1966		1970		1975		1980	
Ciudad Guayana and	Truck	Ship	Truck	Ship	Truck	Ship	Truck	Ship
General cargo								
Maturín	33	—	74	—	158	—	283	—
El Tigre	24	—	58	—	124	—	227	—
Guárico	5	—	8	—	14	—	22	—
Puerto la Cruz	35	—	68	—	159	—	282	—
Caracas	131	65	269	154	552	318	936	581
Maracay	40	12	69	28	131	57	203	105
Valencia	110	54	252	129	493	267	839	487
West of Valencia	25	—	40	—	68	—	103	—
Puerto Cabello	15	1	23	3	39	5	53	10
Barquisimeto	2	2	5	5	10	11	19	20
Valera	16	—	38	—	86	—	158	—
Barinas	19	—	45	—	101	—	185	—
Apure	4	—	6	—	11	—	17	—
Maracaibo	13	76	35	182	87	376	147	687
Total general cargo	472	210	990	501	2,033	1,034	3,474	1,890
Bulk cargo								
Coro	—	140	—	140	—	350	—	700
Margarita	—	—	—	—	—	100	—	100
Guanta	—	680	—	1,470	—	2,740	—	4,860
Total bulk cargo	—	820	—	1,610	—	3,190	—	5,660

Reprinted from Richard M. Soberman, *Transport Technology for Developing Regions* (Cambridge, Mass.: The M.I.T. Press, 1966), Table 4.8, p. 108.

not be significant in relation to the total value of the goods. For others, shipments might be too small to permit economic handling by ship. Also, the shipping *costs* estimated in Table 4.2 are much lower than the shipping *rates* currently quoted by Venezuelan shipping companies.[7] These companies presently employ much smaller ships than those upon which the cost estimates are based. A substantial potential demand for water transportation would probably have to be demonstrated before shipping companies would incur the initial expenditures for larger vessels. High utilization would also have to be guaranteed before lower rates could be offered to attract the necessary traffic.

Nevertheless, because of the large differential between trucking and water transportation costs, it might reasonably be assumed that almost all finished steel products destined for Maracaibo and at least 50 per cent of the finished steel products (excluding machinery and equipment) for the Caracas-Maracay-Valencia industrial belt would be transported by ship. Most of these estimated commodity flows are steel shapes for construction industries, steel for use in automotive related industries such as assembly plants, and metal for foodstuff containers. Steel requirements for these industries can generally be anticipated far enough in advance to allow sufficient time for shipment by boat. In Table 4.3, therefore, the estimates of truck and ship traffic were made by assuming that all steel products moving to Maracaibo and 50 per cent of those to Maracay, Valencia, Caracas, Puerto Cabello, and Barquisimeto are to be transported by ship.

On the basis of calculations made elsewhere,[8] it appears that the truck tonnages shown in Table 4.3 could be handled adequately by the existing regional road system at least until 1975. Between 1975 and 1980, total capacity of the regional routes would have to be increased either by widening the route via Ciudad Bolívar or by replacing the ferry service across the Orinoco at Ciudad Guayana with a bridge connection to the Los Barrancos highway.

Naricual-Matanzas railroad. The economic justification for a railroad from the coal mines at Naricual to Matanzas depends upon the relationship between the savings in variable costs of transportation obtained by using the railroad and the costs of amortizing the capital investment in the railroad line and rolling stock. Since the railroad would be owned and operated by the government, the analysis is confined to whether or not investment in railroad construction represents an efficient way for the government to spend available funds. Thus we are concerned with *cost* differentials between alternative modes of transportation; the private investor is interested primarily in *revenues*. The government can take into

TABLE 4.4

Comparison of Estimated Portal-to-Portal Transportation Costs Between Ciudad Guayana and Selected Cities by Ship, Road, and Railroad (Bs. per ton)[a]

Destination	Ship[b]	Truck[c]	Naricual-Matanzas Railroad	
			Piggyback[d]	Other[e]
General cargo				
El Tigre	—	34.1	25.5	32.2
Puerto la Cruz	58.0	56.6	38.7	40.4
Caracas	69.0	96.5	83.3	85.0
Maracay	81.6	98.0	89.3	96.0
Valencia	75.6	102.7	94.4	101.1
Puerto Cabello	68.8	109.7	101.1	107.8
Barquisimeto	89.6	125.2	117.0	123.7
Barinas	118.8	146.7	137.5	144.2
Valera	103.6	154.7	145.5	152.2
Maracaibo	77.7	164.2	155.4	162.1
Maturín	—	28.8	61.6	67.8
Bulk cargo				
Naricual	9.98	—	—	7.17
Pertigalete	8.12	—	—	7.62

Reprinted from Richard M. Soberman, *Transport Technology for Developing Regions* (Cambridge, Mass.: The M.I.T. Press, 1966), Table 4.9, p. 109.

a. 1959 prices.

b. Fully distributed average costs, including amortization of investment in ships and terminal charges.

c. Fully distributed operating costs, including terminal charges but excluding any allowance for road construction or maintenance costs.

d. Trucking component as in note c. Rail costs are operating costs only, exclusive of any allowance for investment in railroad construction or rolling stock but including terminal charges.

e. Operating costs only as in note d.

account savings in highway investment that may occur as a result of railroad construction; the private investor has no interest in these.

An analysis of the proposed Naricual-Matanzas railroad must consider differences in the costs of transporting foods to and from Ciudad Guayana by railroad, highway, and ship. For bulk quantities, such as coal from Naricual and limestone from Pertigalete, the relevant comparison is between railroad and ship, since ship costs are much lower than trucking costs for these commodities. For general cargo, the costs of moving goods by railroad from Ciudad Guayana to El Tigre or Puerto la Cruz and from there by truck must be compared with the costs of shipping and trucking to various other destinations in Venezuela. In this case, savings in operating costs on the railroad result from lower line-haul costs per ton-kilometer (approximately Bs. 0.05 versus Bs. 0.12 by truck). These savings, however, are reduced by the additional costs of transshipment at El Tigre or Puerto la Cruz.

Costs of shipping general cargo between Ciudad Guayana and selected cities are summarized in Table 4.4 for ship, truck, railroad (freight car), and trailer-on-flat-car (piggyback) operations. Costs of transporting bulk cargoes from Naricual and Pertigalete by rail and ship are also shown. Note that the costs of ship and truck operations are fully distributed average costs including the costs of amortizing investment in ships and trucks (but not roads), whereas railroad costs include only costs of operation. Cost savings must therefore be compared with equipment costs as well as with investment in construction.

These figures show that the costs of transporting general cargo to various cities in Venezuela are much lower by ship than by railroad-truck alternatives. For all but goods destined to Maturín, however, rail-truck combinations represent a lower cost solution than trucking alone, although most differences are insignificant in view of the uncertainties associated with the basic cost data. Rail costs are also lower for the bulk commodities shown, although for the limestone from Pertigalete a small change in terminal costs could reverse the saving in favor of shipping. Thus for general cargo the railroad would be competitive at best only for the truck traffic estimated in Table 4.3. Some general cargo would continue to move by truck despite the lower rates that could be offered by the rail-truck combination. Traffic in this category would include very small shipments and high-value cargo for which the prospects of an overnight trip to Caracas or Valencia as opposed to two or three days by rail would outweigh the cost advantages of rail transportation. It has been assumed here that 20 per cent of the general overland cargo shown in Table 4.3 would be transported by truck despite the higher costs involved.

Railroad cost savings depend upon the distribution of traffic between freight car and piggyback operations. Since piggyback costs are lower for the proposed route, it would be advantageous to move as much cargo as possible by this method. For some cargo, however, side loading of flatcars (as opposed to end loading of trailers) will be necessary. This cargo is assumed to include from one quarter to one half of all rail traffic, or 20 to 40 per cent of total overland general cargo. For these traffic distributions, and using the cost differentials in Table 4.4, annual savings in transport costs are estimated in Table 4.5. These savings can be compared with railroad construction costs.

Construction cost estimates for the Naricual-Matanzas railroad are shown in Table 4.6. Because of the wide range in the costs estimated for this line, both low and high estimates are given. Cumulative estimates showing the total investment that would have to be accumulated in rolling stock as of the various years are also shown. In Table 4.7 these initial costs have been converted into annual costs for interest rates of 4 to 10 per

TABLE 4.5

Summary of Estimated Annual Savings in Transportation Costs Resulting from Construction of the Naricual-Matanzas Railroad

Savings Between Ciudad Guayana and Indicated Center	Savings (Bs. per ton)[a]	Total Savings (Bs. thousands per year)		
		1970	1975	1980
Bulk cargo savings				
Naricual	2.81	2,360	4,440	7,620
Pertigalete	0.50	330	600	1,120
Subtotal		2,690	5,040	8,740
General cargo savings				
Alternative A[b]				
Caracas	9.88	2,660	5,450	9,250
Maracay	4.28	300	560	870
Valencia	3.96	1,000	1,950	3,320
Puerto Cabello	4.20	100	160	220
Barquisimeto	3.88	20	40	70
Barinas	4.68	210	470	870
Valera	4.68	180	400	740
Maracaibo	4.36	150	380	640
Puerto la Cruz	13.64	930	2,170	3,850
El Tigre	4.20	240	520	950
Subtotal		5,790	12,100	20,780
Alternative B[c]				
Caracas	10.22	2,740	5,620	9,520
Maracay	5.62	390	740	1,140
Valencia	5.30	1,340	2,620	4,450
Puerto Cabello	5.54	130	220	290
Barquisimeto	5.22	30	50	100
Barinas	6.02	270	610	1,120
Valera	6.02	230	520	950
Maracaibo	5.70	200	500	840
Puerto la Cruz	13.98	950	2,220	3,920
El Tigre	5.54	320	690	1,260
Subtotal		6,600	13,790	23,590
Total savings				
Alternative A		8,480	17,140	29,520
Alternative B		9,290	18,830	32,330

Reprinted from Richard M. Soberman, *Transport Technology for Developing Regions* (Cambridge, Mass.: The M.I.T. Press, 1966), Table 4.10, p. 112.
a. 1959 prices.
b. 50 per cent of rail cargo by piggyback.
c. 75 per cent of rail cargo by piggyback.

TABLE 4.6

Summary of Estimated Investment Required in Construction and Rolling Stock for Naricual-Matanzas Railroad, 1970, 1975, and 1980

| | Costs (Bs. thousands)[a] | |
Items	Low	High
Construction costs		
240 km. llanos (plains)	168,000	312,000
98 km. mountains	93,100	245,000
Subtotal	261,100	557,000
Bridge across Orinoco	60,000	60,000
Terminal facilities	9,000	9,000
Total construction costs	330,100	626,000
Cumulative costs—1970		
Locomotives	6,600	13,800
Ore cars	18,700	18,700
Freight cars	21,400	21,400
Total rolling stock	46,700	53,900
Total rolling stock and construction	376,800	679,900
Cumulative costs—1975		
Locomotives	12,000	25,600
Ore cars	34,800	34,800
Freight cars	44,300	44,300
Total rolling stock	91,100	104,700
Total rolling stock and construction	421,200	730,700
Cumulative costs—1980		
Locomotives	19,400	41,400
Ore cars	61,700	61,700
Freight cars	75,700	75,700
Total rolling stock	156,800	178,800
Total rolling stock and construction	486,900	804,800

Reprinted from Richard M. Soberman, *Transport Technology for Developing Regions* (Cambridge, Mass.: The M.I.T. Press, 1966), Table 4.11, p. 113.
a. 1959 prices.

cent. In computing the capital recovery factor at each interest rate, the life of the railroad facility itself has been assumed to be thirty-five years. Equipment life varies with the type of equipment and the section of the route over which it is used. Flatcars running between Ciudad Guayana and El Tigre, for example, are estimated to have longer lives than similar equipment moving to Puerto la Cruz, since the average daily distance traveled will be less.

A comparison of Tables 4.5 and 4.7 indicates that prior to 1980 annual savings are much lower than annual costs for the interest rates shown. By 1980, savings are equivalent to annual costs for the low construction cost estimates at an interest rate between 4 and 5 per cent. In other words, if low construction costs are assumed, traffic volumes predicted for 1980

TABLE 4.7
Estimated Annual Fixed Charges on Investment in Construction and Rolling Stock, Naricual-Matanzas Railroad, for Selected Years and Interest Rates[a]

Annual Charges	Low Estimates (Bs. thousands)			High Estimates (Bs. thousands)		
	1970	1975	1980	1970	1975	1980
At 4 per cent interest						
Construction	19,460	19,460	19,460	36,910	36,910	36,910
Locomotives	850	1,560	2,530	1,810	3,330	5,400
Other rolling stock	3,430	6,700	11,680	3,420	6,700	11,680
Total	23,730	27,720	33,670	42,140	46,940	53,990
At 6 per cent interest						
Construction	26,190	26,190	26,190	49,680	49,680	49,680
Locomotives	930	1,710	2,770	1,990	3,640	5,920
Other rolling stock	3,960	7,760	13,520	3,960	7,760	13,520
Total	31,080	35,660	42,480	55,630	61,080	69,120
At 8 per cent interest						
Construction	34,000	34,000	34,000	64,450	64,450	64,450
Locomotives	1,010	1,860	3,020	2,170	3,980	6,450
Other rolling stock	4,520	8,880	15,460	4,520	8,880	15,460
Total	39,530	44,740	52,480	71,140	77,310	86,360
At 10 per cent interest						
Construction	42,780	42,780	42,780	81,140	81,140	81,140
Locomotives	1,100	2,030	3,290	2,350	4,330	7,020
Other rolling stock	5,120	10,070	17,530	5,120	10,070	17,530
Total	49,000	54,880	63,600	88,610	95,540	105,690

Reprinted from Richard M. Soberman, *Transport Technology for Developing Regions* (Cambridge, Mass.: The M.I.T. Press, 1966), p. 114.
a. 1959 prices.

are sufficient to provide an internal rate of return of 4 to 5 per cent on the investment in the railroad. When an allowance is made for saving a bridge crossing to Los Barrancos or widening the road to El Tigre, the return on the low construction cost estimate increases to between 6 and 7 per cent by 1980. In either case, the return on the investment is extremely low for a capital-scarce developing region. In view of the risks associated with such an undertaking, there would be little justification for constructing the railroad prior to the 1975–1980 period even if a return of 6 to 7 per cent were to be considered acceptable. There are several reasons for this conclusion.

In the first place, the range of construction cost estimates is too broad to place any reasonable degree of confidence in the estimated returns. These estimates are based on typical average costs that are unsatisfactory when a specific railroad line is under construction. Cost estimates based on actual quantities obtained from preliminary route surveys could reasonably be expected to fall within 10 per cent of real costs.

Second, the difference between shipping and railroad transportation costs for coal and limestone are too small in view of the uncertainties involved in these estimates.[9] A small change in terminal or transshipment costs or in the initial cost of the ships themselves could upset the balance in favor of shipping.

Third, uncertainty as to future volumes is also very great, as discussed previously. If this uncertainty is reflected in higher interest rates, then the annual costs of the railroad will be considerably higher than the annual savings for those traffic estimates. While this uncertainty exists for shipping and trucking too, the risks involved are much smaller. For the railroad, an investment on the order of Bs. 360 to Bs. 660 million is needed just to go into operation; the necessary investment in roads, on the other hand, has already been made, and further investment in trucks and ships can be made in accordance with traffic increases.

Conclusions

An important problem suggested by this analysis concerns shipping rates. Lower shipping rates, consistent with the low real costs of this mode of transportation, could have important effects on the region's growth. If shipping rates are lowered, delivered prices of regional outputs would also be lowered, which in turn would lead to greater demand for the products of the region. Shipping rates also affect the cost of living in the region through their effect on import prices, which eventually affect the costs of production. Thus lower shipping rates could result in lower costs of producing goods in the region.

Lower rates might be obtained by pricing regional outputs such as steel products f.o.b. La Guaira, Puerto Cabello, or Maracaibo. In this manner sufficient ship cargoes would be guaranteed to permit lower rate schedules, make it worthwhile for shipping companies to purchase larger vessels, and thereby incur lower costs. Attempts could also be made to reduce the high port handling charges. In particular, methods of eliminating the cumbersome customs regulations governing the transportation of domestic goods by water should be investigated.

This shipping rate problem illustrates a characteristic problem encountered in transportation planning for underdeveloped regions: their transport problems often appear to be more administrative than physical. Failure to mobilize excess capacity in the shipping industry through a proper pricing policy may yet lead to excessive investment in other modes of overland transportation.[10] In addition to causing this unwarranted investment, the failure of the rate structure to reflect true transport costs may ultimately introduce distortions into the spatial pattern of economic activity. Where these administrative problems are so apparent, some sort of government policy of subsidization may be desirable in order to reduce the social costs of transportation. In the case of shipping, for example, infant industry arguments might justify rate subsidies inasmuch as lower rates might result in sufficient cargo being diverted to this mode to permit shipping companies to realize economies of scale that would eventually be passed on to shippers. Examples from other countries indicate that such administrative difficulties (namely, bringing rates into line with economic costs) may well be characteristic of developing countries in general.

Barring these administrative problems, however, one must conclude that for the Guayana region the lack of adequate transportation facilities does not represent a bottleneck in its economic development.[11] By and large, improvements in the basic regional transportation system can be scheduled as the needs arise and can be carried out by the government agencies normally charged with this responsibility rather than by the CVG. Existing highways and deepwater shipping facilities are more than adequate to satisfy the transportation needs of the region during the planning period under consideration, although some increase in the capacity of such northern ports as La Guaira may be necessary. With the exception of obtaining lower shipping rates, therefore, the planning of regional transportation facilities appears to be one area with which the development agency need not be greatly concerned during the next five to ten years.

Chapter 5

Migration and the Population of Ciudad Guayana

John Stuart MacDonald

How attractive is Ciudad Guayana to migrants? Is the city being overrun by poor migrants? Is the city approaching a saturation point, making advancement harder for new arrivals? Are the hopes that bring migrants to the city realistic? The planners of Ciudad Guayana needed to know the answers to these questions, but the city lacked the sources of demographic data used in more advanced parts of the world. The population of Ciudad Guayana is obviously growing rapidly, so the national census of 1961 is far out of date. A current population register is not feasible for administrative and political reasons. Although everyone is supposed to carry an identity card, the records rarely reflect changes of residence. The national vital registers are incomplete, and even the best vital registration system could not hope to catch all births and deaths of residents and, at the same time, separate those occurring to temporary visitors. Thus the population of the city would have remained largely unknown until the next decennial census if the Corporación Venezolana de Guayana (CVG) had not taken the initiative in demographic studies by arranging for occasional sample surveys.

The Central Bank was commissioned to take multipurpose household surveys in August 1962 and February 1965. Although the main focus of these surveys was on economic characteristics, they have also made up for some of the important deficiencies in the demographic statistics, particularly data on migration and the city's total population by age and sex. In order to supplement the population statistics of the Central Bank surveys and lay the foundations for a cumulative series of field studies on a

TABLE 5.1

Ciudad Guayana: Distribution of Male and Female Population, by Age Group, 1961 and 1965 (as per cent of total population)

Age Group (years)	1961[a]		1965[b]	
	Men	Women	Men	Women
0 to 4	10.1	9.7	10.4	9.9
5 to 9	7.2	7.0	9.0	8.8
10 to 14	4.8	4.9	6.2	6.4
15 to 19	3.6	4.0	4.2	5.2
20 to 24	5.5	4.7	3.8	4.5
25 to 29	6.2	3.7	4.2	4.1
30 to 34	5.7	3.1	3.8	2.9
35 to 39	3.8	2.0	3.0	2.4
40 to 44	2.7	1.5	2.0	1.4
45 to 49	2.1	1.3	1.4	1.2
50 to 54	1.3	0.9	1.1	0.9
55 to 59	0.9	0.7	0.5	0.6
60 to 64	0.5	0.4	0.4	0.5
65 to 69	0.3	0.3	0.2	0.3
70 to 74	0.2	0.2	0.4	0.4
75 to 79	0.1	0.1	—	—
80 to 84	0.1	0.1	—	—
85 and over	—	0.1	—	—
Total	55.2	44.8	50.5	49.5
0 to 14	22.1	21.6	25.6	25.1
15 to 29	15.3	12.4	12.2	13.8
30 to 44	12.2	6.6	8.8	6.7
45 to 59	4.3	2.9	3.0	2.7
60 and over	1.2	1.2	1.0	1.2
Total	55.1	44.7	50.6	49.5

Sources: Banco Central de Venezuela, *Encuesta sobre Características Demográficas, Ingresos Familiares, Características de la Vivienda, Tipo de Transporte Utilizado de las Familias de Santo Tomé de Guayana, Febrero 1965* (Caracas, 1966; mimeographed), Table 12, p. 16; and special unpublished tabulations drawn from the Ninth General Census of Population, February 26, 1961.

Note: Totals may differ because of rounding.

a. The entire Distrito Caroní, including a small minority of rural population.

b. Urban agglomeration only.

variety of economic subjects, a survey office was opened under the supervision of the CVG's Department of Economic Studies and Planning. Its first task was a migration survey, not only as an important end in itself but also as a trial run of the new office.

Principal Findings of the Survey

The principal substantive results of the migration survey (taken in May 1965) identify the composition of migration to Ciudad Guayana, show the relationship between employment and population growth, explain the mechanisms of migration, map settlement patterns and the ecological dimension of the class structure, measure the socioeconomic mobility of migrants after arrival compared to their careers in other places, reveal the economic welfare achieved by the mass of migrants, and relate attitudes toward aspects of life in the city with propensities for migration elsewhere.

The age and sex composition of migration to Ciudad Guayana runs counter to the common contention that a population pyramid fed by migration will grow with an irregular shape unless its migrants are drawn from a cross section of a "normal" population under the impetus of persecution or catastrophe. Examination of actual cases, however, shows that the age and sex selectivity of migration for employment often does not result in an irregular population pyramid, at least in the long run. The age-sex pyramid of Ciudad Guayana (see Table 5.1) has gained a "normal" smooth shape in an extraordinarily short period, as shown graphically in Figure 5.1.[1] An explanation can be found in the characteristics of the eastern Venezuelan social structure.

In Mediterranean, African, and South Asian countries rural migrants

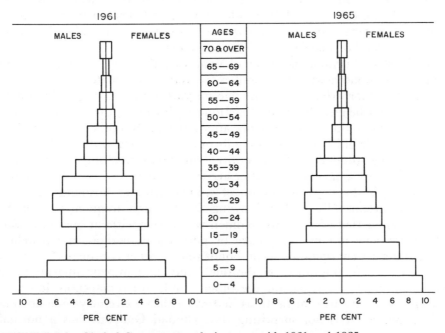

FIGURE 5.1 Ciudad Guayana population pyramid, 1961 and 1965.

to the city as a rule leave their women and children behind for long periods or never bring them to the city; women are rarely permitted to migrate alone. The resulting urban population pyramid is irregular because of the excess of working-age males. By contrast, in northern Europe and North America whole families may migrate immediately or within a few weeks of their breadwinners; and single women may migrate alone as often as or more often than single men. Depending on the balance between these two tendencies, the resulting urban population pyramid has either an excess of working-age adults of both sexes or a normal smooth shape.

Ciudad Guayana is of this last type, but for different reasons. Its age-sex pyramid has been smoothed by a combination of family migration, lone male migration, migration of women with children but no husbands, and the high fertility of women after arrival in the city regardless of their marital status. The traditionally seminomadic existence of the shifting agriculturalists, cowboys, prospectors, miners, oil workers, riverboat men, and fisherfolk in eastern Venezuela, combined with the ease of erecting or dismantling a shanty over night, smoothes the way for migration of whole families and of women with children. Thus there would no doubt already be an excess of adult females in Ciudad Guayana (as in so many other Latin American cities) if it were not for the counterbalancing effect of the city's labor market, which favors males.

In Ciudad Guayana and much of Venezuela the process of forming and re-forming households and families is very complicated, particularly among the poor. Men of working age migrate alone, leaving their women and children behind. Some of these lone males bring their previous wife or concubine to their new residence after a period, but others permanently abandon their old family and may form a new family with another mate in their new residence. Those entire households that migrate together may break up sooner or later after arrival. Parallel to this male-centered movement is the large migration of women without husbands. Female migrants are usually mothers, owing to the high frequency of births among unmarried adolescents. Women who arrive without husbands usually enter new unions, temporary or permanent, without much delay.

In eastern Venezuela the social bonds that in other continents link (and thus encourage) migrants, on the one hand, and impede migration by certain groups of people, on the other hand, are remarkably loose. A society without firm institutions naturally has extremely free-flowing migration. So it is not surprising that Ciudad Guayana has a normal sex-age pyramid.

The proportion of small children in the city's population shows that its fertility must be the highest of any urban-industrial center in the world. It is almost identical with that in eastern Venezuela as a whole, the region with the highest reproduction rate in this most fertile country. The great majority of the city's women come from this high-fertility region. Moreover, since half of them have arrived in this decade, and few grew up in large towns, they have not yet had much opportunity to "urbanize" their fertility. In addition, large tracts of Ciudad Guayana are not really urban at all;[2] and the contacts and flow of information between different sectors of the city are poor. The upper- and middle-class housing developments of the city have lower fertility than the rest of the city, but there seems to be very little opportunity for the diffusion of birth control information to the high-fertility sector. (However, more than one doctor practicing in the shantytowns has been actively spreading birth control information, through clinics and public lectures.) The lower-middle-class people living outside of the housing developments have slightly fewer children than the shanty dwellers. This may be due not to birth control but rather to a higher age at first birth for mothers in the lower middle class, who are more often formally married than girls in the shantytowns. Over time there is considerable movement from shanties to houses built individually outside of the housing developments. Since among the families living in such independent houses the first birth may be delayed awaiting formal marriage, the continuing trend toward transforming shanties into houses, indicative of upward social mobility, should be accompanied by a slight reduction in the city's fertility rate. But there is a strong counter trend: as long as the city continues to attract mass migration, new arrivals will replace all the established families who move out of the shantytowns.

Both interviews and circumstantial evidence show that employment is the primary motive for migration to Ciudad Guayana.[3] Eastern Venezuela, the source of most migrants, has been almost completely free from civil disturbances and disasters. Long-distance migrants come predominantly from the urban middle class, which has been little affected by the violence in other parts of the country. The relationship between the city's expanding employment opportunities and the migration flow is affected by (a) the "push" from stagnant or declining opportunities in the sending areas, (b) the competition from opportunities in other receiving areas, (c) the migrant's tolerance of unemployment in the city, (d) the means of transportation at prospective migrants' disposal, (e) the flow of information about the city's opportunities that actually reaches prospective migrants, and (f) the aid available to migrants during their settling-in period.

The economy of the eastern region has scarcely advanced during this decade, and it may be declining. The eastern oil fields, prime movers of employment expansion in past decades, have remained stationary or have closed down. There are no evident prospects of large-scale development in the East that might discourage intending migrants from leaving their hometowns for Ciudad Guayana. Venezuela's larger cities are competing strongly for Ciudad Guayana's potential migrants, but unemployment rates are practically the same in all of Venezuela's major cities except Valencia, which has a small advantage. The strength of the push from the sending areas can be appreciated from the fact that half of the migrants in the early 1960's had been unemployed before moving to the city. More than a third had been unemployed over one month; nearly one fifth had been out of work for six months or more.

Initially migrants have not been faring better in Ciudad Guayana than in their previous residence. Not only do two thirds fail to get a job in their first days in the city but one third remain without work for more than a month and one tenth for over six months. After the first difficult months, however, recent migrants have about the same unemployment experience as the whole population. Thus after six months, the unemployment rate of migrants is only one fifth of that experienced in their place of origin.

It is puzzling that there is no direct relationship between stability of employment and length of residence after the six months' settling-in period. This is probably due to the rapid, persistent labor turnover in all fields of employment, particularly at the steel mill and in construction jobs. While a great deal of employment is by nature temporary, especially in construction, there is also a rather cavalier attitude on the part of much of the labor force toward steady jobs. Settled residents cannot and do not count on a progressive improvement in their employment chances with the passage of time and the accumulation of contacts and experience.

A migrant's first job varies, depending on when he arrived in the city. We can distinguish among three phases of migration. Those who came in 1964 and 1965 and in the 1950's entered less skilled, less responsible, and less independent positions than those who arrived in the early 1960's. The latter enjoyed extraordinary opportunities because it was then that the steel mill and other CVG offices were under construction.

Almost the same differentiation obtains for the present occupations of the migrants arriving in these three periods. The migrants who came before the last census have remained in lower occupational ranks than subsequent arrivals. Indeed, those who came before 1961 have been no better off occupationally than the most recent arrivals, who have scarcely had time to adjust to city life. Migrants of the 1960's generally have, after a year or two, risen higher than earlier arrivals because the CVG's activities, coinciding with the reduction of foreign immigration, have created high- and medium-level opportunities that scarcely existed for Venezuelans before. This has attracted migrants who were better qualified than the earlier arrivals. Yet much of this movement is simply a replacement of foreigners by Venezuelans from the central highlands and northwest; it does not greatly alter the position of the great majority at the bottom of the occupational structure. Because these contrasts have occurred principally at the top of the occupational structure, however, the proportion of people in the lowest income brackets scarcely differs in terms of periods of arrival.

Few migrants have had their transportation paid for by others. The costs of going to Ciudad Guayana from the eastern region are not great, however, for one day's wages at the lowest rate suffices to pay for the trip from most parts of the East. The trip from Caracas, the central highlands, the central plains, and the farthest reaches of the eastern region is more expensive: three day's wages at the lowest rate. A large proportion of the people coming from the central highlands and the northwest migrate under the auspices of an employer, who pays their passage. This means that few unskilled workers come from outside the eastern region: transportation costs are negatively correlated with opportunities in this case. Except for those who have specific opportunities in Ciudad Guayana, it is not worth migrating from a long distance; on the whole the job opportunities are no greater there than in other developing regions. Indeed, Valencia has achieved considerably less unemployment, while the other major cities, including Caracas, have no more unemployment than Ciudad Guayana. The Guayana is attractive to long-distance migrants only for specific jobs in specific projects. For example, technicians and managerial personnel are often sent to the city from the head office when their firms open a local branch. The same process brings in civil servants from the various government agencies, particularly the CVG. The long-distance migrants who enter small businesses are generally foreigners. Practically no formal or informal channels exist by which information about the Guayana can reach the population at large in the center or west of the country.

There is, however, a network of information all over the eastern region. The opening up of the eastern oil fields in the last three decades drew people across the Orinoco River from the hinterland of what was to become Ciudad Guayana. When the city began growing on the doorstep, as it were, of their old homes, many returned with the families they had founded in the oil fields of the adjacent states. The Iron Mines Company used Puerto de Hierro in the far northeast of Sucre State for the transshipment of ore. When better loading facilities were built in Ciudad Guayana, employees moved in from Sucre and established a bridgehead for a large stream of migration from that state. The passage of ships and small craft up and down the Orinoco provides another means of diffusion to neighboring states. The river traffic has brought in sailors from Nueva Esparta, the island state beyond Sucre, whose seafaring people have been spreading along the whole coast of Venezuela. In many parts of the East, transistor radios pick up stations broadcasting from the Guayana just as easily as from the central highlands. The baseball and basketball teams of the main eastern towns and cities, including Ciudad Guayana, regularly exchange visits.

In addition, chain migration has provided an already established network of information for a considerable part of the movement.[4] Half of the migrants in the 1960's have received no assistance to move to the city. Only a quarter have been assisted by kinfolk. Yet despite the remarkably high proportion who have received no definite aid, practically every migrant has known somebody in the city before he arrived. Since, among the poor, friends and relatives do a great deal of casual sharing of material possessions, the mere presence of such people has been some assurance against adversity during the settling-in period. In any case, the great majority come from adjacent states and are quite accustomed to moving around.

The loose networks of relatives, compadres, and friends who may sustain new migrants are not dependable enough to prevent frequent distress, especially for mothers without husbands. Among the poor, not even the family is strictly dependable. For many, there seem to be no alternative institutions for direct assistance. A few hometown associations are beginning to form, along the lines of those in Caracas, but they are very weak and tend to restrict themselves to the more successful migrants. Neither fellow townsmen nor migrants from the same region settle together in compact neighborhoods that would provide a bridgehead for those who follow them. (One shantytown, Dalla Costa, has a remarkably high concentration of people from Sucre State, but Sucreños are also scattered widely in other sectors of the city.)

Migrants from distant regions have rarely come with the assistance of

kinsmen. This is especially true for the residents of the housing developments, where most of the long-distance migrants and most of those brought
in by employers are concentrated. Migrants from adjacent states have
often arrived without a job awaiting them, and their relatives and
friends have not always been in a position to help them get a job. Long-
distance migrants have, as a rule, gone to Ciudad Guayana only when
employment was prearranged.

The difference in economic positions enjoyed by easterners and noneasterners is a foundation for the socioeconomic structure of the city, which
is expressed quite clearly in its urban ecology. Practically no long-distance
migrants live in shantytowns, and relatively few in the better houses built
outside of the developments. Of the tiny minority of families in independent housing or shanties who were born outside the eastern region, most
had previously lived in an adjacent state. Of the few barrio residents whose
last residence was in a distant state, most were born in the East or had
lived there at some time.

The distinction between easterners and noneasterners is not clear-cut.
A large minority of easterners have already moved up the occupational
ladder. A considerable fraction have moved from shanties to houses.
Although the housing developments have a high proportion of noneasterners and foreigners, there is a considerable proportion of easterners
at all levels of the socioeconomic structure, except perhaps at the very
top.

While the population of the city has been growing by about 13 per cent
each year since 1960, that in the housing developments had more than
doubled by 1965. In early 1966 a new housing development increased the
population of this sector of the city by another two thirds. The population
growth of the individual houses and shantytowns cannot be estimated
with any precision, but it obviously has been much slower. Between mid-
1962 and early 1965, while the population of the housing developments
doubled, that in independent housing and shanties grew by less than a
third. There was very little crossing over from the individual houses and
shanties to the housing developments or vice-versa. Migrants settling
initially outside of the housing developments remained there, as a rule,
until the new low-rent housing schemes were opened in 1966. Up to the
time of the migration survey in 1965, most moving had occurred only
from the shanties to the individually built houses. This is shown by the
lower proportion of recent arrivals living in the latter, for the transformation of shanties into houses takes months or years. Although many
poor migrants go first into shanties and do not yet show any signs of

transforming them into houses, the clear trend outside of the housing schemes is to upgrade the dwellings eventually. The low- to medium-income housing units completed in housing developments since the survey have made it easier for better-off people to move up from the rest of the city, since these units have lower rents than any previous housing schemes. They are not being filled by long-distance migrants as were the previous housing developments.

In other countries, successive waves of migrants with different group loyalties typically enter separate residential areas; and either the first or the last migrant group becomes dominant, while the other waves of migration take up intermediate positions in the socioeconomic ladder. Such a hierarchy of ethnic groups is a product of the different opportunities that a city offers at different stages of its history, as well as of the time of arrival of each migrant group and the ability of each group to seize such opportunities. In North American and European cities the oldest migrant groups are usually dominant and the newest subordinate. In Venezuelan cities, in the period since oil accelerated economic growth, newly arrived foreign groups have tended to predominate in the upper levels of the socioeconomic structure, sharing this position with old white *criollo* families and lighter-skinned peoples from the western Andes. Darker-skinned families are mainly concentrated in the slums, although they also make up a considerable fraction of the population in the lower-middle-class individual housing and the more modest housing schemes, where the majority of southern Europeans, West Indians, and Latin American immigrants are concentrated.

There are no signs that forms of ethnic succession are developing in Ciudad Guayana. All the national, regional, occupational, and racial categories of the city have arrived at approximately the same time. However, practically no North Americans live outside of the better housing schemes, and practically no dark Negroes live in the best housing developments. Relatively few southern Europeans live in shanties, and few West Indians or Latin American immigrants in the worst shanties, where eastern Venezuelans bulk largest. But it is not differences in time of arrival that have put one category in a favored position over another. The main reason for this separation is educational in the broadest sense; for eastern Venezuelans typically are poorly educated and have had little experience with modern occupations.

Racial segregation is not institutionalized, and ethnic barriers are not clear-cut, although there are definite correlations between residential type, on the one hand, and nationality, skin color, regional origin, occupational rank, income, education, and positions of power. Except at the very top, among the high executives of the CVG and the larger Venezuelan and foreign corporations, these correlations are well below unity and should not be taken too seriously. Generally the people take only income, power, and nationality seriously; a person of humble origins, such as the descendant of slaves, can rise in the social hierarchy as soon as he can acquire money or position. There have been enough opportunities for doing so to blur the family origins and hereditary advantages of the elite; the main social cleavages are between Venezuelans and foreigners, the rich and poor, the powerful and powerless, not between Venezuelans of different colors.

Although the tiny majority of household heads who were born on the site of the city have fared poorly as the new socioeconomic structure has taken shape (they have the highest unemployment rate), some of them are found at all levels, except the very peak, of the socioeconomic ladder. Migrants from the eastern region are also found at all levels, but they are exceptional at the top. Dark-skinned Venezuelans and foreign Negroes are found in considerable numbers in what might be called the middle-middle class. Some persons of evident African descent are at all levels, although they are rare at the very top. Formal marriages and consensual unions across all of these categories are common, again with the exception of the peak and between extreme types.

Ciudad Guayana's socioeconomic class structure is certainly not more rigid than that in other Venezuelan cities. Apparently it is more or less akin to the systems in the more modern and liberal areas of Brazil, Panama, Mexico, the Dominican Republic, pre-Castro Cuba, and the Philippines. The evidence is not clear whether the city's class structure is tending to become even less rigid.

The cleavage between white foreigners and Venezuelans of all complexions is the most evident point of social friction. The great majority of foreigners live in housing schemes or independent houses, while more than half of the Venezuelans live in shanties. Before the CVG entered the scene, the socioeconomic distinctions between foreigners and Venezuelans were more definite.[5] The CVG has greatly accelerated the Venezuelanization of all levels of the local class and power structure.

Residents' opinions about the cost of living in general and food costs and rents in particular are highly unfavorable. Half of the residents do not consider Ciudad Guayana their favorite city, and an equal proportion do not advise their hometownsmen to go there. But these attitudes really have little bearing on remigration from the city, which is small. The great majority consider earnings in their line of work in Ciudad Guayana superior to those in their former residence and foresee a good economic future in the city for themselves and even more so for their children. Only a slight fraction regret having gone to Ciudad Guayana, and few are either thinking of leaving or looking for work in other places. These attitudes toward remigration are realistic. For the unskilled and semi-skilled easterner, competition with more experienced labor in the developing cities of central Venezuela would put them at a disadvantage, even in Valencia, where unemployment is considerably lower. For the skilled and educated from central and western Venezuela, Ciudad Guayana can offer relatively good opportunities in particular jobs, with little competition.

The opinions and plans of the Venezuelan long-distance migrants in the housing schemes are not more negative than those of the population at large. Being tied to a narrow range of specific jobs, they are more likely to leave *if* they lose their employment. Since in fact they do not suffer unemployment and consider their present and future earnings in an even more favorable light than the rest of the population, they rarely have plans for leaving.

Two thirds of the residents own real estate in the city. Some of these properties are merely insubstantial shanties and certainly do not mean that their owners have put down roots in the city. Nevertheless, the proportion of property holders is higher than in the migrants' last place of residence. Moreover, half of those who held real estate in their previous residence sold it subsequently. A considerable fraction are currently engaged in buying real estate in Ciudad Guayana, while an infinitesimal number have bought it in other places since they moved to the city. Thus migrants have not been accumulating savings in the city in order to invest them back home; the city is fortunate in avoiding this drain on its capital formation. This supports other evidence that there will be little remigration from the city under current conditions. (A search for a small sub-sample of eastern Venezuelan respondents six months after the migration survey showed that only about 1 per cent had left the city in that period.)

Since the Central Bank survey of 1962 the population as a whole—the blue-collar workers and people outside of the housing developments especially—has advanced on a number of fronts. There has been a marked upward shift in occupational rank and level of skills, after initial losses during the difficult settling-in period. After a few months, inmigrants achieve as high a rate of employment as can be found in Caracas and Maracaibo, and scarcely lower than in Valencia. Employment and income have risen, not only for the population as a whole but also for the workers and the lower-middle class. Housing for workers and the lower-middle class has also improved. Home ownership, which is an indicator of economic welfare among families in individual houses, has increased considerably. Thus the city's attractiveness has increased from the standpoint of the mass of migrants, as distinct from just the middle and upper classes. The movement to the city is realistic in this sense, and it certainly is not resulting in the city's being swamped. In view of the superior positions held by post-1960 migrants, even during their first months in the city, it is not becoming more difficult to settle in the city.

Some Planning Implications

The smooth shape of the age and sex pyramid of Ciudad Guayana implies greater educational, housing, and health responsibilities than had been expected. A preponderance of adult males naturally would have made small demands on schools, housing, maternal and child health services, and emergency aid for needy children. The "normal" age-sex composition also means that the city has a firmer hold on its residents. The first large wave of children born in the city has almost reached maturity; within the next few years a considerable fraction of the labor force and heads of household will have been city-bred and have some roots there. The rapidity with which women have settled in the city poses a problem of female employment that will not be solved by the program for expansion of heavy industries. The problem is increased by the extremely high fertility among women in unstable unions. Although fertility in the housing schemes is low by eastern Venezuelan standards, there is no clear sign that it is declining in the rest of the city.

The unemployment rate is an essential element in the population projections, which are derived from projections of the city's economic growth. The migration survey shows that the continuing inflow of migrants is not the main determinant of unemployment; if the inflow were cut by half or even stopped completely, unemployment would still be high. The persistence of high unemployment among the settled population may be reduced by shifting more of the shanty dwellers into modest housing developments. Presumably voluntary unemployment will decrease as family stability and responsibilities increase. This stability could be promoted by better housing and the long-term responsibilities of paying it off.[6]

If the CVG wanted Ciudad Guayana to become a magnet for internal migration on the national level and expand its catchment area to Venezuela as a whole, some middle- and low-level workers from other regions might be recruited by providing assured employment and by increasing wages to the levels prevailing in the urban central highlands and the northwest.

A small number of workers brought in from distant states and provided with good job opportunities and living conditions could serve as a bridge-head for chains of migration from their hometowns. Some modest assistance might be afforded hometown clubs representing distant regions, so that they might help to promote a greater mixing of migration streams to the city, especially in the poorer sections of the city and in the lower-middle-class housing schemes. In any case, these clubs could serve as a kind of travelers' aid society, a function they have long performed in other countries and in Caracas.

Whether Ciudad Guayana *should* be composed of a greater variety of people from all parts of Venezuela is debatable. Perhaps the city should prepare eastern Venezuelans for urban and industrial life before it confronts them with the competition of more experienced and skilled people from the most developed states. Venezuela is especially subject to the formation of dual economies when its regions develop rapidly. If sufficient experienced labor had been brought in from the more advanced districts at the beginning of the city's growth, eastern Venezuelans might have been left behind by development. The city performs an important social function by drawing eastern Venezuelans into the modern sector of the national economy.

Over the long term, there is a strong tendency toward residential segregation by socioeconomic levels in Ciudad Guayana. It is not yet too late to deflect this process. As in all advanced Venezuelan cities, the recent introduction of homogeneous housing schemes—which naturally go first to the upper and middle classes—and the rapid proliferation of homogeneous shantytowns have introduced a much clearer separation of classes than hitherto. Coupled with the differences in regional origins of the two social extremes, this tendency could threaten Ciudad Guayana with a turbulent political future. In fact, however, the city is tranquil, due in great part to the still sufficiently numerous exceptions to the over-all correlation among socioeconomic characteristics. The recent completion of large housing schemes that are within the reach of the lower-middle class and many semiskilled workers from the rest of the city, combined with the new first-rate high school accessible to students from poorer families, are steps in the right direction. A delicate balance has to be struck between providing attractive environments for elites who are reluctant to leave the larger cities and opening avenues for social mobility from below.

The mood of the people is one of overriding optimism tempered by real complaints that are not serious enough to provoke remigration. This may simply mean that the improvements in income, living conditions, and status experienced by so many migrants have resulted in a positive balance of satisfaction. It remains to be seen whether the complaints will be translated into political action, since the alternative—remigration—is ruled out by the vast majority. The small percentage of people planning to leave and the indirect evidence showing that actual remigration is slight indicate that the population will most probably have a very low turnover if development keeps up its present pace. The retention of upper- and middle-class migrants from the central highlands and the northwest is one of the main goals of the development program. The responses to the attitude questions in the migration survey suggest that these people are, on the whole, in favor of staying in the city.

Recommendations for Improving Data Collection

The migration study incidentally served as a check on the key socio-economic statistics from the multipurpose Central Bank household survey of February 1965.[7] Since this earlier study was conducted by an organization without continuing experience in the city, it required independent confirmation before it could be used with real confidence. The two surveys are in very close agreement; this equivalence of results suggests that the sectors of the city are much more homogeneous than expected. Thus future surveys could be reduced in size from the 2,500 families studied by the Central Bank toward the 600 interviewed by the regional survey office. If the number of cells in the tabulations were reduced by concentrating surveys on particular problems and narrow cross-classifications, the number of interviews in each sector could be brought down to as few as 60 without a loss in confidence, effecting a great economy. In any case, more narrowly focused surveys could be more easily digested.

Multipurpose surveys are uneconomical in such a small population. Generally speaking, a sample has to be the same size in Ciudad Guayana or Liechtenstein as in the United States or India. In a large population, sampling saves a great deal of money and effort. Moreover, acute casual observation can scarcely compete with sample surveys in a large population. Rather than cut down on sample surveys in Ciudad Guayana, it would be advantageous to apply the same survey budget to the larger population of the whole development area between the Guri Dam site and the delta, including the towns and hamlets on the northern banks of the Orinoco opposite and downstream from the city. For the sake of comparability with past and future national censuses, however, it would be best to cover the entire state of Bolívar and all of the Amacuro Delta Federal Territory, plus those districts in the states of Anzoátegui and Monagas along the Orinoco. The immediate repercussions of the CVG's various activities spread far beyond the city. For example, Upata, once a remote county seat, is already practically a satellite and suburb of Ciudad Guayana, while Los Barrancos is a direct extension. Yet there is scarcely any information about changes outside the city proper. Comparative information about the several districts within the development area would provide the CVG with a greater sense of perspective and would discourage treating the city as if it were on the moon.

Sample household surveys are not a good method for calculating population. Aerial photographs of dwellings, taken yearly on the same date as the last national census, are needed to estimate, first, the increase in dwelling places and, then, the total population. The average number of occupants per dwelling place can be calculated on the basis of a sample check made on the ground, distinguishing among the major types of dwellings identified by aerial mapping.

Traffic-counting mechanisms set up at all roads leading to the development area's urban centers would show the volume of vehicles entering and leaving. The average number of passengers per vehicle of each major class could be calculated on the basis of observation of a small sample of vehicles at random intervals.

The impossibility of measuring the actual correlation between migration and economic conditions exemplifies the lack of a basic statistical system in the city. Without migration and economic activity statistics taken at frequent intervals or continuously, the coefficients on which the population projections are based cannot be checked. Rather than rely solely on sample household surveys, the economic picture should be measured indirectly by counting the flow of long-distance telephone calls, cables, letters, parcels, airline passengers, long-distance bus passengers, housing starts, traffic across main intersections, banking transactions, heavy vehicles entering and leaving the city, motor vehicles registered, and employment in establishments with five or more employees.

The statistical services of the CVG should be placed outside the operating and technical studies departments. It is fashionable to insist that all offices do research, but experience in many countries with mature statistical systems shows that a more or less autonomous statistical office serves operating agencies best. The latter cannot indulge in basic comparative or long-term studies, or in those statistics that are of *general* interest. Yet it is these sorts of incidental background data that give planners a sense of perspective grounded in previous experience. In any case, a specialized statistical office will take greater care to use nationally and internationally accepted definitions that will permit its "consumers" to make their own comparisons. Furthermore, the CVG should prepare to farm out its statistical responsibilities—as it has its operational functions—by setting up an office that could eventually "spin off" into the hands of state and local government or an eastern regional interagency committee. It would be worthwhile to join forces with the interagency, interstate Commission for the Development of the North-East (Comisión para el Estudio de la Región Nor-oriental del País). At present the CVG is delegating some of its operations to regular agencies without making its statistics available to them, when the diseconomies of organizing a statistical service for such a small population dictate that the CVG should shed this burden, too.

Chapter 6

The Evolution
of the
Linear Form

Willo von Moltke

Ciudad Guayana is located at the focus of a region with almost unlimited sources of energy, enormous deposits of iron ore, and a high-capacity water transportation route. These are significant advantages for the development of its economy. The physical site is also exceptional. The dramatic spectacle of rapids and falls, the gently rolling terrain, the extraordinary hinterland of forest and savanna offered challenging opportunities to the designer to encourage the development of an efficient and memorable city that would serve both the needs of its inhabitants and the development of a heavy industry complex.

The Site

The climate is hot, but there are usually refreshing breezes from the east-northeast. Fortunately the hottest time of the day—around four o'clock in the afternoon—occurs when the breezes are strongest and the relative humidity the lowest. The vegetation is sparse, except in the many small valleys and along the shores of the rivers. The river levels fluctuate considerably between the dry and the rainy seasons; the Orinoco varies by as much as forty feet. However, the level of the Caroní above the rapids and falls will eventually be stabilized by the Guri Dam. Once a year large areas along the shores of the rivers are flooded. (See Figure 6.1.) Fortunately most of these lands are sandy or wooded and not swampy. Nevertheless the constantly changing relationship of the city to the shores poses a special design problem.

The land is generally flat, about 420 feet above the level of the Orinoco, and slopes gently to the shores of the rivers. Although not spectacular,

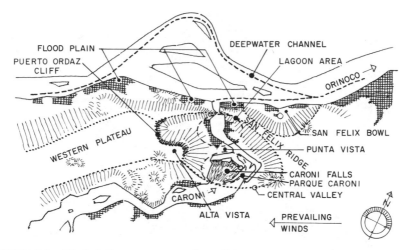

FIGURE 6.1   Ciudad Guayana, natural conditions.

except in the area of the rapids and falls, the terrain offers variety and forms distinct visual units.

At the eastern edge is a concave bowl, with the Las Delicias lagoon and the town of San Félix at the focus. The next visual district in a westerly direction is the central valley, between the San Félix ridge and the edge of the western plateau above Puerto Ordaz. The valley encompasses two subareas: the lagoon area to the north and the Parque Caroní, the area of the rapids and falls, to the south. The two are linked by the Punta Vista peninsula, which lies at the focus of the central valley. To the west is a large plateau bordered by the shores of the Orinoco to the north and the upper Caroní to the south. It includes Alta Vista, a promontory projecting into the central valley beyond the crescent-shaped cliff west of Puerto Ordaz, at the apex of a convex mass.

Stage of Development in 1961

When the Corporación Venezolana de Guayana (CVG) began its task in 1960, a number of settlements existed, and various facilities had already been built (see Figure 6.2): the vast new government steel mill; Puerto Ordaz, a settlement developed by the Orinoco Mining Company to serve its ore-loading port; a second ore-loading facility and camp at Palúa; the Macagua hydroelectric dam; the 100-year-old commercial and political center of San Félix, eighteen miles east of the steel mill; and a series of settlements scattered along a seven-mile corridor. The CVG also inherited a number of problems resulting from previous piecemeal decisions.

The location of the steel mill had apparently been chosen solely to fit the company's needs rather than on the basis of any broader planning considerations. Thus a large flat area close to a natural port location was selected, even though it was eighteen miles by road from the nearest settlement then existing.

An excessively large tract of land had been granted to the Orinoco

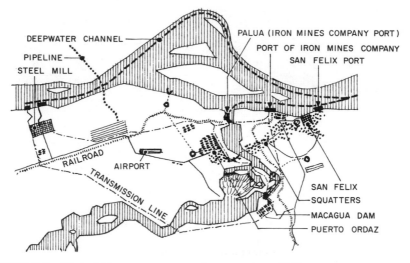

FIGURE 6.2   Ciudad Guayana, man-made constraints, 1961.

Mining Company for the development of an ore-loading port and a town (Puerto Ordaz) to serve the port. This tract is close to the heart of the proposed new city and even includes part of the future business center.

The Ministry of Public Works had developed a plan for the city, which focused on a center overlooking the existing town of San Félix. One element of this plan, a major circumferential road, had already been constructed. The CVG had also inherited the decision to construct a general-purpose port east of San Félix to serve a proposed industrial area east of the city. This commitment was made without the benefit of a plan and without major industry in the vicinity. (See Figure 6.3.) The location

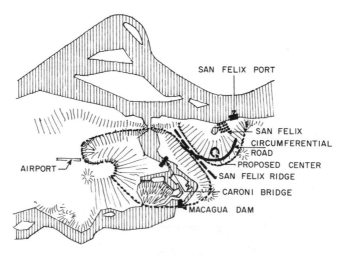

FIGURE 6.3   Elements of Ministry of Public Works' plan for Ciudad Guayana.

might help to develop the economy of San Félix in the future. Its present location at the far eastern end of the proposed linear city puts it at a disadvantage in relation to the dominant source of employment, the heavy industry complex that is being developed at the western end at an average distance of about fifteen miles.

Another inherited decision—to locate the western end of the first bridge across the Caroní on the peninsula of Punta Vista—proved to be very fortunate. Thus the Cachamay Falls could become a part of the daily experience of many people, which would not have happened had the bridge been placed at the mouth of the Caroní, the other possible site.

Thousands of inmigrants had already flocked to the site in search of work. They were arriving without financial resources and had to provide shelter for themselves as well as they could. There was no organization to receive them and few areas where they could settle in an orderly manner. The result was spontaneous, scattered growth, predominantly along the seven miles of road between San Félix and Puerto Ordaz. A number of clusters gave this sprawl some nodes, resulting in areas with a sense of identity.

When the CVG's Urban Design Section started its work, the economists had just begun to collect data and had only rough notions about the future size of the city. The physical planners were beset by urgent daily problems —where to place a school, a hospital, or a playground, where to develop a road or a sewer, where to settle the constant stream of inmigrants. They had to make these decisions without the benefit of any socioeconomic guidelines or general land-use plans.

In addition, they faced constant pressure from the administration of the steel mill to build a settlement near the plant. The steel mill is required to compensate its workers at half-time pay for time spent traveling beyond 1.25 miles to the nearest housing they can afford. Since the nearest appropriate housing was ten miles away, in Puerto Ordaz (and even that was not yet completed), the steel mill was bearing a considerable financial burden in the especially difficult shakedown period. And there was no housing at all for the technicians and administrators whom the steel mill needed desperately.

The Urban Design Section resisted this pressure. They felt that building such a settlement would have created a company camp, with all its un-desirable social and economic effects. It would have generated political opposition from the elected representatives of the existing political center at San Félix. It would also have been much more expensive to start an entirely new infrastructure in an undeveloped area than to enlarge an existing infrastructure with some elements already designed and developed for an increased demand. Finally, a building program south of the steel mill would have delayed the creation of an urban community with a density high enough to support public services economically and to attract and hold the skilled workers and managers needed for industrial development.

Preliminary Design Decisions

This was the situation when the urban design group of the Joint Center for Urban Studies arrived in September 1961. The most important decisions could not be made until the economists and others had done their work. Meaningful design studies could not be undertaken without some knowledge about the nature of the industrial base, the population composition and income distribution, and the size of the city. Elementary data were needed before one could make firm decisions about the location of economic activities, the provision of transportation and other public services and facilities, and the appropriate form of the city to serve these various functions. Yet despite the lack of information, many immediate decisions had to be made about the location of certain minimum facilities needed by a rapidly increasing population.

Various assumptions and hypotheses were quickly formulated and tested in order to provide some guidance for these decisions. For example, at the outset the Caroní River was looked upon as a barrier between Puerto Ordaz and San Félix, the two major communities. This suggested the development of "twin cities." The idea did not survive very long, for a strong urban image was also needed to help overcome the sense of isolation in this frontier area. Since we thought only a unified city would be able to satisfy this goal within a relatively short span of time, attention was given to locating an appropriate site for a center that would provide one dominant focus for the entire city.

The earlier plan to locate the center in the San Félix bowl was examined and promptly abandoned. This proposed site had no visual relationship to the central valley, the area that contains a rapidly increasing proportion of the total population, encompasses the rapids and falls (the outstanding natural element of the site), and is close to the dominant center of employment. Furthermore, this site would not be on the primary channel of intracity movement, making its development difficult if not impossible.

The first new proposed site for the center was on the San Félix ridge that separates the El Roble–San Félix area from the central valley. (See Figure 6.4.) It was to be right on the main road between these two settled areas. This site had two distinct advantages: it was visually prominent from both the San Félix bowl and the central valley, thus uniting both sectors of the

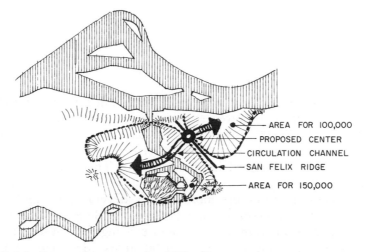

FIGURE 6.4 Proposed center on San Félix ridge.

city, and it was on the main line of movement, a prerequisite for its successful development. It was a good site for a city of 250,000 inhabitants (at that time the estimate of its ultimate size), all of whom could have been accommodated in these two areas: 100,000 in the eastern valley and 150,000 in the central valley.

However, this location was criticized for not having a close relationship to the river system, the greatest natural asset of the area. The next site studied was on the eastern shore of the Caroní lagoon. (See Figure 6.5.) The hope was that this area would overshadow the Puerto Ordaz center in the west, so that the city would develop around both sides of the lagoon,

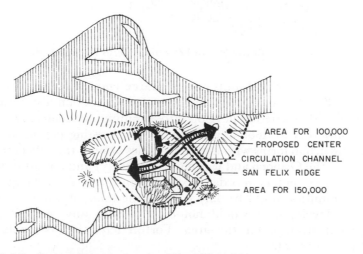

FIGURE 6.5 Proposed center on east side of Caroní lagoon.

making this body of water a unifying rather than a separating element. Further study indicated, however, that this site was entirely out of scale for a city of only 250,000 inhabitants. Also, it was not on the dominant channel of movement between the eastern and western shores of the Caroní, which would retard its development. Therefore, this site, too, was abandoned.

In the meantime, to ensure more orderly development, and to locate housing areas for different income groups, the design staff decided to develop plans and programs for the major existing units of settlement: the El Roble–San Félix and the Puerto Ordaz areas. (See Figure 6.6.) Both

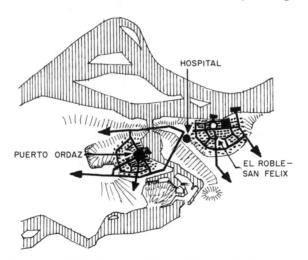

FIGURE 6.6 Design for El Roble–San Félix and Puerto Ordaz areas.

areas form distinct visual units and are large enough for communities of 60,000 to 100,000 people. In each the terrain focuses on a natural center that had already started to develop into a community center. In planning for these subareas we took advantage of these existing factors and developed simple urban forms with higher densities around the subcenters (near the shores of the Orinoco and Caroní, respectively) and a road system that focuses on these centers in order to strengthen them. We were aware that these communities would be only parts of the total city, but we assumed that their development would not conflict with any over-all physical development strategy for the area. Fortunately, this assumption later proved to be correct.

The constant flow of unskilled inmigrants, estimated to be as high as

1,000 people a month, also required attention. The plans for the El Roble–San Félix and Puerto Ordaz areas provided the framework for the identification and design of reception areas for these inmigrants. At this time the concept of *mejoramiento progresivo* was developed, in order to permit and encourage the gradual development of self-help housing from a minimum shelter to a substantial house. The residential units were to be grouped around a common recreation area. In the early stages, this area would also contain the only source of water and common laundry facilities. This concept was used in the layout of a number of residential areas.

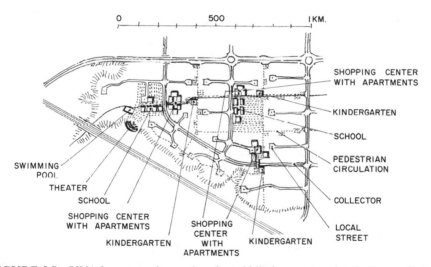

FIGURE 6.7   UV4 demonstration project for middle-income housing in Puerto Ordaz area.

In addition to choosing sites for schools, playgrounds, commercial areas, churches, and the first general hospital (see Figure 6.6), the design group also developed plans for a demonstration project for middle-income housing. This housing project, in the Puerto Ordaz area, called "Unidad Vecinal Quatro" (UV4), was planned for the many specialists who could not find suitable quarters in the rapidly growing city. (See Figure 6.7.) The main features of its design were

1. separation of pedestrian and vehicular traffic
2. parking areas, sufficient for all cars, near the houses in small groupings under shade trees

3. provision for different incomes and household compositions: two-story row houses for families with children, and walk-up apartments for smaller households
4. the highest possible density, to reduce the cost of development, make mass transportation more feasible, and create a sense of urbanity
5. connection of the pedestrian system to principal destinations: bus stops, kindergartens, schools, play areas, and commercial areas
6. a system of small streams, shade trees, and orientation toward the prevailing winds to provide coolness, repose, and delight.

The plan was that this demonstration area would be built soon. However, four years later only the first segment had been completed.

During this preliminary phase of planning we also attempted to analyze the traffic flow and to speculate about the form of the city. However, these attempts were rather theoretical without basic data.

The Effects of the Economic Studies on the Physical Plan

By the fall of 1962 the economists had completed the first phase of their tudies. In substance they envisioned a resource-oriented, integrated heavy industry complex and projected an urban population of 650,000. This changed the designers' perspective drastically. A city of 250,000 might have been contained in the San Félix bowl and the central valley, but a city of 650,000 needed a much larger area.

Given the economists' projections, the designers had to reconsider the location of the city center. Punta Vista now seemed to be the best location. At the focus of the central valley, it united two subareas—the rapids and falls and the lagoon of the lower Caroní. As the site of the western end of the bridge over the Caroní, it was on the dominant movement channel of the city.

Additional support for this idea came from a visiting consultant, Edmund Bacon (Executive Director of the Philadelphia City Planning Commission), who called our attention to a curious geometric relationship. The axis of the bridge and the main street at the base of Puerto Ordaz, which parallels the shore of the lagoon, intersect on the island that is flanked by the Cachamay and Llovizna falls. This is the focus of the rapids and falls. If you bisect the angle formed by these two axes, the line will pass through the narrow mouth of the Caroní before it joins the Orinoco. This discovery led him to develop a city form that consisted of four corridors extending from the center at Punta Vista in four directions along the shores of the rivers. The southeastern corridor would have

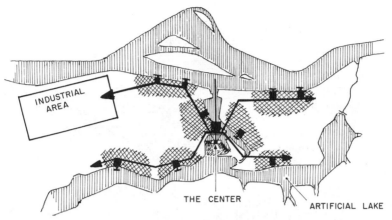

FIGURE 6.8   "Bacon concept."

extended along a projected artificial lake created by flooding a low-lying valley to the south of San Félix. (See Figure 6.8.)

This concept had a forceful emotional appeal for the designers. Its dominant idea was a city developing along the shores of the two magnificent rivers, with subcenters following the shore lines, with water-borne mass transit, and with the center at the visually most significant site (Punta Vista).

However, at that time the designers did not know enough about the locational requirements of industry and assumed that a considerable portion would be located on the eastern side of the Caroní. Aside from other considerations, Bacon's idea had to be abandoned when it became evident that most of the industries would be located in the vicinity of the steel mill (on the western edge) and that it would be impossible to find appropriate land uses for the huge areas between the two western corridors.

At the beginning of 1963 the design group's emphasis shifted from emergency assignments to an analysis of the elements of the urban form and then to a synthesis leading to the form itself. After thorough analysis the designers became convinced that

1. The major part of industry would have to be developed in the west, near the steel mill. The many linkages of the other heavy industries with the steel mill made it mandatory that they be developed adjacent to the mill. This location had a number of other advantages for industry. (See Figure 6.9.) The five miles of shoreline close to the deepwater channel of the Orinoco offered an opportunity to construct special ports for the industries, and the heavy industry freight traffic could reach domestic markets to the northwest without passing through the city. Furthermore, the prevailing winds would carry the polluted air away from the city. Finally, there was an ample supply of flat land for future expansion.

2. A linear city with a series of nodes connected by a central transportation spine would be the form that would best fulfill the goals of efficient and memorable physical development. Only a linear city could tie

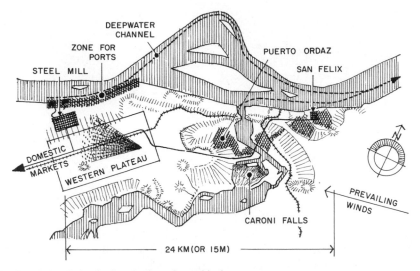

FIGURE 6.9   Criteria for the location of industry.

together the existing developments, scattered over a distance of seventeen miles, and thus help to overcome one of the site's major physical problems —the extreme dispersion of existing facilities. The resulting unity and greater urban density would provide a stronger attraction for the many people with the special skills that were needed. Also, contiguous development—as opposed to a series of camps, twin cities, or a new city on the Caroní south of the steel mill—appeared to offer some political, social, economic, and visual benefits. Linkage with San Félix might bring about more political cooperation. Contiguous development might help to overcome some of the isolation in the different parts of the city. It would also mean expanding the existing services and community facilities, rather than building complete new systems, and thus reducing their cost—especially important in the early stages, when demands for public capital are very great. Finally, it would increase visual unity and provide a continuity of experiences within the city.

Once these general lines of development had been established, the designers again turned to the question of the city center. A linear city is in conflict with the single-center city, since it spreads high accessibility along a line. This tendency might be arrested by a powerful center. A new site, Alta Vista, now competed with Punta Vista for this role. Alta Vista is a promontory on the western plateau and the natural site for a visual link between the western plateau and the central valley. Alta Vista offered many advantages (see Figure 6.10):

1. an adequate supply of level land for both the initial development and the future expansion
2. enough surrounding land suitable for high-density residential development to support and enliven the center

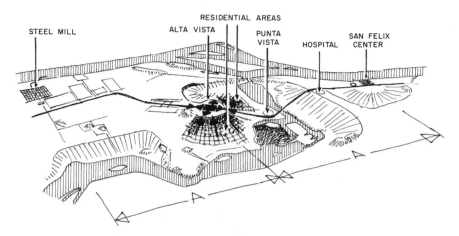

FIGURE 6.10 Advantages of Alta Vista as city center.

3. access from all directions except the north
4. location at the midway point between the extreme ends of the city—the steel mill in the west and San Félix in the east
5. an elevated site, making visual control essential only at the edges and along the central spine.

Although Punta Vista had a number of points in its favor, it also had three major disadvantages as a site (see Figure 6.11):

1. The beauty of the peninsula would have been destroyed through development: to look down from the heights of Alta Vista or the San Félix ridge onto large parking areas and the roofs of sprawling commercial buildings would have been dismal. This would have been unavoidable without strict design control. But strict design control was undesirable because it would hinder the development of the center by private enterprise—a basic goal of the CVG.

2. Access was too limited to accommodate the traffic that a successful center would generate.

3. Land for the development of high-density residential areas close to the center was much too limited.

After some efforts to define the goals of the city and to develop other alternatives, and after some extensive argument—some of it impassioned—the design group finally chose Alta Vista. Their decision was also influenced by a computer model, which identified the places where residential areas might develop in relation to the fixed centers of employment and then identified the point of maximum accessibility to these population distributions. The distance of that point from Alta Vista was negligible.

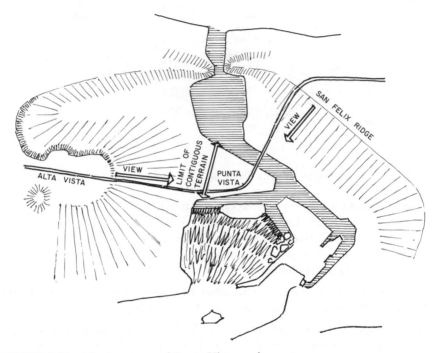

FIGURE 6.11   Disadvantages of Punta Vista as city center.

The choice of Alta Vista as the center did not mean that Punta Vista's advantages would be neglected, however. The institutions of higher learning and those symbolizing law, order, and permanence (city hall, courts, and churches) could be developed on this magnificent site.

The 1964 Comprehensive Physical Plan

By 1964 the fundamental design decisions had been made: the site would be developed as one linear city, with industry predominantly in the west, and the business center at Alta Vista. These decisions formed the basis for the comprehensive physical plan.

The design group set a number of general and specific criteria for their plan. The design must be congruent with the terrain, the natural conditions, the forces acting upon it, and the functional organization of activities. It must fulfill the human needs of its inhabitants and further social adjustment. It must accommodate change over time. It must offer interesting visual experiences. It must create order, a sense of unity, and a memorable image. It must give a sense of beauty that will foster pride in and loyalty to the city.

A basic objective of the plan was to connect the city's three major visual units—San Félix, the central valley, and the western plateau—along a central spine. This spine, Avenida Guayana, would join all the major existing elements into a series of intervisible nodes providing continuity for all the activities and experiences along it. Going from west to east along Avenida Guayana, five major development areas would be developed (see Figure 6.12):

1. In the west, extending from the steel mill to the airport, the heavy industry complex would be developed.

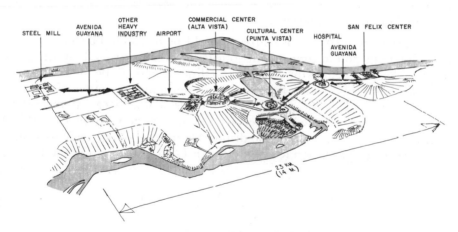

FIGURE 6.12   1964 comprehensive physical concept for Ciudad Guayana.

2. Halfway between the steel mill and San Félix, the Alta Vista commercial center would establish intervisibility between the western plateau and the central valley. This site dominates the central valley and is the symbolic focus of the urban area. Furthermore, even at the beginning of the city's development, all traffic from existing residential areas to the western industrial district, the dominant center of employment, and to central Venezuela must pass through it. Also, the location of the airport just to the west will increase its importance. Moreover, it would be further strengthened by the development of high-density residential areas in its vicinity and by designing the street system to converge on it.

3. The next center to the east would be at Punta Vista. This important focus would be the site for the cultural center, institutions of research and higher education, a center for city-wide recreation, and residences of high quality—the activities that symbolize a city's highest aspirations. The buildings would be clustered according to their functions, in a park-like setting, creating a unique environment at this unique site.

4. On the eastern side of the Caroní, on the San Félix ridge, would be located the medical center, including the 280-bed general hospital that has since been constructed. This node would establish visual continuity between the central valley and the San Félix bowl.

5. Finally, at the eastern edge, around the lagoon of Las Delicias and adjacent to San Félix, would be grouped clusters of apartment buildings, sports areas, a club, and a shopping center. The lagoon ends at the San Félix waterfront, with its *paseo*, marina, and *mercado libre* (the traditional Venezuelan farmers' market).

The price entailed in this strategy would be a sizable burden in transportation costs and in time for the journey to work, especially in the early stages of development. Moreover, the facilities would not be used efficiently because of the tidal traffic flow between the dominant center of employment at one end of the system and the residential areas at the other. It was estimated that when the city reached a population of 250,000 approximately 15 per cent of the disposable income of its residents would be spent on transportation (compared with 12 to 15 per cent in the United

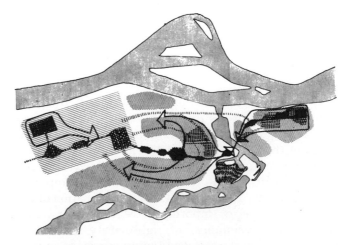

FIGURE 6.13 Growth from outside-in and bypasses.

States). However, as residential development grows westward and industry grows eastward, commuting distances and the proportional cost of transportation will be reduced. (See Figure 6.13.)

It was quite apparent that in the long run the central spine would be unable to accommodate all the east-west traffic. The designers therefore planned bypasses to the north and south, which could be built when the concentration of traffic became heavy. These bypasses would be expressways, thus reducing the time for the journey to work. Avenida Guayana would then serve only the activities developed directly along it.

To implement this general, over-all plan, the design group also made more detailed plans for the first phase of development. They proposed to provide housing for all income groups in all sectors of the city and to use the staging of residential development to further city-wide goals. The first three steps would be (see Figure 6.14):

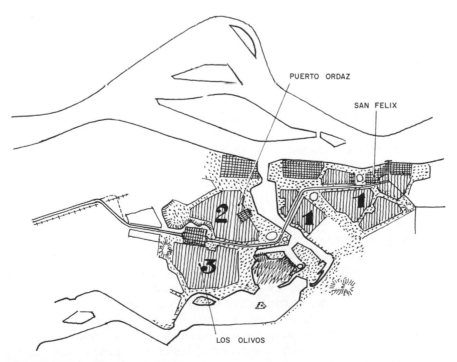

FIGURE 6.14 Housing strategy.

1. to bring order to the existing scattered settlements east of the Caroní by revising street layouts and to increase the densities there wherever it could be done without disturbing existing structures
2. to open up new residential areas in the Puerto Ordaz area for a wide range of income groups
3. to develop new housing for a variety of income groups in the Los Olivos area south of the proposed Alta Vista center to strengthen the center and to further the city's westward development. The collector roads in Los Olivos would focus on the center.

Housing density needed to be increased, particularly near the Alta Vista center. Where that was not possible under present conditions, the infrastructure in designated areas would be designed to make a future increase in density possible.

The designers recommended beginning the development of the center at Alta Vista as soon as possible. The first elements would be a shopping and office center north of Avenida Guayana, a bus terminal on it, and a *mercado libre* south of it. They would be bounded on the east and west by a system of paired one-way streets, which would also be the links to the Puerto Ordaz and Los Olivos areas. (See Figure 6.15.)

They also planned a system of public open spaces in the Alta Vista area, culminating in an overlook plaza at the eastern end of the central pedestrian walk. From the plaza, at the edge of the cliff above Puerto Ordaz, there would be a view of the entire central valley, the rapids and falls, the lower Caroní, and a long stretch of the Orinoco.

The first stages in the construction of Avenida Guayana would be the sector east of the Caroní and, most important, the sector from the airport to the eastern end of the Alta Vista center. This latter sector should have a high standard of design in order to promote the image of the center and of the city.

Modifications of the Plan since 1965

The plan developed in 1964 has withstood a number of tests and remains basically the same as of this writing. However, it has undergone a number of modifications in response to criticism in two areas: the alignment of the central artery between the heavy industry area and the airport, and the design and character of the center and of Avenida Guayana within it.

To increase the sense of continuity between the airport and the heavy industry area, the alignment of Avenida Guayana in this sector was changed. The aim was to make the movement more continuous and at the same time improve the vertical alignment, which was quite unsatisfactory in the earlier location.

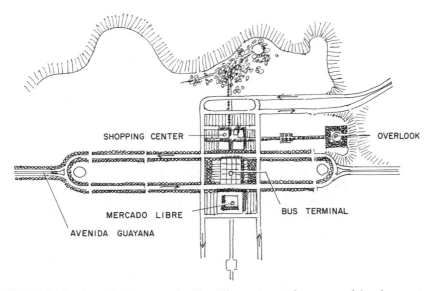

FIGURE 6.15   Avenida Guayana in Alta Vista center—first stage of development.

To strengthen the new center, the planners decided to establish at least the first construction phase of the institutions for higher learning and research south of Avenida Guayana at the eastern edge of Alta Vista overlooking the rapids and falls. The new additions would also include public cultural facilities, such as a large auditorium. Since in the previous plan these facilities had been located at Punta Vista, these changes would affect its character, too. The facilities remaining at Punta Vista would be recreational—a luxury hotel, yacht club, marina, amphitheater, aviary, museum, restaurants, and cafés.

The most significant modification affected Avenida Guayana where it traverses the center. There had always been a dilemma about this section of the road: it was needed in order to generate activity for the center, but once it had done this it would be inadequate to carry through traffic, which would have to be diverted over a bypass to the south. Furthermore, as the center developed on both sides of the avenue, the road would become a barrier between the northern and southern sectors.

To overcome these problems, the plan was modified to split the avenue into a pair of one-way streets about 180 meters apart. (See Figure 6.15.) The land between the roads would remain in public ownership and could be rented temporarily to businesses that require little investment in structures such as automobile-oriented commerce. After development has taken place to the north and south of this center strip, traffic will become congested, and land values in this central corridor will increase. At this point, the leases for the strip would not be renewed, and a depressed highway would be constructed so that through traffic could pass below the business center without interfering with local traffic. (See Figure 6.16.) The central

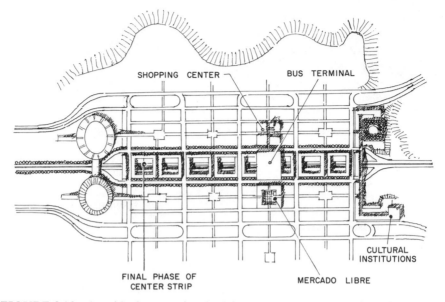

FIGURE 6.16   Avenida Guayana in Alta Vista center—later stage of development.

strip is wide enough to permit construction of a six-lane expressway at a lower level and of parking areas and commercial buildings above, along the northern and southern edges. This design will not only improve traffic movement in the early stages of development but will also be a visual asset, since it will call the traveler's attention to the center—as he approaches it, he must slow down and turn toward it. Moreover, the road will be less of an obstacle to pedestrian movement across it.

Conclusions

There were difficulties and inefficiencies in the process of developing the urban plan. As noted earlier, the design group arrived before the economists and therefore had to work for a year without an over-all economic framework or population estimates. And even after all the planning specialists—economists, social anthropologists, education specialists, political scientists, various engineers, as well as designers—had arrived, the required interdisciplinary collaboration was not easy to achieve, despite the universal willingness to do so. People in the different fields just have different approaches, techniques, and languages, and it takes time and effort for them to work together effectively.

The small size of the team and the lack of developed analytical methods in urban design also explain the slow and ad hoc evolution of the plans. In addition, the tremendous number of uncertainties—goals based on assumptions, often untested, lack of basic social data, doubts about the economic future, lack of cost estimates, and lack of controls—created difficulties that more analysis might have helped but not eliminated. Delays also came about because of sharp disagreements in the design and general planning group about the relative importance of certain goals, for example, aesthetic versus instrumental goals. But perhaps these differences contributed to as much as they detracted from the evolution of the plans.

The urban design group has frequently been criticized for having chosen Caracas instead of Ciudad Guayana as its seat of operation. However, this location was most appropriate in the initial phase: Caracas was the source of most of the information needed for long-range planning. In addition, it would have been impossible to evolve a long-range development strategy under the daily pressure of local problems and without the kind of perspective that comes only with physical distance. But once the over-all plan and strategy had been developed, the design group should have moved to the site, except for a small liaison section in Caracas, where the major decisions are made. And even during the first phases some designers should have been permanently on the site, with authority to deal with day-to-day problems. For instance, all lotting should have been carried out locally.

A design group at the site could have worked closely with the local people, controlled developments through inspection, and gathered data on local conditions. This would have improved communication with the site, which was practically nonexistent. The inhabitants of Ciudad Guayana did not understand the planning ideas and at times acted in ways detrimental to the implementation of the over-all plan. A program of continuing discussions of the plans with the local people would have removed most of the conflicts and would have provided constructive feedback from the site.

The designers' work was also hampered by their inability to enforce decisions at the detailed design stage on the site. The engineers did not understand the planners' ideas, and they were anxious to proceed with the greatest possible speed and to employ the highest engineering standards, even when inappropriate. For example, they cut unnecessarily wide swaths through woods for the construction of roads or utilities, and they made borrow pits wherever convenient, without regard for appearance, future land uses, or soil erosion. If a designer had been assigned to the engineers, with power to deny payment if the engineers failed to comply with design recommendations, much of the damage that resulted form the engineering operations could have been prevented.

Despite these difficulties, the resulting over-all plan is well suited to the constraints and opportunities of the situation. The design is congruent with the terrain and the conditions acting upon it, and, as we have seen, it can accommodate change over time without losing its visual consistency. Indeed, it uses predictable change as a tool to implement the development strategy (such as the change from auto-oriented retail trade to a more substantial commercial use of the center strip of the business center, or the change from low-density to high-density residential use in the vicinity of the center), and planned obsolescence where appropriate. Starting with a chaotic situation it attempts to create order and a sense of unity, and at the same time it offers interesting visual experiences. Ciudad Guayana will develop a memorable image that will be an inspiration to the inhabitant and visitor alike.

Chapter 7

The Guayana
Program in a
Regional
Perspective

John Friedmann

What can be learned from the Guayana experiment in regional resource development? Is it a unique experiment that bears no special lessons for other planners, or will it become, like the Tennessee Valley program, a model inspiring similar efforts in other parts of the world? Its similarities to the Tennessee Valley effort are in many ways striking. Here is the same bold scale, the same determination to bring under a central authority of the national government the management of natural resources within a broad geographic area, primarily for economic ends. But the contrasts between the two gigantic undertakings are more interesting. A comparative analysis may lead to a clearer understanding of the Guayana's important contribution to the theory and practice of regional planning. The relevant points of divergence between the Guayana and Tennessee Valley programs may be summarized as follows:[1]

Guayana	*Tennessee Valley*
Purpose	
Economic development of the nation through the coordinated development of all resources, including but not limited to water, in a relatively new and sparsely populated region; regional consequences considered secondary to the national significance of the program.	Economic development of a depressed region through the coordinated development of primarily its water resources for a number of related uses and appropriate land management; national consequences considered secondary to the regional significance of the program.

147

	Guayana	*Tennessee Valley*

The region

A remote resource frontier loosely defined geographically but focused upon a new and rapidly expanding urban-industrial complex within a national economy in the process of industrializing.	An old and economically backward area defined as a river basin and as a power service area, within an already industrialized and technologically advanced national economy.

Program emphasis

Manufacturing industry, electric power, urban development, mining, transportation, agricultural development.	Water and land resource development and conservation, agricultural and rural development, forestry, electric power, river navigation, tourism.*

Local participation

A national design imposed upon the region with only minor participation of local, state, or regional interests; political support sought and obtained on a national basis.	Importance of local, state, and regional participation emphasized as a matter of doctrine; major efforts to strengthen local institutions and to obtain political support within the region.

Planning style of development agency

Planning institutionalized; long-range planning studies for both the economic and the urban-physical development of the region.	Informal planning only; absence of long-range planning studies for the economic growth of the region; such planning left to the states and to private institutions.

Performance criteria

Number of new industrial plants; industrial production, exports, and total employment; regional population growth; integration of the region with national economic development.	Financial solvency and economic efficiency of development authority; physical measures of increase in regional output (electric power, river traffic, acres reforested, etc.); electric power consumption per capita; growth of regional per capita income relative to that of the nation.

These contrasts in the approach to regional development in the Guayana and the Tennessee Valley are remarkable. They reflect differences primarily in the structural conditions for planning. The Guayana

*To the extent that the TVA has completed its task of multiple-purpose river development and has turned its attention primarily to the question of producing and selling electric power, it has become interested in industrial development. This interest, however, has remained essentially a passive one, and the Authority has continued to rely on state, local, and private groups to further the growth of manufacturing industries in the region. Similarly, the TVA has stimulated the regional coal mining industry during recent years as it has begun the construction and operation of a number of huge thermoelectric plants. But at no time did the TVA consider becoming actively involved in the development problems of the coal mining industry.

is an emerging frontier economy in a country with a unitary government and an economy that is still transitional to industrialism. Administration is highly centralized; local participation in public decision making has not yet taken root; and the private sector still lacks a strong institutional base. The Tennessee Valley, on the other hand, was a backward regional economy with a long history of settlement, a large agricultural sector, and a substantial urban population divided among a number of medium-sized and smaller cities and towns. The United States has a federal government in which both states and municipalities enjoy considerable autonomy. Its economy during the 1930's was already the most powerful industrially in the world, and its private institutions were and continue to be imbued with a strong sense of independence.

Each program of regional development may therefore be regarded as a type. The Guayana experiment is an apparently successful response to the problems of resource frontier areas in developing economies organized as unitary states; the Tennessee Valley program represents an equally successful, if much older, effort to cope with the problems of regional economic backwardness in an advanced industrial society organized as a federation of states. The lessons of the Guayana appear for this reason particularly appropriate to countries in South America, Africa, and the Middle East, which offer similar conditions and in which resource frontiers may come to play a decisive part in national development.[2]

Resource frontiers are remote from their country's principal centers of population. They come into existence as the result of a commitment, usually by private firms, to exploit important natural resources or resource complexes on a commercial basis.[3] Typically, they are isolated from the rest of the country by natural barriers to transportation such as deserts or mountain ranges; they are, at least initially, controlled by foreign concerns that operate the mining or other important economic establishments in the region; their economies are focused upon a city or quasi-urban settlement that, however, has very limited central service functions because of the great emptiness that surrounds it; their future depends to a great extent on the behavior of foreign markets and, in the longer term, on the strategic resource reserves that can economically be exploited; and they acquire a social system that, although it is extremely transitory, is yet highly stratified.

The Guayana met all of these conditions when the government of Venezuela decided in 1958 to transform this distant frontier area into an integral part of the national economy, creating on the Orinoco River a major center of manufacturing based on iron ore, hardwood forests, hydroelectric power potential, natural gas, and petroleum. This move was attractive to Venezuelans not only because of the obvious wealth of the region's natural resources but also because of a general dissatisfaction with the continued growth of the national capital, Caracas, at the expense of the provincial periphery. Thus two important national goals were invoked in support of the proposed development scheme: the diversification and strengthening of the country's export base, and the regional decentralization of productive activities and population. Ciudad Guayana came to be regarded as a counterweight to Caracas and began to compete with the capital both for investment and for professional and managerial groups.

How this problem was attacked may be studied by analyzing a number of decisions that affected the course of the Guayana's development in a major way. Admittedly the choices were not always made with complete awareness of their implications or of all the relevant alternatives.

Plan Implementation: Coordinative versus Corporate Planning

One important question was whether the development of the Guayana's resource economy could be carried out efficiently and expeditiously through the coordinated action of many public agencies or whether the complexity and scale of the task would require an organization endowed with broad executive powers. The choice is a familiar one in regional planning.

In Venezuela the government opted for the corporate solution and created the Corporación Venezolana de Guayana (CVG), vesting in it full powers to plan, program, and implement the investments that would have to be made. What were the reasons for this far-reaching choice? Some were subtle and intangible, yet extremely important to the ultimate success of the enterprise. First, a development corporation would underscore the determination of the new government to assign top priority to the Guayana program among all the pressing claims for its attention. Second, decisive coordinated action could be more readily achieved, it was thought, by concentrating in a single institution all the necessary authority and economic power. Third, resources for regional development could probably be mobilized more readily through the agency of a corporation, with its comprehensive but exclusive responsibilities, than through a dispersed, haphazardly coordinated program involving many centers of power. Fourth, only a corporation would be able to take a global view of the program and of the strategic interrelations among mining, industry, urbanization, transportation, housing, agriculture, forestry, social services, and electric energy, to name only the major sectors.

In short, the very complexity of the program suggested the necessity for a concentration of powers capable of overcoming the many limitations inherent in traditional government bureaucracy. Experience with inter-agency coordination in Venezuela had rarely been happy and argued strongly for a centralized institutional structure to ensure rapid progress. The national planning agency (Oficina Central de Coordinación y Planificación—Cordiplan) or the national development corporation (Corporación Venezolana de Fomento—CVF) might indeed have been given a leading role in the over-all coordination, but Cordiplan was to be carefully isolated from executive responsibilities, and the scale of the Guayana program was too ambitious to be entrusted to the CVF as one of its many activities.[4] Above all, in view of the traditional autonomy of the ministries, no one would have been clearly accountable for the program. Finally, a regional development corporation was probably thought to be more capable of dealing energetically with the powerful foreign mining concerns that were active in the area than a program in which responsibilities would be divided and whose ultimate authority would justifiably be regarded as uncertain.

Regional Boundaries: Fixed or Indeterminate

A question of perpetual concern to regional planners is the delimitation of the area to be planned. In the case of the Guayana, the problem was to determine precisely the area within which the CVG would have authority to make decisions. The problem was complicated by the fact that there were no clear natural boundaries. The geographic concept of the Guayana itself was ambiguous, a loose designation for all of the area south of the Orinoco, encompassing two thirds of the nation's land area. The river-basin concept, on the other hand, would have been inappropriate in view of the CVG's concern with the development of resources other than water. In the absence of definite physical criteria, it was difficult not to be arbitrary in the drawing of boundaries.

A novel solution was finally found. A region is a time-space continuum. Why, then, invest it with Euclidean properties? From the outset it was evident that the major impact of the CVG would be on a small and tightly circumscribed zone in the area surrounding the confluence of the Caroní and Orinoco rivers. This would be the focus of the CVG, and it was care-fully described by a coordinate system in the legislation establishing the Corporation (though the corresponding map was never published). Within this development zone (*zona de desarrollo*) the CVG would have complete responsibility. But—and this was the novelty—the Corporation was legally entitled to undertake investment programs *beyond* this zone if their relevance to activities within it could be demonstrated.

As a result of this decision, the CVG now operates a coal mine on the coast, some 250 miles from the *zona de desarrollo*, is helping to finance road-building projects throughout the eastern provinces, and has initiated a large land reclamation scheme in the Orinoco Delta. This ingenious device for regional delimitation serves to constrain the Corporation's powers by establishing a criterion of relevance, but it leaves the Corporation flexible to cope with problems that could not be foreseen at the time of the initial legislation. Above all, this device helps to concentrate the attention of CVG planners at the same time that it minimizes potential conflicts with provincial governments and national ministries.

Regional Strategy: Developing a Core Region

From the beginning the *zona de desarrollo* was conceived as primarily an urban region of metropolitan size. In the language of regional theory, the decision was to create on the frontier of Venezuela's effectively settled space a core region (*pôle de croissance*) whose successful development was believed essential to the attainment of national objectives. Ciudad Guayana was expected not only to stimulate the economy of the Guayana and the eastern provinces but also to help to integrate, as a functionally specialized element, the Guayana's wealth in resources with national development. The CVG's planners were therefore confronted with a unique and very difficult task: to coordinate the physical development of a new metropolis with the economic development of an extensive resource complex.

This task was defined as an empirical problem; to avoid it would have been impossible. Initial construction of the steel mill, the first of a series of hydroelectric dams on the Caroní River, and related facilities such as local access roads and workers' housing attracted large numbers of migrants from all parts of eastern Venezuela. Within a few years the population of Ciudad Guayana increased more than tenfold. The additional investment in urban service facilities for this growing population reinforced the attractiveness of the core region for migrants from rural areas, who kept streaming into the region at the rate of about 1,000 a month. The rate at which new jobs became available was insufficient to absorb the steadily swelling labor force, and this created pressures for expanding the economic base of the community. Thus was set into motion a rapidly upward-turning spiral that contributed to the political urgency of the enterprise and gave to urban development an importance at least equal to that of economic programs in the region.

This interaction was more visible in the Guayana than in Caracas, where the economic development function was obscured by the urgency to find solutions to the urban problems of this rapidly expanding metropolis. Housing and physical planning in Caracas were typically handled in gross ignorance of underlying economic forces, with results so clearly unsatisfactory that high priority was given to urban decentralization as a national policy objective.

In the Guayana, on the other hand, the physical planning of the metropolis was done in close correspondence with the economic planning for the region. This was reflected in the distribution of types and location of houses, in the selection of the appropriate structure of community facilities, and in the main outlines of the internal circulation network. It should be emphasized, however, that the physical plan for Ciudad Guayana was not wholly derived from the economic plan for the region but made a significant contribution of its own. Interregional competition, especially with Caracas, suggested the need for creating in the Guayana an urban environment that would be able to attract and hold professional and managerial groups. The aim of urban development, therefore, was not merely to provide minimum facilities for the industrial labor force but to create a socially diversified community by attending to the needs of the middle class for cultural and physical amenities of a type that exceeded the functional minimum of a purely industrial city.

Three conclusions may be drawn concerning this close, interactive relationship between urban and economic development. First, the long-term growth of the city was set into motion by concentrating initially on the export of manufactured products from the region. The export of raw materials alone did not lead to urbanization. And, without a local market of sufficient size to support by itself an industrial structure capable of generating further expansion, the Guayana's economy became vitally dependent on the series of industrial projects that would, in the first instance, serve primarily international and national markets. To assure the competitive advantage of Ciudad Guayana as a location matrix therefore became a major objective of development policy for the region. This called for a careful adjustment of physical and economic planning to each other.

Second, the full potential of urban development could be realized only by going outside the urban nucleus itself and developing the natural resources in the surrounding areas on which the city's growth as a manufacturing center would have to depend. The natural resource wealth of the region would be brought together and organized by the city through its several industrial complexes. The interests of city and region were thus viewed as complementary to each other, and the city, acting through the agency of the CVG, would have to reach out and assure for itself an adequate supply of the basic materials on which its own progress depended. Equally important was the concentration upon the city of a network of transport routes that would channel raw materials and energy (roads, railroads, pipelines, high-tension transmission lines) to its industries and carry the city's products to other parts of the nation and to the world (waterways, highways, airports).

Third, the development of this core region would have a major impact on other areas of the nation. Thus the rural areas from which the city obtained its population would be drained of much of their manpower and would have to readjust their local economies accordingly. Complementary market-oriented industries and services would have to be established in other urban centers, particularly along the coastal belt in the eastern provinces, which would obtain from the Guayana intermediate products for final processing. Little attention was given to this phase of the regional development effort, partly because the problem was regarded as lying outside the specific responsibilities of the CVG. In the absence of a national policy for regional development and with an intensification of regional development efforts in other parts of the country, full advantage could not be taken of the Guayana program. This problem will be discussed more extensively later in this chapter.

Locational Efficiency: Projects versus Programs

The locational strategy of the Guayana program was clearly aimed at maximizing so-called external economies that might be obtained from the coordinated implementation of a group of related industrial projects. Since it is practically impossible to measure external economies with any degree of precision, this strategy was more an act of faith than a fully rational determination. The alternative would have been a fragmented approach in which each project would be separately evaluated in relation to similar potential projects in other locations. What would have been the optimal location for a steel mill? Which would have been more economical: a number of small thermal plants using natural gas and located in the vicinity of the large consuming centers, or Guri Dam, with its power potential of several million kilowatts? What port improvements in what locations would have the largest payoffs for Venezuela's economy as a whole? It might well be true that some of the investments that eventually came to be located in Ciudad Guayana would have been better located elsewhere, had each determination been made separately and independently of all other projects. But a dispersal of the individual components that made up the Guayana program would have left the region more or less as it had been during the early fifties: a typical resource frontier dominated by foreign interests, an exclave mining economy on the periphery of the nation. The mobilization of resources for projects unrelated to a regional program would have been more difficult. Internal political forces might have been set into motion that, ultimately, could have fought each other to a standoff. A new core region might not have come into being, and possibly fewer resources might have been incorporated into the stream of national production.

In the Guayana program we have a case where the locational efficiencies of its separate projects can be measured only after the fact, for the maximum benefit from externalities can obviously be obtained only when the program has attained maturity and all of its component parts are in place. The Guayana scheme must therefore be viewed as primarily a program for establishing the conditions for efficient industrial location. The ultimate test will be the vitality and capacity for further growth of Ciudad Guayana and its region once public investments decline to levels comparable to those in other Venezuelan cities.

Planning Strategy: Imbalance versus Balance

The general planning strategy for the Guayana was closely related to the decision on locational strategy, with its emphasis on external and agglomeration economies. The two important alternatives were imbalance or balance in the development of the different sectors of the regional economy. The case for imbalance has been effectively argued by Albert Hirschman, that for balance by Paul Rosenstein-Rodan in his theory of the "Big Push."[5] A strategy of imbalance would permit a development agency to concentrate its resources on a few key sectors or projects without taking into account complementary investments. The resulting imbalances would, according to Hirschman's theory, create political pressures for action on other fronts and eventually lead to a reallocation of resources on an emergency basis. Thus the pendulum would swing back and forth from crisis to crisis, all the while maintaining a high degree of forward momentum.

It is doubtful whether such a strategy would have worked in the Guayana, where the CVG controlled all essential elements of the program. In the absence of "countervailing powers," imbalances might very well have remained imbalances as the Corporation strove for dramatic breakthroughs in a few key sectors—say, the steel mill and Guri Dam. The CVG was in fact created precisely for the purpose of doing "balanced" planning, since it was feared that the imbalances created by alternative organizational arrangements would not be self-correcting. It was primarily for this reason that the CVG instituted a formal planning process whose aim was the simultaneous advance on a number of roughly balanced fronts. (The TVA, acting in a richer institutional environment, could dispense with formal planning and internal balances.) By rapidly building a balanced physical and economic environment, the CVG hoped to engender the dynamism that would assure the sustained growth of the region, create an efficient location matrix, and exude the magic of success so necessary to an enterprise on the scale of the Guayana. On the basis of this experience, it may be suggested that the theory of the "Big Push" probably has greater application to the activation of core regions in transitional economies than to national economic development with its more complex institutional setting.

Control: Order versus Growth

The approach to planning through a series of internal balances automatically gives preference to the aesthetics of order over the dynamics of rapid growth. If every component of a balanced program were to be put in its right place and its timing determined with precision, then indeed the whole arrangement might be subjected to an aesthetic criterion that would render the plan exceedingly rigid and resistant to modification in the course of its implementation. The problem may be reduced to a question of control: to what extent should spontaneous forces be controlled in the interest of harmony and order? During the early years of the CVG the desire for controlled order was very great; it reflected the typical planning bias in favor of equilibrium arrangements intended to maximize community welfare in the long run. But soon the impossibility of reconciling order with growth became apparent, as the several elements of the program refused to fall into place in accordance with the plan. The desire for total control had therefore to be reduced to a desire for *strategic* controls. As a result, planning became less and less precise as a means for imposing a preconceived scheme but gained importance as a general framework for making decisions. Neither the actual physical form of the city nor the temporal sequence of industrial investments could be determined beforehand by the CVG's planners; their planning had to reflect the spontaneously evolving reality of the region's economy. If balanced or comprehensive planning contributed to the institutionalization of the planning function within the CVG and argued for the full exercise of formal powers of control, the exigencies of spontaneous growth steadily gnawed away at planned formalism. The CVG's planners were unable to control decisions from the top; they had to contribute to decisions with the specialized knowledge they acquired from their studies and long-range projections.

Interregional Relations: Improvisation versus National Policy
One unanticipated consequence of the Guayana program was the intense interest it generated throughout Venezuela in regional development planning. There was an awakening of regional consciousness and of a desire on the part of provincial interests to participate more actively in the great task of national transformation. The CVG was so obviously successful in concentrating financial resources for the development of regional resources that it was natural for other parts of the country to wish to imitate this experience and to put pressure on the central government for the creation of development corporations with equally extensive powers. It was obvious that this was done without sufficiently differentiating among regional problems. While the CVG appeared to be an eminently successful means for integrating a remote resource frontier into the national economy, the problems of backward, downward-transitional areas such as the Andean region might call for a totally different approach. The national planning office, Cordiplan, resisted these pressures as much as it could, because it feared that the extension of the regional planning concept to other areas would divert energies from the main tasks of national development. On the other hand, it lacked a clear vision of the regional economy of Venezuela, of the country's urban structure in terms of functional specialization, and of the close interrelationships among the problems of regional development. It failed to see, for example, that the backwardness of the coastal belt in the eastern provinces might be aggravated by the Guayana program farther to the south or that this program might be used in combination with other efforts to overcome the traditional economic problems of that region. What was lacking, then, was a national policy for regional development that might be used to guide the newly found enthusiasm for regional development into constructive paths and to forestall such obviously mistaken measures as the creation of the Corporación de los Andes on the pattern of the CVG.

The difficulties in implementing a national policy for regional development would indeed be numerous if, at the same time, one wished to avoid the multiplication of the development corporation concept as a means for overcoming them. For at any one time a country the size of Venezuela can ill afford more than one concentrated and centrally administered regional development effort. The difficulties inherent in the normal processes of coordination led to the creation of the CVG; other regions, however, would have to be content with less imposing organizational arrangements. But even the first steps in this direction could not be taken until Cordiplan acquired the intimate knowledge of Venezuela's regional economies and the relations among them that would be needed to provide central guidance in this area of public policy. The failure to develop such expert knowledge left a critical gap between a national investment policy elaborated along sectoral lines and the implementation of specific projects. It also left Cordiplan incapable of exercising the leadership necessary to prevent regional development initiatives from working against the basic purposes of national development. The issue is still unresolved, but it appears that Cordiplan is taking a closer interest in the problem than heretofore and may be gradually acquiring the expertise needed to fill this vacuum of public policy.

Conclusions

The preceding analysis demonstrates, I believe, the relevance of the Guayana experiment to other nations. As a means for transforming a resource frontier into an integral part of the national economy and for activating a potential core region as part of this effort, the experiment must be considered an outstanding success that holds important lessons for regional planning, in theory as well as practice.

It would have been relatively easy for the program to go wrong. The critical points of decision were many, and the possibilities for mistakes—in the absence of a clear theory—were obviously great. One need only imagine what would have become of this experiment if alternative choices had been made:

1. if loose coordination had been substituted for corporate planning
2. if an essentially arbitrary spatial system of references had been permanently fixed in legislation, with the consequent diffusion of energies and the chance inclusion (or exclusion) of strategic resources
3. if, instead of concentrating on the activation of Ciudad Guayana as a core region, a number of focal points had been chosen simultaneously or, worse, if urbanization had not been brought into functional relation with resource development
4. if, instead of a regional development program, individual investment projects had been evaluated without taking into account mutual complementarities and external and agglomeration economies
5. if a strategy of imbalance had been followed in the hope that imbalances would ultimately be self-correcting through the mechanism of political pressures or autonomous action on the part of private entrepreneurs and public institutions
6. if planned order had been preferred to a more flexible framework of planning adapted to the exigencies of a rapidly changing situation.

It does not matter that some of these alternatives would have been inconsistent with others. One or two wrong choices would have been sufficient to reduce dramatically the effectiveness of the program.

In the Guayana experience one basic idea seems to run as a constant theme through all decisions affecting the program and was, more than anything else, responsible for making correct choices more often than not. This is the idea of *integration*: the integration of the Guayana's resource economy with the national economy, the integration of the Guayana's empty spaces into the effectively settled space of the country through a functionally specialized core region, the integration of the urban economy of Ciudad Guayana, and the integration of urban physical development with planning for the city's economic base. It would be quite appropriate to call this the master idea of regional planning. Where it is ignored, or where ineffectual measures are taken to implement it, regional development planning in transitional societies cannot be expected to be successful.

Part 2
Implementation
Issues

Chapter 8

The Promotion
of Economic
Activity

Roberto Alamo Blanco and Alexander Ganz

Although the Corporación Venezolana de Guayana (CVG) had at its disposal very substantial investment resources, they were expected to be less than one fifth of its total investment needs. Even the development authority's own projects would require a substantial addition of loan capital. In effect, for the creation of a heavy industry complex in a new city in a new region, virtually everything had to be promoted: resource development, heavy industry, light industry, housing, and urban infrastructure. The Guayana program, with its eighty principal projects covering the full spectrum of economic activity, provides a unique case study of the promotion and implementation of economic activity.

This experience encompassed a variety of approaches to promotion, including techniques that departed from accepted practices in addition to the more traditional devices. Serious problems were encountered in all projects, even when promotion was successful, as in the large-scale ventures. The most important problem was the substantial time lag between the feasibility study and the implementation of a project; another was the slow response when traditional promotion techniques were used. This chapter reviews the whole range of experiences with the promotion of economic activity, the methods used and their results, the problems of time lags in implementation, and the possibilities for improvement.

General Characteristics of the Promotion Effort

Half the battle was won by the extremely detailed definition of the development possibilities and the subsequent selection of the enterprise most suitable for fulfilling these possibilities. The principal focus of the promotion effort was a handful of large-scale projects using modern technology: electric power, heavy industry, the city's principal shopping center, and middle- and upper-income housing projects. The promotion and implementation of these projects have been accomplished through the identification of a few large established industrial enterprises with advanced technology.

While this special approach to large-scale projects has dominated the whole character of the promotion effort, more traditional techniques have been used for other industries and service activities. Industrial parks were developed for the small and medium-sized industrial enterprises (mainly producers of construction materials and light metal products) that were attracted by the growing local markets. For low- and middle-income housing, a variety of incentives, aids, and institutional arrangements were organized. For light industry, analyses and projections of the market in retail trade were formulated. Projections of demand for agricultural products complemented a program of experiments on agricultural production possibilities. For transportation, projections of the movements of goods and people were undertaken. For personal services, analyses and projections of demand were carried out. In general, these projects were on a smaller scale, used a more traditional technology, and were not as clearly defined as the large-scale projects.

Industrial promotion has traditionally centered on the effort to mobilize interest among a broad and varied spectrum of potential investors with an enticingly presented portrait of the attractiveness of a given location, from both an economic and an amenity viewpoint, sometimes sweetened with an array of incentives and inducements. Hard facts on markets, transport, labor, and power costs are blended with a kindly picture of the area and its citizens and impressive references from happy, solid enterprises that have previously succumbed to this open welcome. Inducements and incentives frequently include tax abatement, lease or purchase financing of plant and equipment, and special manpower training programs. The usual objective is to promote fuller use of an area's existing manpower resources; the appeal is directed at footloose enterprises that are equally at home in any area with suitable labor, power, and transport costs. The attraction of footloose businesses requires an approach to a wide range of potential investors.

The promotion of economic activity in the Guayana, however, had to have a wholly different approach. This sparsely populated region contains a combination of resources that may be unique in the Western Hemisphere:

abundant, cheap hydroelectric power potential; high-grade, easily mined iron ore; convenient ocean transport; forests suitable for pulping; and nearby reserves of oil and gas. These resources, when matched with the Venezuelan economy's needs for industrial diversification and substantial new exports, meant that certain specific kinds of industrial production, with specific technologies, markets, and scales of production, could provide an extraordinary competitive potential. In short, the enterprises to be developed in the Guayana were easily identified, specific, and few, but they were important enough to be capable of providing as much as one fourth of Venezuela's industrial output by 1980.

The unique resource combination (described in Chapter 3), when related to market perspectives and national goals, suggested an industrial complex centered on iron and steel, upgraded iron ore, aluminum, heavy machinery and metal fabrication, ammonia and certain other chemicals, and pulp and paper. These industries are composed of a relatively small number of large-scale producers and require high initial investment and modern technologies. Thus there was a limited handful of known potential investors for each project.

Furthermore, most of these potential investors were already aware of the possibilities in the Guayana; at a very early date in the life of the regional development authority, they had taken the initiative to solicit the authority's support, collaboration, and participation in the promotion and development of their projects. As a consequence, before the development authority had even finished defining the areas of industrial potential, a handful of enterprises in each of the principal fields had demonstrated serious interest and intent to promote and develop new enterprises, and they frequently requested participation by the development authority in a joint venture. In effect, the nature of the promotion effort was virtually predetermined by the nature of the development program.

The promotion effort for the large-scale industries responded to the particular needs of these enterprises by arranging for market and feasibility studies and organizing specific investment ventures. No special tax or financing inducements were to be offered because the principal reason for the development program was the region's competitive potential; industrial diversification and exports were the main targets rather than expanded employment (which would be spurred indirectly). In essence, the promotion instrument was a highly accurate rifle rather than a shotgun. With this kind of approach, an expensive, loosely defined promotional effort is avoided; promotion and development energies can be efficiently spent on projects with a high prospect for success.

The Promotion of Heavy Industry and Power Projects

Even with the unique resource and location advantages of the Guayana and with comprehensive feasibility studies indicating favorable returns on investment, the implementation of the Guayana development program has encountered many trying problems.

The over-all design of the industry and power complex is taking shape along the lines originally envisioned in 1962, but the projects have taken considerably longer than planned to move from feasibility study to earth-moving, and some important projects have been begun on a substantially lower scale than would appear to be justified by demand or by economy of operation. There has been serious hesitation and foot-dragging in carrying projects to successive stages of development. The trials and tribulations of outstanding projects as they made their way through the gamesmanship of both partners in a joint venture and the interminable red tape of a multilayered government hierarchy have been frustrating and nerve-wracking for the planners.

The roles of the public and private sectors in the Guayana's industrial development have been largely determined by the interplay of national government policy and the venturesomeness of the private sector. The industrial promotion effort has operated within the limits of this framework. Hydroelectric power would be developed by the public sector; the government was determined to develop electric power in all areas of growing demand outside the rich big-city markets served by private power. The Orinoco Steel Mill was a public enterprise; no private Venezuelan group had the financial capacity to launch a venture of this magnitude. On the other hand, enriched iron ore and the direct reduction of iron ore, suited mainly for export markets and involving new technology, would be developed by the private sector. For most of the other key industrial projects—aluminum, pulp and paper, ammonia, metal fabrications—private initiative was encouraged, with public sector participation in joint ventures available when needed.

Private sector, public sector, joint venture enterprises—each type had its own criteria for feasibility. Private ventures were especially concerned with external economies: the prior availability of electric power, gas, transport facilities, housing, schools, technical training facilities, hospitals. They were also sensitive to national tax policy. Joint ventures, in addition, counted on external economies and on direct and indirect assistance with equity and long-term loan financing. Public enterprises operated under schizophrenic criteria: although their social responsibilities and their important role in making external economies possible required the supply of goods and services at low prices, they would inevitably be judged on whether they made a profit or experienced a loss. In a sense the development program was a jigsaw puzzle in which each piece could be placed only in sequence and within a limited amount of time.

In retrospect, it may be said that the stretched-out lag from blueprint to construction, the reduced initial scale of some projects, and the red tape all were understandable. The magnitudes of investment involved were large. A new industrial complex in a newly developing region, with the success of enterprises highly dependent on promised but delayed external economies (power, flat steel products, transport facilities, housing, education, and other urban facilities) and worried by the vagaries of world markets, had many elements of uncertainty. It appears that these problems are not likely to recur—at least not on the scale experienced in the first five years of the program. The initial installations are going up, urban facilities and amenities are being provided. Expansion of scale is already in an advanced planning stage, and new projects and enterprises are entering what is now a going and fully viable venture—the Guayana power and industry complex.

In the beginning each major enterprise had its own share of difficulties. Their range and variety provide an ample textbook for industrial development and are of some interest for that reason. The following is a summary of some of the most important problems faced in the promotion and implementation of some of the key enterprises.

Guri Dam. The Guri Dam project is one of the largest hydroelectric facilities in the Western Hemisphere. Designed for 1,750,000 kilowatts of electric power capacity on the completion of the first stage, with ten generating units, it is presently exceeded in capacity size by only two dams in the Western world, the Grand Coulee Dam on the Columbia River and the Robert Moses Dam at Niagara Falls. The Guri Dam is designed to provide abundant and extremely cheap electric power for the smelting of iron and steel, aluminum, and certain other minerals and chemicals that make up the heart of the Guayana industrial complex; it is also designed to supplement the electric power needs of the Caracas area, 300 miles away, at a lower cost than would be possible with alternative gas or petroleum thermal units. With Guri Dam producing electric power at an estimated average cost of 3 mills per kilowatt-hour, the development of the industrial complex would be assured. By 1980 the Guri-Macagua complex will be providing 40 per cent of the entire electric power capacity of Venezuela. Without Guri, the growth capability of the industrial complex would be severely limited.

The Guri Dam project required a very large investment—$120 million in the first stage and about $300 million for total capacity. Although this was well within Venezuela's saving and foreign exchange capacity, it was considered essential to submit the project to an international agency (the World Bank) for financing, in order to have the independent review and verification of the merits of the project (with all that this would mean for confirmation of the Guayana program).

The technical part of this project had been under study since the late 1950's, but estimates of the electric power demand and needs of a Guayana industrial complex were not developed until 1962. Consequently, when the World Bank surveyed the economic development needs and possibilities of Venezuela in 1960, it noted the absence of studies of the industrial possibilities and demand for electric power in the Guayana and tabled the dam project for the time being.[1] Two years later, when the World Bank re-examined the Guri project, the Guayana program had taken shape, with specific, detailed analyses of electric power demand and the potential role of the Guayana in the achievement of national development goals. A firm commitment to smelt aluminum in the Guayana had been made. This time the World Bank reported that "the Guri Project is feasible," and "consideration could be given to an early construction of Guri."[2]

Engineering plans were completed, and the competitive bid for the prime construction contract was won by a consortium headed by Kaiser Engineers Inc. The World Bank offered a loan of $80 million, covering two thirds of the first part of the first stage of the dam; the remaining one third, representing local cost of materials, manpower, and services, would be financed by the CVG. Construction began in September 1963.

The Orinoco Steel Mill. Recent studies indicate that the site of the Orinoco Steel Mill is potentially the most competitive location for a new steel plant in Latin America and the western coast of Europe because of the area's unique mineral and energy resource endowment and the possibilities for easy ocean transport.[3] Despite this potential, the Orinoco mill, whose construction was begun in 1956 and completed in 1963, was saddled from the start with fundamental problems whose only long-term solution lay in expansion, diversification, and experience.

Designed for the Venezuelan market of the 1950's, the Orinoco mill was ill prepared for the market of the 1960's. It was geared to produce large-diameter pipe for the petroleum industry, and construction bars and shapes, but no flat products. The Venezuelan market of the 1960's, however, has lower requirements for pipe and greatly expanded needs for flat products, tin plate, and durable consumer goods—the demands of a rapidly urbanizing population with a rising level of income. The need for a flat steel products mill is urgent, both to meet the demands of a growing Venezuelan market and to make the steel plant financially viable by enabling it to achieve full economies of scale and to produce goods that command a higher level of value added per ton.

The present Orinoco Steel Mill has the highest output per worker of any fully integrated steel plant in Latin America and is the only Latin American mill selling steel products in the domestic market at international prices. (Other mills maintain substantially higher internal prices behind high walls of protection from imports.) The management of the mill is young, able, and dynamic and has made extensive use of outside expert consultant and advisory groups. However, productivity in the steel mill is substantially below U.S. levels (though above that in Latin American mills) and cannot be improved significantly without expansion in the scale of output. Expansion is contingent, in part, on the possibility of producing flat products. But the management of the Guayana development authority is reluctant to commit an additional $100 million of investment for the production of flat products before an improvement in the mill's productivity has been demonstrated.

The resolution of this apparent dilemma is crucial. The Orinoco Steel Mill is the largest industrial enterprise in Venezuela and a significant source of employment. It also represents more than half of the total fixed capital assets of the CVG.

Enriched iron ore. Venezuela's resource endowment makes possible the production of a uniquely competitive export product—enriched iron ore, prereduced by a gas process to a pellet with an 80 per cent iron content. This is substantially more advanced than the pelletizing in the U.S. Mesabi Range and in Canada, which raises the iron content of ore from 30 per cent to 50 per cent. The Guayana product can take advantage of the easily mined high-grade ore with 60 per cent iron content, cheap natural gas for prereduction, and easy ocean transport to foreign markets. With world steel capacity expanding at a phenomenal rate (exceeding 450 million tons), U.S., West European, and Japanese requirements for iron ore seem insatiable. Prereduced ore is highly preferred because it increases the iron-smelting capacity of steel plants and thus the output per unit of investment. Of all the ore sites in Latin America, Africa, and Australia, only Venezuela is presently able to produce and ship a pellet with an 80 per cent iron content.

Attracted by these competitive advantages, one iron-ore exporting company in Venezuela is building a plant for the production of enriched iron ore. The initial capacity of one million tons (with an investment of $40 million) is scheduled to be raised rapidly. The economic returns of this project may be sufficient to encourage the substitution of exports of enriched iron ore for exports of iron ore, substantially increasing the level of value added to Venezuelan exports.

However, there were two preconditions for the successful implementation of this enriched iron-ore project. The gas pipeline from Anaco to Ciudad Guayana, planned by the government through the Corporación Venezolana de Petroleo, must be completed. The government and the iron-ore companies must resolve litigation on tax liability and the legitimate price base for calculating gross income when subsidiaries supply parent companies. The latter appears to have been satisfactorily settled, and the pipeline has been given high priority in the Venezuelan national plan. Nevertheless, the planning timetable of the CVG for the provision of supporting urban facilities and the promotion of complementary industrial activities was highly sensitive to these key decisions, which could be resolved only in a national policy context.

Direct reduction of iron ore. A recent technological development of importance to Venezuela is a process for the direct reduction of iron ore, bypassing the need for furnaces and coke to produce a product similar to pig iron. The technique, which uses natural gas or petroleum, is especially suitable for Venezuela, with its abundance of gas and oil and its dearth of good cokable coal. The Venezuelan oil company that developed the process is interested in establishing a plant for fluid iron-ore reduction in Ciudad Guayana as a joint venture with the Corporación Venezolana de Guayana. The product would be a highly competitive export, and the projected initial and subsequent output capacities represent important contributions to the Venezuelan economy. But decisions to embark on this venture are tied in with the over-all relations between the oil companies and the national government. Although the tax litigation, including controversy on the price base for calculating gross revenues from the sale of oil, has been resolved, the planned launching of this project in 1966 was delayed. The planning effort could do nothing about this delay. Objective resource, market, and technological factors indicate that this or a similar project should be launched in the fairly near future, nevertheless, and the Guayana program has included this project as part of the "potential" plan alternative.[4]

Aluminum. In 1961 Reynolds International and the Corporación Venezolana de Guayana formed a fifty-fifty joint venture, Aluminio del

Caroní Sociedad Anónima (Alcasa), for the smelting of primary aluminum in Ciudad Guayana. This was one of the earliest major enterprises; it was also the first joint venture effort of the newly established (December 1960) CVG. The project held great promise for the competitive production of primary aluminum because it could be supplied with its most important single input—electric power—at rates that would be among the lowest in the world (2.2 mills per kilowatt-hour). (Although the average cost of Guri electric power was estimated at 3 mills per kilowatt-hour, the cost would be reduced to 2.2 mills for an extremely large bloc, around-the-clock consumer such as an aluminum smelting plant.) The enterprise was also important for demonstrating that there was an effective market for electric power, which would provide the economic justification for the Guri Dam project.

Although this promising venture was begun in 1961, ground was not broken for the construction of the plant until early 1966. Furthermore, the plant has been designed for the lowest economic scale, 10,000 metric tons, which is below present domestic market needs. However, Reynolds International, which is managing the enterprise, has shown renewed interest in the possibility of doubling capacity even before the installation of the present plant is completed, and thereafter rapidly expanding capacity to 80,000 tons, to take advantage of the export potential for a product whose world demand is rising at a rate of 7 to 10 per cent a year.

These shortcomings reflect all the classic problems of a small country dealing with a private foreign enterprise that has production and marketing know-how and is part of the monopolistic industry. Simply put, each party to the joint venture operated within a different framework of interests. For the CVG this was an opportunity to take advantage of the expertise of foreign private enterprise in the industrial processing of a resource (electric power) and the creation of an essential part of the industrial complex, which would diversify industrial production, create new exports, and provide productive job opportunities. The interests of Reynolds International, on the other hand, were to obtain a foothold in the Guayana region, with its attractive cheap and abundant electric power, with the minimum capital commitment at the lowest feasible scale of production. It was actively engaged in smelting, fabricating, and exporting aluminum from many plants all over the world to many markets; exports from Venezuela might compete with other Reynolds operations in the world market, and plans for export capacity had to be judged in this context. Within the outlines of these general considerations, the project experienced delays while a series of issues were favorably resolved.

These included a foreign investment guarantee, an antidumping protection regulation, a long-term loan from the U.S. Export-Import Bank, and the decision to use traditional rather than experimental technology.

The development program has survived these postponements, and it appears that the timing of the availability of electric power, aluminum capacity, and urban facilities will be conducive to minimizing capital charges for idle capacity. But the effect on the planners was one of frustration and self-doubt. Aluminum was needed to justify electric power; aluminum and electric power were needed to justify building housing, schools, and urban infrastructure. All three were required to attract other regional export industries with the possibilities of industrial linkages and external economies. In the early years it was hard to tell whether we were dealing with wishful hopes or reality.

Pulp and paper. The Guayana region contains the largest reserves of forest resources in Venezuela. The domestic market for paper is growing rapidly and is only partially filled by the handful of domestic paper mills, which use principally imported wood pulp. These factors, together with the recent successful commercial use of tropical hardwoods for the manufacture of pulp and paper in Brazil, Colombia, and elsewhere, suggested the possibility of attractive opportunities for the production of pulp and paper in the Guayana. Feasibility studies by the CVG confirmed these prospects, and the Inter-American Development Bank indicated interest in providing long-term loan financing for the project. The CVG succeeded in attracting the main paper manufacturing concerns of Venezuela, representing 84 per cent of the country's paper and paperboard capacity, to form an enterprise, C. A. Pulpa Guayana, and to contribute the main capital investment. The CVG and the World Bank investment subsidiary, the International Finance Corporation, are providing a small complementary capital investment.

Plans were going well until 1964, but since then the participating paper companies have progressively reduced the size of the project—first by eliminating the paper mill, then by further limiting the planned capacity of the pulp mill. This has been done despite the resultant higher unit costs and the expanding needs of the Venezuelan market. Criteria of minimum capital risk, reflecting the lack of both financial capacity and venturesomeness, are prevailing.

Nevertheless here, too, it is presumed that, after the initial birth pangs have passed, objective economic and financial criteria of market opportunities and needs will prevail, and the scale of operations will be expanded.

Metal fabrication. The Venezuelan market is too limited to support the mass production of machinery, but the construction, petroleum, mining, and transportation industries are an important potential market for certain types of foundry and forge products, metal fabrications, and heavy machinery that are traditionally custom produced on a limited scale. For such products, where transportation to market is a miniscule proportion of total sales value, the Guayana region, with its linkages to the Orinoco Steel Mill and the Alcasa aluminum smelter, has important locational advantages.

A detailed feasibility study carried out by the Battelle Memorial Institute of Columbus, Ohio, for the CVG fully confirmed the possibilities of competitive production of a range of forge and foundry, metal fabrication, and machinery products. In line with these prospects, private investors have designed a number of projects to produce these goods for the transportation and petroleum industries.

The scale of investment interest developed thus far, however, is smaller than that expected. This may reflect the greater complexity of ventures in this field and the element of timing, as well as the limited promotional effort undertaken. Ventures in metal fabrication and machinery, requiring both external economies and a clearly visible market, may be expected to develop more readily once flat steel sheet and plate are produced in the Guayana and the basic enterprises in iron-ore reduction, enriched iron ore, steel, aluminum, and pulp and paper are in full swing.

Problems in the Promotion of Other Economic Activities

In contrast to the pinpointed promotional technique applied to the key large-scale projects, a more traditional approach has been used to stimulate investment in light industry, medium- and low-income housing construction, trade facilities, agriculture, transport, and services. Here the promotion effort has been less effective, and more substantive work needs to be done.

The rationale for this relative neglect was complex. Under the general thesis of "first things first," these sectors were slighted in the allocation of manpower and resources for planning. There was also the thesis that these traditional activities could best be left to the operation of market forces to arouse investor interest, with the provision of a minimum background of market analysis and prefeasibility studies.

There was a whole set of difficulties in dealing with these sectors. Markets were smaller and more complex to evaluate. Traditional technology, suitable for a wide range of small- and medium-sized potential investors, was involved; these investors were a more cumbersome group to attract and judge. For the same promotion effort, the yield would be smaller for these projects.

Nevertheless, these activities are important for the successful growth of the heavy industry complex, and their relative neglect was a serious oversight. Much was done, but more could and should have been done. The following sections compare the promotion effort actually undertaken with the need in a number of these areas.

Promotion literature. As part of the long-term projection and definition of the growth of the regional market, two promotional brochures were prepared by the CVG in 1963.[5] These brochures (1) welcomed private enterprise, describing the assistance offered by the CVG with respect to industrial site preparation, project development, financing, and manpower training; (2) described the investment opportunities in manufacturing, housing, trade, transport, and services; (3) set forth the resources of the Guayana and the mandate of the CVG; (4) reported on five case histories of enterprises that had already been established or were in some significant stage of promotion, including joint ventures; (5) evaluated the nature of the expanding local market; and (6) pictured the future amenities of Ciudad Guayana. The *Portfolio of Investment Opportunities* also presented summaries of key information for thirty types of projects: analyses of the market, technology, investment requirements, materials, and manpower needs. These brochures, in editions of 7,500 each (5,000 in Spanish and 2,500 in English), were circulated to enterprises and individuals, in Venezuela and abroad, who had expressed an interest in the Guayana program. But this literature should have been only a beginning. It should have been followed by feasibility studies and promotion efforts in each field.

Light industry. For light industry, three industrial parks, covering a total area of 1,750,000 square meters, have been developed. A number of small- and medium-sized industrial enterprises have been established in these industrial parks, but they are concentrated principally in the construction materials field. These include enterprises producing clay products, concrete products, wood products, and other construction materials, metal fabrication, and insulating materials. Also established are a bottling plant, a shoe factory, a print shop, and a cold-storage plant.

Incentives offered include the usual plant and equipment financing by the Venezuelan government that is available to industrial enterprises nationally, the appeal of an expanding local market, attractively designed industrial parks with full urban service facilities, and the urban development program, with educational and technical training institutions and urban amenities.

On the other hand, the development of food processing, clothing, furniture, and house furnishing enterprises has been inadequate, and local prices reflect the high cost of long-distance transport of some of these items. The new city provides inadequate employment opportunities for women. The CVG has not studied or promoted any enterprise to fulfill this need.

Housing. With a population that doubled in the short span of five years, housing construction in Ciudad Guayana has lagged behind needs, and the housing shortage has proved to be a serious obstacle to the achievement of production goals. With a popultion of 90,000 in 1966, the city already had a deficit of 8,000 dwelling units, even with the construction of more than 3,000 housing units in 1965 and the first half of 1966. If potential employment targets are achieved, 50,000 additional housing units will be needed by 1980.

Given the existing demand, defined by family income levels and payment capacity, and eager builders, the promotion of housing construction required the creation of new financing instruments and institutions. Their absence was indeed a major obstacle in a new city with an unseasoned real-estate market, in a country without a mortgage guaranty institution or an established secondary mortgage market.

In these circumstances promotional efforts for housing activity centered on establishing a savings and loan association to finance mortgages, organizing the Foundation for Community Development (Fundación de Desarrollo de la Comunidad y Fomento Municipal—Fundacomún) to finance low-cost housing, and attracting private U.S. investors to build middle- and upper-income housing under the U.S. Housing Investment Guaranty Program. The results have been uneven. Institutional devices to facilitate the construction of very low-income (under $1,350 per family) and medium-income ($1,350–$2,500 per family) housing have been inadequate and deserve more attention.[6]

Agriculture. Ciudad Guayana is already a food-deficit area, and there is a danger that high food costs (caused by the need for long transport hauls) could mean high labor costs, thereby neutralizing the locational advantages of Guayana's abundant low-cost resources. To prevent this, a number of agricultural development projects are being carried out. The most important of these is the flood control and land reclamation project in the Orinoco Delta, about sixty miles east of Ciudad Guayana. The delta, with an area of 22,500 square kilometers of flat alluvial soil, is believed to be the country's largest contiguous expanse of new land susceptible to agricultural development. The first stage of the project could protect some

900,000 hectares, of which some 200,000 are considered suitable for agricultural exploitation. Plans are well advanced for the immediate use of some 20,000 hectares; the form of agricultural exploitation and the selection of crops to be developed are under study.

Other agricultural projects being carried out by the CVG include a small irrigation system near Upata, south of Ciudad Guayana, in a fertile enclave in the arid Guayana soil, an agricultural experiment and demonstration station in the Yocoyma Valley, and a study of the possibility of developing a citrus-growing area on the north bank of the Orinoco near Barrancas.

Commerce, transportation, and personal service activities. The rapid growth of Ciudad Guayana has been accompanied by an apparent lag in the development and supply of service activities, including trade and distribution facilities, transportation, and personal services as well as public services. This shortage of service activities shows up both in quantitative measures (such as the structure of employment by economic activity, and the composition of family expenditures for goods and services) and in the mundane daily problems confronting the casual observer—a complete absence of some services, such as telephones, and an inadequate supply of others, such as produce markets, wholesale distribution, and retail sales facilities. Background studies on market and investment requirements have been made for virtually all service activity areas, but serious substantive development and promotion activities are under way only for the Alta Vista business center. The study of produce distribution and the design of marketing facilities are described briefly here. The Alta Vista business center and the region's goods transport needs are described in other parts of this volume.

In addition to the programs to increase the food supply just described, a complementary effort centers on the shortage of facilities for distribution, marketing, and cold storage. Produce arrives at irregular intervals, marketing facilities are rudimentary, and storage facilities are virtually nonexistent; thus produce deteriorates at a rapid rate. As a consequence, the food supply fluctuates widely, producers' earnings are affected, and the consumer pays higher prices.

To study marketing and distribution needs, and their seasonal variation, surveys of the flow of agricultural products to Ciudad Guayana, by point of origin and type of product, have been carried out on a continuous basis since 1964. Surveys conducted in 1965 covered about two thirds of the estimated agricultural crop and fresh fish products and about half of the meat and fowl consumed in the city.

Based in part on this information, facilities have been designed for marketing, distribution, and storage. But thus far no substantive effort has been made to promote investment in these much needed facilities.

Conclusions

A development plan has little worth without implementation; successful promotion is the payoff. In a private enterprise system, where a development authority can use only persuasion and its own investment leverage, planning must recognize and take into account the probability of substantial time lags between feasibility studies and groundbreaking. Successful promotion requires a well-staffed, continuous, determined effort.

The promotion strategy in the Guayana program may be said to have been successful with the large-scale enterprises that require a specific modern technology held by a handful of known, well-established companies. The effort to attract small- and medium-scale enterprises, however, has not received a similar degree of dedication. In view of the region's need for the manufacture of construction materials, some types of consumer goods, and certain metal products, the effect of this neglect is not inconsiderable. The same may be said for insufficient promotional efforts in the fields of low-income and medium-income housing, agriculture, trade, transport, and personal services. The slow growth of light industry in the Guayana has also retarded the development of job opportunities for women and contributed to the extremely low labor force participation rate. This is doubly serious because of the significant proportion of women who are heads of households. Thus, although the basic strategy of industrial promotion is a good one, it should be complemented by a small-enterprise promotion operation, including research, development, and financing.

Chapter 9

Urban Transportation

Anthony Penfold

There are four major interrelated considerations that guide the choice and design of an effective and feasible transportation system for a new urban settlement: the physical conditions of the site; hypotheses that describe the form of the city and its regional relationships over time; estimates of future travel demand in terms of volume, direction, and type; and land expropriation, construction, maintenance, and user costs implied by alternative designs.

In recent years, objective techniques have come into use to help shape urban form, estimate future traffic demands, test the effectiveness of alternative transportation systems, and approximate costs. The impact of these methods on the planning of new towns has been slight, although they are now becoming fairly commonplace in the planning of existing cities. In recent new town planning, the impact has been more evident in forecasting traffic demands on the basis of explicit hypotheses derived from studies of travel behavior in an increasing number of established cities.[1]

However, none of the plans of the early postwar British new towns, such as Stevenage, Basildon, and Crawley, took into account calculated estimates of future travel demands over time based on explicit assumptions. Other physical planning considerations, particularly urban form, must have assumed an exaggerated importance when confronted by the poorly stated requirements of the transportation element. Similarly the plans for Brasilia and Chandigarh—the new capitals of Brazil and the Punjab— lacked the support of quantitative assessments of future traffic requirements.

But there may be times when conjecture is the only practical means at one's disposal, as in the planning of Ciudad Guayana's first two communities, Puerto Ordaz and San Félix; and it contrasts with the subsequent use of systematic techniques to describe the transportation problem through time of the new city as a whole. Thus Ciudad Guayana exhibits side by side two approaches to the urban transportation problem and provides a useful opportunity for discussing the implications of each for planning and implementation.

The "Crash-Action" Planning of Puerto Ordaz and San Félix

The reasons for relying on conjecture in planning the transportation systems of Puerto Ordaz and San Félix were compelling. In 1950 there were some 4,000 inhabitants in the area of the new city, but by 1962 this population had reached 50,000, three quarters of whom were living on the eastern banks of the Caroní, mostly in or near San Félix. The remainder were in Puerto Ordaz on the other side of the river. The need for housing and essential urban services was urgent. Families were erecting their own shanties in disorganized settlements with poor access and inadequate services. In 1961 the Corporación Venezolana de Guayana (CVG) decided that Puerto Ordaz and San Félix could not be left on their own during the time required to plan the future city. The physical planners were therefore asked to design the two communities.

The task confronting the planners was unenviable. Two substantial communities had to be planned as part of a rapidly growing new city, the form of which was undefined. Of course, ideas were aired about its form, based on unsubstantiated assumptions; one idea that took root during the planning of the two communities envisioned both industry and residence equally divided on both sides of the Caroní River, with the center of the city at Punta Vista. But this city-form hypothesis was neither firm enough nor sufficiently quantitative to permit forecasting on an explicit basis the travel patterns for the city as a whole over time. This in turn meant that traffic-demand studies of Puerto Ordaz and San Félix could not be made, for to do so without considering the city as a whole would be totally misleading. For instance, if a major portion of the city, including heavy industry, were located on the San Félix side of the Caroní, the transportation requirements of the two communities would be quite different than if the city were largely centered to the west of Puerto Ordaz.

Perforce, the planners conjectured the communities' future transportation requirements. This was reasonable, but there was a pitfall. This type of judgment making is not necessarily time demanding or constrained by the need of special expertise. Consequently each member of the planning team found himself making his own ad hoc judgments, some more explicitly based than others, to justify or oppose alternative design proposals. This facile process of transportation planning was reflected in the staff organization, for no experienced person or group was deemed necessary to look after the transportation element; therefore, no one sifted the individual judgments and weighed them in a context of emerging, albeit rough, transportation hypotheses for the two communities. Not surprisingly, transportation played "second fiddle" to other physical planning determinants. At one time, for instance, to achieve the objective of major residential areas sited along the waters' edge, plans were based on a romantic notion that the steelworkers would make their daily trips to and from the steel mill, ten miles or more from the two communities, in river boats. Disenchantment with this assumption came only slowly, when the competitive advantages of more flexible forms of overland transportation for moving 5,000 workers or more twice a day were again seen in a proper perspective; meanwhile valuable time had been wasted.

The transportation network for a community in a city has to accommodate all traffic movements generated within the community as well as some generated elsewhere in the city and beyond. It is only a part of a comprehensive system that is roughly scaled to the needs of the city and region as a whole. Since Ciudad Guayana's physical development plans were extremely tentative in 1961, the designs of Puerto Ordaz and San Félix tended to be "community oriented" as distinct from "city oriented"; and since estimates of future traffic demands could not be made, the physical planners had to be guided by their own good sense regarding the location, scale, and character of the network's components, consistent with topography, land-use hypotheses, visual considerations, and access to regional routes.

Puerto Ordaz had to be planned in about nine months, and San Félix in three to four. Taking population capacity as a measure, the equivalent of two British new towns was designed by a skeleton staff in a little more than a year. This was no mean feat and should be born in mind while discussing some of the results.

The community development areas of both Puerto Ordaz and San Félix are in shallow semicircular depressions facing rivers, one the Caroní and the other the Orinoco. Undoubtedly the similarity of the two sites was a factor that contributed to highway networks that in many respects were conceptually akin. Figures 9.1 and 9.2 show the road networks for Puerto Ordaz and San Félix planned in 1962 and 1963 before a hypothesis had been prepared for the development of the whole city.

Aside from their flirtation with waterborne modes of transportation, the

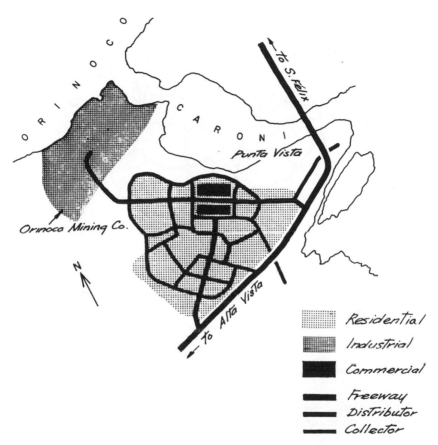

FIGURE 9.1   Road network planned for Puerto Ordaz in 1962 and 1963.

planning team believed that the bus, *por puesto*,[2] and private automobile would adequately cope with all nonpedestrian travel within the two communities. Any assumed relative division among these three modes over time was never made explicit. For both communities, the team adopted the formal or traditional solution, evident in many waterside towns, of a network of arcs or semiring roads intersected by radials. This solution was more clearly articulated in the plans for San Félix, though it was less consistent with the proposed land uses and regional ties of San Félix than with those of Puerto Ordaz. Preoccupation with pattern, unrestrained by estimates of future traffic requirements, resulted in a symmetrical network for San Félix, whose focus—the intersection of its three most

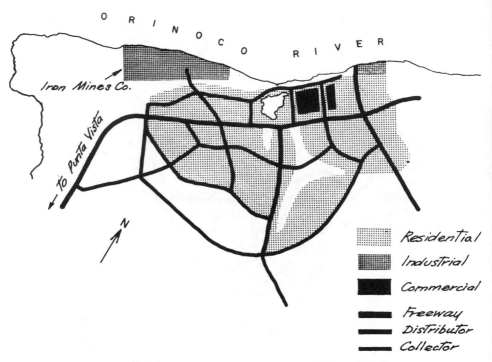

FIGURE 9.2 Road network planned for San Félix in 1962 and 1963.

important radials—was not designed to coincide with the commercial center of the community as in Puerto Ordaz. Consequently the basic symmetry of the San Félix highway system exhibited a "hollow climax" at its most important and accessible point.

Lack of specialists' advice enabled exaggerated weight to be given to some questionable criteria concerning highway location. For instance, the planners attached great importance to the need for panoramic views from the major road system, especially if the rivers could be featured. This was justifiable. It would provide a source of both enjoyment and orientation. But there were severe shortcomings when this value was expressed, for instance, in terms of a criterion requiring that major roads, when possible, be placed on ridge lines. For a ridge road is not necessarily the best location for providing maximum local accessibility, nor does it present an interesting horizon when viewed from the side. Furthermore, and most important, a ridge location can (and did) result in alignments that are unsightly and costly owing to adverse topographical conditions.

Without estimates of vehicle flows to guide the scale and character of the roads in the two communities, the planners tended to play for safety and designed generous facilities. Although a hierarchy was devised, almost all roads except the lowest in the hierarchy—frontage access streets within subdivisions—were specified to have at least four lanes, a median divider, and green strips alongside sidewalks; and access to property fronting these roads was prohibited unless agreements for existing developments had to be respected. In effect, almost all the roads in the major network were given these characteristics on the principle that they would carry the majority of the communities' vehicle trips, and the interstices of the network would then be free from bothersome "through" traffic. The application of this planning principle, to be economical, requires a careful balance between the potential generation of vehicle trips in each interstice or "environmental area" and the capacity of the roads surrounding the area, after taking into account "through" traffic flows. Reliance on conjecture, however, particularly in the planning of Puerto Ordaz, led to an excessive density of roads of this type. Some medium-density residential areas of fifty acres or less were limited on all sides by four-lane divided roads with no frontage access. Besides being expensive, a road network dominated by facilities of this character can give the community a monotonous façade, since frontage development, lacking direct access, will not normally attract expressive, vital, and varied land-use activities. In fact, if frontage development to such roadways—often the side or rear of properties—is not carefully supervised, the community runs the additional risk of presenting an ugly aspect to the people driving by.

Ideally engineering drawings of the major road system should precede the designing of adjacent subdivisions. These drawings would enable sympathetic adjustments in level to be made in the subdivision designs where they abut the major road network, particularly in zones of difficult topography. But the nature of the "crash program" prevented this sequence; routes for major roads were shown merely on a small-scale plan (1:5,000). Based on this plan, construction drawings of the road networks for the communities were made piecemeal, in accordance with the house-building program. Consequently the design of one section in the network often created problems for the engineer of a subsequent section. Occasionally the control points established by lengths of road already designed or built so restricted the vertical alignment of an intermediate section that undesirable differences in level occurred between the road network and adjacent development. Sometimes even minor changes in the horizontal alignment, recommended by the engineers, could not be accepted because new subdivisions, located and built in accordance with the development plans, already had fixed control points and rights of way.

The insensitive application of generalized designs for rights of way—one for collectors, another for distributors, and so forth—untailored to the conditions of local topography and existing and planned development further exacerbated the relationship of the major road system to adjacent areas. The highway engineers, hired to design the roads, applied the standard rights of way conscientiously but rigidly, with the result that the rights of way were constructed by cutting and filling across their total width to bring them to the same level as the road pavement. Existing property owners and the designers of subdivisions alongside the major roads assumed that gentle transitional slopes joining road and property levels would be made within the right of way. In fact, ugly vertical cuts or steep inclines of fill were constructed in these areas near the property lines. Expensive remedial measures will have to be taken in the future when funds are available. With the undulating topography of Ciudad Guayana, rights of way should not be standardized, nor is it recommended that they should be in flatter terrain, for occasional changes provide opportunities for visual variety.

Many lessons were learned from the Puerto Ordaz and San Félix "crash program." Some errors were seen in time to be corrected, while others only gradually emerged and are now quite evident on the site.

The City

With the plans of Puerto Ordaz and San Félix in the hands of the CVG's Planning Department early in 1963, the physical planning team turned its attention to the city as a whole. The economists now had a list of industries likely to be attracted to the Guayana; and, on the basis of industrial production targets, they forecast employment and population levels for the city in 1970, 1975, and 1980. These economic hypotheses, coupled with the knowledge of the natural and man-made conditions of the site, constituted the most immediate data at the physical planners' disposal.

The scale of the problem facing the physical planners called for a tighter staff organization. During the analysis stage, each staff member took responsibility for some element of the city, such as industry, housing, or urban transportation. This change gave the transportation element a separate identity and enabled it later to expand its role into the design stages of the planning process. A local firm of highway engineers was appointed as consultants.[3]

After the experience of the years 1963–1966, certain distinct steps stand out as being critical as the transportation planning of the city proceeded:

The location of heavy industry. Industrial location studies soon dispelled the tentative hypotheses that heavy industry would be distributed equally on each side of the Caroní River. In fact, the best zone for most of the heavy industry was found to be on the west side of the river, to the east of the steel mill. Preliminary estimates showed that some 60,000 employees out of an active population of 200,000 would work in the industrial zone in 1980, which implied a transportation problem of some magnitude, especially if a city of 600,000 inhabitants was to be centered around Punta Vista and the mouth of the Caroní eleven miles away. These estimates were to contribute to a radical reappraisal of the city's form.

Urban form and growth. Because Ciudad Guayana is a new city, located in an isolated part of a developing country, its design presented a problem in a context that is unusual but not unique. Canberra is one example, and Brasilia another; but they are national capitals, whereas Ciudad Guayana is an industrial city. This is a fundamental distinction with implications for both urban form and transportation.

These implications can be explained in the following way. In the interests of a national economy it may be necessary to let a heavy industry plant seek the site that best satisfies its locational demands. If the site is isolated and there is no local planning authority to regulate development, then residential, commercial, and other dependent activities will tend to maximize accessibility and settle in the shadow of the plant. If, however, a local planning authority exists, it may reduce environmental incompatibility by establishing a minimum "buffer zone" between the plant and the nearest permissible community area. In this case, there is a "trade-off" between accessibility and environment. If the local planning authority is very energetic, it may recommend that residential development takes place only in an area it has identified, where there is a fine scenic and climatic environment and where some urban development may already exist. But this locality may be distant from the plant and thus give rise to a critical question—at what point should environment be sacrificed to accessibility in the shaping of urban form? Lack of an immediate answer to this question, raised in much the same way in the Guayana project, created for a time what we may call the "Guayana dilemma."

New capital cities do not pose this dilemma. Nor do other types, except heavy industry cities and perhaps port cities. A new capital city does not call for major uses that are environmentally incompatible. All its activities are relatively "footloose"; all of them will seek sites in an area that is physically pleasant; and once the area is selected, all of them will juggle on the ground or on the planners' drawing board for the best locations they can afford compatible with the character of the city within a single emerging "field" of accessibility.

The "Guayana dilemma" split the physical planning team in the Guayana project into two camps: those who thought that environmental considerations should dominate in determining the form of the city, though this would mean that the proposed city center (in Punta Vista) would be eleven miles from labor-intensive heavy industries; and those who believed that in the long run the residential areas would grow toward the industries, thus improving accessibility, and that the choice of a city center location should be consistent with this assumption.

Those who emphasized accessibility and its corollary, transportation cost, turned to objective techniques in the form of mathematical models to allocate urban growth and forecast intra-urban travel. The "environmentalists" had little sympathy for these methods, for models are inept at weighing values, and value judgments formed the basis of their hypothesis. The division of opinion in the planning team in some respects reflected C. P. Snow's "two cultures"—the arts and the sciences. But these contrasting attitudes stimulated one another; and they eventually found the necessary balance to ensure rational proposals for achieving an attractive urban environment.

Those who disagreed with a city focused around Punta Vista based their case on the hypothesis that the direction of urban growth would tend to be toward the steel mill if the declared policy of the Corporación Venezolana de Guayana to encourage the participation of the private sector in industrial and urban development was not to be frustrated. Of course, the Corporation could try to attract the private sector to sites distant from the industrial zone by simply reducing the sale price of its land where development needed to be encouraged. However, this would not only lower the Corporation's income but would also deter industry from going to Ciudad Guayana. Venezuelan labor law compels industry to supply transportation to its employees to and from work if a plant is more than 1.25 miles from a "center of population";[4] and under the terms of its contract with the steelworkers' union the steel mill must also provide half-time pay for the journey beyond 1.25 miles. These additional overheads at present are considerable for the steel mill; and any measure to reduce the distance of the journey to work for all industries would be a major asset to the development program.

To demonstrate how the city might spread to the west, the transportation planners constructed a model, to be processed by a computer, to allocate urban growth. This model was based on an accessibility model devised by Hansen.[5] The most valuable series of experiments investigated stages of city growth at discrete levels of employment and population, with the assumption that a planning authority would not intervene in the selection of residential areas and a city center. Each model in the series was similar in principle. All land considered feasible for middle-income residential development between the steel mill and San Félix was divided into seventy-five zones. The measure of accessibility of any one of these residential zones to a zone of attraction possessing employment opportunities was considered to be indirectly proportional to the straight-line distance separating the centroids of the residential and attraction zones, and directly proportional to the number of employment opportunities in the zone of attraction. The summation of a residential zone's accessibility to all zones of attraction indicated the zone's accessibility "potential" to all employment under consideration. After computing the accessibility potential of all residential zones to all major zones of employment (excluding a central business district), the residential zones were ranked in order of potential. A sufficient number of the top-ranking zones were then selected to supply the land area needed to give the predicted population of the city a given average "community" density, fixed according to the city's stage of growth. The city's population was then allocated to these selected zones in proportion to their potentials. Each zone had its own density limit, depending on its topography. The excess population of any one zone was redistributed among the others.

Once the population was spatially distributed, the theoretical location of the business center, one that would be consistent with the city's particular growth stage, was found by computing the accessibility potential of each residential zone to all other residential zones possessing an allocated population. Based on these values, a series of isopotentials were drawn on a site plan to find, by extrapolation, the point of highest potential accessibility to all the population. This point was considered the theoretical center of the city.[6]

The model was incremental; that is, the population distribution for any one growth stage was incorporated as a given in the next. Thus the inertia inherent in fixed urban investment was acknowledged. The results showed that in the early stages of the city's growth the population would settle in Puerto Ordaz and San Félix—in much the same way as it has done—and that in the long run, as the city increased to 650,000 inhabitants, residential

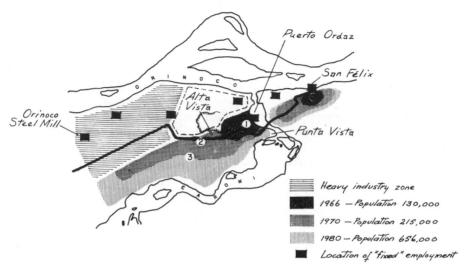

FIGURE 9.3 Residential development, 1966, 1970, and 1980, as forecast by population allocation model.
Note: The forecasts shown here assumed the property of the Orinoco Mining Company (enclosed by dotted line) would not be available for development. The theoretical locations of the city centers for the three forecasts are indicated sequentially by the numbered circles. Population densities are not indicated.

growth would move westward from Puerto Ordaz in a broad band toward the steel mill, leaving only a minority of the population in San Félix. The theoretical location of the city center did the same; in the beginning it was near Puerto Ordaz, and then, as the city grew in size, it moved westward past Alta Vista. It always appeared west of Punta Vista. (See Figure 9.3.)

But a city center is not something on wheels; nor can it always be located at some theoretical point of high accessibility, if only for topographical reasons. Furthermore, its location exerts a strong influence on the form of a city in spite of competing attractions elsewhere, such as industrial activity. The model therefore was varied slightly to enable an allocation of urban growth to be made over time, with the assumption that the Corporation had decided on a location for the city center. The implications of different locations—Punta Vista, Alta Vista, Puerto Ordaz, and an isolated location south of the steel mill—were investigated. The model distributed residential population on the basis of each alternative city-center location in combination with the other fixed points of employment. The Alta Vista hypothesis indicated an urban form for a population level of 450,000 grouped around the city center; but in the next stage of growth, at a population level of 650,000, a westward "suburban" expansion to the south of the industrial zone exploded this strong form. In each of the two stages, about three fourths of the population were accommodated on the west side of the Caroní River.

The results of the models were as good as the rough but explicit assumptions on which they were based. They showed only general growth tendencies. But these were enough to demonstrate that considerations of accessibility could shape the form of the city in a very distinctive way, and that a strategy of development adopted to promote such a growth form would be most effective.

The indication that a location in or near Alta Vista would be consistent with the western growth of the city weighed heavily in the final decision to locate the center there. It also seemed that Punta Vista, largely surrounded by water, could not easily contain the estimated "center-seeking" activities required by a city of 650,000 inhabitants, and that the trips generated by these activities would call for high-capacity transportation facilities that would be difficult and expensive to arrange on such a small promontory.

Estimates of intra-urban traffic. The "Guayana dilemma" was resolved by designating Alta Vista as the city center and Punta Vista as a park, and by the adoption of a development strategy that would stimulate city growth to the west of the Caroní. The city-form hypotheses developed around these decisions were used by the transportation planners in forecasting first approximations of intra-urban travel demands.

To make these calculations, a gravity model[7] was selected because of its ability to predict changing traffic patterns over time in a rapidly expanding urban area. A possible alternative might have been a growth factor model. But this model bases its predictions on a description of present trip patterns and thus has difficulty predicting trips to and from previously vacant residential and employment zones. The growth factor model is useful for making short-term forecasts and can be used for longer-run forecasts if most urban growth in the future is expected to take the form of an intensification of presently located activities. Neither condition applied to Ciudad Guayana, since forecasts were required for a period of twenty years, and great physical, economic, and social changes are expected to take place there within that time.

The gravity model is an expression of the principle that trips originating in any one zone are attracted to all activity points offering terminals to these trips, and that these trips distribute themselves in direct relation to the number of trip terminals at each activity point and in inverse relation to some function of the distance between the zone of origin and each activity point. Morning peak-hour rather than average daily travel was thought to be a more reliable estimate and much easier to approximate, given the lack of data about urban travel habits. Data for the United States were a help, but they did not, for instance, take into account such Latin habits as the long midday siesta and the tendency for extended families to live in the same city, both of which lead to a high number of daily trips per automobile, with the morning and evening peak periods virtually merged into one another.

The city-form hypotheses showed, by income group, the population distribution of each residential zone and the number of employment opportunities in the major work shift at each "fixed"[8] place of activity. Using these values in conjunction with straight-line distances between residential zones and activity points, the gravity model was processed by a computer to obtain "basic" travel patterns for each income group during the morning peak period.[9] These "basic" results were adjusted to account for person trips to employment locations "distributed" with the population (such as schools), for nonwork trips, and also for commercial journeys.[10] Next, modal split factors, a set for each income group, converted the "adjusted" person trips into vehicular trips—private automobile, *por puesto,* bus, and taxi. (Rail rapid transit was not thought to be warranted in a city of well below one million inhabitants.) A final conversion reduced these results to morning peak-hour vehicular trips. The trips for each of five income groups were then summed.[11] Each city-form hypothesis was evaluated in the same manner.

Basic network design and testing. The estimates of the total number of vehicle miles traveled during the morning peak hour were so similar for each city-form hypothesis that the urban designers could select the preferred city-form alternative on the basis of other factors. The new year (1964) was approaching, and a preliminary scheme for the city had to be published in the annual report of the Corporation. The hypothesis selected gave priority to city growth on publicly owned land south of the steel mill rather than on private land to the north of the airport near Alta Vista.

Nine alternative highway networks to suit the chosen city form over time were successively sketched out and tested by assigning the estimated traffic flows to each. Minimum distance was the criterion for the selection of vehicle routes, and each road was given a maximum vehicular capacity. When the system became overloaded, the capacity limit of major roads was raised. All assignments were done by hand, as this method was much faster

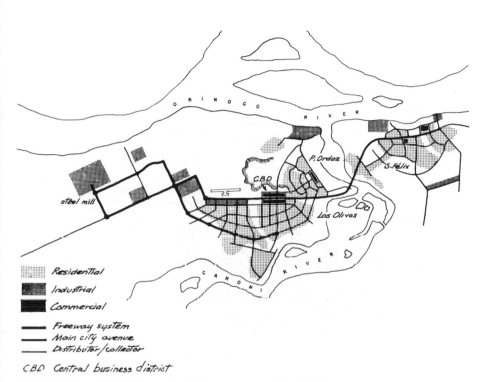

Residential

Industrial

Commercial

Freeway system
Main city avenue
Distributor/collector

CBD Central business district

FIGURE 9.4   Preliminary city highway network for 1970.

than assignments by computer for testing alternatives at the degree of accuracy required.

The alternative networks were designed on the principle that all but the most local trips would be made on freeways and on distributor roads in order to preserve a high standard of environment in the developed areas within the interstices of the network. The networks formed by the freeways were too fine in these preliminary designs. This resulted from a decision to limit freeways where possible to four lanes, with the assumption that they could lend themselves more easily to widening if necessary in the future. Flexibility to adjust to changing growth forms of the city and an inherent clarity of structure were two important considerations in the choice of a network adequate to serve population needs at levels of 250,000 and 650,000 inhabitants. However, only major topographical features were taken into account at this stage. Cost was a factor inasmuch as route mileage and the number and complexity of freeway interchanges were

FIGURE 9.5 Preliminary city highway network for 1980.

taken into account. Land costs were ignored because the Corporation owned most of the site of the future city.

In the network selected (shown in Figures 9.4 and 9.5), the Ciudad Bolívar–San Félix road was strengthened between the steel mill and the new Caroní Bridge at Punta Vista. The plans already provided for a connection between the bridge and the port of San Félix. Thus an important road, some eighteen miles long, which could act as the backbone of the city, would be formed between the heavy industrial zone and San Félix. In the early stages of the city's growth this road would be a fairly high-speed route, until development at points along it, such as the central business district in Alta Vista, made it congested. When this occurred, a freeway would be built south of Alta Vista, enabling morning traffic to move rapidly from the Caroní Bridge to the steel mill. This freeway would also, in the later stages of city growth, carry traffic from the residential areas in the west to the business district, thereby ensuring its full utilization

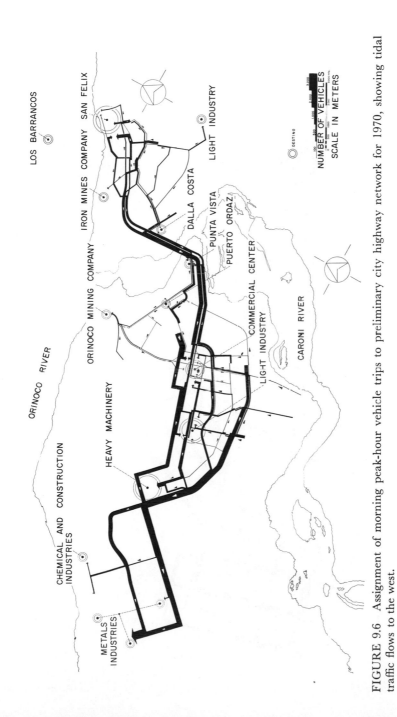

FIGURE 9.6 Assignment of morning peak-hour vehicle trips to preliminary city highway network for 1970, showing tidal traffic flows to the west.

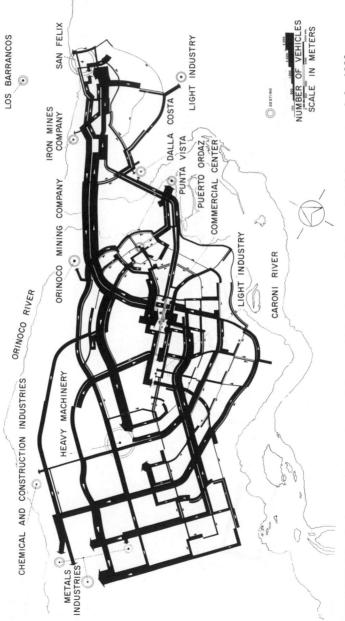

FIGURE 9.7 Assignment of morning peak-hour vehicle trips to preliminary city highway network for 1980.

in both directions during peak hours. In contrast, much of the rest of the network would have to carry "tidal" traffic flows. (See Figures 9.6 and 9.7.) This is unavoidable, since many of the heavy manufacturing industries will be to the west of the city.

Engineering studies of the basic network. Before the sketch network could undergo engineering studies, the task of incorporating it into the outline hypothesis for the city's form had to be carried out. This stage resulted in a series of more refined land-use plans. The highway system and the urban activity structure were adjusted to reinforce one another, and major nodes of activity such as the center of the city in Alta Vista changed from general design concepts to much clearer statements of intention.

Rather than develop the engineering design of the highway network piecemeal and have many of the same problems that were being experienced in San Félix and Puerto Ordaz, the planners decided to obtain basic network layout studies from the consulting engineers. These would be sufficiently detailed to give a high degree of confidence in the location and functioning of the system. The system could then be tested by assigning the results of a more refined set of gravity model predictions based on time-distances measured along the network routes and more numerous and precisely defined zones of residence and activity. Once the network passed the test, rights of way would be reserved, and any proposed services or other installations could be readily located before highway construction began.

The implementation of this decision has met with only partial success. Pressure to develop the residential area of Los Olivos, south of Alta Vista, forced the engineers to do preliminary construction drawings of this sector, including the center of the city, before they had time to look at the city network as a whole. In addition, detailed location studies of heavy manufacturing industries in the industrial zone to the west took much longer than expected. It was thought that the results of these studies would influence highway alignments in the industrial zone and in turn affect the rest of the city network. To date, basic engineering studies have been completed for only the commercial center of the city, for Los Olivos, and for the residential areas lying south of the Alta Vista airport.

The consulting engineers were asked to seek alignments that would preserve and take advantage of the natural features of the site and in particular to minimize cut and fill. This would enhance the visual character of the road system, reduce the cost of construction, and avoid a repetition of the unsightly differences in level between the major roads and the adjacent subdivisions experienced in Puerto Ordaz and San Félix. Minor

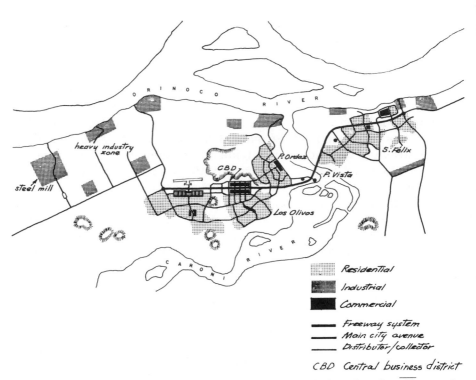

FIGURE 9.8 City highway scheme for 1970 after completion of engineering consultants' design study for 1970 network.

differences in level could be dealt with in the subsequent designs of the subdivisions.

The distances separating interchanges on the freeway system called for a careful balance between the constraints set by the geometrical standards of freeway design and the need to tie the subordinate roads to the freeway system at frequent intervals. In spite of this, and in spite of some very difficult topography that required the elimination or drastic realignment of some routes, the conceptual form of the preliminary network was maintained. (See Figures 9.8 and 9.9.) A simplified freeway network envisioned higher-capacity facilities than those proposed in the preliminary design.

Network revision. Although the consulting engineers' basic layout studies were done in close association with the transportation team, there was a growing concern that the network no longer "looked right" on paper. It was true that its pattern or geometry was not so clear in concept after its encounter with the realities of the site. But this general observation was

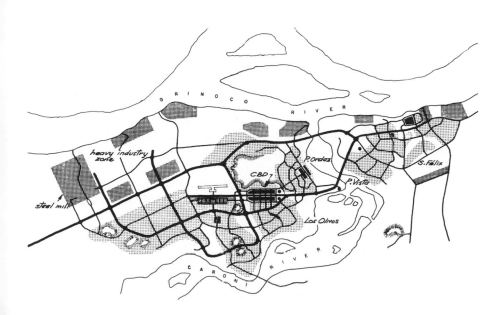

FIGURE 9.9   City highway scheme for 1980 after tentative appraisal by engineering consultants.

also mixed with a detailed criticism of the location of a north-south freeway immediately to the west of Alta Vista. The route of the freeway was through a deep natural gully, where it could meet traffic requirements without using good residential land. However, the gully is full of trees, and some would have to be cut to build the road. This was thought to be intolerable, even though a carefully landscaped road in this location would be one of the very few that would be enclosed in a beautiful setting and provide the automobile driver with some relief from the enormous horizons experienced on most of the city's other highways.

But by this time it was difficult for the transportation planners to defend their position against those who saw the highway network as a means of providing the land-use plans with an agreeable pattern of lines to emphasize on paper the city's future form. Though the transportation planners considered many aspects of highway alignment, including visual factors, they relied heavily on traffic-demand estimates to support their recommendations and decisions. But this prop little by little was withdrawn from them by the economists, who drastically reduced the industrial production targets of the city and so called into question the validity of the traffic estimates.

There was no time to revise the traffic-demand estimates. All available staff were kept busy on day-to-day problems; the Corporation was calling for a report from its own members and the Joint Center to be ready in six months (by June 1966), setting forth major policies for development.

To prepare this report, some compromises had to be made, and the plans of the city underwent considerable reappraisal. Growth strategy now calls for developing residential areas north of the airport near Alta Vista prior to opening up the land south of the heavy industry zone. The offending freeway in the gully has been eliminated, a more direct connection has been devised between Alta Vista and the steel mill, and the highway system south of the airport has been restructured. (See Figure 9.10.) Although agreement has been reached, these changes are still only in sketch form and will have to be carefully evaluated, following studies of revised sections by the engineering consultants.

Discussion

Lack of time and a shortage of staff were two important constraints that the traffic planners had to contend with in their program to provide the city with transportation plans. Time was a major problem because the need to develop the Los Olivos area for steelworkers' housing became so urgent that the longer-term planning of the city became a second priority. In this sense, Los Olivos became another "crash" program like those of San Félix and Puerto Ordaz—programs that seriously retarded the planning process on a city-wide scale.

Skilled physical planners are scarce in Venezuela, and staff in the office was in such short supply that those who were working on the city-wide scale were gradually withdrawn when other areas, like the central business district, called for detailed examination. Consequently, during the engineering studies of the transportation network, the transportation planners, consisting of one staff member and the consulting engineers, had to make decisions by themselves about the highway network without sufficient studies of related land use. This was unfortunate because the urban designers harbored a fear, from the time the consulting engineers were appointed, that the engineering profession would have too much sway in the planning of the city and that this would result in a clinical design—a city devoid of character. On seeing the alterations to the network (Figure 9.10), some thought this fear was justified. The subsequent revisions of the

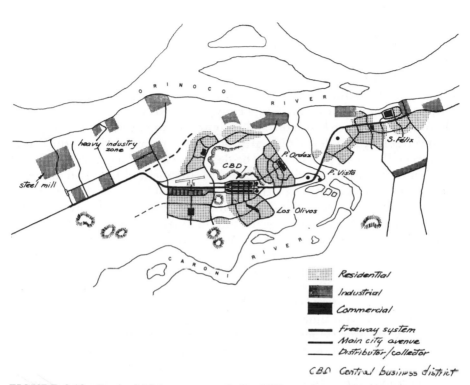

FIGURE 9.10 Revised highway network for 1970 consistent with northern growth strategy, showing improved continuity between steel mill and central business district in Alta Vista.

network design in preparation for the June 1966 policy report represented to a great extent an effort by the physical planners to redress the balance by concentrating their attention once more on the city as a whole, particularly its activity and visual structures.

Another factor that curtailed the transportation program was the frequency with which the economists revised their targets. To an economist this means the production of a new set of numbers; but to physical planners this change may mean the radical reappraisal of the urban transportation system, some of which may be in an advanced stage of design. Without a plentiful supply of time and staff, it was not practical to repeat the procedural steps of the network design to evaluate each of the economists' major revisions. Instead, it had to be assumed that the staging of the network need only be retarded without altering its basic layout. The network could then be considered to have a longer period of adequacy than previously expected. But it was hard to defend this approach with others on the urban design team who saw, parallel with the reduction of the economists' targets for 1980, a reduction in the scale of the network, particularly the freeway system—not merely a modification in staging. Had the economists commenced their studies some two to three years before the physical planning program was begun, it is possible that the physical planners would have had more stable figures to work with.

Nevertheless, in a developing area where the uncertainties of the future are especially great, plans have to be flexible. The transportation planners found it difficult to reconcile this fact with the method they had adopted, which provides an answer to a transportation problem only if the problem is defined fairly precisely. But though one may "bracket" the problem, it is still difficult to describe it in a flexible manner as it progresses into the future. Much depends, therefore, on how the results are interpreted. In this sense, gross tendencies of trip movements are important; and a good understanding of the relationships that control these tendencies provides a useful framework within which to judge the implications of changes affecting the transportation system. This flexible attitude toward results developed only with time in the Guayana project, when the instability of projections became evident. In contrast, the growth allocation model was never expected to provide more than a crude approximation of a gross tendency of population settlement, and it performed its task of demonstrating a hypothesis very effectively during the period of the "Guayana dilemma."

Aside from Puerto Ordaz and San Félix, some limited sections of the major road network have already been built, as for instance in Los Olivos. Since the construction drawings of these roads preceded the detailed designs of related subdivisions, many problems experienced in Puerto Ordaz and San Félix are being avoided. One difficulty that seems to defy solution is the control of the location and form of borrow pits and dumping areas during construction. This is in part because a comprehensive landscape plan is still lacking and in part because of an inadequately developed means of site supervision. Furthermore, it has not yet been possible to integrate satisfactorily the engineering and the landscape aspects of highway designs. Highway engineers in Venezuela have not overcome the prejudice against working closely with landscape architects; to date, only a short length of the freeway south of Puerto Ordaz, leading to the Caroní Bridge, has been studied by landscape architects to provide a "cosmetic" treatment to the right of way following the building of the road.

Ciudad Guayana is now seven years old—virtually nothing in the life of an existing city, but critical in the formative period of a new city. It is the time when its foundations are being laid, and the success of its subsequent growth will indicate the worth of the preparatory work that has already been done. The transportation planners have been conscious of groping in the future of a developing area—a future full of uncertainties. In scale with the resources at their disposal, techniques were used to shed some light on the future, techniques that may have turned out to be too inflexible when adaptability to changing circumstances is paramount. However, the planning process is a continuous one, and the repetition of procedures through time with firmer economic estimates and plentiful "feedback" information may do much to counterbalance this limitation.

Chapter 10

Creating a Land Development Strategy for Ciudad Guayana

Anthony Downs

Building a truly viable "new city" in accordance with a rational plan is one of the most difficult tasks that can be undertaken. Moreover, the hardest parts of this task have received the least attention from those who have done the most thinking about "new cities" in general. Most such planners have never actually had the responsibility of building a "new city." Therefore, they have not grappled either intellectually or practically with the enormous and intractable problems of translating their aesthetically neat "end-product" visions into a concrete settlement inhabited by real men.

In general, creating a rationally planned city can be divided into three steps: (1) developing the over-all plan, (2) creating a basic strategy for converting that plan into reality, and (3) implementing the strategy. The basic physical plan for Ciudad Guayana had already been formulated when Real Estate Research Corporation was asked in 1964 to review the assumptions of the plan and to submit recommendations on the best methods of putting the plan into effect. Our assignment was therefore to develop answers to the following questions:

Which parts of the envisioned city should be developed first, and which last?

Were the land-use patterns created by the planners economically sound? If not, how should they be revised?

How fast would various types of land (such as residential or commercial) be put into use, given certain predicted population growth rates? As a result, how much land of each type would have to be developed each year?

What land disposition policies should the city developers follow? That is, under what conditions should they sell, rent, or otherwise dispose of various types of land?

In essence, this meant developing that part of the city-formation strategy concerned with land use (as opposed to other parts concerned with education, political institutions, and social policies). By strategy, we mean a generalized plan indicating the nature, sequence, and approximate magnitude of those actions that would most effectively culminate in the kind of city envisioned in the basic plan. Whereas a plan is a depiction of the entire city as of a given moment in time (usually after most of it has been built), a strategy is an envisioned set of actions distributed over time —a "flow" rather than a "stock" or "state." Yet a strategy also differs from a program: the latter is a "flow," too, but it is far more detailed and includes precise quantities and schedules for the actions concerned. Thus a program contains the tactics implied by a more general strategy. In practice, however, strategy formation tends to overlap both planning and programming to some extent. In fact, every part of the city-building process is continually modified by feedbacks from other parts that, on the basis of pure logic, both precede and follow it.

At the outset we decided to use a systems analysis approach to creating a land development strategy for Ciudad Guayana. This approach entailed

1. explicit formulation of the objectives being pursued by the builders of the city
2. analysis of alternative methods of achieving those objectives, where practical, rather than concentration solely on one possible method
3. evaluation of these alternatives by comparing their relative desirability in terms of the objectives being pursued
4. quantification of variables wherever possible.

Although we tried to formulate alternative policies at each stage of the analysis, we often settled on one alternative before proceeding to the next stage. This was necessary to reduce complexity to manageable proportions, as will become clear when we describe all the stages involved.

Estimating Residential Land Absorption

Because the Corporación Venezolana de Guayana (CVG) and the consultants from the Joint Center for Urban Studies had already drawn up the basic physical plan for the city—including general land-use patterns —we were able to concentrate mainly on "pure" strategy formation rather than on planning itself. The first step was to estimate the rate of speed at which the city was likely to develop. As the single best indicator of over-all development—and one relatively easy to manipulate—we chose total population. Our population forecasts for the city were based upon a combination of induction (from recent population growth rates) and deduction (from the states of economic development to which the CVG and Joint Center economists aspired). They were considerably lower than the earlier estimates of the CVG and Joint Center economists.

Moving from total population forecasts to estimates of land absorption rates for specific types of land uses required the following steps:

1. We converted total population into number of households by using a simple persons-per-household factor of 5.5, based upon recent census data.

2. We estimated the percentage distribution of households in each of five income groups for each year covered by our analysis (1964–1970). For the first year we used the income distribution revealed by the latest census. We then assumed gradually increasing prosperity; that is, the proportion of households steadily declined in the lowest income group (from 26.9 per cent in 1964 to 13.8 per cent in 1970), rose in the highest group (from 4.1 to 8.2 per cent), and changed congruently in intermediate groups.

3. By applying these percentage estimates to the total number of households forecast for each year, we calculated the absolute number of households in each income group in each year. Then we subtracted the total for each year from that for the following year to obtain the absolute change in the number of households in each income group in each year.

4. The next step was to convert changes in the number of households in a given income group to changes in the demand for housing appropriate to that group. *The distinction between these two variables is crucial, for shifts in household income differ sharply from shifts in the income structure of housing demand.* This is especially true where net changes in the number of households in a given income group result from large movements into the group by some households and out of it by others. For example, in one year we estimated that the lowest income group had a net rise of only 19 households. But this resulted from (a) inmigration to Ciudad Guayana of 1,550 low-income households, (b) natural increases of 241 low-income households, and (c) a loss of 1,772 households to the next higher income group because of rising incomes. However, not every family that moves into a higher income group shifts houses; many merely upgrade their existing dwellings by addition or improvement, especially in underdeveloped countries. Therefore, we estimated that the housing demand generated by households in this income group would rise by 1,259 units in that year—even though there were only 19 more households in the whole group.

5. Whenever incomes in general are rising, but significant inmigration of low-income households occurs, net shifts in the number of households in each income group grossly understate changes in the demand for low-income housing and overstate changes in the demand for high-income housing. By preparing estimates for each income group of inmigration, natural increase, upward income shifts, and the probability that such shifts would cause moving rather than mere upgrading, we were able to forecast changes in the demand for housing units appropriate to each group. Here "demand" refers to the number of households desiring or needing new units, not necessarily to the number capable of paying for them.

6. Since our analysis had thus shifted from effective demand to needs, the remaining steps dealt with converting these needs to the amount of land that would be absorbed by meeting these needs if they were met in accordance with certain standards of housing quality considered minimal by the city's planners. The planners supplied us with estimates of the minimum amount of land per household associated with housing in each income group for (a) single-family homes, (b) multifamily homes, and (c) shacks (for the lowest income groups only).

7. We estimated the proportion of increases in housing needs in each income group that would be met by single-family homes, apartments, and shacks. Then we multiplied these totals by the appropriate land amounts supplied by the planners to obtain the net residential land absorption for each income group.

8. The final step was to convert net residential land needs (land actually occupied by dwelling units) into gross land needs (residential land, including allowances for local streets, parks, churches, and other facilities). Whereas the planners had suggested that only 50 per cent of the gross residential land be used for housing, we recommended a shift to a 67 per cent ratio (compared to the 75 per cent often used in the United States). This would allow the CVG to realize 33 per cent more revenue from any given gross amount of residential land than would be possible following the ratio originally suggested. Thus by multiplying net residential land absorption by 1.5 (so 67 per cent of the result was covered by housing), we obtained a final estimate of the gross amount of residential land that would be absorbed each year if housing demands were met in accordance with our minimum planning standards.

I have set forth these steps in detail because they reveal quite clearly the complexity of just the land-use part of the strategy formation process. This complexity is usually glossed over by studies that discuss city building only in the abstract. Moreover, these steps imply two other important conclusions. First, every strategy analysis involves a compromise between (1) what is likely to happen if things merely go on as they have in the past and (2) what might happen if the city developers are successful in implementing their plans. In our estimation of residential land absorption, almost every step involved such a compromise, partly because lack of information forced us to rely upon aspirations as well as "facts." For example, our estimate of the rate at which incomes would rise was influenced by the goals of the Joint Center economists as well as by our estimates of what was actually likely to happen. Aspirations played even more central roles in our estimation of housing "demand," since we assumed that every household that needed a housing unit would somehow get one. Moreover, for all but the lowest income groups we further assumed that the housing units they obtained would conform to the minimum lot-size standards set by the planners. Although we did estimate that many low-income households could not afford standard housing and would therefore live in shacks falling below minimum house-quality standards, we nevertheless devised minimum lot-size "standards" for shacks and assumed they would all meet such standards. As a result, our final estimate of residential land absorption was a mixture of actual trends and hoped-for developments, with such strong emphasis on aspirations that it really described needs or requirements rather than likely outcomes. This is a necessary step in strategy formation; the developers of a city need to start their operations with a strategy that embodies their aspirations and yet is realistic enough so that they can conceivably carry it out if everything happens in an optimal fashion. It is certain that everything will not happen optimally, but coping with these deficiencies can then be done at the tactical level, in day-to-day programming.

The second important lesson is that planning standards can have profound economic consequences for the city's developers—as the builders of Reston and Columbia (two "new cities" near Washington, D.C.) have belatedly discovered. Planners may, for aesthetic or other reasons, make decisions about lot size, street width, density, and the provision of ancillary nonresidential uses without fully appreciating how much this may increase the amount of land needed to serve a given population. This not only decreases the revenue that the city's developers can realize from a given amount of land but also increases utility and other development costs for a given population. Hence land economists can play a key role in planning new cities (or even old ones, for that matter), because they can test the economic consequences of schemes developed by physical planners and recommend modifications on the basis of their findings.

Estimating Commercial and Industrial Land Absorption

Estimating commercial and industrial land absorption was easy in comparison with estimating that for residential use. This was true because we assumed that (1) commercial land use would be a function of population and incomes, and (2) industrial land use need not be forecast at all, since the existing supply appeared adequate to meet all needs remotely conceivable for the next three decades. We developed modified versions of the relationships between commercial land needs and population and income that we had often used in the United States by examining land-use patterns in Caracas, Valencia, Ciudad Guayana itself, and other Venezuelan cities. However, we devoted much less effort to making these forecasts than we had to the residential land forecasts because the amount of land likely to be needed for commercial purposes was both much smaller and much less subject to possible variation than that likely to be needed for residential purposes.

Strategic Goals

Our strategy analysis began with estimates of future land absorption rates because it was vital to know in what major ways and how fast the city was likely to expand before we could develop a strategy for guiding that expansion. Another factor necessary for developing the strategy was a definition of the developers' objectives. It was clear from the legal mandates given to the CVG that urban development was only one facet of its major task: economic development of the entire Guayana region. But the CVG had never spelled out any specific urban development objectives in writing. So we articulated those we believed properly expressed what the CVG was actually trying to do, and discussed them with CVG and Joint Center officials.

The result was a conception of the CVG's urban development objectives as one primary goal subject to three major constraints. The primary goal was rapid and efficient development of the urban services necessary to support and attract new industries and other economic base activities to the region. The derivation of this goal from the CVG's basic regional economic development function is clear. The three major constraints, which could alternatively be called secondary goals, were as follows (not necessarily in order of importance):

1. capturing a satisfactory financial return on the CVG's investment in the area

2. minimizing the managerial and other developmental responsibilities of the CVG by turning over as many functions as possible to the normal action of the market or to other public agencies

3. maintaining the planning and land-use controls necessary to create an attractive and efficient city that would provide maximum long-run satisfaction to its citizens as well as a nucleus for the attraction of industry.

At first glance, these goals may appear to be so broad and general as to be in the "motherhood" category, that is, both obvious and operationally useless. However, although our later analysis of urban programming required breaking these general goals down into a number of much more specific objectives, even this broad statement was operationally helpful for several reasons. First, it established economic development as having higher priority than any other objectives—such as making profits, achieving high planning standards, or reducing the CVG's managerial efforts. Thus, whenever some action crucial for economic development conflicted with one of the other goals, the choice was clear. Many ambiguous conflicts arose among the goals, and it was not always easy to judge just how "crucial" to development any given action might be. Nevertheless, even this simple priority ranking proved quite helpful.

Second, the CVG's desire to limit its managerial efforts meant that urban development was not a potential empire-building game for the existing bureaucracy. Third, it also meant that the CVG favored encouraging private entrepreneurs to play as large a role in urban development as possible. Hence the CVG was willing to sell land to private developers if that was necessary to get them into action.

Fourth, the CVG's desire to maintain good planning standards whenever possible meant that many things would not be sacrificed to development, profit making, or reduction of responsibilities. As a result, the physical quality of Ciudad Guayana will probably differ strikingly from most other Venezuelan cities—if the plan succeeds. Thus even these extremely broad goals had very specific implications crucial to the formulation of a land development strategy.

The Concept of Paced Development

For maximum encouragement of economic development in Ciudad Guayana, the facilities necessary for each step in urban expansion should become available at the same time that the need or demand for them appears. For example, housing should be constructed so that it comes into existence at the same rate as the population grows, so that neither shortages nor surpluses arise. Such pacing appeared essential in order to (1) prevent bottlenecks from slowing down expansion, (2) conserve resources so that excessive supplies of certain facilities would not waste labor and capital, and (3) minimize the managerial efforts the CVG would have to devote to coordinating various phases of urban development.

Since it would be completely unrealistic to expect perfect pacing of all aspects of development, we attempted to distinguish between those urban facilities vital to development that the CVG should try to provide slightly in advance of the need for them and those that could be allowed to lapse behind demand. What this actually meant was picking facilities that would have the shortest lags behind the need for them. These top-priority facilities were

1. well-located industrial land suitable for plant construction
2. roads and utilities serving industrial land, main housing areas, and main commercial centers
3. low-income housing and planned vacant lots on which inmigrants could erect shacks. This was vital for controlling the location of squatters, which will be discussed later.

Lower-priority facilities, which could be allowed to lag further behind the demand for them, were housing for middle- and upper-income groups and commercial land of all types. These types of land use were much closer to being economically self-supporting than the higher-priority ones mentioned earlier. Therefore, when the demand for them became strong enough, entrepreneurs would step forth to supply them, with minimal assistance from the CVG. True, the speed at which entrepreneurs appeared might seem like a snail's pace in the United States. But the relative likelihood of getting facilities of various types without major CVG effort, plus the relative importance of such facilities in the economic development process, dictated the choice of priorities.

It should be emphasized that the scope of these priority recommendations was confined to major types of land uses. Hence these recommendations did not cover other uses of resources that could play even more significant roles in economic development, such as improved industrial and commercial promotion and schools.

Land Disposition Policies

A major issue for the CVG was the proper disposition of land in Ciudad Guayana. Since the CVG owned most of the land (except for some key pieces still held by the Orinoco Mining Company), it had a unique opportunity to use this major asset both to control and to finance urban development.

A previous Joint Center consultant had recommended that the CVG refuse to sell any land in order to capture all future gains in value likely to occur because of rising land prices. He thought the CVG should only rent land to developers, particularly land for commercial uses. The CVG, however, since its primary goal was rapid development, would not want to adopt any disposition policies likely to exert a strong drag on the speed of development—and, given the general investment situation in Venezuela, it was not likely to get many private developers to build either residential or commercial facilities if it would not sell them any land. The possibility of receiving capital gains from rising land values was a major incentive for their participating in the development of Ciudad Guayana. Furthermore, if the CVG failed to get private developers involved, it would have to build all the housing and commercial facilities itself. This would violate another of its goals—minimizing its own managerial efforts—and further slow down development. In fact, the resulting slowdown and administrative tie-ups might significantly diminish the rise in land values that would be the major benefit expected from not selling the land.

Therefore the CVG should sell residential land to developers as fast as possible—but also retain certain well-located pieces so as to capitalize on future land price rises. (The location of these pieces will be discussed later.) In order to minimize its own administrative efforts, the CVG should both sell large tracts and try to get private developers to do as much as possible, such as installing local streets and utilities. On the other hand, the CVG would have to provide lots for individual households in the lowest income groups. They were the single largest set of residential land consumers, and so had to be provided for; but no private developers could make any money dealing with them—hence none would do this job.

Regarding industrial land, we concluded that the CVG should tailor its policies to fit the needs of individual users and should adopt virtually any disposition arrangements that would encourage industrial firms to locate in Ciudad Guayana. This would mean preserving some areas with large tracts for sale to big firms and developing some with small tracts or even parts of completed buildings for rent to small firms. The industrial land should be manipulated not primarily to make financial profits but to create employment.

Since commercial land was likely to rise in price both faster and to higher levels than any other type except high-rise residential, it would certainly be desirable for the CVG to retain ownership and to rent to developers whenever possible. Nevertheless, at least in the initial stages of urban development, it was essential for the CVG to offer whatever terms were necessary to get developers into motion. This probably meant that the CVG would have to sell some commercial land at first, especially around the new commercial district it hoped to start in an almost completely vacant area. After development was well under way the CVG could demand terms more favorable to itself—such as rental with an option to buy, straight rental, rental with escalation clauses concerning rates, percentage leases, or leases with rent-renewal options. In essence, it should strike the best land disposition bargains it could at any given moment that would be consistent with attaining the speed of development desired at any moment.

Here, too, the CVG ought to retain certain well-located parcels so as to capture the long-range appreciation that would probably affect them. These parcels could be used as parking lots, baseball fields, or parks, or even rented for low-intensity commercial purposes involving minimal building coverage, until the CVG felt the time was ripe for higher-intensity commercial development. Arranging identical lease expiration dates on adjacent small parcels rented for interim uses would avoid difficult reassembly problems when the time for more intensive uses arrived.

Two other aspects of the CVG's land disposition policy are also noteworthy. First, the CVG ought to purchase all the remaining vacant land in Ciudad Guayana—especially that owned by the Orinoco Mining Company. Ironically enough, that company owned both the existing commercial center of Puerto Ordaz and the planned (but then totally undeveloped) commercial center of Alta Vista. Moreover, the company was selling prime commercial land in the competitive Puerto Ordaz downtown area at prices far below true market value (largely through ignorance of what that value was)—thereby pre-empting some of the potential tenants of the planned Alta Vista development.

Second, it appeared wise for the CVG to adopt a policy of not giving final title to any land until the buyers had received approval for the particular improvements they planned and had actually started making them. Some such control mechanism was necessary to ensure that developers' improvements would fit into the city's master plan.

The Balance of Development East and West of the Caroní River

At the time of our study, about 60 per cent of Ciudad Guayana's population lived in the older and more run-down San Félix area on the east side of the Caroní River. The remainder lived on the west side, where nearly all existing modern housing and commercial structures were located and almost all future urban growth was planned. Thus the planners' concepts called for a dramatic reversal of the existing population balance on both sides of the Caroní River.

Just how dramatic a reversal was required is shown by our estimates of the future growth patterns necessary to achieve several different east-west balances by the target date of 1970. We set forth possible future balances (ranging from 75 per cent to only 49 per cent on the west side) and indicated what percentage of all growth from 1964 to 1970 would have to occur on the west side to attain each outcome. For example, to go from the 1964 balance of 40 per cent on the west side to a desired 75 per cent by 1970, 99 per cent of all population growth in the interim would have to occur on the west side (given previous projections of total population growth from 1964 to 1970). Since about 65 per cent of all growth had been occurring on the east side, we did not believe the CVG could suddenly drop this fraction to 1 per cent, even though it had just built a bridge connecting both sides.

We concluded from these estimates that a 1970 balance of 60 per cent on the west side would be a more realistic objective than the 75 per cent the planners had previously called for. The 60 per cent target still contained a significant element of aspiration, requiring a sharp change in growth patterns: the proportion of all growth that would have to occur on the west side rose from 35 per cent to 75 per cent. This quantitative analysis of alternatives—the heart of the systems analysis approach—thus had great practical implications for the plans.

The quantitative analysis also pointed up the inconsistency of two different policy objectives. On the one hand, all CVG officials were agreed that the west side should be dominant and should receive a preponderance of future growth. On the other hand, some top officials also wanted to keep all modern developments on the west side and relegate squatters' shacks and other aesthetically substandard structures to the older east side. Their goal was to build a thoroughly modern and attractive "new city" free from surrounding squatter villages—and therefore more attractive to potential executives and leaders than other Venezuelan cities already permeated with squatters.

However, the analysis showed that inmigration of very low-income households formed a large part of the total future population growth. It would therefore be impossible to confine the expansion of this group to the east side and still have a preponderance of total growth occurring in the west side. This posed a dilemma: should the CVG sacrifice the aesthetic and social-class "purity" of west-side development in order to shift most growth to that side, or should it sacrifice the size dominance of the west in order to maintain its "purity"? We favored shifting total growth to the west side as much as possible and developing a heterogeneous mixture of social classes there, partly because this would unify the city politically. The alternative growth pattern would tend to create two groups that were very distinct from each other socially and economically as well as spatially—and therefore much more likely to split into two separate legal entities as well. Since the city had only recently been created by unifying these two areas anyway, such a combined social-economic-spatial stratification would prevent it from ever really becoming a single city. However, there should be a planned segregation of income groups on the west side into different neighborhoods, so that each household could choose a neighborhood-sized environment that was homogeneous in relation to its own socioeconomic status.

The Time-Space Strategy of Development

Most cities grow outward from an initial center. The outward movement can be either concentric (in all directions at about the same speed) or radial (out along a few transport arteries or geographic corridors faster than between them). In either case, the transport economies of locating as close as possible to existing facilities tend to keep growth from leapfrogging any distance out into the hinterlands over intervening vacant land (though this has occurred more frequently around U.S. cities in the past twenty-five years).

This "inside-out" growth pattern was the one the CVG and Joint Center planners had projected for the development of the "all-new" Ciudad Guayana on the west side of the Caroní River. The initial center they had selected was the planned commercial district of Alta Vista, on the main road connecting downtown Puerto Ordaz and the bridge to San Félix on the east with the steel mill on the west. However, Alta Vista was still totally vacant in 1964, with no residential development anywhere near it. This fact reinforced their desire to build up residential areas quickly all around it (except north toward the Orinoco River where the terrain was forbidding) so as to create nearby consumers who would make the planned commercial center economically viable. Thus the planners sought to duplicate the normal historical process of urban growth around an "artificially" (that is, nonhistorically) selected center.

This strategy involved significant disadvantages. First, it meant that the CVG would be unable to capitalize on the appreciaton of land values created by its own activities. A study of the history of urban land prices reveals that the greatest increases occur in the parcels at the center of a city. As the periphery of development moves farther and farther from the center, more and more time and effort are required to travel from undeveloped land to the center and its facilities and amenities. Thus centrally located land enjoys an ever-increasing relative accessibility advantage, so its price goes up as the city grows larger. However, land at the margin of development is always the least expensive in the urban area, since it has the poorest accessibility to the center.

If Ciudad Guayana were developed on the traditional "inside-out" pattern, the CVG would always be selling peripheral land to private developers in order to expedite the next "concentric ring" of growth. Hence it would receive the lowest prevailing price for land at every stage of urban growth. Moreover, as the value of the centrally located land rose, the beneficiaries would be the private developers who had previously bought that land—not the CVG. Unless the CVG retained and developed central land itself, it could not capture any of the substantial central-land value appreciation likely to occur because of urban growth. But such self-development would violate the CVG's principal of minimizing its managerial responsibilities. It would also force the CVG to tie up in construction some resources that could otherwise be used to create more infrastructure, thereby encouraging much more private construction. True, the CVG could sell some land to developers and hold onto major parcels at the center without developing them at all, thus retaining its ability to capture the future appreciation of those parcels. But if such parcels covered any significant area, then the CVG would not really be following an "inside-out" pattern, since large areas at the center would remain undeveloped.

The second major drawback of "inside-out" growth is that it creates undesirable residential settlement patterns that generate a need for urban renewal. In general, households prefer single-family dwellings to higher-density residences—particularly multistory high-rise apartments. This is especially true of low-income households in developing countries. They contain many children, and it is hard to care for children in high-rise buildings; they would like to grow some food in backyard garden plots; their normal social and economic affairs involve frequent trips in and out of the home, which are inconvenient in an elevator building; and they are simply not used to high-rise structures. We have already indicated that low-income households will comprise a high proportion of Ciudad Guayana's population growth in the near future. Moreover, it is unrealistic to suppose that these households will all be provided with new, modern apartment projects similar to the public housing in Caracas; it is likely that much of the residential settlement during the next few years will consist of single-family shacks erected by the occupants themselves. If an "inside-out" growth pattern is followed, such settlements will be located close to the center of Ciudad Guayana, because all growth will occur in concentric circles outward from the center.

As a result, when the city has become fairly large in population and area, its center will consist of a high proportion of slum dwellings. Even standard dwellings erected near the center will then be the oldest standard units in the city (since the center will be built up first); hence many may have deteriorated (depending upon how fast the city grows). Moreover, most of both the standard and the substandard housing around the city's center will be low-rise units (though in some shack areas they may be close enough together to create relatively high densities).

One of the planners' key concepts was to keep the city a single-nucleus settlement, with a vital and dominant downtown area. In this respect it would differ from Caracas and most large U.S. cities, which are rapidly becoming multinucleated thanks to the automobile, although the once-dominant downtown is still the largest nucleus. According to this concept it would be desirable for the center of Ciudad Guayana to be surrounded by relatively high-density residential areas, including those occupied by upper-income and middle-income residents.

Yet the "inside-out" growth pattern in Ciudad Guayana would result in a pattern of settlement quite different from this desired outcome. The downtown area would be surrounded in large measure by low-density substandard dwellings occupied by the lowest income groups. Assuming that the general level of incomes will rise over time, upper- and middle-income families would form an ever-increasing proportion of the total population. But since they would appear on the scene later, they would tend to locate relatively far from downtown on then vacant land. This would encourage the development of outlying commercial nuclei serving these better-off economic groups, as has occurred in Caracas. The result would be a downtown area patronized primarily by daytime office workers and nearby low-income groups, as in almost all the largest U.S. cities.

Then the only way this pattern could be converted to the desired high-density, mixed-income-group central residential area would be through extensive urban renewal. Such renewal would consist of clearing out the slums near downtown and replacing them with high-rise apartments serving both low-income groups (in public housing) and middle- and upper-income groups (in private housing). But clearance programs of this type are highly undesirable, especially in a developing country, for the following reasons:

1. Urban renewal is expensive. It ties up both money and trained administrators in the process of buying existing homes, demolishing them, creating additional homes elsewhere for the displaced persons, relocating them there, and finally building new structures.

2. The persons displaced from renewed areas form a strong source of political opposition to the government doing the renewing. This resistance is likely to be especially bitter in a country with an absolute shortage of housing. Dislocated households cannot move into vacant existing homes, since none exist. Few democratic governments are willing to destroy many housing units under these conditions—particularly when they destroy units occupied by the poor in order to build new ones occupied by the rich.

3. It is difficult to undertake renewal over a large enough area all at once, so that a really complete change in residential environment occurs. Yet such a change is needed to attract upper-income and middle-income households into predominantly lower-income areas.

These shortcomings of urban renewal have prevented it from becoming effective over any very large proportion of the residential land, even in U.S. cities—which have vastly more resources than cities in developing countries. In fact, for the reasons just given, it is extremely unlikely that any major urban renewal programs would actually be undertaken in Ciudad Guayana during the next three decades. This means that use of the "inside-out" strategy for developing Ciudad Guayana would not result in the type of city desired by its planners but in a weak downtown surrounded by slums and competing with powerful outlying commercial subcenters.

As a result of these considerations we drew up a general land development strategy that we called "outside-in with corridors." The basic concept is to anticipate future growth by building each type of residential settlement in the location that will prove "ultimately" desirable after the city has become very much larger than it is now—say, containing 250,000 persons. Hence low-density and low-quality housing would be located relatively far from downtown, in a ring of settlements encircling it. Higher-density settlements—such as moderate-rise and high-rise apartments—would be placed closer to downtown, with the highest density ones closest. These closer-in settlements would initially be grouped along a few radii connecting the downtown with the lower-density and lower-quality outlying settlements. As a result, the many outlying settlements of low-income residents that would be constructed in the near future would be linked to downtown by other settlements grouped along a few corridors lining major traffic arteries. Such contiguous grouping would partly offset the higher initial utility and transportation costs involved in an "outside-in" strategy.

Large areas of land lying between these few settled corridors would be held by the CVG for later development. These reserved parcels would include some land right next to the downtown area. Therefore, this strategy would allow the CVG itself to capture much of the future appreciation of the central-area land values. In addition to this financial boon, preventing slum housing from surrounding the downtown area would obviate the need for urban renewal later. Furthermore, the existence of sizable vacant, publicly owned parcels at varying distances from the city center would greatly increase the flexibility with which the government could respond to future growth pressures that are hard to predict now. (Think how delighted many U.S. mayors would be to have such flexibility today!)

This strategy admittedly has some significant drawbacks. First, it imposes higher initial utility and transportation costs upon the city. Early settlements will not be packed together close to the center, and residents of outlying areas will have to travel farther to get to the center. However, these costs can be reduced by concentrating all initial development along or near the end of one or two corridors leading outward from the center. Such a pattern would retain contiguity, thereby reducing utility trunk-line costs. It would also provide nearly continuous visual linkage with settled areas for people traveling between outlying areas and downtown. Furthermore, the land lying between outlying settlements and downtown would be likely to rise in value more quickly than if settlement radiated outward from downtown. These interstices will be such obviously good locations for added development that the kind of "linkage pressure" described by A. O. Hirschman may lure entrepreneurs to act faster than they would in an "inside-out" pattern.[1]

The second disadvantage of the "outside-in" strategy is that it results in a weaker focus of commercial demand upon the downtown area, especially in the first few years. Since many initial settlements will be distant from downtown, retailers may not want to build stores there. This was especially serious in Ciudad Guayana because the planned downtown did not yet exist and had to emerge in competition with already booming downtown

Puerto Ordaz. Consequently, there might have to be at least some low-density or low-quality housing near the planned downtown just to generate enough demand there to get things started.

The third problem inherent in an "outside-in" strategy is that it assumes that squatters will not inundate the large reserved vacant areas near the city center. In many developing nations, inmigrants have erected whole cities of shacks in public parks, on planned malls and parkways, and on other government-owned parcels that are both vacant and conveniently located. In a democratic country the government is reluctant to evict such squatters—particularly if it has no immediate alternative use for the land concerned.

However, if the government cannot prevent squatters from invading vacant land, it will never be able to carry out any effective land development strategy. Instead it will be at the mercy of squatters' residential location preferences, since they can then pre-empt any desired public land not already covered with buildings.

Two policies could effectively prevent squatters from moving onto reserved land. The first is to provide alternative locations for squatters, with enough attractive amenities (such as streets, water, electricity, and well-laid-out parcels) to compensate for their less central position. If the CVG could get ahead of the inflow of squatters by creating enough of these plots in "planned slums" so that each new inmigrant household could occupy one immediately, this would in effect intercept the squatters from settling on vacant land held for other future uses. The second crucial policy is to encourage interim uses on reserved land that would generate enough activity there to discourage squatters. Such uses might include baseball fields, farming, and school playgrounds.

The fact that the CVG owned or controlled nearly all of the land in Ciudad Guayana and was simultaneously responsible for planning its development as a city created a breadth of choice concerning land development strategies that is very rare in urban history. Most cities are virtually compelled to grow in an "inside-out" fashion. The economic pressures generated by private ownership of many fragmented parcels cause each land developer to ignore the long-run social costs of "inside-out" growth in order to reap the short-run private profits it creates. The CVG's land-control monopoly provides an extraordinary opportunity to reverse this process by adopting an "outside-in" approach modified with radial corridors.

Chapter 11

The Business Center

Philip E. Beach, Jr.

In 1963 Alta Vista, a relatively isolated grassy plateau, was designated as the commercial and business center of Venezuela's young, rapidly growing, industrial city, Ciudad Guayana. Designation on a planner's map, however, did not mean that a city center would automatically spring to life in this bare area, particularly since significant and growing competition existed in the populated, highly developed parts of Ciudad Guayana. The challenging effort of promoting the development of Alta Vista by private enterprise will be described in this chapter.

In choosing Alta Vista as the center of the city, the planners were dominated by long-run considerations, such as ample undeveloped land, ease of communication, visibility, and a location that would offer the highest over-all accessibility to Ciudad Guayana's future population and industry. If short-run, or even medium-run, considerations, such as nearness to existing population centers and immediate commercial attractiveness, had been given a stronger role, the center might well have been planned for another area, perhaps Punta Vista or even Puerto Ordaz.[1]

Thus the choice of the best long-run site meant the sacrifice of short-run advantages. Even though Alta Vista had the advantage of being located on Ciudad Guayana's major artery, it was at a commercial disadvantage with Puerto Ordaz and San Félix. The magnetism of the latter contrasted greatly with the savanna of Alta Vista. Whereas Puerto Ordaz and San Félix were established centers of commerce, government services, entertainment, and semiurban residential forms, Alta Vista was a grassy plateau adorned with a few bars and a small sawmill and was located about one mile from the nearest residential area and one and one-half miles from the nearest commercial establishment.

In addition to its location on a main highway, Alta Vista's other qualifications consisted of dreams and schemes: housing projects and apartment developments; civic, municipal, and medical facilities; and commercial and business installations. These plans represented the planners' vision of great accomplishment in Alta Vista during the sixties and seventies.

It was all very well for the planners to speak of an "optimum long-run solution," but where did that leave those who were charged with implementing such a plan? Indeed, what businessman concerned with making profits would be so ill advised as to erect a store or office building in an isolated grassland, the sole merit of which seemed to be a passing highway?

The short-run disadvantages of Alta Vista were compounded by the urgency of the situation. It was becoming increasingly evident that if its development were not advanced as rapidly as possible, the Alta Vista location could be made commercially unviable by the spontaneous growth of San Félix and especially Puerto Ordaz. If events were left to their natural course, all commercial development to the west of the Caroní would concentrate in Puerto Ordaz, and the Alta Vista area would be attractive only when Puerto Ordaz became overcrowded and strangled, in about ten to fifteen years. Therefore, Alta Vista's disadvantages had to be overcome in a hurry if the chosen urban center was to become a reality in the short run and save the city from expensive redevelopment at a later date.

A Commercial Center as the Nucleus of Alta Vista

It was obvious that the desired commercial growth would not occur spontaneously in Alta Vista. In order to attract high-quality commerce and business it would be necessary to stimulate the development of a strong initial project that could create its own locational appeal.

The Centro Comercial de Alta Vista is this project. The Centro was conceived by the Corporación Venezolana de Guayana (CVG) architects as the nucleus of development in Alta Vista. Occupying a square superblock, about one thousand feet on a side, the Centro (see Figure 11.1) will include a large modern CADA (Compañía Anónima Distribuidora de Alimentos) supermarket,[2] a sizable department store for Sears Roebuck de Venezuela, an office building for the CVG, a movie theater, a bowling alley, and large amounts of space for small stores and offices. Total construction will be about 340,000 square feet, and there will be

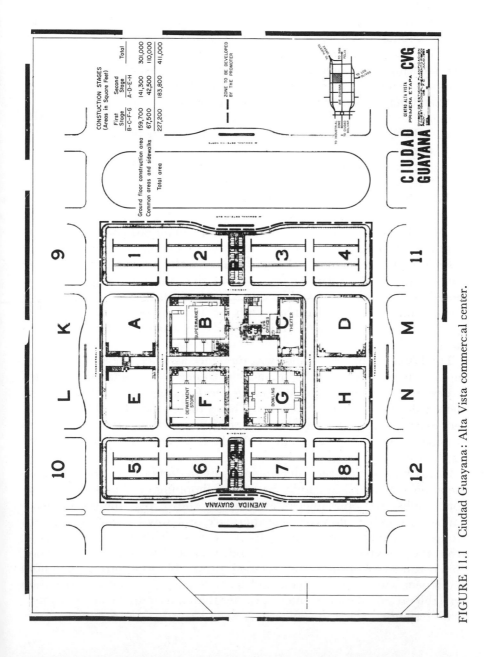

FIGURE 11.1 Ciudad Guayana: Alta Vista commercial center.

parking areas for a thousand cars. Total investment in the Centro will be about $2,500,000.

The major commercial attractions of the Centro will be CADA and Sears Roebuck. Experience in Caracas, Lima,[3] and other South American cities has shown that these two tenants are vital to the success of a commercial center. The presence of Sears and CADA assures a heavy flow of shoppers, which in turn attracts the small-shop tenants, who pay high rents and make the center a profitable operation.

Thus the Centro involved two important levels of stimulus to Alta Vista: CADA and Sears would give strong magnetism to the Centro itself, and the Centro would provide the momentum needed to start the development of Alta Vista. Stated in reverse, Alta Vista would depend upon the success of the Centro, while the latter would be impossible without the tenancy of CADA and Sears.

Strategy for Promoting the Centro

CVG officials often observed that one of the main tasks of the CVG is to create opportunities for successful investment by the private sector. For this reason, not to mention others, it was generally agreed that the Centro was a project for private enterprise and that the CVG's participation should be as limited as would be consistent with the goal of establishing a high-quality commercial center. Only as a last resort should the CVG enter the shopping-center business and construct the Centro on its own.

The CVG's promotion office was therefore assigned the task of seeking out and negotiating with a private developer who would be interested in designing, building, and operating the Centro as a private business. Such a developer would necessarily have to be one of high reputation and experience, with excellent financial connections and the skill to promote successfully the rental of the large amount of space projected for the Centro.

It was known that such developers exist in Venezuela. Private Venezuelan groups had successfully promoted shopping centers, large recreational clubs, and office blocks. It was also known that these groups are limited in number (in Venezuela there are probably fewer than ten such groups) and that they are normally quite busy, with one or more active projects occupying each developer's full time and with other projects on the horizon. It was therefore necessary to be able to approach potential developers with concrete plans and to have enough specific information available to stimulate real interest rather than a friendly "come back next year" response.

The pioneering nature of investing in Ciudad Guayana made this factor even more important. Most of the experienced developer groups concentrate their work in the Caracas area and rarely venture into the cities of the interior, let alone into what they believe to be the harsh growing pains of Ciudad Guayana.

In order to stimulate firm interest on the part of developers, the CVG took three important steps: an outside architect was contracted to prepare preliminary plans for the Centro; feasibility analyses were carried out, which demonstrated the profitability of the project; and of highest importance, the CVG decided to negotiate leases with CADA and Sears, for transfer to the Centro's developer at the proper time. Thus with designs, feasibility analyses, and contracts with the two most important tenants in hand, the CVG would have a firm base from which to promote the private installation, financing, and operation of the Centro.

The Negotiating Process

To a large extent the mechanics and tactical problems encountered during the process of negotiation are separable from the substantive issues that were resolved during the negotiating period. This section will briefly describe the preparations and events that occurred, and the following section will discuss the important differences of position that were raised and the compromises reached in the negotiations.

Preparations. The negotiation preparations that were of the most immediate importance to the promotional effort were the preliminary architectural plans,[4] the financial models and feasibility analyses, and the demand analyses performed for CADA and Sears. (See Figure 11.2.)

When the sketch plan was completed in mid-1964, an outside architect was hired to prepare the preliminary plans. These drawings were not begun until three months later, however, because of delays encountered in obtaining the CVG Board's approval of the architect's contract.

Work on the financial models and feasibility studies was begun simultaneously with the plans. The first important use of the financial models was in guiding the architects. If a commercial center is to be financially successful, economics must be a major factor in its design. The financial models were the means by which this fact was made a reality to the architects.

The balance between the major tenants (CADA, Sears, and others) and the small tenants is critical. The major tenants are of great importance in drawing shoppers and, hence, small shopkeepers to the center. But the major tenants pay a relatively low rent, which generally does not justify the erection of a building for lease to this type of tenant alone. The small shops bring profitability to a center. In Venezuela small shopkeepers

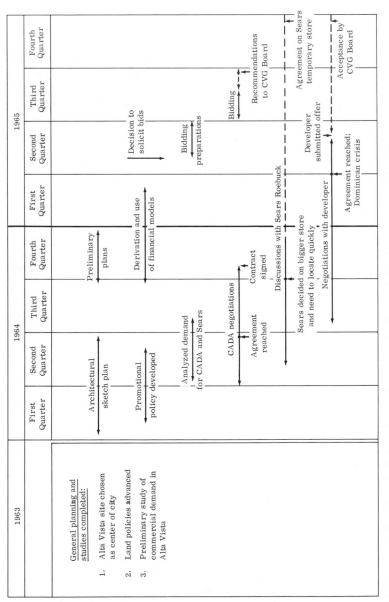

FIGURE 11.2   Historical time chart: the use and misuse of time in promoting Alta Vista.

normally pay up to three times the rent per square foot offered to the major tenants.

Thus there must be enough small-tenant space to bring a center up to satisfactory profitability but not so much that the owner will have trouble keeping the space rented. The financial models were instrumental in finding this delicate balance and incorporating it into the preliminary plans.[5]

A second important use of the financial models was to develop a feasibility-study presentation for use in promoting the project to potential developers. This presentation made use of the data and techniques of the financial models to demonstrate that the Centro would be an attractive investment by Venezuelan standards.

Demand analyses were prepared for the lease negotiations with CADA and Sears. The demand estimates were derived from the projected income distributions, purchasing power, and consumption patterns of the city's population. The highest weight was given to those consumers who would be living in the housing developments near Alta Vista. The population of the San Félix area was not a highly significant factor in the analyses.

Negotiations with CADA. With the aid of the demand analyses the negotiations with CADA proceeded rapidly during April and May 1964. Agreement was reached in May, but obtaining approval from the CVG Board required five more months, and the lease contract was not signed until October. The contract specified the terms under which CADA would lease space in the Centro from the CVG or from any third party upon whom the two parties agreed.

Negotiations with Sears. Discussions were begun with Sears in May 1964 and were still continuing at the time of this writing. Toward the end of 1964 it was mutually decided tht the final conditions for Sears' tenancy in Alta Vista would be worked out directly between Sears and the developer group. The developer with whom the CVG was negotiating at that time wanted to have the rental terms decided directly between himself and Sears. Thus it turned out that the developer was satisfied to make an offer to build and operate the Centro on the basis of the CADA lease contract and an assurance of firm interest on the part of Sears.

Negotiations with the developer. In mid-1964 preliminary discussions were held with several Venezuelan developer groups. Most of these groups either had little interest in the Centro or were willing to consider Alta Vista only under terms unacceptable to the CVG, such as low-grade construction and free land. One group was found, however, that had the combination of strong interest, experience, financial capability, and the willingness and vision to take on the Alta Vista project under suitable terms. This group, hereinafter called "the developer," had been responsible for significant construction projects in Venezuela, including the successful design, construction, and promotion of a 6,000-member, $10-million private club on the Caribbean coast.

Discussions with the developer were started in July 1964. When the preliminary plans and the feasibility study became available toward the end of that year, detailed negotiations began, and a verbal agreement was finally reached at the end of March 1965. Since the developer and the CVG negotiators believed that the agreement would be acceptable to both the developer group and the CVG Board, it was decided that the developer would submit the offer to the CVG with a formal letter.

At this time a revolution exploded in the Dominican Republic. Surprising though it may seem, this revolution on a small Caribbean island had serious short-term repercussions in Latin American financial circles. It was felt even in Venezuela, which has a democratic government and a sound economy and currency. As for the Centro project, the immediate effect of the crisis in Santo Domingo was to prevent the developer from submitting his formal proposal until June 1. At the time, however, the CVG officials did not realize that the Dominican revolution was the cause of the delay, and as the weeks went by there was growing uncertainty, indeed apprehension, that the developer might have lost interest in the project.

This uncertainty caused the CVG to decide to contact other interested groups with the hope of developing one or more alternative proposals. Two additional reasons for this decision were that some members of the CVG Board had expressed the opinion that a government body should not negotiate with one group to the exclusion of all others, and there might be a possibility that the CVG would receive a better offer from another group.

The CVG decided that negotiations with other groups would take the form of a private bid; the CVG would distribute a descriptive brochure of the project to a small number of select groups and invite each group to make a formal proposal.

The promotional brochure[6] was written during May and June 1965, and the bidding period was to be July and August. At the end of June the brochure was distributed to seven additional groups, some of which had been approached during the preliminary negotiation stage in mid-1964.

The months of July and August went by without any offer from the seven groups. Although this invitation to bid did not produce an additional offer, it did awaken firm interest on the part of three of the groups contacted. The results of this effort showed that

1. it is practically impossible to achieve a concrete offer for such a complicated project by means of a bid
2. it was unlikely that further negotiations with any of the interested groups would produce an offer significantly more advantageous to the CVG than the existing one.

The bidding procedure failed to produce a concrete offer because the process does not provide for discussing complicated issues at length in a give-and-take atmosphere. The earlier negotiations with the developer had taken place in such an atmosphere and had eventually produced a concrete offer out of what were initially just ideas and concepts. Since the developer's offer was necessarily a confidential document, conclusions and compromises reached during its negotiations could not possibly be discussed with the groups participating in the bid. It was also inadvisable to enter anything like detailed (or give-and-take) negotiations with the participating groups because such action would run the serious risk of partiality.

The participants were thus left with the general ideas, conditions, and limitations put forward in the promotional brochure. With these alone, and without further urging or discussions, they were expected to come up with detailed propositions. This expectation proved to be far too optimistic. Given the normally heavy work load of such important and influential businessmen, they were unable or unwilling to devote a significant amount of time to what seemed to be an interesting, but relatively uncertain, project. Thus the results of the bid were the stimulation of firm interest on the part of three additional groups and the awakening of a vague, long-run interest among the other groups approached.

The bid had an important side effect: the CVG was led to conclude that even if extensive negotiations were undertaken with one or more of the three interested groups, there was little likelihood that a significantly better offer would be received. This conclusion was reached on the basis of comments made by the interested parties both during and before the bidding period. The comment heard most frequently was the claim that the CVG would have to "give away the land" in order to establish a successful Centro in Alta Vista. Other comments included the statement by one group that further negotiations would have to be accompanied by a CVG agreement to guarantee (cosign) the bank financing and to negotiate exclusively with the group in question.

A decision. Thus up to September 1965 the CVG had received one acceptable proposition from the developer and had heard helpful, but unpromising, expressions of interest on the part of three other groups.

At this juncture the question of time was rapidly increasing in importance because:

1. CADA expressed a firm desire to have its branch store installed in Ciudad Guayana by the end of 1966. There was an appreciably high probability that CADA would pull out of the Alta Vista commitment and move into Puerto Ordaz if the Centro were delayed much beyond this date. The loss of CADA would mean the loss of Sears, and the Centro would be left as an empty skeleton without its two most important tenants.

2. The commercial growth in the Puerto Ordaz area was fast coming to the point where Alta Vista would be faced with serious competition.

Allowing a minimum of one year for final design and construction gave precious little time to waste. It was therefore recommended to the CVG Board that the proposal of the developer be accepted in principal, with the fine details to be worked out later. This decision was taken in December 1965.

Negotiating Issues: CADA and Sears

Both CADA and Sears had been examining the possibilities of opening branch stores in the Puerto Ordaz area of Ciudad Guayana. They had been delaying their decisions, however, because they had gone through some rather unpleasant market reverses during the boom-and-bust cycles that had occurred during the construction of some Venezuelan oil towns. Thus it was necessary to convince CADA and Sears that the growth of Ciudad Guayana was a healthy, long-term industrial expansion rather than a short-term construction boom.

Visits to Ciudad Guayana and a glance at the long-run industrial development program were enough to mollify the boom-town worries. For example, a detailed tour of the city caused a dramatic increase in the enthusiasm of one Sears official. The manager in charge of all branch stores in the interior saw the large amount of furniture and appliances being sold in San Félix and Puerto Ordaz, and he knew that Sears' quality, service, and credit policy could immediately command a significant share of this blossoming market. Shortly thereafter, Sears' official position toward Ciudad Guayana changed radically. Whereas Sears had been considering a 10,000-square-foot store in about two to three years' time, Sears now wanted immediate space in a 10,000-square-foot store followed by a move to a 30,000-square-foot store two years later.

It was not difficult to persuade CADA and Sears that the location of branch stores in Ciudad Guayana would be more than justified. More challenging was the task of promoting Alta Vista (rather then Puerto Ordaz) as the best site within the city. Three factors were important in selling Alta Vista: the demand analyses prepared by the CVG showed that there would be adequate sales at the Alta Vista location; other things being equal, the normal businessman will go along with, rather than against, government planners; and, of most importance, the planned Centro was large enough to create a magnetism of its own.

The importance of the last point is reflected in the fact that CADA and Sears each insisted that the other be a tenant of the Centro. This is a definite condition of the CADA lease contract.

Sears' newly acquired desire to enter Ciudad Guayana as soon as possible raised a problem because the Alta Vista Centro could not possibly be ready before the end of 1966. In order to satisfy Sears' immediate requirements and still keep it as an eventual tenant in the Centro, it was necessary to find a way for Sears to occupy space temporarily and move to Alta Vista when the latter reached completion. Thus Sears rented a small shop in Puerto Ordaz to use as a showroom for big-ticket items during the intervening period.

Negotiating Issues: The Developer

Before discussing the important issues that were negotiated with the developer, it may be useful to list the apparent goals that the CVG and the developer were seeking to achieve, and to review the resources that each party could call upon to strengthen his bargaining position.

The CVG's most important goals in these negotiations were

1. the establishment of Alta Vista as the center of the city
2. the provision of high-quality, aesthetically pleasing commercial, office, and entertainment facilities
3. a sharp increase in the value of the land owned by the CVG in Alta Vista. Revenues from this land would be used to finance future development efforts.

Strengthening the CVG's bargaining position were

1. the CADA lease contract and the confirmed interest of Sears
2. the CVG's control over the land
3. the completed preliminary plans and positive feasibility study
4. the fact that the CVG was the government authority concerned, which guaranteed that the project would have governmental cooperation.

The apparent goals of the developer were
1. a profitable business investment
2. the satisfaction of a pioneering instinct to enter and become eminently successful in a field from which others shrank back.

The following points were to the developer's advantage:
1. his obvious promotional and organizational ability, demonstrated in previous successes, which would be a strong asset to the Centro
2. his access to financing
3. the uniqueness of his interest. Both sides knew that no other group had shown as strong an interest in carrying through the project.

The issue of land disposition. The question of land tenure was the most important and difficult point to resolve during the negotiations with the developer. Indeed, this issue was in large measure responsible for the unnecessary prolongation of the negotiations.

The CVG's policy on land tenure was not well defined at the start of the negotiations. Top CVG officials tended to take a pragmatic view of the situation: they were willing to dispose of the land in any way that would get the Centro started. Several Joint Center consultants, however, insisted that the CVG should not sell any land in Alta Vista but should offer it only for rent.

The latter position was enforced by cogent arguments.[7] The consultants said that the CVG should recover (and later reinvest) its investments in urban development by means of maintaining ownership in commercial land in the city and making profits as the land increased in value because of urban growth. In this manner the CVG would make enough profits on real-estate transactions to offset most of its previous expenditures for roads, site improvements, and the Caroní Bridge. These funds could be reallocated to future urban development projects.

Ownership of land by the CVG would also provide the city planners with a method of controlling land use that would be more effective than zoning. Moreover, in later years, the redevelopment of important central areas would be much more feasible if the government corporation retained ownership of the land. The CVG's negotiators, who were part of the Joint Center group and who did not have Venezuelan counterparts, therefore found themselves under strong pressure to exclude the sale of land from the negotiations. According to the consultants' recommendations (never formally accepted by the CVG), the Alta Vista land was to be made available under lease terms only.

It was impossible to carry out such a policy and still bring the Centro to fruition through private investment. From the start of the preliminary negotiations, all the private developers exhibited a strong distaste for building anything but low-quality, temporary buildings if the land could be only rented from the government.

The first objection, that a builder could not obtain mortgage financing on rented land, was not a major problem, because the CVG was willing to offer the land as mortgage security.

Three closely related points, however, convinced the CVG negotiators that it would be necessary to sell the land for the Centro. First, Venezuelan law does not allow land lease contracts to be written for terms exceeding fifteen years, with an option to renew for an additional ten years. The impossibility of granting long-term leases raised the serious question of the disposition of the property at the end of the lease term. Would the CVG compensate the developer for the value (how much?) of the buildings, or would the lease be renewed or renegotiated? The uncertainties of Latin American political life had made the developer aware of the fact that he did not know with whom he would be negotiating in twenty-five years' time. Outright ownership of the land by the developer would avoid any such problems.

The second reason was the combination of the expressed desire of the developer to execute a relatively simple contract and the tradition of landownership in Latin America. In Latin America, landownership is the traditional means of saving and increasing one's wealth. Developers almost without exception build on their own land and shy away from entangling lease agreements, especially if the uncertainties of dealing with the government are involved.

The third point was the question of speculation. The developer's frank position was that if he were to take the relatively high risk of building the Centro at Alta Vista, then he should be compensated for that risk by being allowed to speculate in the land in and immediately around the Centro.

In the final negotiations, therefore, the developer asked for and received not one but three land concessions (see Figure 11.1):

1. The sale of about 160,000 square feet of land comprised of areas B, C, F, and G.[8] These four areas lie in the center of the first superblock to be developed in Alta Vista and are the location of the initial Centro buildings as contemplated in the preliminary plans and negotiated with the developer.

2. The sale of areas A, D, E, and H, with a total of about 141,000 square feet of land lying on the sides of the superblock adjacent to areas

B, C, F, and G. The developer will build on these areas "in concert with
the demand for space" and will maintain the same décor to be observed
in the initial construction in areas B, C, F, and G.

3. In addition to the sale of eight areas in the first superblock, the
developer received the right of first refusal regarding the purchase of
areas K, L, M, and N in the two neighboring superblocks opposite areas
A, D, E, and H, and containing about the same construction area as the
latter.[9]

Thus the developer received concessions on about three times as much
land as would be required for the initial Centro construction, a total of
about 440,000 square feet of land that would be one hundred per cent
construction space. The land price that was negotiated for areas A through
H would give the CVG considerable profit on the sale but would not necessarily reflect the future rise in land value that a successful Centro would
bring about.

The decision to sell the land for the Centro was unfortunately taken only
after long and tedious negotiations. When the CVG learned that the
developer would not accept a rent-only arrangement, the negotiations
moved to the possibility of renting with an option to purchase at a price
that would rise over time. The latter was the basis for negotiating for over
four months, until, finally, the developer group said that, for the reasons
described earlier, they would insist on direct purchase of the land.

Thus everyone on the CVG side was eventually forced to adopt a more
pragmatic view toward the land question. Although quite feasible in other
places and under different conditions, the land policy advanced by the
consultants simply was not acceptable to businessmen in the Ciudad
Guayana situation.[10] If Alta Vista were to be developed by private
interests, the CVG would have to follow the usual course of Venezuelan
business and sell the land. When a significant portion of Alta Vista is
developed, enough momentum will be generated so that the CVG may
again consider the application of a rent-only policy.

The financing issue. The CVG is not a financing agency and therefore
did not wish to participate in the capitalization of the Centro. In fact,
with its appropriations becoming more carefully scrutinized by the Congress each year, the CVG preferred to leave the greatest possible part of
the investment to the developer.

Thus it was agreed in the final negotiations that the developer would
not only finance the buildings but would also construct the parking areas
and the pedestrian ways on CVG land and would perform the site

improvements within the dotted line, including areas A through H, on Figure 11.1.

The developer had requested a loan guarantee from the CVG to facilitate his bank financing. The CVG declined to extend such a guarantee but did agree to give long-term (up to ten years) credit for the payment of the land. In this manner the CVG extended credit by deferring its own revenue but did not make an outright investment in the Centro.

Questions of design and cooperative ownership. The CVG wished to obtain the highest possible quality in the design, construction, and exterior appearance of the Centro. The developer therefore consented to adhere to the CVG's preliminary plans and exterior regulations (such as signs and lights) and to submit the final plans to the CVG architects for their approval.

The question of cooperative ownership was raised when the developer expressed his intention of converting the Centro buildings into condominiums.[11] The CVG planners had doubts about the merits of condominiums, because their existence in Alta Vista might tend to "freeze" the center of the city and inhibit the flexibility that a rapidly changing city requires. The inflexibility might be brought about by the Venezuelan condominium law, which requires a unanimous vote of all owners before any significant change can be made in a building.

This point was resolved by agreeing that, if any building were converted into a condominium, the CVG would have a perpetual right of first refusal to buy any units offered for sale at any time.

Results of the negotiations. In summary, the negotiations resulted in gains and concessions on both sides. Although the consultants' land policies were not implemented in the Centro, the CVG did end up with the promise of some profit on the land transaction. Of more importance, the CVG concluded arrangements for the erection of a high-quality Centro (and the start of Alta Vista) by private enterprise with no CVG involvement in the financing.

The developer obtained a challenging business proposition, potentially very profitable, but requiring a strong effort to succeed. The ownership of the surrounding land and the possibility of conversion to condominiums would help in obtaining bank financing, but this task would still be a difficult one in view of the risky nature of the project and the CVG's refusal to offer a loan guarantee.

The Critical Question of Time

In addition to the conclusions already discussed—the importance of the major tenants, the effectiveness of the financial models and market studies, the inappropriateness of a bidding procedure for such a complicated project, and the necessity of compromising the rent-only land policy in order to attract a high-risk investment—some final comments on the use and misuse of time may serve to bring this experience into a sharper and somewhat different focus.

The attractiveness of Puerto Ordaz to CADA and Sears made it clear from the start that Alta Vista was in competition with this area. Upper-level CVG officials were aware of this situation, but they lacked both the will and the power to control commercial growth in Puerto Ordaz. This competition could only become stronger over time as Puerto Ordaz grew and Alta Vista remained undeveloped. Thus a race was on between the two: if Alta Vista were not brought to reality within a short period, the developers in Puerto Ordaz would build so much commercial space that no tenants would be left for the Centro.[12]

Since the time question was appreciated from the start, why did the promotional process take nearly two years? Much time-absorbing work, such as the preliminary plans, the financial and market studies, the negotiations with CADA and Sears, and some of the negotiations with the developer, was indeed necessary, but the following elements of time wastage were clearly avoidable:

1. *Protracted discussions on land tenure.* If the negotiations had been begun with an open view toward the sale of land, less time would have been wasted analyzing and discussing the possibilities of either rental only or rental with option to buy. An agreement might have been reached as much as four months earlier.

2. *The slow process of decision making.* Obtaining a decision by the CVG Board took three months to get the preliminary architectural plans started, five months to sign the CADA lease contract, and three months to approve the offer negotiated with the developer. This unnecessarily slow process has retarded projects other than the Centro; it needs to be streamlined.

3. *Bureaucratic red tape.* When the developer submitted his offer in June 1965, the CVG could have called off the bidding procedure, but did not do so because top officials felt that a government agency should not negotiate with one private group to the exclusion of others. The "private bid," which was a failure, took three months to complete.

An improvement in these elements of time loss could have saved up to nine months. Coupled with the many tasks and handicaps that have been discussed, the time delays made the Centro Comercial de Alta Vista a project that stepped beyond the realms of normal commercial promotion and into the challenging area of reconciling the long-term schemes of planners and the awkwardness of a government bureaucracy with the short-term demands of private enterprise and of a rapidly growing city.

Chapter 12

The Housing Program

Rafael Corrada

The Corporación Venezolana de Guayana (CVG) is not a housing but a regional development agency. Its mandate calls for general planning and coordination and for some direct participation, preferably in areas outside the jurisdiction of already established public agencies. Nevertheless, housing constituted such a critical problem and such an important aspect at the initial stage of development of Ciudad Guayana that the CVG could not afford to stay out of it.

Good housing was essential to recruit the technical and professional personnel needed to initiate and maintain the industrial growth of the area. The high labor turnover in the steel mill and in other businesses was certainly due in part to the lack of adequate housing and community facilities for workers. Good housing constituted an important social and educational experience for the incoming population. The move from a shack without adequate services to a house with running water, cooking facilities, and sewage disposal is a significant challenge for most rural inmigrants.

The construction of housing also offered employment opportunities to unskilled inmigrants. The construction industry incorporated workers of intermediate-level skills into the industrial labor force of the area and familiarized unskilled workers with semimechanized procedures through on-the-job training. Housing construction alone is expected to provide employment for 10,700 workers by 1975 and to generate a total of $250 million in salaries and wages during 1965–1980.[1]

A vigorous housing construction program was also an important promotional asset for other development activities, such as the establishment of construction industries, which otherwise were likely to delay locating in Ciudad Guayana or to demand high locational incentives.[2] About $230 million worth of building materials will be needed for housing construction in Ciudad Guayana during 1966–1980.[3] A going housing program also reflects the existence of a clientele with adequate purchasing power, which plays a vital role in the promotion of commercial development and special shopping facilities in the early stages of city development.

Defining Housing Policies and Programs

Providing a sufficient quantity of adequate housing is not an easy job, especially in a frontier region. Aside from the logistics problems involved, it requires significant administrative innovations, skilled staff, and competent technical research. The financing problems are even more formidable. Housing represents 16 per cent of the total development investment in Ciudad Guayana and 40 per cent of the planned investment in the urban development sector during 1965–1980.[4] The CVG's objective was to maximize the contribution of the private sector, and, if accomplished, approximately half of the planned housing investment would come from that source. (See Table 12.1.) Public funds could then be concentrated in projects for which private financing is not readily available, such as low-cost housing for low-income groups.

One of the CVG's first tasks was to determine the amount and type of housing needed by the different income groups expected to migrate to the city and the appropriate price and rent ranges. The CVG also attempted

TABLE 12.1
Investment Requirements for Housing, 1963–1975, by Source
($ millions)

	Private Savings[a]	CVG	Other Government Agencies[b]	Private Capital[c]	Total
1963–1965	1.5	8.4	7.2	3.9	21.0
1966–1970	19.2	11.2	41.6	41.7	113.7
1971–1975	21.2	9.7	35.2	53.3	119.4
Total, 1963–1975	41.9	29.3	84.0	98.9	254.1

a. Includes imputed value of squatters' labor for low-cost housing.
b. Banco Obrero, Foundation for Community Development and Municipal Improvement (Fundación para el Desarrollo de la Comunidad y Fomento Municipal—Fundacomún), and savings and loan association (Asociación Guayanesa de Ahorro y Préstamo—AGAP).
c. Domestic and foreign.

to maximize the participation of private entrepreneurs and other public and quasi-public agencies in an effort to limit its own direct involvement. The following sections outline the major housing problems in Ciudad Guayana and the programs and policies the CVG devised and implemented to cope with them.

Housing for squatters. The shantytowns—variously called *tugurios, arrabales, villas miserias, callampas, favelas*—surrounding most cities in Latin America constitute one of the greatest problems caused by the process of rapid urbanization now taking place. The socioeconomic process creating this problem is quite different from that responsible for the urban slums in more developed countries. In the latter, most residential districts begin with adequate standards and then deteriorate over time. In Latin America, although the districts start from substandard conditions, there is a noticeable process of spontaneous improvements, despite the chaotic settlement patterns that often discourage such efforts.

The CVG squarely faced the fact that it would not be possible to develop Ciudad Guayana without slums. In 1965 the city already had eight slum areas and around 5,300 ranchos (shacks). (See Table 12.2.)

TABLE 12.2
Existing Stock of Housing, 1962 and 1965

	September 1962		February 1965	
	Number	Per Cent	Number	Per Cent
Shacks[a]	2,816	32.6	5,280	44.5
Low- and middle-cost houses[b]	5,745	66.4	5,965	50.3
Low- and middle-cost apartments	29	0.3	288	2.4
High-cost houses	60	0.7	332	2.8
Total	8,650	100.0	11,865	100.0

Sources: Surveys made by the Central Bank in September 1962 and February 1965.
a. All are substandard and must be replaced.
b. Approximately one fourth of the houses in this category are partially substandard.

Conceivably slums can be avoided if migrants are permitted to arrive only at the rate at which adequate housing is built for them. This *police strategy* implies control of population movements and forceful eviction if necessary. It has failed even in countries with totalitarian governments. The obvious alternative is to undertake a construction program at the expected rate of migration. This *massive construction strategy* requires a huge allocation of resources that were simply not available for Ciudad Guayana. Another possibility is the *confinement strategy* followed in Brasilia. This involves designating an area adjacent to the new city where squatting is permitted. Relocation of the residents in the city proper takes place as housing becomes available. The squatting area is transient in character, and no security of land tenancy is provided. Squatters are not encouraged to invest their labor and money in housing improvements and thus miss the opportunity to better themselves progressively in a stable community. Instead, they generally have to accept an apartment in the new city bearing little relation to their income or social needs.

The CVG decided to test a different approach. Squatting is considered unavoidable and is accepted. The aim was to prevent squatting from taking place at random and from concentrating in a pattern that would make future shack replacement practically impossible. If squatters could be guided into settlement areas within the city and encouraged to place the ranchos according to a community layout, the gradual replacement of the shacks could be greatly facilitated. According to this *settlement strategy*, the key to controlling slums in Ciudad Guayana lies in the ability to control lot sizes and the arrangement pattern for the placement of shacks. In this approach, the rancho is viewed as part of a lot-community-city system, closely interrelated, which cannot be ignored without making the control of slums and the replacement of shacks even more difficult. The designation of settlement areas inside the city where families can squat with security of land tenure was thought to encourage squatters to invest their labor and money in improving or replacing the shacks as their time and incomes permit. In addition, public agencies can install adequate services in the future without incurring high costs for clearance and expropriation.

Ranchos have been expropriated in Ciudad Guayana at an average cost of $310 in two-year-old sites and $890 in ten-year-old areas. These figures indicate an average appreciation rate of $75 per year, mainly as a result of the squatters' improvements. These expropriation costs are much higher than the $47 for a lot and $324 for a lot with minimum public services (water taps, paved streets, and electricity), which were the development costs in the settlement communities.

Still, the question of how to get rid of the ranchos remains. One way to deal with this second aspect was to rely on the spontaneous improvement process evident in most squatting areas. The few areas that develop into hard-core slums could be dealt with as a special social problem. The CVG also contemplated possible ways to speed up and improve the process of replacement. The simplest method was to provide construction materials and technical assistance. This method was especially appropriate in Ciudad Guayana because squatters were adequately motivated to improve themselves economically, utilizing to the utmost their own untrained labor. They normally use their labor to improve the shacks, but when plans, construction materials, and supervision were provided, this manpower became more productive and effective in replacing the shacks with adequate houses.

The CVG experimented with three ways to accelerate shack replacement. One was to develop a construction manual based on the skills common among squatters, so that construction materials were more economically used to build a house of better design and quality. Squatters were not familiar with standard plans and specifications, and a simpler do-it-yourself illustrated construction manual could improve their productivity and workmanship. A second alternative that combines partial prefabrication with conventional techniques, such as the shell house, was also tested. These shell houses (columns, roof, and a plumbing wall) were put up by contractors in certain areas, and the families buying these structures could complete them at the rate permitted by their free time and savings, with the help of an instruction manual. The shell, widely used, can help to prevent random squatting, to bypass the shack building phase, and to achieve a fast rate of construction, but its cost (about $780 for the shell alone and about $2,000 for the finished house) precludes purchase by most low-income squatters. Since these families earn $111 or less per month, they could barely afford such a house with even the most liberal public financing terms available. The third alternative considered, which did not reach the operational stage, was to develop a completely prefabricated unit that could be assembled by squatters with the help of a construction manual and some technical supervision. Theoretically this approach could achieve a faster replacement rate, but it involves a greater initial investment of public money and a reduction of squatters' labor equity.

Working-class housing. A variety of other programs were initiated for families in the next group, with monthly incomes of $112–222. Most of organized labor belongs to this group. (Approximately 70 per cent of the workers in the steel mill, a CVG subsidiary, have earnings within this income range.) Most of these families had permanent employment and enjoyed contract benefits that facilitated buying a house, though they did not have savings. In general it was estimated that this group could and would spend around 15 per cent of its gross income (or about $17–34 a month) for housing. This amount was sufficient to enable the individual to purchase a house costing from $2,000 to $4,000 with the available public financing terms. (See Table 12.3.)

Banco Obrero, the national urban housing agency, has been building

TABLE 12.3
Estimated Housing Needs, 1966–1975, by Family Income
(dollars)

			Income Groups			
	I	II	III	IV	V	
		Approximate Family Income Per Month				
	111 or less	112–222	223–444	445–667	over 667	
		Approximate Housing Payment Per Month[a]				
	11 or less	17–34	45–89	112–167	over 167	
		Approximate Maximum Price for Housing[b]				
	1,600	2,000–	5,000–	12,000–	Over	
Period	or less	4,000	10,000	19,000	21,000	Total
1966–1970	2,800	6,600	5,400	1,700	500	17,000
1971–1975	1,900	5,300	6,100	2,100	600	16,000
Total,						
1966–1975	4,700	11,900	11,500	3,800	1,100	33,000

a. Assumes these groups devote 10, 15, 20, 25, and 25 per cent, respectively, of their total income to housing.

b. Assumes the following terms for financing:

	Down Payment (per cent)	Interest Rate (per cent)	Amortization Period (years)
Group I	0	4	20
Group II	10	6	15
Group III	10	8	15
Group IV	20	8	15
Group V	25	8	10

Other costs (collection, insurance, etc.) are estimated at 10 per cent of monthly payments.

houses for families within this income range. The CVG promoted the participation of a national rural housing agency to increase the supply and the choice of low-cost housing for these families. To facilitate these efforts, the CVG has been providing Banco Obrero and other agencies with tracts of land having peripheral service mains for public utilities. To cover the market demand for this income group more adequately, the CVG also promoted the creation of the Municipal Housing Foundation (Fundación de la Vivienda del Caroní—Funvica) and encouraged it to participate in this market. Banco Obrero and Funvica started to coordinate their efforts by supplying different housing types: the former producing primarily row and apartment housing and the latter concentrating on detached and duplex units. Unfortunately, this coordination was discontinued.

Middle-income housing. The agencies just mentioned generally supply housing at $6,000 or less and in their statutes did not contemplate providing housing at higher price levels. On the other hand, the CVG had direct responsibilities toward middle-income families (about 23 per cent of its workers and most of its office staff were earning from $223 to $667 a month). As the city grows, the number and proportion of middle-income families will increase significantly, according to market projections (see Table 12.3). The CVG could have pursued one policy for its own contract obligations and another for the city at large; the steel mill could have built housing camps for its workers and employees. However, housing camps already existing in Ciudad Guayana permitted the CVG to evaluate the possible outcome of such a dual policy. Significant contrasts exist between the mining company camps of the U.S. firms and the surrounding areas. In the compounds maintained by these companies, the Venezuelan workers enjoy good housing accommodations, medical services, and school facilities while they are on the company's payroll. These facilities contrast sharply with the inferior facilities available in the adjacent urban areas. The steel mill people—both managers and workers—naturally argued for a similar approach, which meant better facilities, living conditions, and exclusive services for them.

The CVG decided to promote the open city approach even though this meant the dispersal of resources throughout the city and less exclusive facilities for the workers on its payroll. No further housing compounds are to be built, and the one built while the steel mill was under construction is expected to be torn down as soon as the city's housing market is strong enough to replace such facilities. The main justification for this policy was that the CVG—unlike the foreign companies—has a responsibility toward the entire labor force (past, present, and future) and must promote housing for all families, regardless of where they are employed. Instead of building a fixed amount of rental housing, the steel mill agreed to provide a financial contribution to help its employees acquire a house in the city, which can remain their own after they leave the company.[5] This program was geared to satisfy a very widespread desire for home ownership. Most participants in this program were families earning between $223 and $667 a month, who could afford houses costing from $5,000 to $19,000 under savings and loan terms of financing.

To mobilize savings and further increase the financing capacity of middle-income families, the organization of a savings and loan association (Asociación Guayanesa de Ahorro y Préstamo—AGAP) was promoted by the CVG in 1963. The objective was not only to channel family savings into housing but also to make available lower financing terms (10 per cent down, 7.5 per cent interest, 20 years) than prevalent conventional mortgage financing terms (25 per cent down, 12 per cent interest, 10 years).

After increasing the effective demand for housing, the CVG shifted its interest to the supply side of the market. The CVG's housing funds now could be invested in various projects throughout the city, and by means of the savings and loan mechanism they could be recaptured for reinvestment. However, a direct investment in housing by the CVG was considered contrary to the development of a "normal" housing market, because it did not tap the traditional banking institutions for construction financing. These institutions supply such capital in other cities of Venezuela; they financed a remarkable construction boom during 1965 in Caracas. Since the institutionalization of such financing was considered essential for Ciudad Guayana, the CVG explored several ways of utilizing its own housing funds to provide maximum guarantees to commercial banks in order to mobilize private construction financing for builders.

To attract commercial banking operations into construction financing, two basic mechanisms were utilized. The first was to defer payment to the CVG for land tracts sold to builders until the housing units were sold to the public. In other words, the CVG accepted a second mortgage so that the banks could have the first mortgage as security for the construction financing. The second mechanism was a sale guarantee to the builder: the CVG committed itself to buy, at a prestipulated price that included reasonable profits for the contractor, any house built according to CVG specifications and not sold to the public after six months of sales promotion. The contractor had the incentive of higher profits for selling the house to the public.

The sale guarantee policy was only partially successful, because of inadequate promotion. Of the 6,266 lots and houses completed or under construction by the end of 1965, 613 lots and 1,530 houses were promoted under these guarantees. Provided the guarantees are issued according to a realistic market demand estimate, this mechanism is likely to save the CVG a significant amount of direct investment in the housing market. It will also promote construction financing operations in the city, which are essential to develop a local financing market for housing construction.

The mobilization of long-term mortgage financing from private sources, local or foreign, posed somewhat different and difficult problems. The conventional mortgage financing available was for short-term loans at high interest rates, plus second mortgages at even higher rates (usually five to ten years, 50 to 60 per cent loans at rates of 10 to 12 per cent for the first mortgage, and 15 per cent or more for the second mortgage). One project was successfully promoted through the U.S. AID guarantee program. This provided housing for middle-income families on relatively attractive terms (10 per cent down payment, 8.5 per cent interest rate, including the 2 per cent guaranty fee and 20 years' amortization). However, AID guarantees are difficult to obtain for other projects in the city because of the AID preference for the dispersion of its investments throughout Venezuela. To test other avenues for obtaining long-term financing for housing, the CVG decided to explore the possibilities of a mortgage guaranty fund.[6] This fund consisted of 10 per cent of the long-term investment and was to be deposited in a foreign or local bank under trust arrangements to cover monthly defaults, foreclosure costs, resale expenses, and currency devaluation. As of 1965, this formula had not proved sufficiently attractive to induce foreign investment outside the AID guarantee program. Venezuelan long-term financing funds are earning more in the conventional mortgage market, with very high security in terms of the product (50 per cent of appraised value) and discount notes.

High-income housing. The highest income group, those with a monthly income of $667 or more, presented few difficulties. This group included executives, professionals, and technicians, who expected high-priced housing—as well as club facilities and schools of high quality—as perquisites of employment. They were drawing on their savings to buy a lot and to hire an architect for a custom-made design. The savings and loan association was expected to provide most of their financing needs, and conventional mortgage lending was also available to them. For this group, the CVG preferred to limit its role to providing land, under conventional or guaranteed sale contracts, to builders interested in developing country clubs and high-cost housing subdivisions.

Land policies for housing development. One of the basic policies adopted by the CVG from the beginning was to acquire all the land expected to be needed for the city. This provided complete control—except for squatting—of the initial phase of urban development. To facilitate urbanization in planned directions and places, the CVG also controlled the provision of public services. Roads and water and sewer lines were built by the CVG and the Ministry of Public Works. Electricity was distributed by a national agency although produced in the Guayana by the CVG.

The CVG's housing policies and goals were reinforced by its land policies.[7] A built-in subsidy mechanism was contemplated to differentiate the price of land on the basis of the price level of the housing market to be served. The simplest way to implement this land pricing policy is to charge a fixed percentage of the selling price of the improved lot or house— around 15 per cent for a lot and 5 per cent for a lot plus house. This policy can permit the CVG to recover a significant portion of its investment in public utilities and to share in the increases in land values as the city grows.

In squatter settlements the lot is leased until the squatter replaces the shack with an adequate house, at which time he can buy the land. This is done to prevent land speculation, which tends to delay the construction of adequate housing. The squatter is free to speculate after building a permanent house and purchasing the land. In all other housing programs land can be bought immediately and thus become a marketable product along with the house on it. In 1965 Banco Obrero was studying the possibility of retaining the land title in its housing projects.

To retain land titles for the entire housing market was against the existing national practices of the savings and loan system and the conventional mortgage practice. Such a national issue could not be decided by the CVG at the regional level alone. It was felt that to retain land titles in public hands would have arrested the city's development program by making it unattractive for private investment. Although it has been done successfully in several countries, in the Venezuelan context it meant a significant obstacle to private investment and an undue control of the city by the regional development agency. Although politically controversial, such a policy could have been implemented, since the CVG was the legal owner of the land. Nevertheless, to adopt it was meaningless because the CVG did not have the resources, nor was it willing to invest sufficiently to maintain the necessary rate of growth for Ciudad Guayana without private investment. Because of insufficient public funds, the housing program requires private investment, and an adequate rate of construction can be maintained only with formulas that will attract private capital.

The major purposes of retaining public ownership of land are to ensure cheaper and easier acquisition of land for future public purposes and to benefit from rising land values in order to finance further public investments. In Ciudad Guayana these goals were pursued in other, less controversial, ways. The CVG reserved large amounts of land for future public uses, and it left vacant land in the midst of developed areas for future sale when the demand for (and value of) this land increased.

Achievements and Shortcomings of the Housing Program

Table 12.4 compares the supply and demand for housing in the 1963–1965 period. The demand estimate made in 1963 was revised in 1965 after it became clear that the city was not growing as fast as expected. Although employment opportunities had increased more or less as estimated, the total population was about 20,000 less than expected.[8] Two factors were apparently responsible for this: a significant number of the people employed in Ciudad Guayana lived with their families in nearby towns, and a larger than expected number of them were living in Ciudad Guayana without their families. Both factors were caused in large part by the lack of adequate residential and community facilities in the area.

The number of houses built from 1963 to 1965 represented only about 33 per cent of the housing program adopted in 1963 and 53 per cent of the

TABLE 12.4
Housing Supply and Demand, 1963–1965, by Family Income Level

	Approximate Family Income Per Month					
	$111 or less	$112–222	$223–444	$445–667	$668 and over	Total
Demand estimated for 1963	4,056	6,041	2,865	961	337	14,260
Supply programmed for 1963	4,159	5,551	2,722	740	224	13,396
Supply expected for 1965[a]	1,092	2,621	412	325	5	4,455
Indicated program deficit	3,067	2,930	2,310	415	219	8,941
Portion of program accomplished (per cent)	26.3	47.2	15.1	43.9	2.2	33.3
Revised demand estimate for 1965[b]	1,590	3,447	2,266	851	281	8,435
Expected actual deficit	498	826	1,854	526	276	3,980
Portion of actual demand satisfied (per cent)	68.7	76.0	18.0	38.2	1.8	52.8

a. According to the housing survey conducted by the CVG in May 1965.
b. Based on revised population-income projections made after the 1965 survey by the Central Bank.

1965 revised demand figures. This is unsatisfactory even if supply were held at around 80 per cent of the estimated demand in order to maintain a fast rate of sale.

Programs for squatters. The El Roble pilot project was undertaken in 1963 to determine the feasibility of the CVG's policies for guiding squatter settlement and replacing shacks.[9] The project disclosed many inadequacies that had to be corrected in order to make it more effective.

The program of settlement communities for squatters became entangled in bureaucratic procedures. Families were carefully screened to make sure that the poorest or most "deserving" ones got the available lots first and that no speculation could develop. As a result, it took nearly a year to allocate 434 lots in one settlement community. Even more disappointing was the effective screening of "antisocial" families by social workers interested in developing "uncorrupted communities." This screening almost defeated the essential purpose—to divert arriving squatters from locating at random or concentrating in places designated for other uses in the city plan. Undoubtedly the settlement communities have fewer social problems, but other areas of the city have a disproportionate concentration of them.

The pilot project also spotted several weak points in the shack replacement program. First, the credit requirements for obtaining construction materials prevented the participation of most squatters: a permanent monthly income of over $67 or a cosigner with sufficient payment capacity was needed. The process of getting the loan and the construction permit was too complicated and discouraging for people who were not accustomed to bureaucratic procedures. The granting of the loan took an average of eighty days after the first interview. Although 80 per cent of the applicants qualified for the loan, only half of them persisted through the negotiations until the loan was granted. Of those who received loans, only half initiated construction afterward.[10]

Second, the squatters were given a choice among three different housing plans to protect them from arbitrary attempts of the architect to model their lives according to his own ideas and prejudices, but they consistently selected the most conventional and rejected the most imaginative designs. Reasonably enough, they preferred the houses most similar to those they were accustomed to seeing and living in. The possibility of innovations in housing design, construction methods, or functional layout essential to city development was eliminated by what was considered to be a democratic requirement.

Third, many participants left their houses incomplete in order to reduce the amount of the loan. Many houses remained without plastering, painting, closets, or even sanitary facilities. The replacement of the ranchos remained incomplete, since 35 per cent of the self-helpers moved into their unfinished houses and stopped construction.

Thus only 104 of 752 families in three settlement communities started replacement activities during a period of two years. At this rate it would take over eight years to replace all shacks with adequate houses in these communities, instead of the estimated five years. Even worse, a third of them did not finish the new house, thus failing to achieve complete replacement. Administrative procedures slowed down the settlement program to about half of the rate of incoming squatters. During 1962–1965, squatters built shacks at a rate of about 85 a month. Only 37 of these were built in settlement communities. In the same period the total number of ranchos increased by approximately 2,500. Thus the program allowed around 1,500 ranchos to be located at random outside the settlement communities.

On the basis of this experience, procedures had to be modified, and the following changes were recommended:

1. Lots in settlement communities should be granted on the basis of "first come, first served." Land speculation can continue to be controlled by a lease arrangement that grants the title to the squatter only after he builds an adequate house. Families should not be screened for need or social acceptability—though records must be kept and referred to in order to avoid granting more than one lot to the same person.

2. Shack replacement should be encouraged by eliminating income requirements in the granting of construction loans. Anybody who is physically able, including the unemployed, should be permitted to build houses in settlement communities. This should be possible, since building

techniques can be simplified, and work can proceed by stages according to a simplified construction manual. Construction manuals should be provided according to designs selected by the housing agency, to expose the families to more novel housing types from which to choose. To maintain sound financing, the squatters should build initially for a housing agency, not for themselves. If the house is completed according to specifications and accepted by the agency, then the ownership of the house can be decided between the agency and the squatter. The legal basis for this arrangement is contained in a self-help contract that offers four options to the squatter:[11]

a. To receive payment for his labor equity, at a price prestipulated in the contract, after he builds the house and turns it over to the agency.

b. To continue building other houses and receive one free of charge for every three built for the agency. This alternative is based on current cost estimates of $324 for the settlement lot, $1,000 for construction materials, and $668 for labor equity.

c. To buy the construction materials and the lot under a long-term loan, provided he has the required payment capacity.

d. To lease the house and pay for the lease with his labor equity. This would carry him for three years, assuming a monthly rent of 1 per cent of invested capital and 10 per cent depreciation for construction materials. During this period the squatter is likely to get a job in the city and be able to buy the house if he wishes. The selling price would include the lot, the construction materials, and the amount of the labor equity consumed in rent up to the purchasing date.

After the pilot project was finished, Funvica was promoted and sponsored by the CVG in order to expand the program on a permanent basis. This arrangement eliminated some frictions that had developed between the CVG and the municipal government because the participation requirements enforced by the pilot project eliminated too many applicants, who then complained to the municipal authorities about discrimination. Also, Funvica used a different financing formula, which lessened the CVG's financial involvement in the program.

The pilot project accomplished its essential purpose. It tested some ideas that are now being applied on a larger scale by Funvica. Representatives of the city government, the CVG, and the Foundation for Community Development and Municipal Improvement (Fundación para el Desarrollo de la Comunidad y Fomento Municipal—Fundacomún, a national agency) are members of its Board of Directors. Funds are obtained from

Fundacomún for housing, from the CVG for land and site development, and from the municipality for operating expenses.

Programs for other income groups. The performance on other types of housing programs varied significantly. The performance was relatively high for working-class (incomes from $112 to $222 a month) housing because of the participation of Banco Obrero, which built 1,670 of the 3,500 units completed or under construction by the end of 1965. However, performance for families with incomes of $223 to $667 a month was poor, because the promotion of private investment was slow and ineffective. No housing was built for the highest income group; the planners apparently focused their efforts on the needs of the numerically larger low- and middle-income families and overlooked the needs of high-income families. The latter include key executives and top technicians, who are badly needed in the area and who usually demand better than adequate housing facilities before they will move to the Guayana.

General deficiencies in the program. Performance lagged behind the goals of the program in time, quantity, price, and design quality. Lack of proper scheduling techniques and controls was mainly responsible for the *time lags*, which on the average were around nineteen months. In 1966 the CVG began to apply more sophisticated scheduling methods to its urban development program.[12] However, not all project delays were caused by poor programming and control techniques. Middle-cost housing was not adequately promoted among private investors and builders. In fact the CVG never organized a promotion unit for housing. Until that is done and the sale guarantee program is publicized and discussed with bankers and builders to ensure its best application, there is little probability of catching up in this sector. The danger, of course, is that circumstances may force the CVG to step in with direct investment in this type of housing, thus delaying the development of a self-sustaining housing market in the city.

Though they will be built more slowly than planned, almost all the houses programmed will actually be built. The *quantity lags* suggested by the slight decrease in number reflect the normal adjustments that occur when general estimates of houses per unit of land are translated into final plans and specifications.

The *price lags* were more serious because the sale guarantee contract was based on estimated demand at programmed sales prices. There were five projects in which housing units were priced above the programmed levels. Since supply was still significantly behind demand, no serious problems developed as a consequence of these price increases. Nevertheless, some of them took place in subdivisions prepared for low-priced housing. In those sales, difficulties developed when houses were expensive in proportion to the size of the lots and the public services available.

Finally, there were the deficiencies in design quality. These deficiencies were significant, but unfortunately they were not amenable to easy measurement and thus did not receive sufficient attention from planners. As of 1965, housing design in the city was mediocre, lacking imagination, novelty of construction techniques, functional quality, and climatic adaptation. These problems had begun to receive serious attention by 1965, and several measures for improvement were under consideration.

Conclusions

The performance of the housing program in Ciudad Guayana was uneven. In a developing country it is difficult both to establish an adequate administrative mechanism and to operate it efficiently. It is even more difficult when most of the implementation of the housing program depends on other organizations, public and private, in a frontier environment that lacks the required social institutions. Therefore, an essential element in judging the Ciudad Guayana housing program is not only the record indicated here but the prospects for the future.

The outlook for the future is more encouraging because of the degree of institutionalization achieved. The national housing agency, Banco Obrero, was slow in getting its program started but has now reorganized its administrative structure and launched a vigorous, large-scale housing effort. A municipal housing agency, Funvica, was created to serve the low-cost market and to expand the settlement program for migrants. AGAP, the savings and loan association, will make available more mortgage funds for middle- and high-income families. In addition, the CVG was considering the possibility of creating a quasi-public urban development corporation (located in Ciudad Guayana rather than in Caracas) to program, promote, and guide development of the city.[13] The CVG established a system to record the status of all building activities to spot problems and bottlenecks before they become too serious. A study was carried out to improve the efficiency of site development decisions on the basis of cost-benefit and systems analysis techniques. The shell house for the settlement program reached the operational stage, and research was initiated to develop a completely prefabricated house, to be assembled by either contractors or squatters, to speed up low-cost housing while increasing architectural variety around a structurally sound frame.[14]

A major question was how to obtain cheaper and sufficient long-term financing for the housing price level best served in the long run by private developers. The risks involved require special guarantees, and the formula tested did not prove sufficient to attract private builders. This effort needs to be continued, since the CVG opted to create a "normal" housing market in Ciudad Guayana. There is much to be said for cities (such as Brasilia and the British new towns) that are almost entirely built by the government; they achieve both a unity of design and a significant supply of housing and community facilities that can set quality standards and act as a stimulus for further development. Although the CVG might have built all of the housing and then returned it to the "normal" market when the basic physical and institutional framework of the city had been developed, it decided instead to operate within the current values, traditions, and shortcomings of Venezuelan society. This meant accepting the limitations of existing government agencies and social, economic, and political institutions and attempting within this framework to innovate and reform in order to achieve a higher level of performance. This approach apparently had a significant negative impact on the quantity and quality of housing. Possibly, an alternative approach might have produced more striking contributions to urban development and planning (though even Brasilia and the British new towns have developed their own kinds of problems), but Ciudad Guayana's experience may be more useful for all those housing development programs that operate within the limitations of similar economic and political institutions.

Chapter 13

Changing
Perspectives on
Residential
Area Design

William Porter

As the urban designers acquired more experience and knowledge, their proposals became increasingly responsive both to the need to build rapidly and to the values and environmental needs of Ciudad Guayana's residents. These shifts in the designers' approach could be seen in the sorts of values upon which decisions were based, the types of elements they sought to control in the environment, and the way in which they sought to control them. The new approach that evolved required a far-reaching reappraisal of the traditional behavior of the urban designer and his role in making the decisions that control environmental form.

The design proposals may be divided roughly into three chronological periods. Because of availability, the designers arrived first on the scene. Partly for this reason, the work in the first period embodied a kind of international high-quality set of designer-held values. In the second period, economic, housing, and social specialists arrived but needed time for studies and analyses. Meanwhile the designers began to focus on long-range plans for the city and on the development authority's own needs and its capability to implement projects. During the third period, the designers were more knowledgeable about the problems, and their proposals tended to reflect the insight of the other specialists and to relate more directly to the needs, values, and perceptions of the people using the environment.

Period One: Designs for Individual Neighborhoods

Having decided to foster the growth of an industrial city in the Guayana, the Venezuelan government and the Corporación Venezolana de Guayana

(CVG) were faced with the difficulties of attracting investors and elite residents to the area. The Guayana had neither the physical, nor the social, nor the cultural climate that appeal to the Venezuelan elite. Creation of a high-quality physical environment was one way of coping with these problems. Urban design could be counted on to dramatize the nation's commitment by producing strong and clear images of a future great city, and to create images of an attractive city—comfortable, efficient, and urbane.

During the first period the designers spent a great deal of their time on jobs on which the Venezuelan staff urgently sought assistance. These tasks ranged from the review of designs for the bridge and the housing projects to the preparation of plans for reception areas for inmigrants. They also devoted some effort to studies of residential neighborhoods for future employees of industry. The design of the neighborhood unit (*unidad vecinal*),

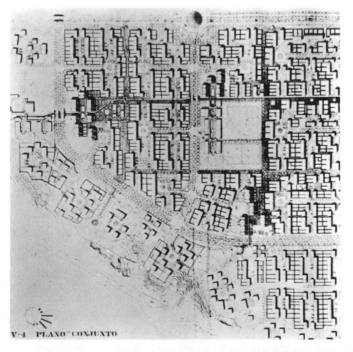

FIGURE 13.1   UV4 in Puerto Ordaz (drawing from the CVG *Informe Anual* for 1961). Urban designers and architects collaborated to specify the form of the physical environment in great detail.

called UV4, for Puerto Ordaz was the most fully elaborated product of this work. Its site plan was specified in great detail, and the row houses were indicated in envelope form. (See Figure 13.1.)

UV4 was to be a demonstration of the CVG's intention to provide high-quality environments for the elite and a demonstration to the residents of Ciudad Guayana of a better way of life. And UV4 was to be an experiment: it was to test whether the implementation mechanism could carry it out and whether people would accept that sort of design. If these tests were passed, UV4 could become a prototype for the residential development of a large portion of the future city.

The relationships between pedestrian and vehicular traffic were carefully calculated so that there was complete separation in some areas and a controlled mix in others. There was a gradient of spaces from public to private, from active and noisy to serene and quiet, and from hard and urban to soft and natural. There were to be shade trees and flowing rivulets. The colors and shapes of the ground and wall planes were chosen to form an ensemble with the larger landscape as well as within the area. The project was never to seem as if it had just been built.

Elementary schools were located within easy and safe walking distance of the residences; higher-density areas, including some apartments, were combined with shopping areas, public walkways, and plazas to create relatively active centers within the neighborhood. It was an elegant way of achieving a medium density of eight families per acre at an average of six people per family.

There were risks. Row housing was the rule only in the older parts of existing cities. Suburban expansion, which had begun on the edges of Caracas and on the properties of the two mining companies in Ciudad Guayana, followed the North American pattern of single-family units at a fairly low density (three or four families per acre and less). Usually the boundaries between the private and the public spheres were rather definite: in the traditional town-house areas, the streets were walled by the houses, which were extremely private within; and in the outlying areas, fences and clear demarcations of property were the rule. This may have been due partly to fear of robbery, partly to tradition, and partly to the characteristic openness of houses to take advantage of the attractive climate. Despite these differences between what was proposed and what was apparently current practice, it was felt that a good design like UV4 could serve as a demonstration and would help to shape tastes.

Architects in Caracas were hired to design the houses. Their designs were in the same spirit as the site design: thoughtfully conceived, very

FIGURE 13.2   UV3 in Puerto Ordaz (drawing from the CVG *Informe Anual* for 1961). Builder's semidetached houses and a conventional street layout were combined with result that the project was quickly built and marketed.

sophisticated, and a little unconventional. Financing was difficult to obtain, however, and perhaps because of that the CVG was not willing to construct the project itself. A contract was finally let with the investment guaranteed by AID; but, even so, only about a dozen of the units had been built by the fall of 1966—four years after the preliminary design had been completed.

When the preliminary design of UV4 was in its last stages, a design for another area in Puerto Ordaz, called UV3, was completed. UV3 resembled a more conventional North American suburb, with its curving streets and small semidetached houses. (See Figure 13.2.) The merits of UV3 were much debated within the staff. The range of types of outside spaces was restricted; there was little difference in either the intensity or the mix of activities in the area; and all vehicular and pedestrian traffic was in the conventional relationship of street to sidewalk.

A large Venezuelan developer, using an existing house design, completed the project rapidly, and the houses were occupied before the UV4 houses had even been designed. Furthermore, the people who actually occupied UV3 were those for whom UV4 had been planned: professionals and technicians, whose income levels were higher than expected for the UV3 occupants.

Because housing was extremely scarce when the UV3 houses became available, a comparison between them and the UV4 houses for attractiveness to buyers is impossible to make. Nevertheless, UV3 had passed the tests of implementation and buyer acceptance. The main tests it failed were those of the designers: it did not demonstrate a high-quality environment, better ways to live, or even new design ideas. But this raises the question of whether the designers were debating the right issues and whether the tests they proposed were the correct ones.

People's needs for housing—even the elite's needs—although easily satisfied early in the development, might become more difficult to satisfy. Constructing UV4 might enlarge the range of choice and influence the demand for housing in the medium- and long-range future. Building only a dozen units was not an adequate test of an idea that required a more complete setting in which to prove itself. But devising a test that will give a short-range reading on a design that might result in a long-range benefit is difficult, to say the least, and a difficulty rather frequently encountered in the profession.

UV4's design had still another role, the importance of which may have been underestimated by the designers. It, and other high-quality design efforts by the staff (such as modification of the Caroní Bridge design and proposals for the new city center), communicated to the administration of the CVG and to people of importance outside the CVG that top talent was engaged in designing the best possible environment for future residents of Ciudad Guayana. Thus not only were designs an essential part of preparing the area for the elite resident but they revealed an activity that had promotional value in itself.

Although UV4 had challenged the traditional design criteria to be used within any neighborhood, it had not challenged the tradition of design by neighborhood-sized units: rather homogeneous physical environments, serving a narrow range of social classes. Whether a challenge to the latter idea would have been successful at this stage is most unlikely. But neither

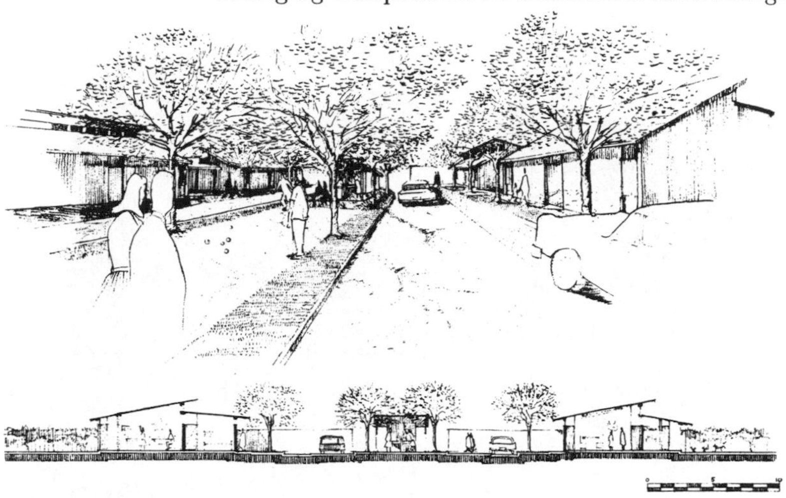

FIGURE 13.3 UV2 in El Roble (drawing from the CVG *Informe Anual* for 1961). Cul-de-sacs for lower-income groups in which an experimental self-help housing program was implemented.

was it contemplated. In any case, parceling out designs in neighborhood-sized units became the rule for the CVG.

While UV4 was being designed for the technical and managerial groups, another neighborhood, UV2 in El Roble, was being designed to complement an experimental self-help housing program for low-income in-migrants, the El Roble pilot project. (See Chapter 12.) Although the effort to design for lower-income groups was not the first in Venezuela, some of the ideas were new. And, like UV4, its middle-income counterpart, UV2 was to be a prototype for future expansion if the experiment proved successful. Lots were arranged around cul-de-sacs; house designs provided for building little by little; and the island in the center of the cul-de-sac could be used for playing, a community garden, or whatever the residents wished. (See Figure 13.3)

The CVG accepted the project design, and organizations were formed to carry it out. The program called for financial and technical assistance for the new residents and for administrative mechanisms to supervise the operations. The approach was substantially different from multifamily, multistory unit designs built elsewhere, or approaches that stressed improvements in manufacturing techniques, notably prefabrication of building units. Prefabrication had failed too often in the past to justify reliance on this device—at least at this early stage. The self-help program also had the merit of developing the construction skills of the low-income bread-winner and of increasing his income directly.

The income levels of UV2's residents were considerably higher than had originally been intended. (See Figure 13.4.) This may have been the result of the careful way the prospective residents were screened. But there was also a misjudgment of the residential needs of the very low-income groups. The typical family, we learned later, does not conform to the model that

FIGURE 13.4   UV2 in El Roble (photograph by author in 1965). Occupants are like those represented in the designers' drawings rather than the lower-income groups for which the project was intended.

designers conventionally carry around with them, expecially in that there is often no male head of household. Also, many of them needed to be very close to employment opportunities: close to the river and to other residences because the livelihoods of many women depended upon taking in laundry; on the main thoroughfares, since the roadside stands, bars, and related activities provided another source of income; and near other groups who demanded services of various sorts. Some features of UV2's design, such as privacy, safety for the children from cars within the residential area, and off-street pedestrian walkways, seemed to have little relation to low-income residents' immediate needs.

El Gallo, another low-income community design, stands in roughly the same relationship to UV2 as UV3 did to UV4; its design was similar to UV3 but inferior by usual urban design standards to UV2. It was meant to complement the second stage of the El Roble pilot project. El Gallo was designed as it was for two major reasons. First, the designers had by that time abdicated the role of designing low-income neighborhoods; those were now part of the action program. (The design was done by a former member of the design group who was serving in Ciudad Guayana as a municipal engineer at the time.) Second, when UV2 was built, it was discovered that the utility costs were very high: the cul-de-sacs were so wide that two utility mains were required instead of one as had been anticipated. On the basis of this one fault the CVG engineers rejected the cul-de-sac idea. This overreaction to the information that was coming in and the lack of attention to information that might also have been important pointed up the need for a continuing program of evaluation of projects. Such a program was recommended and eventually undertaken as an experiment (see Chapter 18), but it has not yet been made a permanent feature of the CVG program.

A shift of administrative strategy enabled the prospective resident first to build a shack on his property in El Gallo and later to build a more permanent house. El Gallo was more successful than UV2 because it actually served low-income families. Relatively soon after the new residents arrived, they became involved in trying to improve their area. They changed the name from "El Gallo" to "Imanuel Piar." El Gallo was the name given by the CVG to the area, after the hill that rose from its edge; Piar is a figure of great importance and prestige in Venezuelan history. Both planner and resident had named the area, each from his own point of view. Residents also began demanding urban services, especially better storm drainage. The lack of services probably had a consolidating effect by providing a cause for neighborhood communication and action. Administrative screening of the applicants may well have helped to attract an industrious group; in any event, the result was the formation of a community moving upward.

The two prototype designs, UV4 and UV2, demonstrated that the CVG intended to provide a more attractive environment for different income groups. However, the partitioning of the problem into designs for middle- and upper-income groups (UV4 and UV3) and designs for lower-income groups (UV2 and El Gallo) ensured that the two groups would be isolated into separate neighborhood units. Moreover, UV2 and El Gallo were on the east side of the Caroní River, and UV4 and UV3 were on the west. Anyone who felt threatened or annoyed by members of the other group would be pleased by such design decisions.

The success of UV3 and El Gallo derived chiefly from their having been implemented easily. But, even knowing that vast amounts of housing were needed, the designers did not examine the standard designs that the private developers and other public agencies already had. The degree of cooperation between the developers and the agencies in working out modifications would have been difficult to predict. Nonetheless, the design profession's reluctance to try such a cooperative approach can probably be attributed in part to their long history of dealing with only a small portion of the total physical development, serving only elite interests.

Period Two: Residential Design in the Context of Total City Development

The CVG's small design staff was forced by the magnitude of the design problem into a supervisory role, including the administration of design contracts and liaison with other agencies and organizations. As a result they began planning on a more general level, relating designs to social and economic conditions, and they began focusing their attention on a few elements they felt to be crucial for the success of the designs. Both shifts in the designers' attention were toward "partial design" and away from the "total design" approach used in UV4 and UV2, for which the site design was specified in great detail. Moreover, the shift in focus and the choice of which elements in the designs should be controlled reflected increasingly the engineering capabilities of the CVG and its need to program, budget, and administer urban development.

In the Los Olivos community design a good deal of attention was given to selecting areas over which to exercise special design control. The special areas selected were the most publicly visible and accessible in the district; they contained the greatest intensity of activities and many of the public buildings and parks over which the CVG would have considerable control.

Design contracts were let with local architects for the residential subunits, with general design criteria set and design review performed by the CVG designers. The specifications included densities, housing-unit sizes and prices, major residential street layouts, and approximate locations for schools and local commerce. These and other specifications, some in sketch form, were given to the local architects as a basis for design review. Some of the criteria were ignored; other criteria were difficult to stick by rigidly because of contradictory information that became available during the course of the design development. Some of the difficulty here can be attributed to the lack of precedent for this approach and the lack of a well-developed symbolic language in which the general issues could be debated; but at least part of the difficulty stemmed from the unwillingness of the architectural professional to deal with problems explicitly and to debate the merits of alternative solutions.

At times the designer at the detailed level worked in another public agency. The part of Los Olivos adjacent to Alta Vista, for example, was to be designed by Banco Obrero, the national housing agency. The power of the purse that the CVG had over a contractor did not exist here. Rather, more detailed sketches were prepared for these areas, and the CVG designer in charge kept in close contact with Banco Obrero to supervise the design development.

The crucial areas were to be designed completely by the CVG, or else more complete design criteria would be established, with frequent design review by the CVG. These design criteria were to include more precise siting of major facilities, specific activity locations, nature of vehicular and pedestrian access, development sequencing, and even choice of street furniture, details, and materials.

During the second period of design the designation of the residential subunits changed from UV, or "neighborhood unit," to UD, or "development unit" (*unidad de desarrollo*); and a numbering system was developed to locate the unit in the city without ambiguity, each major district having its own number series: the 100 series was reserved for the east side of the Caroní and the 200 series for the west. Thus the old UV4 became UD204, and UV2 became UD102.

The shift in numbering was an administrative expedient reflecting the need for more effective communication within the CVG between designers and engineers, with outside contractors in Caracas, and between the Caracas and Guayana offices of the CVG.

The shift from UV to UD indicated the designers' wish to think of many areas in the context of a total development program rather than of residential units in isolation, each with its own self-contained facilities and stable population. It had become evident that facilities and population did not appear all at once, on schedule, nor were they of exactly the types the designers envisioned. Moreover, service areas of all facilities, even the primary schools, did not coincide neatly with the size of the neighborhood (or UV), and there was a growing sense that people from different areas might be able to profit from jointly utilizing certain kinds of facilities and areas. Thus for the residential-community designer, the major road system and its adjacent areas became important design elements for the CVG to control; this was possible because the CVG had the capability to design the roads, finance their construction, and supervise the construction contracts.

Attention focused on the programming of residential development when the deadline neared on a contract between the CVG and the steelworkers' union, which required that the CVG provide 4,180 units of housing for steel mill employees. The early proposals had provided for the completion of all the dwellings in one area at one time. The CVG's strategy shifted when it became evident that it could not supply new dwellings fast enough and still meet the rest of its obligations in the city. As the program was finally worked out, the housing was to be distributed all over the city. Having regularly employed people from the steel mill living close to other people avoided partitioning the population into homogeneous groups; and parts of already existing housing programs in different parts of the city could be used to fulfill the terms of the contract. But this shift to a different development strategy was not precipitated entirely by the exigencies of the situation. The designers were ready because of the views of other specialists and because of shifts in their own thinking in the course of studying the development of the city as a whole.

The mixture of groups was more limited in the new urban areas than in the unplanned areas, primarily because the CVG tended to provide separate neighborhoods for the lower- and upper-income groups on each side of the river. Some designers and top administrators considered this stratification unfortunate and felt that greater mixture would increase communication among different groups and was part of what the environment could contribute to social development.

This goal, to be sure, had to be balanced against the dangers. Providing contact or proximity beyond a certain point might make the upper-income groups feel threatened or intruded upon. Also, upper-income living styles were not necessarily the most helpful models for the poorer families. The wrong kinds of proximities could result in hardening social lines rather than in blurring them or making movement upward appear easier or more attractive. But when development was planned in large units[1] it was not possible to control some of the crucial variables: the sizes, locations, and timing of the new areas of residential development for different groups in the population.

Not every development unit needed to have the same income distribution as the city as a whole. Nonetheless, a rigid stratification appeared likely to exacerbate social conflicts and hinder the learning processes of the lower-income inmigrants. Therefore the CVG wanted at least the large residential areas—say, five or six development units—to contain a broad spectrum of income levels.

The designers had changed their style with respect to residential area design in several ways in order to deal more effectively with the total amount of projected residential growth, but there was still no apparent resolution to the conflict between the residential pattern that the CVG wanted and the current development trends. The CVG's strategy was to develop residential areas on the western side of the Caroní River in order to reduce the distances between residences and the work places in the western industrial zones and to provide a large market for the proposed city center at Alta Vista. However, all new growth areas on the western side were planned, and all excluded shacks; therefore, all new shacks in or out of planned areas were currently being built on the eastern side of the Caroní.

Even though the number of shacks was relatively small—less than one half of the total housing stock—their number was much smaller than the number of households in the city who at one time had lived in shacks. The shacks appeared ever present, but they were not always the same ones nor were they always found in the same locations: many shacks had been improved, or they had been replaced with a substantial dwelling, and new shacks were being built elsewhere. And even though they looked impermanent, their locations as places of human activity were permanent, probably because the occupants regarded the land as their own and were willing to improve it, either for their own use or to rent or sell.

It was thus becoming clear that the initial location of the shacks was important for the ultimate residential pattern. If new areas continued to be planned so that shacks were prohibited and if western locations for them were denied, then the strategy for residential growth to the west would be difficult to achieve.

It was also becoming clear that the shacks had to be seen as part of the process by which people were adapting the urban environment to suit their needs instead of as a sickness of the city.

Other factors combined to create doubts in the minds of the Joint Center leadership and the designers as to the validity of the current approach: new information and insights became available concerning the problems of social mobility, adjustment, and education of the population;[2] and there was increasing interest in obtaining better information about how the local population viewed and used the city.[3] Indeed, what seemed to be required now was a reappraisal of the environmental needs of the city's residents and of how residential design could help to fulfill them.

Period Three: Residents' Needs and Values, and New Prototypes

Squatters are often thought to be rural, low-income, recent migrants who are generally unemployable and difficult to socialize and train for industry. All of these characteristics are then attached to the proliferation of little "unsightly" shacks illegally sited at the edges and in the interstices of the urban area. Although each characteristic exists in Ciudad Guayana, they are not found in the combination just cited; to group them in this way obscures the most important aspects of the problem.

Inmigrants find places in the city roughly in conformity with the existing population distribution. There is one notable exception, the so-called "reception areas"—which have few, if any, recent inmigrants. When people first arrive in the city they find places in pensions or cheap hotels, with family or friends, renting from others, and so on. Shifts are taking place within the city, and these seem to be into areas with better schools and facilities. The residents have fairly high physical mobility, and, given a situation in which they can make a choice, they seem to exercise it sensibly.

Migrants during the years 1964 and 1965 tended to have attained higher educational levels and to have had higher-status occupations before

moving to Ciudad Guayana than migrants in previous periods. It is difficult to infer from the data whether these increases reflect a general trend
over time or whether they are related to specific circumstances in the city
such as the availability of certain kinds of jobs. Except when they first
arrive and for a short period thereafter, recent migrants do not have
lower incomes; in fact, income gains in the city are spread across all groups.

The "unsightly" tin shacks are built by people who are less rural than
those living in mud houses in the city. The shacks are often occupied for
relatively short periods until the occupants can either build or move to a
more substantial home. Unless rented, the shack usually does not require
monthly payments, which would be difficult for the occupant, considering
the unpredictable rate of his income. Similarly he can make improvements
gradually, in accordance with his income and the availability of his time.
Except in some obviously poor areas that have persisted and may continue
to persist, the builder of the shack is on his way up, using the shack as a
temporary living place until he can do better—not so unlike most members
of the middle classes.

Natural increase rather than migration was accounting for the majority
of new growth, and recent arrivals were similar by all available measures
to the people already there.[4] Instead of thinking of the future residents as
somehow different from the existing population, or planning separately
for inmigrants as opposed to residents, it was becoming evident that the
problem was to plan for a city of migrants, some more recently arrived
than others, and that the needs and values of the existing population
would be extremely good guides to those of the future population.

Moreover, instead of thinking of the population as divided into income
groups, with housing areas designed for each, it seemed more useful to
think of housing and residential area design policy as helping the many
different groups in the population to do what they needed and wanted to
do: to find physical environments that suited their current values and
attitudes and contained a minimum of constraints.

Many new residential design ideas that had been partially recognized
in period two were developed: for example, the designer could put more
emphasis on increasing accessibility, so that recent arrivals might be able
to talk with residents of relatively long standing and so that different age,
social, occupational, and ethnic groups might have more places to get
together easily. The environment could show clearly the educational,
employment, and other opportunities through its public information signs
and through the visual featuring of the important institutions, and it could
make evident not only what is happening but also what had happened

and, perhaps, some of the more important things that are going to happen.

While many of the staff felt that these ideas could be achieved within the general context of the way things were being done, others felt that a more radical reappraisal was called for. The city should be "open" in all of its parts to the kinds of development demanded by people at different stages of their development; not only should they be able to distribute themselves all over the city, as was presently happening outside of the planned areas, but also they should be able to move up within any area, to find places that might be right for them in the next stage of their development. This implied not only a self-help type of approach for the lower-income groups but local areas into which they could move later. An "open" city also implied providing equal levels of service and facilities everywhere, so that the shifts within the city would not all be toward areas that were better served.

Whereas in the second period the designers aimed to achieve "partial" instead of "total" design control mainly because they felt that they could not control everything, in the third period there was a growing conviction that while they still urgently needed to control certain elements, they

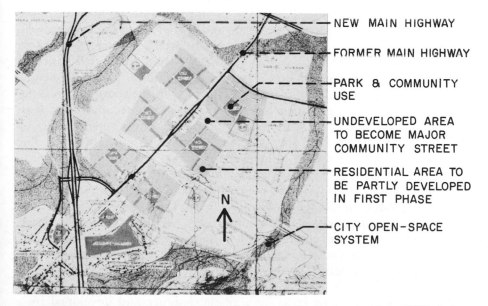

NEW MAIN HIGHWAY

FORMER MAIN HIGHWAY

PARK & COMMUNITY USE

UNDEVELOPED AREA TO BECOME MAJOR COMMUNITY STREET

RESIDENTIAL AREA TO BE PARTLY DEVELOPED IN FIRST PHASE

CITY OPEN-SPACE SYSTEM

N

FIGURE 13.5   Dalla Costa, first stage (drawing by D. Rothstein of the CVG design staff, 1965). Areas to be designed in detail by professional designers were to be small and scattered. Much of the local design was to be done by the residents.

FIGURE 13.6   Dalla Costa, later stage (drawing by D. Rothstein of the CVG design staff, 1965).

equally urgently should not control others. As much as possible should be left to local initiative: local markets for certain kinds of housing or facilities should be allowed to form; and the people should be able to make as many decisions about the local form of the environment as possible.

In this general frame of reference a design was partially developed for a residential area in Dalla Costa. (See Figures 13.5 and 13.6.) The area had existing residences and shacks, some being improved; it was growing at the edges and within the existing pattern; and it had room for new growth. The design task was viewed as an attempt to attack within a single area several different problems of the entire city that demanded different strategies. This area in Dalla Costa was to include a range of income groups representative of the city as a whole in both the short and the long term. It was to be developed for a low percentage occupancy at first. Growth would take place at the edges of the area and in its interstices by filling vacant lots and by opening new streets and adjacent land. The streets to be built later were to have the best access and highest visibility in the area, and the larger lots along them would provide places where those who wished to stay in the community could build larger homes or businesses. We believed that most new areas would increase both in per capita income and in density over time, and we felt that these new streets and adjacent properties could take advantage of the increase in social and economic values. Some spaces in the development pattern were to be kept open—some permanently, others until their use was decided on later by the people living in the area.

Subareas could be designed by a single designer and developed by a single developer, but they would be relatively small (five- to ten-acre maximums); and areas done by the same people would be well separated from one another. Even though Dalla Costa comprised only one or two development units it was to be developed in many different-sized pieces, ranging from individual houses to blocks. We would have tried to scatter social and financial assistance programs also, in order to avoid any one area's becoming identified as "low income" or "recent migrant." But this fragmentation had its dangers. It might be more difficult to provide service for people with specialized needs; and the groups in any area might well be very difficult to organize politically because of a lack of common interests.

There were other difficulties. One was that the utilities might be over-extended and therefore inefficient. But overextension of services can be measured only in terms of time, because in the long term, when development is nearly complete, services will not be overextended; in the short run, the extra expenditures have to be balanced against the possible short-term gains in other goals. Another difficulty was that the areas left open in the early stages might be occupied illegally by squatters. But illegal squatting can be eliminated only if enough legal sites are available. Still another difficulty was that neither architects nor developers nor agencies are accustomed to working in small-scale units. It is much more profitable to design and build in huge tracts; and their other values do not suggest any reason to change their ways of working. This may be the greatest difficulty to remove and may demand much attention in the promotional and incentive programs.

Despite these difficulties, the CVG intended to carry out the Dalla Costa project on an experimental basis.[5] The project could become the prototype for future residential development. However, to make it a worthwhile experiment, two conditions will have to be satisfied rather in-geniously. First, squatting that does not conform to the plan must be prevented. Second, administrative and institutional arrangements must be created to ensure that moving into the project area is nearly as simple as moving anywhere in the city, and that the screening of applicants does not eliminate a large portion of the population either through exclusion, as might happen with the lower-income groups, or through lack of promotion, as might happen with the upper-income groups. These complex administrative mechanisms must at the same time be capable of handling the probable scales of population expansion and development activity.

Moreover, in order to determine whether the experiment is a success, there must be a way of measuring its effects: to assess the way in which the new environment helps or hinders what the residents need to do, what kinds of satisfactions it provides, and the sorts of new activities and perceptions it evokes. One such study was made (see Chapter 23), but, to be useful to the designer, similar studies must be made regularly. The findings from these studies, combined with careful field analysis by the designers, will help in the future to predict the effects of designs before they are built and help the decision makers to choose among alternatives.

Conclusions

It is hardly surprising that the traditional interests of designers prevailed during the early and middle phases of the Guayana project. This was partly because of the pressures to deal with immediate needs and the desire to produce high-quality environments for the low-income groups as well as for the elite. The tardy arrival of the social scientists and the time it took for these specialists to gather data and diagnose the problems eliminated the encouragement they might have provided for new approaches. And a good deal of design effort was concentrated on making plans for the general form of the city and its critical elements: the main linear highway, the commercial center, the industrial areas, and the like.

Meanwhile, the growing knowledge about the residents' needs created doubts about the appropriateness of the original assumptions as to the kinds of residential environments they required. This led to a search for a new kind of residential prototype, one that placed more stress on openness and diversity for all groups in the population. To be sure, these concerns were not shared by all members of the staff—Joint Center or CVG—and it was increasingly evident that the new point of view, emphasizing the social requirements of the population, might well lead to a less traditional, but more challenging, conception of the city of the future and of the role of the urban designer.

Interestingly enough, the unplanned areas of the present city come much closer to this image of the future environment than the planned: sporadic filling in of irregular and small-scale pockets of land, different groups unexpectedly near one another, and an active secondhand housing market juxtaposed to new housing. Development that is full of variety and surprise must be contrasted with the large tracts of residences, homogeneous in design and social composition, being constructed by the large private developers and the public agencies. Even the growing and homogeneous areas of shacks in the eastern part of the city are largely a product of the inadequacies of present programs in reflecting the magnitude of the demand; these shacks are allowed to go nowhere else.

But unplanned areas seldom allow urban services and facilities to be easily introduced, and high standards of health and safety and freedom from erosion are difficult to achieve. Nor is there any guarantee that advantages observed in some unplanned areas will be repeated in others.

In short, there will be a need for an emphasis on design solutions that embody the best of the planned and of the unplanned.

There is no doubt that such an approach to residential area design will involve not only new design ideas but also new administrative and institutional arrangements. And it is probable that new arrangements will create new difficulties for the CVG in the administration of development. The CVG's present activities in residential development reflect the insights of the previous period of design work. The new approach described here would require the CVG to intervene in residential development with much smaller-scale units, to study more carefully what the residents need and want and how they respond to new areas, and to find ways to let the residents decide much more for themselves about how the environment is to be changed. The new approach would require not only new activities within the CVG but also new relationships with the design and construction contractors and other agencies.

If the new approach should result in satisfying the criteria for residential environments of both public agencies and residents, rich and poor, then the CVG might be able to achieve its aim to increase the population rapidly on the western side of the Caroní River by means of planned development.

In the past the CVG has adapted itself to each new approach, creating the necessary programs and activities, not content to sacrifice promising ideas because of a commitment to inappropriate institutional arrangements. The crucial question for the future, therefore, is whether the CVG will be willing to adapt again.

Chapter 14

Education and Regional Development

Russell G. Davis and Noel F. McGinn

The Venezuelan Constitution and the organic law of education state that all children are entitled to a complete and free primary-school education. In the Guayana, although 80 per cent of the children of primary-school age are crammed into schools, there are at present decent accommodations for only 60 per cent of this age group. Less than three fourths of the members of the adult workforce have received sufficient education to attain functional literacy. Closing this gap between the stated goal and the reality could have been made the objective for a strategy of educational development in the Guayana. In this sense, education is a social overhead that must be provided in Ciudad Guayana as in the rest of Venezuela.

The strategy and plan for educational development in Ciudad Guayana prepared by the Human Development Section of the Corporación Venezolana de Guayana (CVG) stressed the productive aspect of education and training, that is, manpower development. The socializing contribution of education was given secondary stress. The Corporation, an autonomous regional development agency funded largely by the central government, has as its primary task the development of the region centering around Ciudad Guayana. First priorities for the Corporation have been the provision of physical infrastructure and assistance in industrial development; social development has had a lower priority. This influenced the rationale for an educational development strategy and plan. While the attempt to fit the plan to the mandate of the Corporation has brought obvious advantages, it has also cut down on social depth and dimension.

The Guayana will not have a rural, agrarian, and authoritarian society with a small elite of *latifundistas* and a vast substratum of peonage. The design of the city calls for a populace capable of coping with the complexities of modern urban life and composed of economically and socially disparate groups living and working in close contact. In the Guayana, members of the workforce and the rest of society must be able to talk to each other. If the community is to flourish, the educational and cultural attainment of its members cannot be too disparate. As Venezuela does not now have a tradition of individual and community development through participation in voluntary organizations, the educational system, by broad definition, must supply those experiences that help a people move toward stability and growth.

To relate educational attainment to productivity in the Guayana, the population, workforce, and economic characteristics of the region had to be assessed for the present, and output had to be projected for some target date. Given current status and probable future trends, targets for education and training could be set.

The economic planners had envisaged a region that in 1975 would generate a product value of $2,200 million. They estimated that by 1975 the Guayana development zone would produce about 5 per cent of Venezuela's gross domestic product and about 15 per cent of total industrial product. Over half of the Guayana output would come from heavy industry marshaled into a complex linkage system. Hydroelectric power capacity would be more than six million kilowatt-hours, and three million cubic meters of natural gas would be available daily. A workforce of over 70,000 and a population of over 200,000 would live in the development zone.

Quite clearly, an ignorant and untrained workforce could not operate the complex industrial machine planned for 1975. The prospect is not for a large workforce underemployed in subsistence agriculture. Educational requirements will be high for the middle- and higher-level workers in the heavy industries of the Guayana of 1975.

Estimating Demand for Education in the Workforce

There is no need to detail the mechanics by which educational targets were set and a strategy of educational development devised for the Guayana. The estimates, reached through successive approximations, are very rough. The 1975 target year labor force was projected by sectors and educational levels within sectors. For the central core of heavy and light industry the analysis scheme

1. projected the output from the base year 1966 to 1975
2. projected the output per worker for the same period
3. divided output per worker into output to get number of workers
4. distributed employment by occupation
5. related occupation to education in the workforce.

In application the analysis was a great deal more complex. For existing industries there are data on present capacity and technology and fair estimates for future output and likely changes in technology. For planned industries there are detailed feasibility studies that provide estimates of the same things. Output and productivity, under varying assumptions of market, capacity, and technology, can be estimated. Employment follows. For industries that will be linked to the central ones (for example, oxygen production to the steel industry), there are also some bases for estimates. For supporting sectors, such as electricity, gas and water, and transportation, there are ways of linking output to the market generated by industrial and private consumer demand. For services and government there are relationships to the size of the population. The method is full of circularity. The workforce can be used to estimate the population, and the population size feeds back to determine the workforce in services and commerce.

There are ambiguities and problems in relating output to occupational distribution and occupations to educational levels. Educational attainment is both a cause and a result of increased production. A great deal of loose definition occurs in occupational and educational classification, and various educational and occupational distributions are possible with differing combinations of factors of production and permutations of technology. But the method provides some targets, no matter how approximate, and the concern here is with the strategy itself rather than with the precision or accuracy of the first round of targets.

The demand for education in 1975 was estimated by taking the existing workforce in the base year, wasting it by death and retirement rates, and subtracting this from the 1975 employment targets. Because educational levels successively feed each other—a secondary-school graduate must also be a primary-school graduate—the targets must be cumulated to provide for both terminal demand at a given level and feed to the next higher level.

These output targets for the schools define only part of the educational task. The targets are expressed in terms of the workforce. The schools must serve the total population, including many who will never join the workforce. In Venezuela employed persons represent about 88 per cent of the workforce; and the workforce in turn represents about one third of the population. The education of persons not in the workforce is essential to generate continued development of skills and understanding among the productive members of the society. For example, educated mothers push their children toward further education, and educated wives encourage their husbands in self-improvement. Targets based on employment are minimal ones, then.

The CVG's strategy has linked educational development to the economic development requirements of the region. The implication of this approach is that, whatever the rights of the citizens to education may be, if the minimal educational targets are not met the growth in output planned for the region may not be attained. This is one significant aspect of a strategy based on manpower needs. One hundred years of entitlement by law has not brought free universal education for the Venezuelans, perhaps because education has been viewed as a burdensome social overhead. Even if manpower analysis provided imprecise data it would still have psychological and political utility as a means of motivating authorities to provide more adequate support for education.

Meeting the Targets

To meet the educational requirement targets set for the Guayana, the population and workforce must grow in absolute terms, and the workers must be trained and educated. The existing population of the Guayana could not attain the required size through natural growth, that is, the excess of births over deaths. The difference must be made up by in-migration, which is currently about 5,000 a year but is destined to rise as the zone's population and economy expand over the next decade. The likelihood is that migrants will come in sufficient numbers, but it is less likely that they will arrive already educated and trained.[1] The Guayana school and training establishments must educate and train people currently in residence and also serve large numbers of uneducated and untrained migrants and their children.

The targets call for 38,000 primary-school graduates by 1975 just to meet workforce demands. (See Table 14.1.) The present annual output of the Guayana primary schools is about 900 graduates. Operating at a much improved degree of efficiency the primary schools of Ciudad Guayana could meet about 70 per cent of the 1975 target demand for the labor force, if *all* primary-school graduates enter the labor force. At the middle-school level the required output can be met if the number of *bachilleres* (graduates of a general preparatory program) increases about tenfold over ten years. Enrollments in technical and artisanal schools must increase eightfold even to meet two thirds of the demand. The graduates of commercial programs must increase at least tenfold to meet half the demand

TABLE 14.1
Supply of Education Projected for the Schools of Ciudad Guayana Compared with Labor Force Demand

Educational Level	1975 Labor Force Demand[a]	Education Provided in Ciudad Guayana 1966–1975[b]	Difference, Demand-Supply
Postgraduate studies	332	—	332
University level			
Architecture, engineering, sciences	1,455	—	1,455
Law, economics, humanities	1,111	—	1,111
Medicine, dentistry	254	—	254
Veterinary, agronomy	56	—	56
Instituto pedagógico	568	—	568
Instituto politécnico	755	—	755
High-school level			
Technical-artisanal	10,190	6,475[c]	3,715
Commercial	6,036	3,280[d]	2,756
Academic	3,120	3,218[e]	–98[f]
Normal	1,220	—	1,220
Agricultural	189	—	189
Nursing	442	—	442
Primary-school graduate	17,215 (21,197)[g]	17,348 (12,973)[g]	–133[f]
4–5 years primary	10,427 (38,412)[g]	12,626 (30,321)[g]	–2,199[f]
0–3 years primary	–8,384 (40,455)[fg]	7,834 (50,781)	–16,218[f]

a. With 1966 labor force wasted out.

b. That is, what could be available to the labor force, assuming maximal increases in numbers of graduates from schools and that all school leavers enter the labor force.

c. All students finishing three or more years in technical or artisanal schools.

d. All students finishing three or more years in commercial schools.

e. Liceo graduates.

f. Negative numbers indicate that the *total* number of people "leaving" school at this level exceeds the *minimal* number required by the labor force. The oversupply of people with very low levels of education suggests that the schools, even though greatly improved by 1975, will still fail to furnish some portion of the population with a sufficient degree of education to contribute effectively to the society, either in the labor force or as educated housewives.

g. Demand for those terminating at this level *and* those feeding higher levels.

projected. These projected increases in primary and middle-level programs are the largest possible for the present system in Ciudad Guayana. Given the time necessary first to establish such facilities and then to produce graduates, no output at the higher education level could be expected by 1975. Hence the entire 4,500 workforce members educated at the post-secondary level must come from outside the region. The targets appear formidable indeed, when it is estimated that about a third of the migrants coming into the Guayana, largely from surrounding rural regions, are illiterate, and fewer than 10 per cent have had any secondary education.

A strategy for meeting the educational needs of the economic development plan would require[2]

1. expanding primary education to the maximum so that a sufficient feed of students is assured to middle-level schools and the workers have enough basic education to profit from shorter special training courses that must be given to cover the deficit of skills in the middle levels
2. expanding middle-level school facilities (*bachiller,* vocational, commercial, and technical programs) to the maximum so that as many middle-level workers as possible can be produced and enough graduates will be available to feed the higher levels of education
3. recruiting higher-level professionals and administrators from outside the region.

The kinds of programs that the CVG and the Ministry of Education must undertake to expand the number of graduates from primary and secondary schools in Ciudad Guayana are discussed later in this chapter.

Many of the professionals in scientific and technological fields must come from outside the country. Because of the political sensitivity that surrounds the recruitment of foreign specialists for higher-level jobs and because of the need to maintain incentives for young Venezuelans coming up through the educational system and the workforce ranks, the recruitment program must be paired with plans for the eventual replacement of foreigners. The recruitment of foreigners without a replacement schedule is not only politically unpalatable; it is socially and economically unwise in the long run. Hence a higher-educational facility must be established in the zone, even though it cannot contribute materially to the workforce by 1975.

Informal Routes to Education and Training
Up to this point we have dealt with only the output of formal educational and training facilities within the region and the inmigration of workers educated and trained outside. There are other, less formal, sources.

Workers may be trained and educated by cooperative programs run jointly by schools and industry. Special centers manned by the National Cooperative Educational Institute (Instituto Nacional de Cooperación Educativa—INCE) may also offer both general educational programs (for example, courses equivalent to the fourth and fifth grades of primary school) and training in specific industrial and artisanal skills. There are also in-industry training programs, currently run only in the largest establishments in the region, the steel mill and the mining companies. Lastly, there is the possibility of education and training from industrial spin-off. While engaged in complex manufacturing processes, the workers acquire a certain amount of informal education and training.

The gap between targets and school output of workers trained at middle skill levels is substantial, perhaps on the order of 10,000.

No joint school-industry programs have yet been launched, but planning and discussions have gone forward. Most school-industry programs will not materially raise the output of middle-level skilled workers but will merely supplement the school program with related work experience. However, some burden will be lifted from the school training shops. Perhaps an increment of 200 trained persons can be expected from this combined source over the ten-year period.

INCE runs various programs. There are artisan programs in construction and in electrical work for fourteen- to eighteen-year-old students who have completed primary school. Present output in these six-month courses averages about 240 graduates a year, and space is available for turning out a maximum of 900 a year. Because of a shortage of instructors this maximum figure is not likely to be met in the next ten years. If present output were doubled, the program would produce about 5,000 trained workers by 1975. INCE also offers general education and specific skill training to workers over eighteen years old who are already employed. The maximum output is 200 a year, and if that were reached—it currently runs about 75—2,000 workers with lower-level skills could be added from this source. Because of inadequate placement services and the rudimentary level of skills generated, there are some difficulties in placing current graduates of INCE in the construction industry. A metals-trade training center was opened in 1967.

The larger industrial establishments in the Guayana will be able to absorb some portion of the training burden, at least for short courses directly related to specific job performance. The mining companies and the steel plant at Matanzas already have had experience in running training programs.

In view of the fact that the steel mill and satellite establishments will employ about 10,000 people in 1975, the size of the present training programs is extremely small. Present steel mill apprentice programs will produce about 50 highly skilled workers a year. The course lasts four years. The steel mill also trains about 500 workers a year in shorter task-related courses in blueprint reading, milling-machine operation, drafting, metallurgical analysis, clerical work, and welding. These courses average about fifty hours each.

The scale of some of the other industries planned for the Guayana makes it unlikely that they will turn out more than 700 trainees a year, largely in specific, short, task-oriented programs that require a primary- or middle-school educational background. Little of the burden of formal training will be taken from the schools.

The future industries of the Guayana must have high productivity if they are to move into Latin American markets now dominated by Europe and the United States. There will be limitations on the extent to which they can shift workers from the production line to training courses. A lack of a pool of educated and trained workers may cause some companies to overlook regional advantages in natural resources, transportation, and markets.

The amount of education and training that will come from spin-off of the production process itself is unknown. Certainly the spin-off will be greater if the workers have a foundation of literacy and computational skills. Over-all, it is not likely that private industry can or will assume a major share of the training, especially the general education required for specificic training.

Educational Level of Migrants

The signs are that large numbers of untrained and even illiterate workers will be pouring into the Guayana. Excluding the professionals who have been brought to the Guayana by the CVG or the Orinoco Mining Company, the average education of the city's adults is between two and three years of primary school. This attainment level is even worse than it looks because most (80 per cent) of the migrants were educated in rural areas or small towns (under 5,000 inhabitants), so that the men who come to the city looking for work have had few of those life experiences necessary for successful performance in an industrial world. They have never worked with machinery and often do not know the uses of basic tools. They have difficulty in self-expression and communication, and minimal reading skills. They tend toward a fatalistic view of life, with the result that their commitments to work are of short duration: they save enough to meet minimal needs and then quit. They are attracted to employment in the service sector because of the low job discipline required.

Rural migrants to the city often are ignorant of the functions of social and political institutions and maintain a life style inimical to their own health, to that of their family, and to the health of the total community. Perhaps most serious, they foster in their children the same characteristics —not just avoidance of formal training but also failure to acquire those social and intellectual skills that ensure success in an industrial city. The barrio people, perhaps the majority of the new residents of the city, are unable to understand the source of their difficulties. They dream of paternalistic welfare programs that the government can ill afford to provide. For political and social reasons, as well as economic ones, the government must provide the educational base to equip workers and their children for life and work in an urban, industrial setting.

Implementing the Program for Educational Development in the Guayana

Education in Venezuela is de facto a charge of the central government, and the enterprise is largely funded and managed from Caracas. This causes some problems in implementing an educational development program in the region. Though state, local, and private sources put some resources into education, about 75 per cent of the support comes from the central government. The Ministry of Education is located, physically and in spirit, in Caracas, about 300 miles from the schools of Ciudad Guayana. The management of schools from distant and isolated central ministries is a problem for Venezuela as for most other Latin American countries.

The charter of the Corporación Venezolana de Guayana is broad and allows it to carry out any programs—including education—that will contribute to development in the region. However, the CVG has no mandate to duplicate the work of ministries. Clearly the Ministry of Education has primary responsibility in its own field, and the CVG has followed a policy of avoiding financial and managerial obligations that more appropriately belong to the Ministry of Education. During the course of its existence the CVG has passed through various stages of involvement with education. At first, the hope was that the Ministry would assume the entire burden. In the first briefing session the President of the Corporation gave the planners a very straightforward charge: "prepare a plan which specifies what must be done in education in the Guayana. CVG will present the plan to the Ministry, and the Ministry, once it knows what must be done, will do it."

The Ministry, then and now, provides education in the Guayana in the same measure it is provided in the rest of Venezuela. The education provided is inadequate. There are reasons for this.

Historically the development of education in Venezuela has alternated between progress and retrogression according to the political orientation of the government in power. With the exception of the period of Antonio Guzman Blanco (1870–1889), public education has declined under authoritarian regimes and enjoyed a resurgence after they have gone. There were serious dips during the reigns of Juan Vicente Gómez (1910–1935) and Marcos Pérez Jiménez (1948–1958) and marked expansion afterward. In the early sixties, at the time the CVG hoped the Ministry of Education would take on the burden of public education in the region, the national educational system was digging out after the reign of Pérez Jiménez, who with skilled and covert strokes and much public self-righteousness had torn the heart out of the system.

Immediately following the departure of Pérez Jiménez in 1958, school enrollments shot up. In the first three years, elementary-school enrollments increased by over 75 per cent; general secondary education doubled in two years; and normal-school enrollments, the key to any meaningful expansion of the primary schools, doubled in each of two successive years. With an expansion of this magnitude, only minimal levels of quality could be maintained. Inputs per student had to be held down to the barest essentials. Enrollments increased but graduates did not. The schools did not produce. No matter how dedicated to public education the central government was, it could not expand the system so rapidly and still maintain quality. Years of demand, backed up during the dictatorship, had to be satisfied. With existing resource limitations, provision could be only minimal. The Ministry could provide no more in the Guayana region than it did in any other. Its charge, after all, was national. What it provided was far less than enough to ensure the educational expansion the region required to achieve growth.

There was then a kind of standoff. CVG policy was to avoid taking on the burden of public education, which belonged in its view to the Ministry of Education. The Ministry for its part could do no more for the Guayana than for any other region in Venezuela, and perhaps might do slightly less, on the grounds that the CVG with its millions and its broad mandate had the funds and the power to provide education in the region if it so willed.

One strategy for the CVG might have been to allow the Ministry to contribute its minimal inputs to public education and then to supplement and enrich the programs where necessary. Manpower targets are based on education at some meaningful level. Increasing the number of students in qualitatively inadequate programs may raise enrollments, but through wastage (retardation and dropouts), significant output in graduates may not be increased at all. The strategy for the CVG would have been to raise the quality in public-school programs by providing textbooks and teaching materials, school libraries, in-service teaching programs to improve the instructional staff, assistance in management, school lunches, health services, testing, placement, guidance, and special instructional programs. The CVG might also have provided assistance with school construction in urban neighborhoods that would be impacted by large-scale housing developments. It could have contributed equipment and supplies to vocational programs and an improved curriculum in the basic sciences and mathematics.

The CVG did none of these things. Until 1964 the CVG put nothing into public education. It did contribute to private education run by church groups. Substantial grants of CVG money went to build and run private schools in Ciudad Guayana. In retrospect it is easy to criticize CVG policy. Instead of adding substance to the public educational program by strategically selected grants to expand and improve the Guayana schools, the CVG underwrote the creation of private schools. There were, however, reasons for this policy.

First, the CVG learned that if it took over any of the burden that belonged to the Ministry of Education it would never get free of it. The Ministry, always hard pressed, would merely reduce its allocations to the Guayana and employ them in some other needy area of Venezuela. As a regional development organization the CVG was responsible for securing maximal allocations to its region, from all sources.

Second, since no higher-education facilities existed in the Guayana, the region could not produce the professionals and administrators to man its industries. All people trained at the university level had to be attracted from outside, mainly from Caracas and a few other established and thriving urban centers such as Maracaibo and Valencia. CVG officials felt that the establishment of quality private schools would attract administrators and professionals who were anxious to ensure the best education for their children. The CVG also felt that the pattern of education preferred by the managerial class would be private and religious.

The CVG hoped it could make initial grants to establish private schools and then phase out more easily than with public schools. This might have been true had private-school authorities come into the Guayana to serve only the upper middle class. The schools could have established a fee structure that would cover future operating expenditures and provide for maintenance and recovery of capital. But the religious authorities did not intend to serve the upper classes alone, and the fee structures established and the number of scholarships offered to poor children made it impossible to run the schools as viable private, profit-making enterprises.

Sadly, the private schools did not even serve the poor. Poor parents did not canvass the private schools for scholarship possibilities. Social distance immobilized the barrio dwellers and put the elaborate private schools, which were built and run with public money, beyond their aspirations, even when books and tuition were furnished. Public schools for the lower middle class sometimes awe the barrio poor and impel them to send their children to neighborhood dame schools where they will be among their own kind. Grinding poverty immobilizes all except the very bold.

The Joint Center planners urged the CVG leaders to reconsider the policy of helping only private schools in Ciudad Guayana. Although the CVG leaders were willing to consider assistance to the public schools, they felt that they could not participate in a joint program with the Ministry of Education until a long-range plan for educational development had been prepared. The plan would limit the goals for educational development, and the Ministry and the CVG could then commit their respective resources to accomplish the task.

In November 1964 the planning staff produced the plan: *Strategy for Human Resource Development in the Distrito Caroní: A Summary*. The steps recommended to implement the strategy are too numerous to detail, but the plan was for the CVG to supplement the Ministry's efforts rather than to supplant them. Supplementary assistance was to be provided primarily in the form of single-outlay capital projects. In general, construction of primary-school facilities was to be left to the Ministries of Education and Public Works. However, the CVG agreed to build six twelve-room schools in areas where new housing and city growth called for immediate action. The reasons for CVG participation here were twofold. First, the areas were already desperately short of classroom space, and the likelihood of a timely Ministry, state, or local response was small. Second, the building of public-school facilities by the CVG would serve as an earnest of purpose that would demonstrate willingness to cooperate in the solution of educational problems in the Guayana.

The strategy also called for enrichment of existing programs in primary education. No schoolbooks were given to schoolchildren in the Guayana or in other parts of Venezuela. Many parents do not buy books for their children, or else they buy what is cheap and available rather than what the curriculum guides recommend. It was and is unrealistic to expect the Ministry to furnish schoolbooks to children in the Guayana when it does not do this anywhere else in Venezuela. Yet with large classes and minimally trained teachers a heavy burden falls on the textbooks. The CVG could make a substantial contribution to the improvement of education by guaranteeing that children have books. The same is true of school libraries, which are indispensable for broadening the teacher's outlook as well as for encouraging students and parents to read. The plan recommended that the CVG furnish textbooks for all students in the Guayana public schools and establish school libraries. This was a grant program to be managed by the Venezuelan Book Bank and would not involve the CVG in continuing obligations.

The planners also recommended that the CVG support the introduction of new curricula in science and mathematics for the secondary schools, that it fund the establishment of in-service teacher-training programs for these new curricula, and that, if and when the comprehensive high-school program (technical, commercial, and college preparatory programs in one school) comes to Venezeula, the CVG assist in the construction and equipping of a model school. A variety of other programs were recommended, all designed to supplement rather than supplant the Ministry programs and to avoid permanent commitments. At the postsecondary level, the Corporation was to build and launch a technological institute.

The plan was presented to the Ministry; the book and library program was launched; the building program was begun; the CVG also gave some supplemental assistance to the public technical school. A proposal to establish a research, planning, and services center, jointly funded and staffed by the Ministry and the CVG, was discussed. The CVG requested the Center for Studies in Education and Development of Harvard University to furnish technical advisers for the center. The center began operation in October 1966.

Planning Educational Development for a Region

Measured against need, effort, and outlay, educational planning and implementation in the Guayana still have a distance to travel. But something has been learned from the attempt to articulate a policy, develop a plan, and devise a strategy for implementation.

The Guayana planning experience foreshadows problems in human resource development that Venezuela and other Latin American, African, and Asian countries must someday face, as institutions for economic and social change and development extend their services into vast hinterlands outside the capital cities. The planning of programs in centralized, national systems has been done in terms of national aggregates and averages. The averages often mask significant differences within a country. Regions might be highly disparate culturally, socially, politically, and economically. In the rush to prepare a "national" plan, regional differences are ignored, and the results are programs that fit no real situation. Ultimately each region must be studied in detail to achieve a plan tailored to fit its particular needs. All of this work is still to be done in development planning. This is not the situation in the Guayana, where the plan, whatever its weaknesses, was created expressly for the region.

A regional plan differs from a national plan by virtue of the smaller size of the region and the close and searching way it can be studied. Rough averages and ratios can be applied in national plans, where the size of the universe will level out nonsystematic errors. On the other hand, the subnational area can be studied in far greater detail. The planner can traverse the entire area and inspect the system for which he is planning. The planner in the subnational area must face and sort out more complexities than in the national situation, where planning is more removed from the confusions and pressures of the real world. At the same time he is more likely to generate a strategy and tactics that go to the heart of the development problem because he is close to specific problems within the region.

In addition to the differences that separate one region from another, enormous differences exist within each region. There are subcommunities and subsocieties, each with its own particular ways and needs. There is a world of difference between the professional man in the Guayana who supports five children with earnings of two thousand dollars a month and a woman who feeds her four fatherless children on twenty-five dollars a month earned by making and selling *arepas* (corn pancakes). For the two, the school cannot even be perceived as the same institution, and its programs cannot be fashioned into one standard product. A vast social distance separates the poor barrio dweller from book and teacher, and programs must be differentially fashioned to bridge this gap.

One limitation of the strategy evolved for educational development in the Guayana is that it stressed the fact that schools must come if the economy is to develop, but it underplayed the idea that education and training must be provided if social harmony is to prosper. Only by being in and of the communities can the planner understand the people's needs and shape the school program to respond to them. This opportunity was not fully exploited in the planning program for the Guayana, partly because the locus of planning was Caracas, far removed from the scene of action. For the poor, underprivileged, and disintegrating families of the barrios the schools must do more than prepare for job performance, although even that is powerful social medicine if it can be accomplished. The schools may also have to serve as parental surrogates and as way stations toward disciplined hope. Such programs cannot be planned effectively by the numbers and from afar.

Within the Venezuelan Ministry of Education each level from primary school through university is under virtually autonomous directorates. Programs across levels are poorly articulated, and there is no view of the educational enterprise as a system. The primary-school curriculum is separate from that of the middle school; rural supervision is divided from urban; the secondary-school teacher scorns the primary and is, in turn, scorned by the university professor. At the national level the very size and scope of authority foster the separation by levels. This division of functions is accompanied by an excessive centralization that denies national planners access to local data.

However, in a regional setting no such isolation is tolerable or necessary. Ciudad Guayana is large enough to permit all the variations within the national educational system from primary through postsecondary. It is also small enough so that programs can be planned integrally, from primary through postsecondary. But if implementation depends on the Ministry in Caracas, the problem of autonomous and conflicting directorates intrudes. For this reason, as noted, a regional research, planning, and services center was established. Such a center will not only permit integral planning at the local level but also provide more detailed data for national planning. The Ministry, far from the scene of local action, has relied too heavily on national aggregate data.

In Venezuela the school establishment has been traditionally isolated from industry, and often unresponsive to the requirements of the economy. The Guayana project offered a unique chance to plan schools that would grow up with the industry of the region, responsive from the outset to the need to train for an ever-changing technology. A major goal of the strategy has been to coordinate educational output with the requirements of the workforce and to make training programs responsive to industry. In an area of rapid population and industrial growth the relationship between education and industry must be close, and maximal flexibility must be maintained in programs. Traditionally the school program drops behind technology, and outmoded vocational programs result. The only strategy possible is to maintain a pattern of continuous request and response between industry and training establishments. Planning in a regional area does permit this.

Institutional patterns unique to the Guayana must influence the policy, strategy, and plan. It is necessary to modify the highly general plans worked out for Venezuela as a whole so that they fit the specific characteristics of Guayana. Guayana is uniquely important to all of Venezuela. The Guayana region had such significance for Venezuela's development that an autonomous development agency was created. This agency, in turn, established an educational planning and service section to work with the national Ministry of Education in the local schools. There has been little open conflict between the two powerful agencies, but communication has faltered, and gaps have appeared in educational development.

Although all things could be planned by the CVG, only some things were within its mandate to perform. Its strategy had to be one of stimulating the Ministry of Education to make a maximal and optimal commitment of resources in some areas, such as buildings and teacher training. The CVG drew back from long-range commitments to programs that the Ministry had the obligation and resources to provide. The CVG played a waiting game. On its side, the Ministry officials knew from the public record that the CVG had vast resources. The Ministry, further, was aware of the pressure on its own resources from the rest of the country. It was natural for the Ministry to play the same game that the CVG was playing. The CVG's initial policy of assisting only private education exacerbated the matter, but the moves would have been wary and sometimes indecisive in any case. Each agency would have welcomed unlimited commitments from the other with no strings of control attached. But both were responsible to higher authorities, and control must follow funds. Inasmuch as neither agency wished to carry the burden alone, although both agencies realized the burden was there, the central objective of any planning had to be the creation of concert between the Ministry and the CVG. State and local participation could come only after the principal national agencies were in harness.

Chapter 15

Legal Issues
of Regional
Development

William A. Doebele, Jr.

Law is one of the least transportable of professional skills. Tied by its nature to the customs and traditions of its culture, it varies significantly among the states of the Union, and to a very marked degree among nations. The situation with respect to the legal traditions of North and Latin America is made even more complex by the fact that the former participates in the common-law system of legal thought, the latter in the tradition of the Continental civil-law system. Nor do difficulties stop there, for in Latin America remnants of colonial and even feudal principles still exist, paradoxically embedded in a general organization of government patterned on that least feudal of documents, the U.S. Constitution.

Yet "institution building" has come to be recognized as an indispensable element of economic development, and was so regarded from the beginning of the arrangements for technical assistance between the Corporación Venezolana de Guayana (CVG) and the Joint Center for Urban Studies. The problems encountered in the execution of certain aspects of the Joint Center's work in this field are therefore worth describing. Though the experience contained many elements peculiar to the situation of Venezuela and the CVG, it also defined a set of fundamental problems characteristic of economic development in general. In this respect it is relevant to almost every project in foreign assistance being carried on today.

The Function of Law in Economic Development

Law, in the final analysis, is a set of secular rules by which men live. Of itself it grows no rice, builds no houses, weaves no cloth, bridges no rivers, creates no goods. Rather, its role is to provide the framework within which the economic, social, and other energies of a country may be most fruitfully mobilized. A well-constructed legal system facilitates the activities needed by a nation to survive and to flourish. A poorly constructed legal system (such as the French Fourth Republic) can frustrate a society that might otherwise be socially and economically vigorous.

The task of law in economic development is therefore to create a total institutional setting that will release constructive forces to do their creative work. In spite of some deficiencies, the general legal framework created for the United States in the eighteenth and nineteenth centuries succeeded in this function by encouraging the rapid economic exploitation of a continent. The international institutions created in Western Europe since the war appear to be similarly well suited to the acceleration of economic progress in that area.

In Latin America the predominantly rural character of society has maintained, in general, a peasant culture oriented toward personal and informal organization rather than formal law. At the other end of the social-economic spectrum, the aristocratic minorities in each nation have also operated through a network of highly personalized, rather than institutionalized, relationships. The emerging middle class, with its need for formal yet flexible methods of dealing, has yet to have a major impact on the legal system.

Modern technological society requires legal arrangements capable of responding quickly and easily to complex and novel relationships. Hence it calls for a legal system capable of great differentiation but at the same time comprehensible to the parties concerned. In developing countries, unfortunately, legal systems have been by and large designed for stability rather than change, and are resistant to the revised relationships essential to the new social order now struggling to emerge. Under these conditions, even the most enlightened social and economic undertakings lack adequate channels for their expression in legal institutions. Good intentions become involuntarily distorted by the instruments through which they must pass into reality. The task of legal reform is indeed a formidable one in Latin America—more formidable than is generally supposed.

Developing countries, in other words, need to execute a particularly complex legal strategy to create institutions to serve their extraordinary needs. They must, by the nature of the modern world, establish a framework of certainty, particularly with respect to the rights of emerging classes, that will permit economic activities to multiply. At the same time they must be prepared to modify old concepts of legal status (particularly property in land) to give play to a new economic order inevitably more fluid and dynamic than the old. Faced with this double set of challenges, developing countries frequently choose the course of least resistance—resolution by ambiguity—an alternative that may be politically expedient, but inadequate in resolving the basic problem.[1]

In the Anglo-American system the process of careful reporting of cases establishes great stability, while statutory revision and judicial review permit decisive breakthroughs when needed. The system of civil law, based on extensive codes, has the stability of written law derived from a single and readily available source, yet it is able to deal with novel situations by extrapolating several sections of the code into the new area. It also possesses the flexibility of direct legislative amendment.

The crux of the matter, therefore, is not a question of whether the Continental or Anglo-American system of jurisprudence is better *per se* but the generic one of adapting any type of legal tradition to the extraordinary demands of a society in the midst of profound and rapid reorganization. The essential difficulty appears to be that legal institutions—like most other institutions—in developing countries have not yet been refined to strike the sorts of balances that law in a modern urban-industrial civilization is called upon to make. In part the very size of most developing nations is in itself a considerable handicap, since (as in the less populated states of the United States) a small (and poor) population will not produce the variety of litigation necessary to force critical issues to resolution. But more fundamentally, the problem of institutional adjustment to extremely rapid change is a general theme in human history.

This chapter cannot, of course, begin to treat this subject as a whole. Rather, it discusses certain specific issues of land tenure and administration as they are related to the problems posed by the development of the Guayana region, and particularly by its major city, Ciudad Guayana.

Institutions Relating to Land Tenure

Squatting. The legal rights of squatters are protected in Venezuela by the doctrine of *bienhechurías* (improvements). Under Article 557 of the Venezuelan Civil Code, any person who improves in good faith the land of another is entitled to compensation upon removal from the land. Historically Venezuela has been a land-rich country, particularly in the southern and eastern regions, including the Guayana. Under such circumstances the law—as in the U.S. Homestead Acts and the liberal doctrines of adverse possession in our Western states—has tended to favor the man who puts land into constructive use.

While the law on *bienhechurías* does provide for the element of good faith, it is in essence favorable to an improver, on the grounds that the person whose land is improved would otherwise be receiving unjust enrichment.

Thus the urban squatter in Venezuela has two protections: the political infeasibility of clearing large areas, and the legal doctrine just described, which applies to large and small areas alike. For these reasons, it was the position of the CVG officials (with some exceptions), and indeed of Venezuelan officials generally, that compensation would be required for the improvements lost when squatters were removed. It was also felt that if the land were not reused immediately, its occupancy by a new set of squatters would entail multiple compensations to keep any particular area clear, except through strong and unpopular policing measures. At the same time the growth of squatter settlements along major traffic arteries and in the most central locations of the new city posed serious problems for the execution of the over-all urban plan.

The CVG responded, particularly on the eastern (San Félix) side of the site, by attempting to convince local authorities to control building permits so that squatting could be prevented in the areas most critical for future development. This approach may have had some impact on more substantial buildings, but the over-all effect was to create a cloud over the legitimacy of the dynamic private construction being carried on by literally thousands of new migrants, which was obviously beyond the power of the local building inspection administration to control. Thus the human resources represented by some of the most energetic inmigrants to the city were not channeled as effectively as if their efforts had been legitimized. In later years of the project, a different approach was adopted by opening up more self-help housing areas. (See Chapter 12.)

For some time, however, the situation was one of mutual ambiguity. Limited by the law of *bienhechurías* and the political constraints on strong action, the CVG and local municipal officials attempted to discourage squatting in the most critical areas, but they could never be fully effective. At the same time the squatters, recognizing the lack of clarity in official policy, continued their building, knowing that they possessed no real title and might be displaced at any moment, but hopeful that condemnation would bring monetary compensation, thus converting their accumulated labor into hard cash. The writer remembers finding on one occasion a large rough barn-like structure in a squatting area, inside which, with infinite pains, a relatively successful inmigrant family was constructing (in semi-darkness) a rather fine house. The plan was to escape the notice of the authorities during the sensitive period of construction, and then, when the proper moment came, to pull down the barn and reveal a *fait accompli* of such proportions that official counteraction would be embarrassingly difficult.

In a similar fashion, many unwritten customs seem to have established themselves throughout Venezuela to rationalize the amorphous relations between squatters and constabulary, the chief of which was the rule of thumb that if a squatter could build his house to the point of having installed the most difficult element—the roof—he could be removed only if compensated.

In physical terms, the results of this legal ambiguity were to produce in Ciudad Guayana large areas of very disorderly appearance but great liveliness and human vitality. By contrast, in Brasilia the government, through strict police measures, has eliminated almost all squatting from the site of the new city, forcing it all into a large and colorful "settlement of the adventurers"[2] several miles from the main development. Ciudad Guayana, with all the chaos that has arisen from its ability to control squatting only partially, retains an urban character and richness that the planned portions of Brasilia have still to generate. It may be that the limitations of choice imposed by the law of *bienhechurías* have forced a more flexible response to squatting that has not been without its advantages. On the other hand, one cannot help wondering when legislation will be devised to achieve the best of both worlds and produce a legal situation of sufficient clarity to capitalize on the constructive energy of urban migrants while permitting a reasonable degree of urban planning for future development.[3]

Disposal of houses in public projects. An interesting variation of the legal ambiguities surrounding squatting arose from the legal instruments used by the public housing authority (Banco Obrero) for the disposal of its units.

When, normally after a long selection process, a family was chosen for such a unit, the house and land were neither given in fee nor leased but granted under a peculiar form of legal transfer known as *enfiteusis*. This doctrine, apparently feudal in origin, permits the ceding of property with an obligation to improve and to pay an annual fee. The possessor (*enfiteuta*) may transfer his rights to another, but he may not create a sub*enfiteusis*. Furthermore, every nineteen years, at the demand of the grantor, the current *enfiteuta* must engage in a ceremony in which formal recognition is given to grantor's rights. On the other hand, the *enfiteuta* may terminate the arrangement and obtain a fee simple interest at any time by the payment of an amount $33\frac{1}{3}$ times the annual rent. (Since rents in Venezuela are normally about 10 per cent, this would represent under market conditions a capitalization of about 300 per cent of the market price.) There are, in addition, other complex rules governing this relationship that need not concern us here.

The important point is to consider this sort of legal device in light of the actors involved: on the one hand, a rural and poorly educated migrant applying for a low-cost housing unit, and, on the other, a junior public housing official with excellent intentions but sorely overcommitted and unable to become involved in further administrative complications.

In the United States, studies have disclosed that even relatively sophisticated suburbanites often do not clearly know whether they are renting or purchasing their homes. In Ciudad Guayana, interviews in the field quickly established that neither the grantors nor the *enfiteutas* were aware of the legal subtleties implied in the documents being executed by the dozen each week.

What had undoubtedly occurred was that the public housing agencies did not want to release a fee simple interest and thus permit speculation and other loss of control in an extremely tight housing market. Yet merely to rent the units would impose on the public agency the duties of maintenance and repair, as well as the psychological problems of a "company town." Lacking alternatives in the existing law it was necessary to use what was at hand: in this case, a very inappropriate instrumentality. The heart of the problem was, of course, that at the time the various low-cost housing programs were initiated, the principal thought had been given to physical and financial factors, and very little attention was given to a workable set of of legal relationships once projects had been completed.[4]

Lack of legal concepts to implement effective over-all land policies. Land tenure policy in a "new town" situation may have two primary objectives: to act as a supplement to "police power" devices to assure orderly development and conformance to a master plan[5] and to recover public investment in infrastructure cost, known in Spanish law as *plusvalía*, in England as "betterment," and in the United States as improvement costs recoverable by special assessment.

If the legal system permits, these two objectives can be achieved simultaneously, and in the British new towns and in large private developments in the United States combinations of leases and restrictive covenants are used for both control and financial purposes. Typically in Britain and North America, commercial areas are leased, residential areas either leased or made subject to covenants to assure that design objectives will be observed, and industrial land similarly restricted to make certain that basic performance standards with respect to nuisance can be enforced.

The mix of legal devices used and the exact policy to be followed with respect to any new town or other large development will of course depend on circumstances. The particular policies relevant to the special conditions of the Guayana are themselves an interesting subject that is discussed in Chapter 10.

For the present discussion, however, the issue is not the specific controls that should or should not be applied to the various areas of Ciudad Guayana but the extent to which Venezuelan law offered a set of legal tools for dealing with the problem. In the Anglo-American tradition, almost 700 years of erosion of the rigidities of feudal land law (beginning with the Statute of Quia Emptores in 1290) have resulted in a system so flexible that it permits the expression of almost any conceivable arrangement between parties in interest to a piece of real estate.

By contrast, Venezuelan law appeared, as of 1962, to be poorly equipped with the instruments that are indispensable for the effective management and disposal of land in a "new town" situation as in Ciudad Guayana. Long-term leases, the most fundamental tool by which commercial property in new developments and redevelopment areas in the United States is disposed of, do not exist in Venezuela, which limits leases to five-year terms. (Even options to renew leases at previously agreed-upon conditions seem to occupy an uncertain position.) This means that one of the most flexible and useful sets of arrangements that could be made between the CVG and potential investors in urban development in Guayana is foreclosed, or at least so limited as to greatly restrict its usefulness.[6]

After leaseholds, the second most useful device for establishing relationships between interests in land in the context of planned development is the restrictive covenant. Although such covenants are apparently in use in certain private developments in Caracas, the opinions of leading lawyers varied as to their enforceability, and no major provisions in the Venezuelan codes cover this important set of devices.

Other more obscure, historically significant devices in Anglo-American law for sharing interests in land—the determinable fee, possibility of reverter, and right of entry—appear not to exist in Venezuelan law, or are actually prohibited. Servitudes and a limited class of easements do exist and were used by the CVG to impose certain types of conditions on the use of industrial land. There were, however, practical and legal limits on the extent to which these devices could be used to solve the more complex problems of disposal of commercial and residential property.

This is not to say that Venezuelan law is incapable of dramatic change. For example, in response to an urgent need for apartment houses in Caracas and other major cities, an extensive body of legislation dealing with "horizontal property," or condominiums, was enacted in 1958. This legislation, apparently copied from Italian legislation on the same subject, has established a legal framework so favorable to apartment construction that few cities in the world have matched the exuberance of high-rise production in Venezuela's capital. In this case, a body of existing property law was in fact swept aside and superseded by a modern and practical new set of principles.

Unfortunately, no ready models exist for a new system of real property law to govern the building of a new city. Indeed, one of the great creative challenges for young lawyer-planners in all developing countries is the invention of just such legislation.

The ejido question. Another interesting aspect of the work in the Guayana was the investigation made during the summer of 1962 of the alleged *ejido* rights of the town of San Félix. Under principles that go back to colonial times, Venezuelan law provides that municipal units have "domain" over lands extending 2.5 kilometers from the center of the town, which may be disposed of by the municipal council. These rights are automatically held by all towns existing before the revolution and may be granted to newer towns by the central government out of national lands known as *baldios,* a concept not unlike the federal ownership of Western lands in the United States. When a town obtains *ejido* lands they are normally divided into three zones: the "urban" zone, the zone of "expansion" (*ensanche*), and the rural zone. Regulations are made for selling to local citizens plots of various sizes at reasonable prices. The objectives obviously are to give the town some measure of control over its development, to permit a growing local population to obtain homesites at reasonable prices, and to establish revenues for the local treasury to offset the costs of growth. It is easy to see how such an institution was well suited to the needs of the eighteenth- and nineteenth-century rural society of Latin America, and indeed even to the conditions of the Guayana before the advent of the iron mining boom and the CVG in the 1950's and 1960's.

Because of the potential importance of this device to the land tenure policies of the Corporation, a study was undertaken in the region's land registry office (at Upata) on all *ejido* sales made by the Municipal Council of San Félix from the coming of the iron mining companies in 1952 to 1962. This research revealed an interesting pattern. In the early years of growth an attempt was made by San Félix to use *ejidos* for the purpose for which they were intended. However, in 1957, the last year of the Pérez Jiménez regime, several hundred hectares of some of the most strategically valuable land on the eastern side of the Caroní River were sold to a few persons obviously intent on land speculation in the Guayana. The fact that these claims could have been authorized and recorded, although they violated the spirit and letter of the *ejido* concept, illustrates another side of the institutional problems encountered in developing countries.[7]

Even aside from the fascinating historical footnote provided by the large speculations in *ejido* lands in the Guayana, the whole question of the land-granting powers of a locality in the face of an expansion as great as that contemplated in Ciudad Guayana is an example of the problem of general cultural lag in developing countries. Institutions well tuned to the needs of another era become ingrained and are hard to change. On the other hand, the Hispanic tradition of communal rights in the process of urban growth could become, if properly updated, an instrument of enormous usefulness.

Administrative Ambiguities

As in Venezuelan real property law generally, the constitutional statutes of the CVG itself contain certain questions of language and power that illustrate a general reluctance to define too tightly certain key relationships; to provide, in other words, enough "play" in the language of legislation to permit methods of personal contact and informal relations to continue to operate.

The legal authority of the CVG rested on two documents: its Organic Act, embodied in the form of a presidential decree (Decree No. 430, December 29, 1960), and its Regulations for Internal Organization, promulgated by the President on November 4, 1961.

The first of these documents, establishing an autonomous corporation having primary responsibility for the development of almost one fifth of the country's area and an annual budget that by 1962 had reached $80,000,000, was frustratingly vague on a number of key points, principally the relations between the CVG and existing governmental entities at the national, state, and local levels. For example, the decree gave the CVG power "to program" (*programar*) the integrated development of the region. In subsequent sections the decree stated that the CVG was "to coordinate" activities of the official agencies concerned with the economic and social problems in the region, but its activities for industrial promotion within the much smaller "Zone of Development" were to be in "collaboration" with the appropriate ministries, "with the concurrence" of the Ministry of Interior Relations, and "in consultation with" the governors of the states affected, the National Executive, and the national planning agency. It was also "to cooperate with" municipal units in furnishing public services.

Similar questions were involved in the Regulations for Internal Organization, which established a Department (*Dirección*) of Urban Development, charged with establishing policy and a master plan for urbanization within the Zone of Development as well as the coordination and actual construction of urban services. At the same time they established a coequal department for over-all regional studies and planning (Dirección de Estudios, Planificación e Investigación).

It is possible, even probable, that these obscurities of language were designed to permit flexibility of approach in a venture of unprecedented scope and complexity in Venezuelan history. Certainly the framers of the Constitution of the United States inserted enigmatic phrasing for precisely these reasons. In a country where personal relations take precedence over legal formalities, it would have been particularly unwise to overturn, in an undertaking already burdened with awesome responsibilities, a style of negotiation to which all levels of Venezuelan leadership were accustomed. And in fact the excellent personal relations among the key staff members of the Corporation did permit accommodation and flexibility in a rapidly changing and complex set of problems. At the same time there is no doubt that the cloudiness in jurisdictional boundaries sometimes required that staff time be spent on purely administrative matters that a more structured concept of organization (both internally and with outside agencies) might have avoided. However relevant and appropriate the Corporation's organic statutes may have been in 1960 and 1961, a clearer and more refined organization has become necessary, and steps have already been taken in this direction.

In a larger sense, the fascination of the art of institution building in the developing countries undoubtedly lies in just this judgment: to be able to determine precisely how rapidly organizational reforms can be made without destroying the essential continuity of the country's administrative tradition.

Conclusions

Drawing back with the perspective of time and distance from the administrative and legal problems of the development of the Guayana and comparing it with the experience of other regional developments, it is clear that the legal infrastructure for such large-scale urban and regional undertakings in developing countries has yet to be designed. If anything, the experience shows the fallacy of believing that any pastiche of existing laws from other countries can meet the growing needs in this field. Scholars and professionals in the field have yet to face the magnitude of the modification of law, even the basic codes of the country, that will be necessary before projects of this scale can be undertaken within a reasonably congenial framework.

Indeed, even in the United States the realization has only recently come that the construction of new towns and the revitalization of depressed regions will require a set of new institutions that we are only now beginning to create. The problem is in fact a double one, involving both the proper *enabling* legislation and an appropriate system of *tenancy* concepts having to do with the very idea of property in land itself.

At the first level, it will be necessary to investigate and compare the organic statutes of the numerous public development corporations in various countries and to discover what principles of organization in the enabling acts of such authorities seem to be successful and what principles are not.[8]

The Venezuelan experience underlined this need. More significantly, it illuminated another and perhaps more fundamental problem: beyond the purely organizational questions there is the matter of the basic real property law of the nation itself as a help or hindrance to effective economic development.

The most promising line of attack on this problem would seem to be to move as quickly as possible toward a system of law that combines *certainty* and *flexibility* with respect to interests in land and buildings. What is called for is a legal system that provides for an enormous variety of partial rights in land, each of which is fixed and defined in itself but capable of combination into an almost infinite number of ownership relations according to the demands of the particular situation.

More specifically it is apparent in all countries, including the United States, that as the pressures of urbanization increase and land must be treated more and more as a limited and uniquely valuable resource, there is a movement toward legal situations characterized by what could be termed *dual* or *simultaneous ownership* in which certain attributes of property are possessed by the private owner and others possessed by the public or semipublic agencies charged with responsibility for development (or redevelopment).

Properly executed, this system combines the advantages of the dynamism of private ownership and the social controls that must increasingly find expression in modern society. The concept is not an esoteric one. It is expressed abstractly in the constitutions of many nations, and in the United States it may be found in many contexts. Such simultaneous interests exist, for example, in the documents of almost any shopping center, by which the original developer of the land rents space to the stores and services that comprise the center itself. In these situations both parties have clear and reasonably defined interests in the same piece of land and in the activities that occur upon it. Title may remain in the developer, subject to long-term leases to the store owners. Management, insurance, provision of parking, and other responsibilities may be shared according to any number of arrangements.

Or, at the residential level, even in the most conventional North American subdivision, the purchaser of a home is soon made aware of the continuing interests of the original developer, which may prevent him from building a fence, making unauthorized additions to his home, or doing a host of other things normally considered to be the rights of ownership.

Recent federal and state legislation encouraging the acquisition by highway departments of so-called scenic easements is an even more direct form of the dual ownership phenomenon, in which two quite separate rights of property, for quite different purposes, exist in the same piece of land. The sale of air rights above highways and railroads is still another example of the possibility of shared interests, as is the "cluster" subdivision.

New cities like Ciudad Guayana are, above all, vast joint enterprises involving both the public and the private economic resources of the nation. Short of complete socialism, they will inevitably involve many types of collaborative ventures for which the necessary legal frameworks must be created. As has been demonstrated in the chapters of this book dealing with industrial development of the Guayana, growth in the economic sector has been possible in no small degree because of the ability of the CVG to enter into flexible, individualized, and mutually beneficial contracts, often of a highly complex nature, with private companies. With respect to land and buildings such arrangements have not yet been possible, and indeed will continue to be difficult under a Civil Code that imposes a five-year limit on leases and is deficient in many other basic concepts by which interests in land could be expressed as freely and accurately as in commercial contracts.

To make the necessary changes in the real property law of the major developing countries of the world is a large and fascinating challenge to the legal imagination, for, unlike commercial transactions, dealings concerning land in all societies connote special emotional elements not present in dealings with other goods. The adaptations that take place must therefore be ones that understand and respect the cultural traditions of the country involved, while forging new tools that will permit the new and more complex simultaneous patterns of ownership that economic development demands.

Part 3
Commentary on Methods and Goals

Chapter 16

Administrative Style[1]

John R. Dinkelspiel

Radical changes in the economic structure of any nation, developed or underdeveloped, often severely strain the capabilities of its political system. For an underdeveloped country without strong political resources and traditions, the management of rapid economic growth and reform is particularly difficult. When the basic form of government is itself a subject of great contention, there are good grounds for skepticism about whether any substantial economic development effort can be coherently planned and implemented. Yet in Venezuela, which in the past twenty years has had leftist revolutionary juntas and governments, rightist military juntas and dictatorships, coalition party governments, and other, less clearly definable, experiments,[2] a major effort of economic development—the Guayana program—has been carried forward under continuous management since 1953.[3]

As other portions of this book demonstrate, the high quality of the economic and technological expertise applied since 1961 in the Guayana has been a major factor in accounting for the recent successes. But this expertise does not account fully for the success of the Guayana development program, any more than European economic integration can be explained solely on the basis of economic factors. The key to the successful development of the Guayana has been the evolution of an administrative style that could cope with the vagaries of Venezuelan politics. This chapter is concerned primarily with an analysis of the origins, nature, and significance of the administrative style of the Corporación Venezolana de Guayana (CVG).

For present purposes the administrative style of a bureaucratic agency may be defined as the systematic way in which it adapts to its environment.[4] The Guayana Corporation's environment consists of such political elements as political parties, other parts of the government bureaucracy, mass communications media, pressure groups, and individual politicians. It also includes such technological elements as the nature and sources of the expertise recruited and the character of the natural resources exploited, as well as such economic elements as regional and national economic plans and programs. A successful administrative style, however, is not created by fiat; it develops over time.

Some Styles of Administrative Failure

That the Corporation's style is the major source of its success can be demonstrated by contrasting it with the style of three other agencies that operated in the Guayana at various times between 1945 and 1960: the national development corporation (Corporación Venezolana de Fomento—CVF) between 1945 and 1948;[5] the Office of Special Studies (Oficina de Estudios Especiales), 1953–1958; and the Venezuelan Iron and Steel Institute (Instituto Venezolana del Hierro y Acero), 1958–1960. The CVG has survived and flourished; these agencies failed.

The development of the Guayana was initiated by the first government of social revolution in Venezuelan history. In 1945 a civilian-military junta overthrew an elected government of the traditional military-landowner oligarchy that had ruled Venezuela for decades. The junta, dominated by its left-of-center civilian president, Rómulo Betancourt, and his party, Acción Democrática, launched a revolutionary program of social reform, industrialization, and economic nationalism, to be financed by a radically new policy of higher taxes and royalties on foreign-owned oil companies.[6] The junta's program sought economic independence from the domination of oil and foreign capital and the creation of a modern industrialized economy. The junta established a national development corporation as the principal means of implementing its industrialization program.

The dramatic discovery of huge iron-ore deposits in the Guayana by the United States Steel Corporation in 1947[7] raised the possibility of building a Venezuelan iron and steel industry. Venezuela's scarcity of electric power and coal led the CVF to conclude that a direct reduction process, using the country's abundant natural gas instead of coal, was the most logical technology to adopt for the production of iron and steel. But no such process had yet been developed, and the CVF's staff did not have the technical expertise to do so. Thus the success of the whole iron and steel venture came to depend on whether consulting firms could solve the technical problems of a direct reduction process. By 1951 it had become clear that none of the consultants could find an economic solution. (Even now no commercially attractive direct reduction process exists.) This conclusion, combined with the changed political circumstances discussed later, made it appear that a domestic iron and steel industry had no future.

In the meantime, a national power study undertaken by the CVF had disclosed the possibility of producing large amounts of cheap hydroelectric power in the Guayana[8]—a discovery that made an electric reduction process well worth considering. Before the CVF could exploit this knowledge, however, a coup d'état in November 1948 had thrown out the Acción Democrática government and established a military junta under Lieutenant Colonel Marcos Pérez Jiménez. The junta was in many ways a resurrection of the pre-1945 oligarchic traditions (its leading officers were a part of the same military clique), and it soon abandoned many of the major reforms and programs undertaken after the 1945 revolution. Those projects and agencies with a strong ideological identification with the Acción Democrática program were particularly vulnerable to the effort to turn back the clock.

The CVF and its ventures in the Guayana were allowed to atrophy to the point of extinction, not because they were intrinsically worthless but because their political coloration was too obvious. The new government ignored the newly revealed possibilities of an electric steel reduction process, and it allowed the study of a direct gas reduction process to run down until it came to a technological dead end in 1951. The study of the hydroelectric potential of the Guayana had even less momentum; it barely crept along, under the guidance of a single engineer—V. Martín Elvira—in the Ministry of Development. When Elvira's studies were ignored by the government, he published their results in a periodical,[9] bringing his calculation of the availability of vast amounts of cheap power from the Caroní River to the public's attention. But while the government continued to be apathetic toward the possibility of a steel mill in the Guayana, this new knowledge encouraged a group of leading businessmen to form a syndicate in late 1952 to explore the feasibility of making steel with Guayana's iron (mined by U.S. Steel) and cheap hydroelectric power. After the industrial possibilities in the Guayana had thus been brought forcefully to the government's attention, the Ministry of Development quickly created its own technical study group, and Pérez Jiménez soon ordered the syndicate to cease its activities in favor of a government iron and steel monopoly.

As soon as the general technical outlines of a feasible steel mill had begun to emerge from the Ministry's study group (in mid-1953), Pérez Jiménez reorganized the group into a small office responsible directly to him and run by one of his closest political and military collaborators—a man with no technical background. The operation was called the Office of Special Studies of the President of the Republic. This reorganization made technology the tool of the personal political aims of Pérez Jiménez, which, among other things, probably facilitated the funneling of a vast amount of graft into the pockets of Pérez Jiménez, the head of the Office of Special Studies, and perhaps a few others.[10] For instance, after the agency had chosen a contractor from among the firms submitting design proposals, the subsequent negotiations greatly altered the mill's specifications—and also considerably increased the contractor's profits. These changes seem to have made a much larger contribution to official graft than to the design of an efficient steel mill. The combination of enormous graft and the low technical competence in the agency considerably lowered the technical soundness of the mill's design and construction (and later operation).

In January 1958 the Pérez Jiménez dictatorship was thrown out by the military with popular support. Although the nonpartisan military junta that took over as the interim government was not sufficiently secure to purge all of Pérez Jiménez' supporters and programs, most of the major figures soon disappeared, and many major projects were either halted or substantially altered. The steel mill was no exception: the Office of Special Studies was quickly abolished and replaced by the Venezuelan Iron and Steel Institute, an autonomous government corporation. The Office of Special Studies was abolished not only because, like the CVF before it, it was ideologically objectionable but also because it was administratively and technically incompetent and was thought to be the seat of enormous graft.

It soon became evident to the Institute that both the financial arrangements with the contractor and the whole construction program and plant design were very deficient.[11] Having assessed the extent of the deficiencies, the Institute had to decide whether to find a new contractor over whom more control could be exercised and with whom better terms could be negotiated, or whether this would lead to so great a loss of time that it would be better to stay with the current contractor. In January 1959 the elected government of Rómulo Betancourt took office, and an immediate legislative investigation was ordered into the contractual arrangements for the steel mill. By the time the investigation was completed so much time had been lost that it seemed far less costly to try to renegotiate than to find a new contractor.

The primary tasks facing the Institute up to December 1960, when it was absorbed by the newly created CVG, were the redesign of the mill and the renegotiation of the contract. That the Institute contributed little to the accomplishment of these tasks seems clear; it had only low-level staff representation on the interministerial committee renegotiating the contract, and it failed to propose any major design changes in the mill. The immediate causes of the Institute's ineffectiveness undoubtedly stemmed from the instability of its leadership (the board of directors was changed three times between 1958 and 1960). But the more fundamental causes of the Institute's ineffectiveness grew out of its vulnerability to the political uncertainties of the period. The political turmoil between 1958 and 1960 was a result of the tentative nature of the interim government, the difficulties of establishing for the first time in Venezuela a coalition government after Betancourt's election in 1958, and the several attempts at counterrevolution by the armed forces and the Right. The Institute failed primarily because it was unable to develop an administrative style that could cope with the great political uncertainty, confusion, and change of the time.

As each chapter of Venezuelan history was closed, the CVF, the Office of Special Studies, and the Institute in turn faded from the scene. The flow of history did not carry these agencies forward; rather, it inundated them. Because each agency was so closely identified with the political style of the regime that created it, each was rejected when a new form of government was instituted. The breaks in administrative continuity that were consequences of the political instability severely hampered the job of developing the Guayana.

A Style of Administrative Success: The Corporación Venezolana de Guayana

Against this backdrop of administrative disaster and political turbulence the evolution of the CVG stands out in striking contrast as an unbroken line of constantly increasing power and responsibility since 1953. How was this possible? What did the CVG do that was so different? Essentially it established a politically neutral, technocratic style of operation that enabled it to flourish under widely varying regimes without taking on the political coloration of any one, while at the same time effectively advancing its own programs.

The foundation for a style of political neutrality was laid in 1953 with the creation of the Comisión de Estudios para la Electrificación del Caroní (CEEC), from which the CVG later evolved. For reasons best known to himself, Pérez Jiménez decided that the dam providing power to the Guayana steel mill from the Caroní should be planned and built by a very different kind of organization from the Office of Special Studies (which was building the steel mill). He appointed a young army major, Rafael Alfonzo Ravard, to head the new agency. Alfonzo, in contrast to the head of the Office of Special Studies, was a trained engineer—perhaps one of the best hydraulic and civil engineers in the country at the time. His ambitions were focused on the development of the Caroní and not, as with many successful officers, on the presidential palace.

As a condition for taking the job Alfonzo Ravard evidently extracted from Pérez Jiménez a promise of great freedom of operations for the CEEC, including a large measure of independence from the rest of the government, the freedom to rely on technology rather than bureaucratic politics in making all significant program decisions, and the privilege of keeping staff selection free from outside pressures.[12] The immediate practical consequence of this freedom of operation was the dissociation of the agency from the politics of the Pérez Jiménez regime. Even though the CEEC was only a small office within the Ministry of Development, its plans for the power dam appear never to have been coordinated within that Ministry (for instance, with those offices concerned with the development of a national electric power system) or even with the Office of Special Studies. Because of its bureaucratic independence, the CEEC was under no pressure from conflicting bureaucratic interests to deviate from the principle that technical criteria would determine all major program decisions on the siting and the design of the dam.

Bureaucratic independence and noninvolvement with politics required the CEEC to exercise considerable restraint in the pursuit of its goals. From its earliest days the CEEC had its eye not only on the dam (Macagua I) but also on the eventual development of the whole Caroní River. But while the Macagua Dam was largely a self-contained project—that is, it was tied exclusively to the steel mill—full development of the Caroní would involve basic national decisions on priorities of development investments and on a national power program. Such decisions would clearly involve the CEEC with a host of other governmental agencies. Therefore, although the CEEC continued to explore with its consultants the possibilities for future development of the Caroní, it gave no publicity to these studies and focused its programs solely on the Macagua Dam (which it built on schedule). Since the agency's charter gave it authority for the development of the whole Caroní, this policy reflected not a lack of authority but the restraint that was basic to the CEEC's style. There is ample evidence that the CEEC felt that such restraint was crucial to its style of operations. For instance, in 1955 and 1956, when the Minister of Development finally began to show some interest in the development of Caroní power,[13] the CEEC (itself a part of the Ministry of Development) did not contribute to these plans, evidently preferring to put off its long-range plans until it could realize them on its own bureaucratic terms. This administrative style created among elite groups an image of the CEEC, and especially of Alfonzo Ravard, as honest, technically expert, and nonpartisan.

The political value of this style became clear in 1958. Unlike the Office of Special Studies and the CVF, the CEEC remained intact after a major revolution; and unlike the Institute, the CEEC not only had the authority to pursue its goals vigorously between 1958 and 1960 but also used it to increase greatly its power and independence. But while the CEEC's style of nonpartisanship, integrity, and technical competence was sufficiently different from that of the other three agencies to account for its ability to survive the political upheavals that started with the overthrow of Pérez Jiménez, it cannot account for the greatly increased scope of the CEEC's activities between 1958 and 1960, or for its expansion into the vastly more powerful CVG. The elevation of the Guayana development program to a major national goal took place largely because Betancourt made this a keystone of his policy of economic development. The transformation of the CEEC into the CVG as the instrument of this policy took place largely because the CEEC's style and the political and administrative skills of Alfonzo were well adapted to the reformist proclivities of the new government. In sum, the CEEC's style was superior to that of the other three agencies on two counts: because it was politically neutral, it assured the survival of the organization during a period of great political instability; and because it exhibited integrity and technical and administrative competence, it was an attractive vehicle by which Betancourt could transform the goals of the CEEC—the development of the Guayana—into basic national policy.

The evolution of the CEEC into the CVG and the expansion of the importance of the Guayana took place in stages between 1958 and 1960. The civilian-military junta established as a provisional government in January 1958 moved very cautiously. Instead of initiating vast new reforms, as had the 1945 junta, the 1958 junta acted mainly as a caretaker government, hoping to maintain a semblance of national unity and to avoid a recurrence of a rightist countercoup as in 1948. Only noncontroversial figures enjoying nonpartisan support were acceptable in such a government. Since the military was a major element in the governing junta, officers meeting these qualifications were especially in demand. Alfonzo Ravard clearly qualified on all counts, and so it is not surprising that he was elevated to the presidency of a revitalized CVF, taking with him the CEEC.[14] Although the CVF is nominally under the Ministry of Development, it is a largely independent government corporation and enjoys considerable freedom of action in allocating vast sums of government investment funds. The shifting of the administrative responsibility for the programs in the Guayana from the CEEC to the CVF gave these programs a much higher priority among the nation's basic goals.

Despite the increased national importance of the Guayana, an effort to accelerate its development during the unstable political situation of 1958 might well have failed. In the first place, the program to develop the Guayana was still little known (indeed, its crudest outlines had hardly been sketched). What little public approval it enjoyed derived from vague national aspirations to develop the Guayana rather than from enthusiasm for the specific projects that might be undertaken, such as a large hydroelectric dam. Second, neither the power of the CVF nor Alfonzo's reputation provided sufficient political momentum to launch the full-scale development of the Guayana. In these circumstances an attempt by the CEEC to push vigorously the Guayana's development would doubtless have destroyed the CEEC's claim to noncontroversiality; this was an asset the CEEC had cultivated too carefully to squander for a doubtful result. Getting actual development under way therefore had to await the injection of the new political energy that was made available with the inauguration of Rómulo Betancourt in January 1959.

Betancourt saw the Guayana as a way to a new Venezuela—a modern industrialized nation freed from colonial status, no longer the treasure lode of foreign oil companies.[15] Within six months after he took office Betancourt had created the Presidential Commission (*Comisionado*) for the Development of the Guayana, which became an additional responsibility of Alfonzo Ravard. The purpose of this move was probably twofold: to underscore the importance Betancourt placed on the Guayana's development and to provide the focus for the development of a permanent body to carry out this development program.

Between mid-1959 and late 1960 a charter for this permanent body was drawn up, and on December 30, 1960 the Corporación Venezolana de Guayana was established. The CVG differed from all previous agencies operating in the Guayana in two fundamental respects. First, its objectives as defined by law were among the highest priority goals of the government and as such received a vast amount of popular support. Second, it enjoyed a unique bureaucratic position of great political power; it was the only operational agency attached directly to the President's office.[16]

Betancourt's endowment of the Guayana development program with broad national support in effect removed it from the arena of partisan politics. The precondition for this "depoliticization" was undoubtedly the large area of agreement among the political parties about the nature of the basic tasks facing the nation. This party consensus grew out of the reaction against the repressions of the Pérez Jiménez regime, a reaction so strong that it had led the major parties to pledge to run a unity candidate for president in 1958. Even though this particular pledge broke down, the consensus on goals was largely maintained. In these circumstances Betancourt's task was to present the Guayana development program in such a way as to appeal to this basic party unity. This he accomplished by making the projected heavy industries of the Guayana the key to national industrialization, which in turn could bring economic independence from foreign oil interests. The CVG was thus the beneficiary of powerful and basic national desires. This enormous reservoir of popular support is the ultimate source of the great power the Corporation has built up since 1960. As will be discussed, an important aspect of the Corporation's administrative style is finding the limits of this popular support and operating within these limits.

The task that faced the drafters of the Corporation's charter was to convert the potential power of Betancourt's endorsement of the Guayana program into actual bureaucratic power. The chief hurdle was interagency relations: relations between a geographically defined agency with broad functional responsibilities and the functionally defined ministries, and between a powerful nonpartisan body and the politically powerful and partisan ministries. The CVG's charter was highly equivocal on this crucial conflict, burying its resolution in the statement that the Corporation was to "coordinate"[17] the activities of all agencies working in the Guayana. Nevertheless the Corporation's charter was drawn up so as to give it later the freedom largely to exclude other government agencies from the policymaking aspects of the Guayana's development.

The Corporation's power was thus founded on the marrying of two potent political assets: a highly successful administrative style and the identification of the Guayana's development with the most deeply felt nationalist sentiments of Venezuela. But the very forces of style and consensus that created the Corporation also defined the kinds of plans and programs that it could undertake and the way in which they could be carried out. By analyzing the Corporation's administrative style some light may be shed on the intricate links between "technical objectivity" and political reality, and some insight gained into the importance to national development of a successful resolution of these potentially conflicting tendencies.

One way that the CVG adapted its style to reflect the new status of the Guayana development program was by rejecting programs that had only regional significance. The identification of the Corporation as the spokesman for the purely regional problems of the Guayana would have seriously threatened its nonpartisanship. As the success of Venezuela's first regional development effort became evident to other regions, numerous regional development agencies sprang up. The largest of these, in the Venezuelan equivalent of Appalachia—the Andes region—was even explicitly modeled on the CVG. Because different parties are dominant in different regions, regional competition for government funds and for location of industries has become a subject of party politics in recent years. Only by keeping aloof from the purely regional problems of the Guayana is the CVG able to stay above this political bickering and continue to assert successfully the high national priority of its own huge investment programs and industrialization efforts. The Corporation has resisted regional pressures, for instance, on its policies for land use, industrial location, and urban and regional development that in its view would divert these policies from their basic national purpose. The Corporation has tended to view proposals for action on local and regional problems that were not coincident with its broader national aims as inspired by partisan political aims.

Threats to the Corporation's policy of noninvolvement in partisan politics have come from other quarters as well. Under Venezuela's system of coalition government (operating since 1958) individual ministries are controlled by one of the coalition parties, with a result that major areas of national policy (for example, agrarian reform) have become identified with one party rather than with the program of the whole administration. Interministerial politics have become interparty politics. From the CVG's point of view, this has meant that the identification of any part of its programs with the policies of another ministry could well involve it overtly in party politics. Maintenance of the strictly nonpartisan and noncontroversial image of the Guayana program has therefore strongly tended to inhibit effective cooperation between the Corporation and other agencies. Even though the effects of this lack of cooperation have been somewhat offset by the personal liaison Alfonzo has maintained with ministers and agency heads, the Corporation has found it increasingly difficult to maintain this policy as its programs have moved from the planning to the implementation stage. For example, the Corporation has found it hard to get funds, particularly in the area of urban development, for projects that are fundamentally the responsibility of other government agencies. Because of this it has had either to neglect its own programs or to secure the active cooperation of other ministries to carry them out. In the area of public schools for Ciudad Guayana, the unpalatability of both alternatives led the Corporation to temporize with a series of rather unsatisfactory expedients before it decided that it would have to begin planning for public education in cooperation with the Ministry of Education.

The desire to undertake only noncontroversial programs has led the Corporation to search out development possibilities it might otherwise have ignored. Providing the burgeoning new city with a local food supply could have involved it in the highly volatile and partisan problems of agrarian reform. It has therefore been trying to develop an alternative, one more congenial to its administrative style, by exploring the possibility of large-scale commercial food production in the Orinoco Delta region. Such a program not only would go a long way toward solving the food supply problems of Ciudad Guayana but also would be large enough to become a major factor in the national agricultural economy. Because the delta region is remote and uninhabited, this program would probably be outside the scope of national agrarian reform. Since the chief problem of food production in the delta is drainage, it calls most for the skills that the Corporation can best provide—hydraulic engineering—and least for the skills that it is least able to provide—solving the social and economic problems of the peasants. The Orinoco Delta program thus has the great advantages of relying principally on technology, of being yet another major program of national scope, and of requiring minimum coordination with other government agencies.

The Corporation's conception of its coordinating power has significantly influenced the direction and content of many of its programs. It has interpreted its powers of coordination in the Guayana as defining a hierarchic, not an equalitarian, relationship. Since the Corporation has the basic responsibility for regional development, coordinated action is achieved, in its view, when other agencies follow the plans and general development strategy it has devised. Thus, insofar as other agencies have been active in the development of the Guayana (for instance, the Ministry of Public Works in road building), the Corporation has tried to limit their activities to program implementation and to exclude them from any long-range planning. This can be seen most clearly in the Corporation's great reluctance, almost refusal, to reveal in any detail its plans for action beyond the current year to virtually any outside body. The only major exception to this rule has been the national planning agency (Oficina

Central de Coordinación y Planificación—Cordiplan). However, Cordiplan's influence on the Corporation's plans has been minimal, largely because Cordiplan has been preoccupied with politically more urgent tasks.

As the CVG has moved outside the area of its technical competence, however, its need to secure agreement on longer-range plans has become increasingly urgent, despite its aversion to coordinated planning. For example, the Corporation for several years did little about public education in Ciudad Guayana. Rather than committing itself to building a public school system or turning the job over to the Ministry of Education, the Corporation provided some support to parochial schools. When it recognized the inadequacy of this policy, the Corporation undertook a study of the city's educational needs and simultaneously began very gingerly to discuss with the Ministry of Education an acceptable division of responsibility for major decisions about public education. It was forced to modify, but it refused to abandon, that conception of the power of coordination that has been essential to the maintenance of its administrative style.[18]

The freedom from bureaucratic and political interference that the Corporation's administrative style has achieved ensures that technical considerations will have the predominant influence in policy decisions. Like the CEEC before it, the CVG follows essentially the courses fixed by expert studies in making and executing policy decisions for its principal programs. The improved technical quality of decisions is one advantage of this style of policymaking and execution. Of equal importance is that it permits the Corporation to reap the benefits that the great popular appeal of modern technology can bestow in a developing country.

The expansion of the Guayana programs after 1960 found the Corporation without the expert knowledge necessary for such unfamiliar tasks as urban planning, industrial development, and steel mill operations. To meet this problem the Corporation chose to employ a large number of foreign consultants on long-term contracts. However, this decision raised the old problem of controlling a large number of technical consultants. The failure to solve this problem and the consequent enslavement to superior outside technology had been an important factor in the administrative and technological failings of the Corporation's predecessor agencies in the Guayana. The CVF's neglect of the possibilities of an electric reduction process, and the Office of Special Studies' mismanagement of the steel mill's design and construction were both in large measure attributable to the lack of adequate technical staff expertise. The CVG's general solution to the problem of controlling its consultants has been rigorously to exclude all but their very highest echelon from access to, and often information about, basic policy decisions. It has also been particularly careful to limit severely the contacts of its consultants with other government agencies. The extreme delicacy of interagency relations is not in itself the principal factor in this attitude; probably most important is the view that technology is and should be politically neutral. If a public agency can show that its decisions simply reflect the technologically best choice, it stands a good chance of sustaining public belief in its nonpartisanship. On the other hand, Venezuelan nationalism is such as to discredit any otherwise acceptable government action that is shown to be strongly influenced by foreigners, even if they are technical consultants. Technology is politically neutral and powerful only when it is indigenously controlled. The CVG has therefore not only kept its foreign consultants under strict rein but has also largely kept from public view the extent to which it is influenced by these consultants. The successful control of foreign consultants has been critically important in sustaining the nonpartisan appeal of technology, which in turn has been a major factor in retaining the wide popular support for the Guayana development program. Technology and the effort to ensure its indigenous control have thus been primary influences shaping the Corporation's administrative style.

Conclusions

The administrative style of the Guayana Corporation has been the means by which the political "energy" of consensus and technology has been harnessed to the task of developing the Guayana. The Corporation could use this political "energy," however, only so long as it acted in a largely noncontroversial and nonpartisan manner. In this light the process by which the Corporation constructed its administrative style can also be seen as the continuing effort to establish an acceptable division of labor, or *modus vivendi*, between the Corporation and partisan elements in politics. For example, other parts of the government, such as the President (or in the case of an explosive steelworkers' strike, the Minister of Labor), take the role of public defender for the Corporation. In return, other parts of the government, usually the President, reap the benefits of the favorable publicity resulting from the accomplishments in the Guayana. The great care that must be taken to prevent the programs in the Guayana from becoming partisan issues leads the CVG to focus on technical and not on "people" problems. "People" problems, such as agrarian reform, public education, and social welfare (all of which are involved in the Guayana's development), clearly are of potentially much greater political volatility than the farming of uninhabited regions or the smelting of iron ore. Finally, the Corporation must refrain from challenging the programs or public positions of any of the major political parties. This requires the Corporation to seek anonymity and to eschew public relations campaigns for the Guayana program, so that it does not appear to be establishing a basis of popular support that would threaten the popular strength of the parties. (Indeed, the Corporation has sought anonymity so assiduously that the nature of what it is planning to do is only vaguely realized by even well-informed Venezuelans.) To exercise power the Corporation had to establish an administrative style that embraced anonymity and noncontroversiality, and to practice political neutrality through technical objectivity.

Insofar as Venezuela is a representative underdeveloped country, it is clear that the political instability seemingly characteristic of these countries creates special difficulties for the maintenance of sustained development efforts. The administrative style of the CVG, to the extent that it has overcome the difficulties created by political instability, therefore represents a high order of political skills. It is not an improbable freak but a logical, if uncommon,[19] expression of Venezuelan politics. This is not to say that the Corporation has completely "solved" the problem of political neutrality. Although the staff of the Corporation places great value on technical objectivity and efficiency, the individual staff members tend to range from the center to the conservative side of the political spectrum. Not unnaturally, the Corporation's style of political neutrality tends in the conservative direction. If the interparty consensus on basic national issues were to break down (a real possibility), or if a radical leftist government were to come to power, the Corporation would be quite unlikely to continue in its present form.

Chapter 17

The Computer-
Based Economic
Planning System

William Morsch

In the early stages of planning the Guayana's development, the important tasks were to establish a steel industry on a sound economic footing,
initiate efforts leading to development of the hydroelectric potential of
the Caroní River (now being realized in the construction of the Guri
Dam), and identify other areas of potential resource development. At the
same time it became apparent that the whole complex of urban infrastructure (as opposed to industrial infrastructure) for a modern industrial
city was needed, and the Corporación Venezolana de Guayana (CVG)
began devoting an increasing amount of its attention to solving these
problems. This in turn led to additional economic planning activities, such
as the analysis of consumer expenditures in the city and of light industry
requirements. Thus the economic planning task has become increasingly
complex, both in its scope (the range of separate economic activities considered) and in its detail (the number of distinct elements relating to each
activity).

The first studies, a series of feasibility analyses for guiding development
efforts, provided the basis for the initial plan. This plan consisted of little
more than a list of production projections to 1975 and 1980 in selected
sectors, direct employment in those sectors, and the implied total employment in the urban complex.

For the second plan,[1] this methodology was refined by using projections
of family income and expenditures based on a detailed survey of household
income and expenditures made in December 1962[2] to obtain direct estimates of employment in the Guayana consumer goods industries. In

addition, a series of studies on resources had eliminated virtually all minerals development possibilities other than iron. The effect was to shift development and promotional activities to iron- and steel-oriented industries—with renewed interest in studies on prereduction processes. These new processes were projected at output levels that essentially made up for the losses in employment resulting from the dropping of other minerals projects. Finally, a series of studies on transportation that became available in March 1963 showed that adequate transportation facilities would be available for foreseeable levels of development, so that the CVG would not have to concern itself with possible bottlenecks in this sector.

The third plan,[3] produced in 1965, used income-elasticity projections of consumer expenditures to obtain better estimates of demand and employment in consumer goods industries, investment requirements for each of thirty or forty industries, and projections of induced construction employment generated by these investment requirements. In contrast to previous plans, these variables were estimated for each year from 1965 to 1975 in order to evaluate the effects of annual variations in investment on employment. The third plan also incorporated for the first time a detailed financing plan for each sector that indicated the possible sources of investment funds and gave some indication of the net inflows of funds that would be required.[4]

More important than the improved methodology of the third plan, however, was the negative aspect of long and cumbersome procedures required to develop the plan. Work was begun in October 1964, and the plan was completed in June 1965. While this may seem a very short time to national planners, it should be recalled that the CVG economic planning group has few problems of coordination with other agencies and that the planning drew heavily on previously prepared studies.

The basic information used in the Guayana plans has come from a series of studies carried out over the period 1961–1966, most of which related to specific facets of the Guayana economy. The extent and content of this literature may be illustrated by the résumé of studies of the Guayana conducted by the Joint Center given in Table 17.1. The coordination of this body of information in itself proved to be one of the most formidable tasks encountered in preparing the plan.

The problem was the increasing size of the plan, which by 1965 encompassed some sixty economic sectors, each requiring some thirty types of data. With this number of sectors it was not feasible to consider more than a relatively few economic interactions, nor was it feasible, for example, to consider both a "firm" plan and a "potential" plan (which we shall discuss

TABLE 17.1
Guayana Economic Studies

Subject	Number of Studies
Population, employment, and income	14
Industry and promotion	13
Natural resources development	11
Transportation	9
General development	8
Investment requirements, public and private	7
Housing	6
Agriculture and forestry	5
Educational and manpower requirements	4
Household consumption	4
Total	81

later). Even more important, it was impractical to test the impact of alternative plans for investment by the Corporation itself.

Another important weakness of the planning methodology was that it could not be easily adapted by the Venezuelan staff in the CVG. This was regarded by some as the major shortcoming of the economic planning effort. No formal, systematic approach to planning had been developed; rather, the studies listed in Table 17.1 tended to be utilized on an ad hoc basis as requirements arose. While Venezuelan staff members could and did participate in most phases of the plan preparation, the lack of a formal methodology for over-all plan preparation was leaving a serious gap in Venezuelan planning capabilities.

These problems led planners to consider data processing as a possible solution. Not only would such a system permit more extensive use of the available data and of improved methodology but it would also constitute a valuable tool that could easily be passed on to Venezuelan planners.

Requirements of a Planning System for the CVG

The Guayana planning system necessarily had to take account of a number of limitations, such as the readily available computing capacity,[5] the amount of data available, and the technical level of assistance. The most fundamental determinant, however, was the context within which the user, the CVG, worked.

The instruments available to the Corporation are quite different from those available to a national government. For example, the Corporation exercises essentially no instruments for directly affecting trade with the rest of Venezuela and the world, the level or composition of household expenditures (with the notable exception of housing), prices, interest rates, or (aside from subsidiaries) production. The Corporation can make direct investments in enterprises, promote or encourage industrial investment by private enterprise, and coordinate and attempt to obtain investment by other governmental agencies, such as the Ministries of Public Works, of Education, and of Health and Social Assistance. Furthermore, it can extend loans, and it can seek to supplement its share of the Venezuelan national budget through international financing agencies such as the World Bank. As industrial development proceeds, the Corporation is compelled either to invest directly or to obtain investment in housing and governmental infrastructure and to encourage development of the necessary human resources by making grants to local schools and by assisting in the coordination and planning of special training courses. One important measure of the CVG's success is the amount of "leverage" obtained with its limited funds—the amount of funds invested in the Guayana by all other sources, private and public, compared with the amount of the CVG's own funds that must be invested.

Since the CVG operates within the context of the Venezuelan national plan, its decisions and plans must be clearly related to the requirements of that plan, and its contribution to national growth must be explicit. The final requirement was that the new planning system would be capable of effectively utilizing the large body of data developed for previous plans.

These factors all tended to indicate, more or less directly, the characteristics that a computer-based system should possess and the manner in which planning personnel should interact with it.

1. Production levels, imports, and exports should be specified directly by the planner.

2. Capabilities for reflecting extensive detail on financial data should be included, so that financial resources could be specified by the planner where appropriate.

3. Although physical investment would be provided directly by the planner, its effects vary with the type of investment, so extensive detail concerning it should be included.

4. Since the Corporation does not attempt to influence household consumption expenditures, these expenditures should be computed internally rather than be provided from outside the system (the usual procedure in making economic projections).

5. Physical requirements for manpower, housing, and urban infrastructure should be provided as an output for use by physical and educational planners.

6. Constant prices should be assumed.

7. The model should be organized on an industry-project basis so that specific projects of interest to the CVG could be considered, as well as industry aggregates, in conformity with previous planning practices.

8. It should be possible to express results in national income accounting terms in order to integrate them with the *Plan de la Nación*.

9. The majority of the data in the model should remain fixed so that alternative plans could be developed with a minimum of data change.

Two additional "desirables," if not requirements, were made possible through the use of a computing model:

1. Any datum in the system would be easy to alter, in the strictly physical sense.

2. We would be able to express the widest possible variety of economic "submodels." In particular, we would be able to allow for increasing returns to scale to reflect the fact that so many Guayana industries are "infant" industries.

The Development of the Computer-Based System

The conceptual framework that seemed most appropriate to meet these requirements was a regionally oriented Leontief input-output model,[6] with a number of modifications that will be described. Such a model permits the inclusion of as much or as little sectoral detail on the regional economy as desired (bearing in mind that we wanted to serve the CVG's interests as opposed to those of the national planning agency) or as data permitted; in particular, an input-output model could be designed to utilize almost all the data developed in previous studies. Our approach was to utilize the computer to integrate within a general input-output framework a number of the economists' simpler mathematical models and to develop their interrelationships numerically rather than through an all-encompassing mathematical formulation. Taken together, such a group of simple models provides results that it would not be feasible to integrate into a single mathematical model.

The set of accounts in Table 17.2 reflects the Guayana planning requirements but is at the same time compatible with the Venezuelan national income accounts. The left side of Table 17.2 lists the elements included in the physical flows of goods and services, and the right indicates the elements of financial flows. Corresponding to each physical flow is the offsetting flow of funds; thus for each input of a physical good or service there is a corresponding outflow of funds. In addition, for financing elements, there are flows of funds without corresponding movements of physical goods. Depreciation and retained earnings do not appear explicitly but are the residual after all other expenses and disbursements on current account, including equipment replacement expenditures; this residual is thus the internally generated fund available for investment.

The organization by industrial sector generally follows previous CVG

TABLE 17.2
The Guayana Planning System Accounts

Product and Service Accounts		Financial Accounts	
Requirements	Availabilities	Sources of Funds	Uses of Funds
Intermediate inputs	*Production	Value of production	Intermediate purchases
Final demands	*Imports		Wages and salaries
Household consumption	from Venezeula		Direct taxes
*Investment	from abroad		*Indirect taxes
Government	*Transfers		*Interest
Inventory change			*Rents and concession payments
*Exports			Imports
to Venezuela			*Dividends
foreign		*Loans (including CVG)	*Amortization
		*Direct investment (including CVG)	Physical investment
			Additions to inventories
			Increases in reserves

Note: The accounts marked (*) are provided directly by the planner. Other data are derived from these, either directly or through the industry structure. Product accounts are maintained in physical, as well as monetary, terms where applicable. "Government" as a final demand refers to public services provided in the region. "Increases in reserves" is a residual after subtracting payments on current account (above the line) from "Value of production."

planning, but with greater reliance on United Nations definitions. Where necessary, classification at the project level is provided, since many individual industrial projects weigh very heavily in their economic impacts on the Guayana region. This industry-project form of specification has distinct advantages from the point of view of data availability. When an industry level of aggregation is used, data are usually available from a number of Venezuelan and U.S. sources. In many cases, however, quite detailed data exist and are, furthermore, specific to the particular project under consideration as a result of the earlier studies.

The industrial sectors also reflect the requirements of the using organization by providing extensive detail when relevant to decision making and by avoiding excessive detail when it would not be useful. In many sectors the Corporation may simply assume that the necessary investments will be undertaken (for example, wholesale and retail trade), while in others it must become heavily, and sometimes directly, involved (agricultural development) or take the major initiative (housing).

Usually planners develop a list of final demands that is then utilized to derive appropriate production levels. In our system, however, production plans are the key element and are taken as the starting point in analyzing the plan. Three reasons for this approach can be cited:

1. In the Guayana region, as in most developing countries, the key problem is one of production rather than of meeting some prespecified set of final demands.[7] Furthermore, production targets for key sectors are set by the national plan.

2. We can include the largest component of final demand, that is, households, in the structure of our model. Sufficient data are available on household consumption to permit the construction of a fairly reliable set of consumption coefficients (described in more detail later).

3. Most planners find it quite easy to work with production as the variable to be controlled.

Working from these production plans (plus the other requirements and availabilities that the planner provides directly, as shown in Table 17.2), we can determine the set of inputs that the plan implies. These are automatically computed through sets of input coefficients once the production plan is stipulated. Thus if production plans are to be met, certain inputs will be required; the inability of the system to provide these requirements results in unbalanced plans. For example, if we plan production in 1975 of 3 million tons of steel this might imply a need for 4.5 million tons of iron ore—but if we plan ore production for the same year to be 3.5 million tons, then our targets are obviously inconsistent, that is, the plan will be unbalanced.

The economic process consists of constantly attempting to achieve physical and financial balances. Therefore we wanted our model to tell us (a) whether over-all requirements for physical goods and services are matched by the over-all supply—either from production or from imports into the region, (b) whether the total sources of funds available to the region balance the total uses of funds—primarily to establish that investment plans are realistic in terms of available funds, and (c) whether the Guayana is in balance with the "rest of world," since, after allowing for outflows of funds from the region, adequate funds must be available both to operate the Guayana economy and to permit fulfillment of the investment plans.

The system outlined here imposes considerable discipline on the planning process. Annual production levels set by the planner may not exceed capacity levels, but to raise capacity levels the planner must lay out an investment program in terms of physical resource requirements, lead times, and manpower development. These requirements in turn must be matched by financial resources through direct investment, loans from outside the region, or internally generated funds of existing sectors. The planner must specify each step in this process.

The system does not attempt to arrive at a mathematically optimal plan, but rather is intended to show and evaluate, in a consistent way, the implications of the planners' own decisions. The planner provides a set of production and investment plans for each sector, year by year. The computer program takes these plans and, multiplying by coefficients that specify the amounts of inputs each sector requires for a unit of output, obtains the required inputs. The input requirements are summed by producing industry, for comparison with that industry's production levels. If there are inequalities, the planner modifies the planned production levels, exports, and/or imports. Eventually a set of consistent production plans is obtained.

Preparation of the first computer plan. In preparing the first computer-produced plan we attempted to use the data that had been utilized in the June 1965 Guayana plan, partly for convenience but also because of our interest in comparing the results provided by the new system with those provided by the old. For many purposes, however, new types of data were required. Since input coefficients, except for employment, had not been used in previous planning, it was necessary to develop an entire set of these over a relatively short period. Some data from the June 1965 plan were reanalyzed and expanded in detail to take advantage of the capabilities of the data processor. These changes included the following:

1. The year 1980 was added to the plan, so that the years 1965–1975 and 1980 were covered.

2. For the years 1971–1975 and 1980 we prepared two plans, one representing the "firm" prospects for development and the other a "potential" plan. In the firm plan we included projects now in being and projects whose promotion and development were sufficiently well advanced that the likelihood of their being carried through to completion is very high. The potential plan added projects or stipulated production levels that are economically justified and have been recommended, but for which the plans were not yet sufficiently well advanced to give them a likelihood of realization.

3. Production and export projections in only eight sectors provide the basis of the Guayana economy; these basic sectors are steel, sponge iron, taconite, iron-ore mining, aluminum, wood pulp, fabricated metal products, and electric power. Therefore, previous production targets for these sectors were evaluated and brought up to date.

4. The ouputs of the other sectors were assumed to be a direct response to the derived demands generated by employment and output in the basic sectors. In each of these other sectors, estimates were made of the extent to which demands will be met by local production and imports. (In some cases an economic scale of production permitting some exports was assumed.)

5. The very important construction sector was directly estimated as a subcategory of investment.

Preparation of input-output coefficients. The difficulties of input-output coefficient preparation can be quite extensive because of their rather technical nature. In a simple economy such as that of Ciudad Guayana, however, the most important relationship is that of labor input per unit of production, from which we can derive employment and from which the model can compute household expenditures automatically. From a variety of sources, these and other coefficients can be inferred if not directly derived. Some of these sources are indicated in Table 17.3. Other sources included ministerial planning factors and eastern Venezuela census data.

Investment projections. No satisfactory way of automatically computing investment requirements in our system seemed satisfactory, despite the

TABLE 17.3
Major Sector Data Sources

Sector	Per Cent[a]	Input Coefficients	Production Projections	Investment Programs
Iron-ore mining	28.1	Operating results	Previous plan targets	Accelerator[e]
Steel	22.0	Operating results	Sidor[b] projections and previous plans	Sidor[b] investment program
Taconite	10.0	Feasibility study	Feasibility study	Feasibility study
Wholesale and retail trade	5.2	U.S. input-output table	Internally generated	Accelerator[e]
Electric power generation	5.2	Feasibility study	Edelca[c] projections	Edelca[c] investment program
Construction	4.0	Contract analysis	Internally generated[d]	Accelerator[e]
Housing finance	4.0	U.S. input-output table	Internally generated	None
State and local government	3.0	Operating budget	Budget projections within the sector	Budgeted investments
Sponge iron	2.9	Feasibility study	Feasibility study	Feasibility study
Natural gas distribution	1.6	Feasibility study	Feasibility study	Feasibility study
Total	86.0			

a. Per cent of total projected value added in the Guayana economy in 1975.
b. Siderúrgica de Orinoco, the Guayana steel manufacturing complex.
c. Electrificación del Caroní, the CVG subsidiary responsible for developing the hydroelectric potential of the Guayana region.
d. Based on total of all other sector investment plans.
e. Based on investment per dollar sales, U.S. data, times the change in total sales.

enormous appeal that such a "dynamic" model might offer. The models that might be considered are those using capital-output ratios to generate automatically the additional investment implied by the output targets specified by the planners.[8] The difficulty with this approach is that it is inappropriate at the detailed project level characterizing the Guayana economic plan. In such cases the existing capital structure assumes such importance in investment decisions that the mechanical application of coefficients is simply not adequate. For example, in the iron-ore mining sector we find that capacity in mining operations (representing 6.9 per cent of the total investment in the sector) is about 18.5 million tons of iron ore annually, the railroad capacity (representing 33.6 per cent of total investment) could move 30 million tons of ore annually, and facilities (representing 17.5 per cent of total investment) could house the labor force that would be required to mine 20 million tons of ore annually. Obviously future investment patterns in this industry will be more complex than would be implied by a simple capital-output ratio.

Although a number of methodological approaches were utilized to refine earlier investment estimates, one major innovation arose directly from the possibility of utilizing a data-processing system to incorporate more detail. This was the preparation of investment plans in terms of their input components, time-phased by year. This in turn assured us that there *was* an investment plan for each sector, as opposed to the less precise statement of investment need; and that if there were changes in circumstances (such as the sharp decline in iron-ore output during 1960–1963) the investment program could be shifted in total to a new date. Since this more detailed investment planning was required in the new system, it led to closer evaluation and projection of anticipated investment and in some cases to a scaling down of previous projections.

Households. Including households within the input-output structure requires only that each income level have its appropriate set of "input coefficients," that is, distribution of household expenditures. The data of the household expenditures survey of 1962 included expenditures on some 450 items, which were summarized into 33 categories corresponding to the sectors in our model. From these summarized data we were able to establish expenditure coefficients for eight income groups.

Household income is determined by sectoral levels of production. Since each sector has labor as one of its inputs, the corresponding outflow of funds becomes household income.

In the case of housing, the CVG planners attempt to influence housing expenditures, so the model uses a "target" coefficient provided by them.

It is thought that households would spend this "target" percentage of their incomes on housing if financing were available; programs to provide such financing are pursued by the CVG.

Urbanization, land, housing, and housing finance. Because of the importance of urban development to the CVG, several relatively small sectors were established to permit focusing on certain aspects of it. Each of these is discussed briefly in order to show how the usual input-output structure can be expanded to emphasize areas of special interest in a particular planning context.

The CVG owns virtually all the raw land surrounding Ciudad Guayana. From the beginning it has attempted to utilize this land as an instrument for promoting the growth of the city by offering urbanized land to builders and individuals under favorable financing conditions and by offering raw industrial sites to industrial investors. The Corporation had been confronted with the problem of determining how much land to release to purchasers; too much would encourage undesirable speculation, while too little would retard growth.

Projections of land requirements would provide a useful guide in making decisions about land use. These projections are provided by the "land" sector. Requirements for land are generated by projected construction of industrial, commercial, institutional, and residential space. Land requirements for the first three are obtained by using simple coefficients that convert meters of space to meters of raw land.

Residential land is developed by the CVG and thus requires substantial CVG investment. Because of these commitments, a special analysis of the sector's input was made in order to lend more credibility to cost figures and thus provide projections of funding requirements for urbanization. Raw land requirements by type of housing were also generated. With this information the CVG can complete financial and contractual arrangements far enough in advance to assure the availability of both raw and urbanized land when needed.

We have already noted the CVG's special interest in housing. To reflect this interest we established five housing sectors corresponding to five income levels for whom specific types of housing are planned. Since each type has different inputs, shifts in demand will have varying economic impacts that can be reflected in the over-all plan.

As a final note, a special sector, "housing finance," was established as a collection point for household expenditures on housing. This, matched with household investments in new housing, reflected the net demand for mortgage funds from outside the region.

Results from the Computer-Based System

Plans under both "firm" and "potential" hypotheses were prepared to 1980. Operationally the "potential" plan can be generated as a relatively simple addition to the "firm" plan, but because of the highly speculative nature of the "potential" plan, little effort was expended in resolving its many inconsistencies; furthermore, because of our interest in "calibrating" the model, the continuous period 1965–1975 was emphasized. It is the plan for this period that we shall compare with the previous Guayana plan (that of June 1965) and whose further development by the Economics Section of the CVG we shall trace.

Since a "plan" consists of some 145 pages of computer printouts, a complete analysis is not feasible in this limited space. What we shall do is examine differences between the June 1965 plan and the first computer-based plan (June 1966) in terms of two key variables—employment and investment.[9] We single out employment for discussion because a stable, growing level of employment in Guayana is a key objective of the CVG, and we select investment because the CVG may vary its own direct investments as a means of achieving its objectives.

Investment projections were lower in the first computer plan as a result of applying the investment planning criteria described earlier. This downward revision of investment targets was further accentuated by the simultaneous reduction of many production targets and the elimination of some projects altogether. The effects of these many adjustments are shown in Figure 17.1, where total investment under the two plans is compared. As can be seen, the later investment levels are substantially below those of the June 1965 plan.

The effects on employment can also be clearly seen in Figure 17.1, where the two employment projections are increasingly divergent. In terms of annual impacts, the June 1965 plan overlooked the effects of fluctuations in investment on employment, apparently because of the limited number of interactions that could be traced through the economy with the previous methodology. For example, the very sharp decline in investment from 1967 to 1968 occurs in both plans but was reflected in the June 1965 plan by only a moderate slackening in the growth of employment, and the decline from 1971 to 1972 produced a similar difference in effects.

Turning to the problem of imbalances, it was simply not feasible, using a manual system, to interrelate fully the goods and services side of the Guayana economy with the financing side; nor, indeed, was it practical to develop over-all requirements for goods and services so that they could be compared with planned availabilities. The production and investment

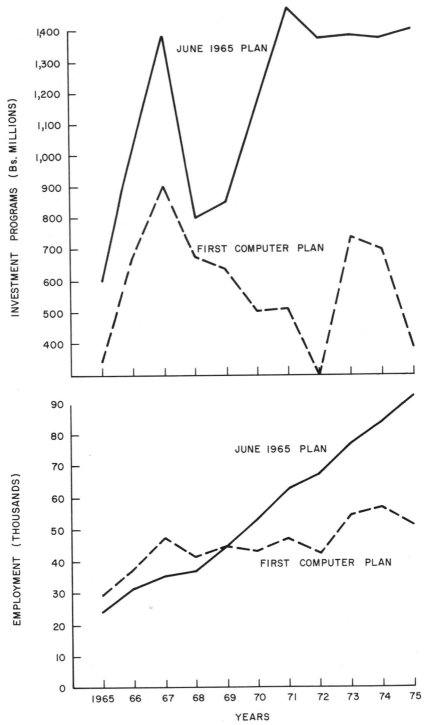

FIGURE 17.1 Investment and employment projections: comparison of June 1965 plan and first computer plan (June 1966).

levels projected in the June 1965 plan implied several inconsistencies in the apparent flows of funds to and from the region, a fact that had been recognized in a qualitative way as a result of earlier studies (in August 1965). However, effective tools for dealing with these inconsistencies were lacking at that time, and no formal solution was developed. To the extent, then, that the data of the June 1965 plan were utilized in the first computer plan, the imbalances of the latter were simply a reflection of those of the June 1965 plan and thus provide some insight into that plan's inconsistencies.

It is clear, looking at the imbalances plotted in Figure 17.2, that the lack of a production balance implies the necessity of increases in production levels where shortages exist, reduction of export goals in order to reduce intermediate requirements, or increases in imports. These types of modifications will serve, in turn, to offset part of the large excesses in balances of regional payments and available investment funds. While this excess in investment funds is partly attributable to the sharp decreases in investment compared to the June 1965 plan, the balances exceed the differences in investment levels between the two plans. From this we concluded that more fundamental balance problems existed. In particular, we found that transfers (dividends paid from depreciation reserves) by iron-ore mining companies far exceeded the level assumed in the previous plan. There is, in addition, a much stronger tendency for all sectors to accumulate reserves than had been previously assumed; in previous planning it was assumed that all depreciation funds were automatically reinvested in physical assets, an assumption that runs counter to the experience of some of the larger sectors in the region over the 1960–1965 period.

It would thus seem that the June 1965 plan was not feasible. This infeasibility was a result of the various imbalances that it produced; these in turn are due to the fact that production in the region cannot reach the levels originally assumed, nor, more basically, can it reach the levels implied by total requirements. It was infeasible also in the sense that the physical investments necessary to reach the projected production levels would not be matched by the necessary financial resources.

In summary, the June 1965 plan presented two problems: the lack of balances in key variables, and excessive fluctuations in key variables. The computer system provided a mechanism for dealing with these problems, and it is to this aspect that we now turn.

The first adjustment sought was the matching of our employment estimate for 1965 to an estimate of employment based on a survey conducted early that year. The survey-based figure of 25,000 was considerably

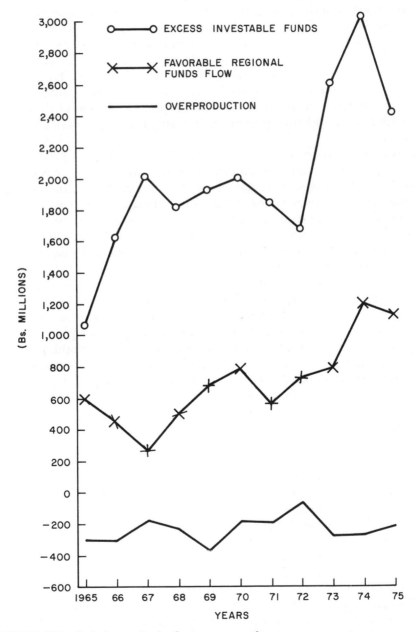

FIGURE 17.2   Imbalances in the first computer plan.

below the 28,955 figure generated by the first computer plan. Substantial reductions in the production requirements balances brought the employment figure generated by the model somewhat closer to the survey figure. The greater portion of the difference, however, could be resolved only by concluding that the levels of production that had been previously assumed for 1965 were too high, and that a higher proportion of goods and services had been imported than had been estimated in the June 1965 plan. Scaling down production levels, along with the reduction of imbalances for 1965, eventually gave us an acceptable 1965 employment of 25,315 in the second computer plan.

One investment program alone, that of the steel mill, was found to be generating the major part of the fluctuation in total regional investment. Since the steel mill had, concurrently with the preparation of the second computer plan, taken steps to postpone or eliminate major portions of its proposed investment program, this new plan was incorporated in the second computer plan. The resulting total investment figures are shown graphically in Figure 17.3. Whereas the annual investment levels in the first computer plan averaged Bs. 581 million, with a standard deviation of Bs. 271 million, the corresponding figures in the second computer plan were Bs. 493 million and Bs. 161 million, respectively.

With this new investment plan and other minor changes, substantial smoothing in the total Guayana plan was achieved. In particular, fluctuations in employment were substantially reduced. (See Figure 17.3.)

The foregoing analyses are but a small sample of the range of studies and evaluations that were possible with the data generated by the computer-based planning system. The purpose here has been primarily to show that there are significant differences between the results produced by the present computer-based planning system and those produced by the former system, and to show that these differences are a result of the more complete analyses possible with the present system.

The question of whether the planning system can be utilized by CVG staff members is answered by the improvements in the second computer plan as compared with the first. The reduction in imbalances, the attainment of the correct 1965 employment level, and the reduction of employment fluctuations were all accomplished, unassisted, by the CVG staff; there was a smooth transition from heavy dependence on outside consultants to reliance on Venezuelan staff economists. The new planning system has apparently provided an effective means of organizing planning activities, and data requirements are unambiguous and explicit, thus providing clear direction for planning efforts.

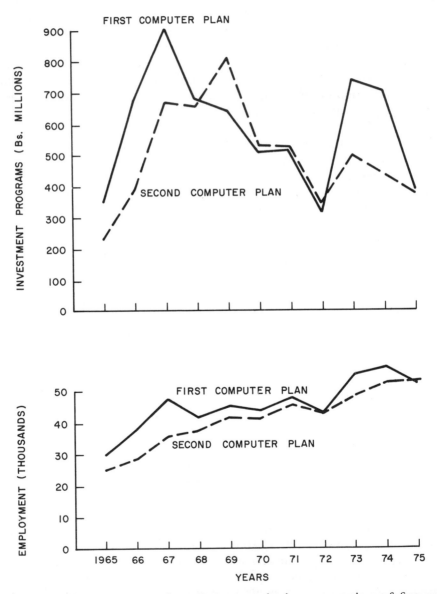

FIGURE 17.3 Investment and employment projections: comparison of first and second computer plans.

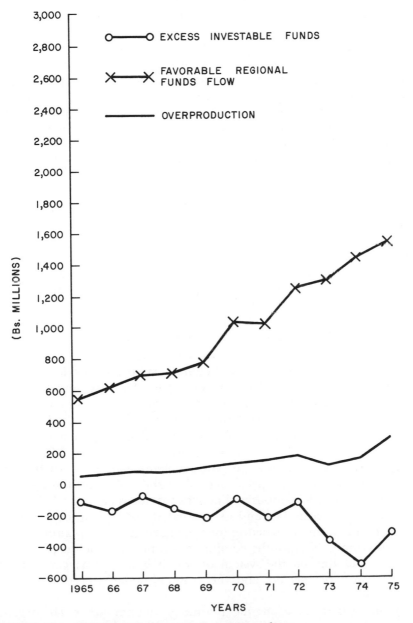

FIGURE 17.4   Imbalances in the second computer plan.

The problem of achieving balances proved to be substantially more difficult than had been expected. Because of interindustry relationships, relatively small adjustments in various sectors constantly caused maladjustments in many others. As a result, imbalances persisted even in the second computer plan, as Figure 17.4 shows. Although it would be possible to have the computer generate automatic balances (by appropriate adjustments in production, exports, or imports), we had earlier rejected this solution as tending to remove the planner from too much of the decision making in the plan. We have already noted the somewhat analogous case of investment—it would be quite convenient (and not very difficult) to have the computer generate investment programs appropriate to the production projections.

Another shortcoming of the planning system is that, having based costs on the level of production alone, we do not consider technological changes that are a function of time—such as an annual increase in productivity and wage and salary payments.

Although features such as these are not included in this planning system, they are clearly within the capability of computer-based systems in general. The problem is in determining to what extent the planner should become involved in detailed decision making. The greater his involvement, the more detailed are the inputs required, and hence the more cumbersome it becomes to make changes or prepare alternative plans.

Data Processing as an Aid to Development Planning

The development environment is characterized by considerable disorganization. Objectives are frequently vague, roles are undefined, and subjective criteria are prevalent. To some extent such disorganization is inherent, but to a large extent it must be attributed to a lack of personnel sufficiently skilled in management and planning. Experience with the economic analysis of the Guayana program shows that difficulties in specifying objectives are an important problem—especially when there is heavy dependence on the special technical skills of consultants who are available only for brief periods and hence must focus on limited objectives. The computer-based model and its associated system help overcome this problem by providing a structure for the organization of planning activities. Furthermore, because the computer is a precise machine, it imposes a certain discipline on the system of which it is a part: concepts and quantities must be specific, and the computational procedure must be explicit.

Most important for economic planning, the computer can organize data, that is, it can bring dispersed data elements into juxtaposition for calculation and comparison and then distribute the results of the calculation into widely diverse, but nevertheless related, areas. Although a relatively unskilled clerk can accomplish any series of steps that a computer can accomplish, the range of tasks that it is feasible to do clerically is soon exceeded by the computer due to its speed, accuracy, and organizing capability. The Guayana economic planning system described in this chapter could have been implemented without a computer, but in fact it would not have been.

The first objection to a computer-based system is usually based on lack of data, which are rarely available in the forms and quantities needed for the problem at hand. However, much of the available data is frequently unexploited because it fails to fit the planner's own conceptual model and because he fails to seek out the economic implications of the data that are available in order to utilize them in his own model. Sometimes his model might easily be altered to take advantage of existing data.

Also, for many data the planner relies on judgment, and although his judgments may be as good as (or better than) those based on limited or spurious statistical data, he is frequently reluctant to quantify them. However, factors set aside (in the planner's mental model) as requiring only the vaguest quantitative values cannot be very important, so the number used in the computer, no matter how unsubstantiated, cannot be important either. The system, by demanding an explicit response, aids the planning process by clarifying for the planner the implicit assumptions on which his projections rest. Furthermore, it may well be that efforts to improve some data are not worth the trouble, since their impact on the final results will be negligible over any possible range of values they might assume.

Another valuable contribution of a computer-based system is that it continues to provide results with whatever data it has. As these data are improved—a process that lack of time and resources will surely require to be incremental—so are the results generated by the model. As planners gain more experience and as decision makers' interests change, the system must incorporate changes—not in any fundamental structural way, but rather in the way data are utilized. New projects must be considered and frequently incorporated. A sector previously developed in very gross terms may be broken down to incorporate a list of detailed projects, while other sectors may be aggregated when their importance is downgraded. Meanwhile, improved data, as they become available, are mechanically incorporated in an economic plan that automatically reflects this improvement.

Since the emerging countries are noted for their high unemployment and lack of advanced technology, it must seem paradoxical to suggest that the techniques of data processing can play an important role in their development. However, data processing brings capabilities that serve to fill those gaps in the structure of the underdeveloped economy that most retard development—the systematization of the development planning process itself.

Chapter 18

The Implementation of the Urban Development Program

Rafael Corrada

The preparation of plans and programs is a relatively easy task compared to their effective implementation, especially when implementation depends on the cooperation and coordination of agents outside the direct control of the planning agency. Ciudad Guayana provides an excellent example of some of the fascinating problems associated with the implementation of an urban development program. Ciudad Guayana is a Venezuelan city and not a camp of the Corporación Venezolana de Guayana (CVG). Therefore, its development depends upon a series of decision-making processes outside the direct control of the CVG. The principal institutional agents in the development process of Ciudad Guayana (as in any other city in Venezuela) are the national agencies, private enterprises, and the municipal government. Thus the effective implementation of the development program for Ciudad Guayana depends to a large extent upon the CVG's administrative efficiency, and foremost upon its ability to enlist the active participation of these other institutional sectors.

The CVG's performance compares favorably with that of other government agencies in Venezuela and in Latin America; even though similar to others, its efficiency and effectiveness have been uneven.[1] The analysis of this uneven performance may help to evaluate the possibilities of implementing the plan within the existing organization and to clarify the nature of the CVG's future urban activities, after the bulk of the urban planning effort was completed in 1965.

Clarifying the CVG's Administrative Performance

Although conflicts between thinkers and doers generally develop in most organizations, they are usually brought together on the assumption that the benefits accruing from such a confrontation normally outweigh the disadvantages. The CVG experience provides examples of some of the best results of such attitudinal interplay, even at the price of occasional conflicts that affected the implementation of the urban development program.

One of the basic requirements for effective implementation is continuous collaboration between executives and planners,[2] in order to ensure the incorporation of planning into the decision-making process of the organization. Often the planner thinks or acts as though the executive were merely an instrument for the execution of his plan, even though conscious that the executive is responsible for the key decisions and actions that put a program into effect. Sooner or later the planner confronts the hard fact that the decision-making mechanism existed before planning evolved as a separate discipline, and it can continue operating without the specific help of planners, although the outcome may not be as good (or so the planners maintain). According to the jargon, the planning process supposedly is a useful tool to help executives (a) identify the decisions to be made, (b) study the alternative solutions available, (c) select the most effective solutions, (d) determine the most adequate form of implementation, and (e) evaluate the effects and implications of action. In this view, planning is ineffective unless it is incorporated into the decision-making process as a tool for executive action. The urban development program for Ciudad Guayana cannot be properly implemented unless the decision-making process within the CVG, and the other institutional sectors, which largely determines the city's development, is taken into account. Otherwise, the program is likely to end up as an expensive, interesting, and historical document bearing little relation to actual developments on the site.

During the development and implementation phase of the Guayana program, the potential conflict between executives and planners became a real one, sparked by the planners' usual bid for time. An initial planning holiday was granted; construction in most of the site for Ciudad Guayana was frozen until the planners could draft a preliminary development plan. This was a significant concession extracted from the action-oriented executives. But a fast-growing city like Ciudad Guayana had its own dynamics. Squatters continued to invade the land. In order to enforce the freeze, police measures had to be taken to protect the CVG's land and to guarantee an orderly development. Municipal authorities sided with potential voters. Pressures and criticisms mounted against the CVG and its executives. The CVG's executives became impatient as they realized that planning is a "continuous process," that the plan is never "complete" or "definite," and that planners are notorious for their lack of time sense.

This situation started to polarize planners and executives into conflicting positions. Once polarization started, rationalization began, and their positions became clear and fixed. The executives felt that three kinds of cases required immediate action, whether planning was done or not: (a) orders from a higher level of authority (from the Venezuelan government or the CVG hierarchy); (b) opportunities that must be seized at once or perhaps lost forever; and (c) problems that might get out of hand or develop into major crises.

The planners' reaction to these situations was unsatisfactory to the executives. Usually they insisted on postponing decisions until adequate analyses had been made and proper recommendations worked out. During the process of polarization, the planners did not adopt a defensive attitude but actively opposed the executives with equally reasonable arguments. They contended that action is not necessarily better than inaction and often is worse, unless it is the correct move. Also, they argued, orders or decisions should be dictated by the development programs and not by circumstances outside it; opportunities should not be seized, but created. Lastly, they felt that the major problems so upsetting to the executives required an attack on their causes, not on their manifestations, in order to prevent their recurrence; or, if they are recurrent by nature, a permanent institutionalized mechanism should be established to take care of them.

The planners insisted on ignoring some of the immediate problems confronted by the CVG, thus increasing their detachment from its normal decision-making process. Occasionally, they were asked to justify a decision already made—to rationalize it with data and concepts; but they were seldom asked to evaluate it or its implementation. When the planners did not cooperate, the executives proceeded to create a separate section or department, one with new personnel fully committed to carry out a given mandate. This bypassing mechanism became a normal executive move.

The polarization of executives and planners was apparently further emphasized by the presence of the group of foreign planning consultants, who, although they advised both executives and planners, invariably sided with planning but were not directly involved in the implementation of programs and the execution of projects. In fact, terms and attitudes usually associated with labels such as "antiplanning" and "antiforeign" were used and assumed interchangeably.

One of the most significant results of the planner-executive split was improvisation, either outside the limits of the urban plan or in areas not properly defined as yet. Although the improvisation was imaginative at times, it proved in the end to be expensive in time and money and deficient in quality. This situation did not last long. Executives and planners alike became aware of the need for improvements on both sides and conscious of being partially right and partially wrong. They gravitated toward a middle ground, searching for a compromise in order to improve performance.

To reach a consensus was not easy. In the first place, a compromise depends on the ability to communicate—the capacity to think explicitly and the willingness to talk openly. These requirements cannot be taken for granted in most developing countries. Explicit thinking can be checked and found to be correct or erroneous irrespective of the position of the person expressing it or making a decision. Knowledgeable executives can inhibit action or change decisions by playing the game according to rules more satisfactory to them. For such purposes, withholding information is one of the basic strategies. Often they claim intimacy with facts or events that cannot be disclosed or discussed in order to retain the prerogative of acting unilaterally and maintaining the image of power and authority. This posture deflects criticism. Responsibility has been given to them, they claim, and they might as well be totally responsible for the outcome. Such an attitude tended to jeopardize certain operations and deteriorated the CVG's performance. Therefore, to enhance the possibility of implementing the urban development program more effectively, responsibilities began to be defined.

The definition of responsibilities posed another problem. Most organizations in developing countries can be described in terms of Parsons' ascriptive, particularistic, and diffuse norms: *ascriptive,* because their top personnel are selected on the basis of social status as well as professional competence; *particularistic,* because they are selected personally, not through an impersonal job recruitment process; and *diffuse,* because they are expected to contribute beyond their field of competence as a result of the relationships of confidence and friendship that bind them to the organization. This system of selection and operation seems logical and reasonable at the developing stage of society that characterizes Latin America today. It is a system that maximizes honesty, loyalty, and dedication—values that are not considered in the abstract but are usually associated with and attached to certain individuals—as a way of coping with the unstable and transitional character of the social structure.

Effective implementation calls for a clear definition of responsibilities, with sanctions for transgressors. But sanctions within the type of organization described are very difficult to apply. Efficiency is not yet the guiding organizational criterion that, taking honest administration for granted, permeates the entire organization in order to obtain higher levels of performance. Efficiency does not make sense unless it is built upon administrative honesty. But if honesty and loyalty are musts at a given stage in the process toward efficient organizational performance, at that stage it is difficult and perhaps unreasonable to impose sanctions for inefficiency. To apply sanctions in the name of efficiency implies a substitution of the initial criteria used to set up the organization, a change in the rules of the game. It implies that loyalty, friendship, and family ties are something apart from and perhaps irrelevant to competence and efficiency. This distinction is difficult to make within the circumstances affecting developing countries. The CVG is likely to become more aware of the fact that organizational efficiency and effective implementation require a definition of responsibilities, with sanctions for transgressors.

The middle ground sought by executives and planners implied gains and losses to both sides, which is the essence of compromise; but it created at the same time an opportunity for the parties to indulge in a battle of wits. Outwitting is an outcome of the mechanics of compromise and can be observed in most organizations composed of different professionals having diverging points of view. In this atmosphere agreements are not necessarily binding, because they are often viewed as one move in the organizational chess game in which one group has temporarily outwitted the other in a given circumstance. The game never ends.

How can these problems be overcome? Sociologists talk about integration as a third possibility available to organizations. (By *domination*, one party gets everything, and in the process the organization may win or lose; by *compromise*, both lose and gain something, and the organization may win or lose; and by *integration*, both win more than they lose, and the organization wins more than it loses.) There are two major prerequisites for integration. First, there must be a continuous search for a broader issue encompassing those in conflict. This seems to call for the active participation of a third party over and above the conflicting ones; the organization needs a clear hierarchy, providing at each level an opportunity to arbitrate conflicts affecting the level below. Second, this arbitration must be based on a clear and objective understanding of the situation and its demands, divorced from the personalities involved. Thus there should be a feedback mechanism providing accurate information about the development situation. It is more difficult for conflicts to develop within the framework of facts and figures; the organization works under the pressure of the development situation, and planners and executives have to react to it and perform according to its demands. Both share responsibility for failure or success in terms of their handling of the situation and implementation of the program.

All that is easier said than done. What mechanism or administrative procedure can bring about the integration of planners and executives? Explicit thinking and regular meetings seem to be essential conditions. The CVG has failed to adopt procedures to facilitate the continuous exchange of ideas, to bring into the open the conflicting criteria that often undermine effective performance. It never has institutionalized staff meetings. In addition, plans for the creation of an information center in charge of providing accurate feedback data on the situation in Ciudad Guayana, to facilitate the decision-making process and the evaluation of the effects of the programs and projects being implemented, were discarded.

Determining a Key Role for the CVG

Even if the administrative problems within the CVG are resolved, it would be a mistake to assume that effective implementation would be ensured. The urban development program calls for total investments of around $900 million until the city reaches a population of 300,000. At the present rate of budget allocations for urban development ($6–13 million annually), it would take the CVG between 70 and 150 years to develop the city. However, inmigration continues at a rate likely to reach that number of people by 1980. Therefore, effective implementation cannot depend upon the CVG's capabilities alone; if it did, Ciudad Guayana would probably become a shantytown inhabited mostly by squatters. The prospects of additional national government allocations to the CVG are dim, since present Venezuelan public policy seems to prefer a diminishing role for regional agencies in urban development.

If the CVG is to implement the development program successfully, its investments must promote other investment. The 1965–1968 plan requires that each CVG dollar should promote about *five* dollars from other public and private sources. However, for each CVG dollar invested during 1961–1965, other sources invested *one-half* dollar. This was not surprising, because the CVG was not organized to promote investment in urban development. It had had spectacular success in the promotion of certain basic industrial projects (such as the Guri Dam and the aluminum and pulp and paper factories) that essentially required two-party negotiations. But it was never effective in undertaking more complicated promotional efforts to enlist more active participation by other national agencies, the municipal government, and small- and middle-scale private enterprises.

Promoting the participation of other national agencies. Until 1965 the CVG approached the task of developing Ciudad Guayana as if it were dealing with another project under its direct control (such as the dam and the steel mill). The coordination of the activities of other public agencies in the Guayana is an explicit function granted under the CVG's charter. However, no specific powers were given to enforce such coordination; in the last analysis, it depends on the CVG's ability to enlist their participation. At the beginning, it was rather difficult to convince the other public agencies of the need to maintain a high rate of investment in Ciudad Guayana. Normally, budget allocations in these agencies are based on the demonstrated needs of an existing population and the influence of political pressure groups, including the municipal governments. To develop a city at a fast rate of growth in an almost uninhabited area sounded like a planner's dream, too ambitious and unreal (in fact, the population estimates for 1962–1966 turned out to be twice as large as reality) to convince other public agencies that they should have invested heavily in Ciudad Guayana.

Whenever other public agencies were slow or reluctant, the CVG went ahead and acted unilaterally in their place. This was a necessary and wise move until a certain stage of development was reached; Ciudad Guayana could not possibly have gotten under way on the basis of a coordinated effort among the various public agencies that normally participate in city development and improvement programs. Although the CVG was forced by the circumstances to develop the city's basic structure to reach a point where its growth would be irreversible, this strategy breeds its own difficulties. It created an image of secrecy for the CVG because it cannot be publicized, since fundamentally such a strategy implies aims different from those held by other agencies. In addition, the CVG developed a self-image of direct action, a we-can-do-everything mentality, that is difficult to replace with the less commanding one of promotion.

Although at the beginning other public agencies were reluctant to assist the CVG in the task of urban development on the basis of plans and projections, they reacted violently when they saw development under way and activities that were normally within their jurisdiction conducted by a hybrid regional agency. Whereas they were not needed to start development, their participation became crucial by 1964 to avoid their blocking or distorting further growth. By then the strategy had to change in order to allow other agencies to jump on the bandwagon and take it over. This policy was successfully implemented with Banco Obrero, but a systematic effort is still needed with other public agencies. The enlistment of other agencies is basically a promotional effort; it calls for (a) project plans and specifications and (b) land grants to attract their investments since those two essential requirements are not readily available in other Venezuelan cities. In part, this process was under way by 1965 after the Guayana program was integrated into the national plan; and the national planning agency (Oficina Central de Coordinación y Planificación—Cordiplan) began earmarking funds for investment in Ciudad Guayana through other public agencies.

Promoting the development of the municipal government. The state legislature, with the active encouragement of the CVG, created a municipal district encompassing the entire area of the planned city. Since then the CVG has been assisting the municipality financially in such typically municipal activities as garbage collection, property registration, municipal engineering, and city planning, and in 1963 collaborated with the municipality to create a local housing agency to take care of the squatter settlement program and low-cost housing, in cooperation with Banco Obrero. These basic institutional efforts have been the CVG's most significant contributions to the municipality.

Nevertheless, the Municipal Council has had little or no participation in the preparation of the city plan or in the development of most projects. Until 1965 it felt that its environment and activities were attached to strings mainly controlled by the CVG. It claimed that the CVG wanted to transfer to the city the deficit operating activities (such as low-cost housing, the water system, and garbage collection) that represented a financial burden while retaining the profit-making operations (such as the commercial center, hotels, medium- and high-cost housing). For its part the CVG claimed that the principal responsibility of the municipality was to attend to the needs of low-income people, who constitute the majority of voters; that the municipal organization did not have the technical capacity to undertake profit-making enterprises, nor the mentality to supersede provincial issues in order to pursue the national goals at stake.

Promoting private investments.[3] The CVG estimated that half the investment requirements for urban development could come from private sources, local and international, attracted by the profit-making possibilities in Ciudad Guayana. To divert the flow of investments presently going to other Venezuelan cities with a thoroughly tested market and building experience constitutes one of its major problems. Special incentives were initially needed.

Since the market was unknown and investors did not go by planners' projections, one of the first steps taken was to prepare a sale guarantee contract. This type of contract guaranteed that the CVG would purchase, at a prestipulated price, any house that remained unsold after six months of sales promotion efforts (these efforts were spelled out in terms of so many ads per month, sales office, billboards). Since construction experience was also limited, the contract tried to incorporate a cost-plus concept, allowing for price increases in cases of higher costs due to factors beyond the control of the builders. The contract was also intended to promote the package-deal concept in order to alleviate the CVG's promotion task; that is, a single contractor could be responsible for the entire development of a tract of land, subject to step-by-step approval by the CVG—from plans and specifications to sale operations. The normal promotional effort was too time consuming, since it called for many separate negotiations—plans for the subdivision, plans for the houses, subdivision construction, housing construction, sale of urbanized lots, and sale of houses.

The sale guarantee clause was used in about half of the projects promoted during 1961–1966, but some of its clauses failed to become general practice. CVG officials contended that the package-deal concept was unrealistic within the Venezuelan context; the planners suspected that the CVG executives' lack of interest was due to a preference to control the granting of numerous, though smaller, contracts for purposes of power and prestige. The executives contended that the package-deal contract called for a more sophisticated and complicated type of promotion, since it implied the sponsoring of big business, building associations, and consortia of bankers, architects, engineers, builders, sales specialists, and other professionals. Undoubtedly the CVG was not equipped to handle this sort of operation, nor, for that matter, mentally disposed to undertake it.

The two major objectives of the package-deal contract were to promote the availability of construction financing through local banks and to encourage long-term mortgage financing through the creation of a savings and loan association. These objectives were attained with only partial success because of inadequate promotional efforts, although the package-deal concept is becoming a normal development practice in Venezuela.

These comments apply mainly to residential construction, but the same approach, efforts, and results characterized the promotion of small- and medium-scale commerce and industry.

Searching for an Organization to Promote Urban Development
Unlike the CVG's other projects, Ciudad Guayana is a political unit and, therefore, its most sensitive area. The CVG's mandate and reputation

had been based on development areas outside the jurisdiction of existing agencies and political units. Although CVG action in areas within the jurisdiction of other institutions was necessary to start the city's development, this approach is likely to continue breeding mounting problems, since it affects the balance of power and the division of influence among agencies and invites similar transgressions into the CVG's realm.

It was therefore thought to be crucial to the success of the CVG's unique regional effort to change the nature of its role in the urban development sector. The effective implementation of the Ciudad Guayana development program calls for a unique organization, one capable of promoting investments by other public agencies and private sources and of assisting the municipal government in the organization and administration of its city services within the context of the CVG's development plan for the city. To this end the CVG considered the desirability of creating such an organization, as a subsidiary agency, in order to achieve three major purposes:

1. To create a structure better suited for the implementation of the city's development program. This requires an organization oriented toward promotion and indirect participation. The CVG could then concentrate on regional efforts, which it is better equipped and mentally disposed to handle. Moreover, if the CVG gradually reduces its direct involvement in the urban program on behalf of the local political structure and other national agencies, it can increase its regional effectiveness.

2. To shift most of the personnel engaged in city planning, programming, and implementation from Caracas to Ciudad Guayana. The present Caracas-based operation has always been criticized by both the local people and the international experts and technicians on the grounds that close contact with the operations at the site is essential for more realistic planning and successful implementation. In the beginning the Caracas location was justified, but after the initial stage of urban planning and programming was over, on-the-site implementation seemed likely to prove more fruitful.

3. To attract more local and foreign capital. This was thought possible by issuing stocks and bonds based on the profit-making potentials of the real-estate development. The securities could be sold to Venezuelan and foreign investors, and their salability could have been enhanced by the prospective revenues from the commercial and high-income residential developments and by certain government guarantees.[4]

Clarifying the Nature of the Promoting Organization

It was considered at first that an organization to accomplish these three tasks would have to be controlled initially by a majority of CVG officials appointed in consultation with Cordiplan, the state, and the municipality and a minority of representatives from the private sector. The CVG officials could gradually be replaced by representatives of the municipal government. In addition, an advisory committee composed of representatives from various agencies and distinguished local citizens was contemplated as a necessary element to ensure local acceptance and backing.

In developing countries the administrative structure of an organization is usually developed in one of two ways. One is to start with available or easily identifiable people of proven loyalty and leave in their hands, subject to final approval from the top, the task of organizing themselves to fulfill the assignment. In informal conversation this approach was usually referred to as "plowing with the available oxen" or "giving the message to García."[5] The other is to start with a provisional organization with a very broad and vague mandate; over time, tasks become clarified and the administrative structure defined or enlarged in order to improve effectiveness. One way emphasizes the people, the other an organization capable of undertaking practically anything.

The virtues of these two approaches are supposed to be simplicity and economy. All too often they merely waste time and money. After costly improvisation the organization has to analyze its tasks and reorganize itself accordingly. Meanwhile, nepotism is rampant and sufficiently strong to postpone the adoption of appropriate procedures for the selection of qualified personnel. Both approaches are typical of developing countries and, in turn, tend to perpetuate a low level of performance. Both ways have in common a vaguely defined set of tasks.

An alternative approach was contemplated: to define the most important tasks, deduce the administrative structure from them, and adopt tentative but clear procedures. Then personnel could be given specific training, and their efficiency easily evaluated. The setting of measurable tasks usually provides a challenge for the personnel involved and encourages high-level performance. With tasks tentatively specified, it seems easier to adopt an adequate organization to carry them out. For the proposed urban development subsidiary, the CVG undertook a series of studies to deduce the administrative structure from the programs and activities that the new organization was expected to carry out.

Major tasks. The CVG's direct investment in the urban development sector for the period 1965–1980 was planned to be about 13 per cent of the total requirements (declining from about 28 per cent in 1965). Thus the fundamental task of the subsidiary agency, as embodied in the development program, was to promote investment in urban development from sources other than the CVG's. Given this general objective, the principal activities of the agency called for the following tasks:

1. acquiring and disposing of urban land as a tool to promote other public and private investment
2. preparing plans, specifications, and brochures for public utilities, public services, and private services in order to promote investment from other public and private sources
3. undertaking site improvements whenever needed to promote further investment
4. providing guarantees to attract private investment for short- and long-term financing of projects
5. assisting the municipal government to establish and manage all necessary city services.

Major line operations. The pursuance of the tasks just listed implies a sequence of stages in urban development, namely, (1) acquisition and disposition of urban lands, (2) development of the urban infrastructure, (3) development of residential facilities, and (4) development of community facilities. To a large extent each stage depends on the completion of the previous one.[6] Also, each stage involves particular operations and problems that call for special arrangements in the administrative structure. The "line" departments of the proposed subsidiary could correspond to the stages indicated: real estate, public utilities, housing, and community facilities.

These "line" departments do not coincide with the present CVG departments. They are based on a different approach. Each except real estate has a section for plans and specifications, with its own engineers, architects, and draftsmen.

This different type of organization was thought to have several advantages. First, it emphasizes final products in the field, not intermediate ones in the office. Each department controls all the necessary steps in a project, up to its promotion in Ciudad Guayana. Departmental efficiency can then be measured not by office output but by field performance. In contrast, the present plans and specifications department judges its efficiency by the quality and amount of plans and specifications turned out rather than by the number of projects effectively promoted, under construction, or completed. The latter is undoubtedly a more important measurement of effective implementation. The pursuance of final products in terms of field activities tends to move the organizational machinery faster from planning into field action.

Second, an organization oriented to field performance could develop more administrative specialization, which in turn tends to increase productivity, efficiency, and effectiveness. Architects, engineers, and draftsmen specialize in certain tasks, such as public utilities, housing, and community facilities. This specialization tends to increase the knowledge and skills of the technical staff in the various line operations.

Major staff and service functions. The major staff function contemplated for the CVG's urban development subsidiary was promotion, which constitutes its central task. Experience until 1965 indicated that the CVG's line departments tended to overlook promotional efforts and consistently preferred to contract directly. A separate staff department with specialized personnel tends to exhaust its promotional efforts before making direct commitments.[7] The top executive, together with the heads of departments, could determine what activities had to be promoted and for how long.

Such functions as general planning and strategy, programming, financing, and research were also recommended for inclusion in a specific staff department advising the chief executive on the kinds of activities undertaken by the line departments. The intention was to protect general planning and strategy from the daily operations and to segregate functionally personnel of different attitudes and skills.

Finally, the new subsidiary had to include departments for such service functions as legal counseling and administration (personnel, purchasing, general services, and accounting).

Horizontal coordination. Since some decisions call for the participation of men with different specialities, and some projects require coordination of various participating departments, the chief executive needs a formal mechanism for consulting the heads of departments on decisions affecting their work program, such as when to promote or directly develop a project. An executive committee composed of the heads of the line and staff departments was recommended to facilitate this type of horizontal coordination, even though the chief executive remained ultimately responsible.

A housing project requires the horizontal coordination of all departments. Shacks need to be acquired, public services installed, plans and specifications prepared, and certain community facilities (such as commerce and schools) sponsored. The designation of project teams headed by a project chief was also recommended to formalize this type of horizontal coordination. The project chief could be a member of the department with primary responsibility for a given type of project and would participate in the promotion of the project together with the negotiator from the promotion department.

Another activity requiring horizontal coordination was the selection and hiring of architects and engineers to prepare plans and specifications according to certain design criteria. The lack of good urban design has remained a major problem despite the fact that a practically new city like Ciudad Guayana provides plenty of opportunities for innovation in design. Interdepartmental coordination of design contracts was considered essential to secure a more impersonal control of contracts, to check favoritism, and to increase scheduling efficiency. Other factors besides design were essential to ensure proper implementation, such as housing-market analyses to check quality, price, time, and location of the units. A special administrative procedure to maintain these controls was recommended for the new organization. A strategic point of control is the act of contracting, and it was thought that a contract review committee to review and check all contracts before they reached the board of directors would improve performance significantly. This committee could also improve the participation of different specialists in the drafting and management of those contracts that have diverse effects and implications for the urban development program.

Lastly, an information center operated by the planning and programming department could help in establishing proper horizontal coordination by maintaining performance communications among all departments.

Conclusions

After 1965 the successful implementation of the urban development program for Ciudad Guayana seemed to depend upon the CVG's ability to change from its role of direct actor to the indirect one of a promoter. This different strategy is likely to have a better chance of incorporating the active participation of other public agencies, the municipality, and private enterprise. The activities and roles of these other sectors will determine whether Ciudad Guayana becomes another Venezuelan city, instead of a CVG camp, with its own spontaneous capacity to grow along the lines considered most convenient by the major participants and in harmony with the development program. The CVG was not structured adequately nor was it mentally disposed to undertake this vital shift in the implementation strategy. The creation of a subsidiary organization of the CVG seems indispensable to achieve effective implementation under the direction of the CVG, or else the other sectors will impose the new strategy and reduce significantly the chances of implementing the urban development program. The new agency that has been recommended calls for a special organization structured on the basis of the tasks involved; a first approximation has been sketched in this chapter to outline the form it might take.

Chapter 19
Evaluating the Allocation of Resources to Urban Development

Anthony Downs

A long-run planning-and-action process can effectively accomplish desired goals only if it includes frequent evaluation of just how successful it has been up to the current date. Such an evaluation requires comparing actual performances with those rates of performance needed to reach the desired goals within the allotted time. Any particular areas in which actual performance has fallen behind "targets" are then analyzed. This leads to revision of the goals themselves, the actions planned to attain the goals, the methods of accomplishing the planned actions, or some combination of these. Such a feedback process is essential if plans are to become more than mere rhetoric.

Yet, historically, governments have been extremely reluctant to conduct accurate evaluations of their performance. The main reason is that they fear exposing their own failures. The government as a whole does not want to let the public know what mistakes it has made or what shortcomings have occurred in its efforts to reach planned objectives. And within the government, individual officials are often afraid to give their superiors an unvarnished view of their own and their subordinates' accomplishments.

Underlying these nearly universal fears is the embarrassing fact that most government programs fail to reach their planned targets on time. There are certain exceptions to this generalization, but it is applicable enough to produce a widespread governmental bias against accurate program evaluation.

There are three basic reasons why most government programs fall short of their planned accomplishments. First, officials tend to create unrealistically optimistic plans to start with. Planning has several functions that are not entirely consistent with each other. On the one hand, plans serve as ideals or aspirations designed to evoke maximum performance. This function requires that plans be grandiose enough to inspire "heroic" efforts that will "stretch" the capabilities of those involved. Specific targets should therefore be somewhat beyond the existing capacity of the actors. On the other hand, plans serve as means of developing concrete action programs and schedules. To fulfill this function well, targets must be realistically tailored to the capabilities of the actors involved and the resources available to them. But this practical function of planning is less glamorous than the inspirational function and does not have its political impact. Therefore, politicians and top government officials normally announce plans that paint glowing pictures of desirable outcomes without mentioning—or perhaps realizing—that these outcomes are beyond their present capabilities.

A second cause of failure to reach planned targets on time is expressed in the Law of Surprise: "It takes much longer, and costs much more, to do anything new than you originally think it will." The substantial accuracy of this law stems from the immensely complex and uncertain nature of the world. Planners of large-scale undertakings are often compelled to oversimplify reality in formulating their plans; otherwise they would never complete them at all. As a result, those in charge of carrying out such plans frequently run into unforeseen difficulties and fall behind schedule because of them. This is particularly likely in underdeveloped countries because they are attempting to accomplish things never done before, are plagued by acute shortages of experienced and skilled managers, and often have rapidly changing and relatively unstructured environments.

A third cause of divergences from plans is the pursuit of self-interest by individual officials. Their own goals inevitably differ from the formal plans of their organizations to at least some degree. As a result, every large organization, public or private, in every nation, developed or underdeveloped, is plagued to some extent by internal power struggles, dissensions, conflicting activities, and diversions of scarce resources into actions that are not designed to help accomplish planned goals. Top officials—even the most scrupulously honest ones—know that these kinds of activities are certain to be going on among their subordinates, although they may not know specifically what the activities are. Hence these top officials are sure that any thorough evaluation will uncover some embarrassing activities for which they will be administratively responsible.

Two other major factors have also inhibited governments from accurately evaluating their programs in the past. First, program evaluation is often extremely difficult, as will be illustrated later in our analysis. It is much more difficult than evaluating programs undertaken by private business, since there is no single measurable yardstick like profits to use in judging success. Second, in democratic countries most government reports—even internal ones—are accessible to the public and the press. As a result, frank and critical analyses that could be kept quiet if done by private firms are likely to be made public if done by government agencies.

In spite of all these factors that generally tend to inhibit government program evaluation, the Corporación Venezolana de Guayana (CVG), on the recommendation of the Joint Center for Urban Studies, asked the Real Estate Research Corporation to study the resource allocations involved in the urban development of Ciudad Guayana from 1961 to 1965. We were to concentrate particularly upon the roles played by the CVG in actual development and in promoting and coordinating the participation of other government agencies. This assignment was undertaken directly for the CVG, under the general supervision of the Joint Center. The study had four main stages. The first three steps were to describe, analyze, and then evaluate the effectiveness of both actual resource allocations and the operational procedures employed by the CVG directly or through other government agencies. The fourth step was to prepare conclusions and recommendations concerning ways in which development goals and targets could be achieved more effectively and administrative efficiency could be improved. This chapter concentrates upon the evaluation phase, drawing upon other parts of the study as necessary to explain how the evaluation was carried out.

A Brief Description of the CVG's Attainments in Urban Development

The main purpose of our study was to improve future resource allocation in the urban development of Ciudad Guayana. However, as in many future-oriented studies, we had to start by examining past procedures and achievements. The first task was discovering what the CVG had actually accomplished during the five years from 1961 through 1965.

In this period Ciudad Guayana grew very rapidly, thus presenting the CVG with a difficult challenge. The population increased at an average rate of 15 per cent per year, rising from 50,000 in September 1962 to 73,000 in February 1965. This growth created the need for about 1,200 additional housing units each year and for many schools, utilities, shopping facilities, and other municipal services.

Full quantification of the CVG's planning attainments is presently impossible for three reasons. First, a considerable portion of the CVG's effort was devoted to preparing general plans and designing projects that have not yet been completed. Second, there is not enough information about actual performance to evaluate some of the activities that have been carried out. Third, some of the products of planning are so intangible as to be difficult or impossible to measure—such as fostering community spirit through the aesthetic impact of a certain urban design. Nevertheless, it is clear that the CVG carried out a major program of urban development in Ciudad Guayana from 1961 through 1965, and many of its components are quantifiable:

1. The CVG was directly or indirectly responsible for the creation of nearly 3,600 housing units from 1962 to 1965. Most (88 per cent) of the new standard housing was built for middle-income groups; about 200 adequate units were built for the lowest income group. The CVG also provided a few areas in which low-income families could build their own units.

2. Fifteen schools were built, providing places for 8,600 students.

3. Ten kilometers of major roads were completed by the CVG and the Ministry of Public Works. Another 30 kilometers of provisional roads had been constructed, and 22 kilometers of major roads were under construction. In addition, the Orinoco Mining Company had built 4.5 kilometers of major roads.

4. Electrical service was provided to nearly all of the standard housing units and to about 60 per cent of the occupied shacks.

5. About one half of all households had adequate water and sewer systems.

6. Other community facilities provided included four social centers, a religious center, an expanded hotel, a major river port, some parklands, and a 280-bed hospital (not quite finished in 1965).

Although it does not take much space to list these achievements, taken together they represent an impressive total result of the urban allocation process.

Criteria for Evaluating the Urban Development Program

Measuring and analyzing the CVG's performance in urban development do not provide sufficient grounds for evaluating that performance, no matter how accurate our measures are, because every evaluation consists essentially of comparing an actual performance (or a measure of it) with some standard of what it "ought to be." Without a standard it is impossible to arrive at conclusions about whether a performance has been adequate or inadequate, efficient or inefficient, or even desirable or undesirable. For example, the fact that 3,600 housing units were constructed in Ciudad Guayana from 1962 through early 1966 does not in itself allow us to arrive at any conclusions about the quality of the CVG's performance concerning housing. We must also have some standard about how many units were needed, or should have been built, before we can make such an evaluation.

Standards of this kind are referred to in this article as *criteria*. Each criterion must be stated in some types of measurable units, or *indices*, that are identical to the units in which actual performance is measured. Thus the criteria for housing could be stated in terms of the number of units constructed per year, square feet of housing built per year, or number of households provided with housing per year.

An over-all evaluation of performance regarding urban development can best be made when several different types of criteria are employed simultaneously. Therefore, at the outset of our analysis we developed the following possible criteria to use in evaluating the CVG's urban development performance:

1. *The maximum developable potential of the area.* This potential, when adequately quantified, represents a standard of the best possible performance the CVG could attain if given relatively unlimited resources for urban development. Since no one has unlimited resources, it might appear that this criterion is useless in practice. On the contrary, criteria based upon maximum developable potential have played a major role in the CVG's urban planning from the very beginning. The urban population projections made by the economic planners in the early stages of the development process were based upon presumed maximum exploitation of the natural resource potential of the Guayana area.

2. *Specific development goals or targets stated by the CVG.* Insofar as the CVG had set up particular goals or targets for its urban development program, we could evaluate its performance by comparing actual achievements with the stated targets.

3. *"Adequate" facilities for existing or projected population in the area.* The concept of "adequate facilities" is very often used in urban planning as a standard against which to measure existing conditions. Criteria of adequacy are based upon a physical or aesthetic analysis of living conditions as they "ought" to exist in some assumed "ideal" or "acceptable" environment. For example, experience in U.S. cities has led to the widespread use of a standard of five acres of neighborhood parks for every

thousand residents as a criterion of "adequacy" in recreational space. Standards of adequacy have the advantage of being applicable to existing conditions rather than to some rather vague and hard-to-define "maximum potential" conditions. However, such standards are also subject to both controversy and change over time.

4. *The maximum output capacity of the CVG, given the resources available to it.* An urban development performance that falls far below the "maximum developable potential" or even contains a high proportion of "inadequate" facilities may nevertheless be the best performance the CVG could possibly have achieved with the limited resources available to it. Therefore, in order to measure the efficiency of the CVG's urban development efforts, it was necessary to have some standard based upon the maximum output that the CVG might have achieved if it had utilized all its resources with the least possible amount of wasted motion or ineffectiveness. We can develop such a standard in terms of either the quantity and quality of output achieved per unit of inputs or the methods or procedure used in the development process.

5. *The cost of achieving similar developments elsewhere.* Since the CVG spent a certain amount of money for urban development and achieved a certain measurable set of results, we could develop a set of costs per unit of output for the CVG's performance that could be compared with the costs of developing similar outputs elsewhere.

6. *A "balanced" degree of adequacy or need-attainment among different types of development.* Since urban development involves a large number of different kinds of elements (such as housing, roads, sewer systems, water systems, and electrical services), it is possible for the degree of "adequacy" achieved in some elements to differ from that achieved in others. For example, even if 60 per cent of the households in a city lived in "adequate" housing units, perhaps only 20 per cent of them would be located on "adequate" roads. This would represent "unbalanced" development, as opposed to a "balanced" situation in which all elements had been built up to about the same degree of adequacy. Sometimes "unbalanced" development may be desirable. (For example, it is usually necessary to build roads before adequate housing units are constructed.) However, a large degree of "unbalance" may indicate that reallocations of resources from one kind of construction to another are in order. Therefore, the concept of "balanced" development can be used as a standard by which the over-all urban development performance can be evaluated.

At the outset of our analysis we intended to use all of these criteria in evaluating the CVG's urban development performance. This would have enabled us to assess both its effectiveness (relation to needs or potentials) and its efficiency (relation to available resources). However, we encountered a number of obstacles that made it impossible to use some of the criteria.

The first major problem was that the CVG has set forth very few specific goals or targets for development, either in words or in numbers. True, extensive economic analyses had been made of the maximum developable potential of the Guayana region and of the implications of such a maximum development for the ultimate need for urban facilities in Ciudad Guayana. But none of these potentials had been officially adopted as development goals or targets for the CVG. However, annual reports and other CVG studies did contain quantified estimates of the development potential for Ciudad Guayana, and we adopted two of these alternatives as "targets" in the absence of any officially adopted targets. These "targets" were based upon analyses of the natural resource potential of the region—analyses that assumed that the maximum potential would in fact be developed as fast as conceivably possible. From these quantified estimates of development potential we developed a description of a "target city" to be used for evaluation, as explained later in this section. Thus we were able to make limited use of the first criterion.

However, the absence or inadequacy of specific development goals—verbal or quantified—made it impossible to use the second criterion: comparing performance to official goals. Nevertheless, in order to make use of this approach in principle, we formulated a complete set of suggested goals and objectives for the CVG's urban development effort and then compared these goals with the actual achievements. Since the goals and objectives were stated in words, and the achievements in numbers, we used the concept of "adequacy" of facilities—the next criterion—in making this comparison.

Even here we encountered some significant problems. Few data exist on the quality of many facilities in Ciudad Guayana (for example, the quality of housing constructed under auspices other than the CVG). Moreover, planning standards used in Caracas or in other countries are not necessarily applicable to Ciudad Guayana. Nevertheless, by comparing the number of households served by "adequate" facilities (such as housing and water-supply systems) with total population, we were able to obtain some measures of "adequacy."

Another major problem was the difficulty of compiling accurate information about the real cost of specific developments. Limitations on the extent and reliability of this information greatly hindered our ability to use any criterion of evaluation that required accurate data concerning the cost of various developments in Ciudad Guayana.

For this and other reasons we were unable to employ the criterion based upon estimating the maximum quantity and quality of the output capacity of the CVG staff, given the resources available to it. Our information about the linkages between specific outputs and specific inputs was not sufficient to develop real costs for such outputs. Another factor was the impact upon urban development of forces beyond the control of the CVG: the pace and results of the CVG's development efforts depend not only upon its own behavior but also upon the decisions and actions of other government agencies, private developers, local citizens, and a host of other factors. The unpredictability of these factors made it difficult to calculate the total amount of development that the CVG "ought to have" achieved in any given period.

However, we did assess the procedures it used in making decisions and compared them with the procedures it "ought to have" used. In fact, this was one of our major criteria for evaluation.

We were unable to use the fifth criterion—comparing development costs for given projects in Ciudad Guayana with those in other parts of the country—for two reasons. First, we could not calculate the total costs of specific projects in Ciudad Guayana accurately, for the reasons already described. Second, conditions in Ciudad Guayana are so different from those in other parts of Venezuela and the world that such comparisons would be of doubtful value even it they could be made.

The sixth criterion—the "balance" among different types of construction—is one we were able to use in conjunction with the first criterion—the "target city" concept.

In summary, we used the following approaches in evaluating the CVG's urban development performance:

1. We compared the annual rates of construction required to provide sufficient elements for alternative "target city" populations of 225,000 and 300,000 persons by 1975 with the highest rates actually achieved in Ciudad Guayana from 1961 through 1965.

2. We compared the verbalized goals and objectives formulated by us for the CVG with the actual development performance attained as of 1965, and estimated the degree of "adequacy" with which each objective was being met.

3. We analyzed the procedures used by the CVG in carrying out urban development and compared them with the procedures that we considered

would have been (and would be in the future) "optimum" for conducting such development.

4. We used the "target city" comparison described under the first criterion to calculate the degree of "balance" among different types of construction.

The first two approaches yielded evaluations primarily concerned with the effectiveness of the CVG's urban development efforts, whereas the last two yielded evaluations primarily concerned with their efficiency.

Evaluation in Terms of Goals and Objectives

In the absence of specific official development goals—verbal or quantified—we formulated a complete set of suggested goals and objectives for urban development, based on the CVG's primary regional goal: to develop the full potential of the Guayana region in keeping with the goals of the Venezuelan national plan (*Plan de la Nación*). The primary urban development goal derived from this is to provide in Ciudad Guayana the urban structure and services essential to industrial growth.

We established two basic categories of objectives related to this urban development goal. Attainment objectives are those subgoals related to the substantive contents of development (such as how many houses are built or schools erected). Procedural objectives are those subgoals related to the methods by which the attainment objectives are sought.

Any task as complex as building a city involves multiple objectives that are always in partial conflict at the margins. It is frequently necessary to make decisions affecting two or more conflicting objectives. In order to make these decisions contribute most toward the primary goal it is essential to assign priorities, preferably by creating a "hierarchy" of objectives. We prepared a priority rating of objectives by classifying all items according to three categories: "A" for critical objectives, "B" for important but not critical objectives, and "C" for the rest. These priority ratings were our own subjective judgments of the relation of each objective to the primary urban development goal.

In addition, we divided the attainment goals into three main types. Each component of a city usually serves only certain segments of the population, or serves different segments in diverse ways. Moreover, various groups have unlike objectives regarding any one component of the city (such as housing). Thus the objectives of urban development can best be stated in terms of the aspirations and needs of specific groups of people rather than in terms of the requirements of the population as a whole. While the community can be divided into many groups, we believe that a three-way breakdown is adequate for setting general attainment objectives. These three groups are (1) the low-income group (Bs. 1,000 or less per month), (2) the middle- and high-income group (over Bs. 1,000 per month), and (3) economic and institutional activities.

In considering the CVG's urban development attainment objectives, it is important to remember that the CVG's intention is to emphasize promotion and coordination efforts first. Only if these efforts are not successful does the CVG wish to become directly involved in providing physical elements of the city.

Because the goals and objectives we formulated were stated in rather vague words rather than quantitatively, we were able to make only a general evaluation of the "adequacy" of urban development attainments related to them. In making this admittedly subjective evaluation, we used the following classification: "A" for excellent or good progress toward achieving objectives, "B" for fair progress, and "C" for poor progress.

We rated the CVG's performance regarding its procedural activities as "fair" in most respects and "poor" in others. It is very significant that the CVG's procedural performance was rated "poor" for the two objectives we rated "critical" to urban development: encouraging more city government participation and promoting maximum private participation.

Comparison of the priority ratings with the performance ratings for the twenty-seven attainment objectives can be summarized as follows:

Performance Rating	Critical (A)	Important (B)	Other (C)	Total
Good (A)	4	1	1	6
Fair (B)	5	8	3	16
Poor (C)	1	2	2	5
Total	10	11	6	27

Tables 19.1 and 19.2 set forth (1) the urban development objectives we formulated, (2) the priority ratings assigned to them, and (3) our subjective ratings of actual performance for each.

There was a strong positive correlation between the importance of the attainment objectives and the CVG's performance related to them. Thus, although the CVG's performance was not as good as it might have been in terms of the over-all urban development needs, in general it was directed toward the most important objectives.

TABLE 19.1
Priority and Performance Ratings of Procedural Objectives

Objective	Priority Rating	Performance Rating
To encourage city officials to take an increasing role in urban development and administration	A	C
To minimize the administrative responsibilities of the CVG by promoting		
Maximum participation by other government agencies	A	B
Maximum participation by private interests	A	C
To guide the physical development of the city in accordance with planned objectives	B	B
To make the best use of land, money, personnel, and other CVG resources	B	B
To capture a satisfactory financial return on the CVG's investment in the area	C	C
To stage construction projects so as to maintain employment levels consistently as high as possible	C	B

Comparisons of Actual Attainments with Targets

As indicated previously, the CVG had few official targets pertaining directly to urban development. One set of such targets can be derived from the housing program for steelworkers. We reviewed this program and its attainments in order to illustrate the usefulness of having established targets in evaluating the effectiveness of the CVG's urban development efforts. In addition to this microevaluation, we made a macroevaluation involving a comparison of actual attainments and major elements in our "target city."

The steelworkers' housing program. In 1963 the CVG and the steelworkers' union entered into a contract that included a commitment on the part of the CVG to assure the provision of adequate housing for steelworkers. The CVG developed a program (published in June 1964) for the construction by February 1966 of 4,180 housing units suitable for families with incomes of Bs. 500 to Bs. 2,000 per month. The demand was expected to total 3,830 units—2,730 by June 1965 and another 1,100 by February 1966.

Our analysis of actual progress indicated that of the 4,180 housing units planned, fewer than 1,100, or roughly 25 per cent, had been completed. Most of the twelve projects in the program differed substantially from the original plan, and none of the houses were completed on time.

Moreover, not only had the targets been missed but the CVG had not officially amended the program. Thus, although the original program appears to have been well conceived, the failure to modify it rendered it almost useless.

The "target city" concept. In lieu of a set of official CVG targets covering the many elements of urban development, we developed the concept of a "target city," as noted earlier.

The quantities of the elements that make up a city vary in approximate proportion to the size of the city. The CVG had not prepared a comprehensive set of targets for providing these urban elements, but it had made estimates of future production and employment, and from these it had derived population estimates. By assuming that the city would grow according to these estimates, we derived the quantities of urban elements that this "target city" would need. The standards used for determining the appropriate quantity of each element were obtained from CVG personnel.

By comparing the quantities of existing elements with those required for the "target city" as of a particular year, it is possible to determine the average annual progress rates that would be required to meet the needs of the "target city." These future progress rates can then be compared with past progress rates to ascertain the degree to which past performance rates must be increased, or perhaps decreased.

As of late 1965 the industrial production and employment estimates of the Economic Planning Section indicated that by 1975 Ciudad Guayana could support a population of 300,000. Subsequently the production and employment estimates were reduced, resulting in a supportable population of nearly 225,000 by 1975. Consequently we decided to use both "target cities." By so doing, we in effect established a range, thereby permitting the ready derivation of other "target cities" with different populations and different target dates.

Having established our alternative "target city" sizes (population based on employment), our next step was to decide on the major elements of urban development to use in our analysis. We worked with various officials of both the CVG and the Joint Center in selecting the elements and in assigning quantities to them. The quantities or values thus established became our unofficial "targets" for 1975 development. Any year can be used, but one of medium range is preferable. We selected 1975 because it is often used in the CVG's future estimates and projections.

We obtained actual values for each element as of 1965 and then calculated the annual rates of progress required to move from these levels to the 1975 "targets." We then compared these required rates of development with estimates of the greatest annual increase for each element during the five years under the CVG. (These accomplishment rates had to be rough estimates because of lack of detailed information.)

TABLE 19.2
Priority and Performance Ratings of Attainment Objectives, by Community Group

Urban Development Category	Low-Income Group			Middle- and Upper-Income Group			Economic and Institutional Activities		
	Attainment Objective	Priority Rating	Performance Rating	Attainment Objective	Priority Rating	Performance Rating	Attainment Objective	Priority Rating	Performance Rating
Land	Provide adequate and properly located reception area sites and other sites for low-cost housing and community facilities to serve this group	A	B	Provide adequate and properly located housing areas and sites for other facilities desired by this group	A	B	Provide sites with characteristics and locations that will best foster these activities	A	B
Utilities	Provide at least minimum standards of water, sewage, and electric service to the greatest possible number of households at low costs	C	C	Provide high-quality water, sewage, and electric service to all households	B	B	Provide high-quality water, sewage, and electric service to all who desire it	B	B
Transportation and communication systems	Develop systems that provide adequate services at low costs to users	C	A	Maximize convenience and minimize time at reasonable costs	B	A	Maximize accessibility and quality of service at reasonable costs	A	A
				Provide high-quality telephone service to all households		C	Provide high-quality telephone service for all who desire it		C
Educational facilities	Provide facilities for elementary education for all youth, secondary education demands, and desired adult-training programs	B	B	Establish high-quality educational facilities as demand warrants at elementary, secondary, and college levels	A	B	Provide facilities required to train enough persons with various skills to meet employment demands	A	B
Housing	Provide properly located housing sites, facilitate creation of minimum-quality housing, and encourage upgrading	A	B	Provide medium- and high-quality housing in desirable, stable neighborhoods	A	B	Provide appropriate accommodations for these activities at best locations	A	B

Urban Development Category	Low-Income Group			Middle- and Upper-Income Group			Economic and Institutional Activities		
	Attainment Objective	Priority Rating	Performance Rating	Attainment Objective	Priority Rating	Performance Rating	Attainment Objective	Priority Rating	Performance Rating
Health	Provide adequate public hospitals, clinics, and sanitary facilities at low costs	B	B	Provide both public and private hospitals, clinics, and other health facilities of the high quality desired by this group	A	C	Provide health facilities that are adequate and conveniently located to serve these activities	B	B
Social, cultural, and recreational facilities	Provide facilities for activities that can be enjoyed at low cost and will satisfy the leisure-time needs of these people	C	B	Provide facilities to house all the social functions and the art, theater, other entertainment and recreational activities deemed desirable by this group	B	C	Locate these facilities in convenient proximity to the locations of the economic and institutional activities	C	B
Commercial facilities	Provide land for low-cost stores and services convenient to low-income housing areas	C	B	Provide medium- and high-quality shopping and service areas convenient to middle- and upper-income housing areas, and encourage the creation of a full array of stores desired by this group	B	C	Locate commercial areas so that they are mutually beneficial to other economic and institutional activities	C	C
Urban form	Provide a suitable environment that will serve the needs of this group and inspire them to make improvements	B	B	Provide a setting that will attract and keep people in this group in Guayana by enabling them to live in a convenient and satisfying environment	B	B	Provide a setting that will be both attractive and efficient	B	B

TABLE 19.3

Annual Rates of Progress Required to Provide Elements of 1975 City of 225,000 Population (Compared with Best Past Performances)

	Estimate in 1965	Target in 1975	Required Average Annual Increase to Reach Target	Estimate of Greatest Annual Increase, 1961–1965	Required Annual Rate as Per Cent of Greatest Past Annual Rate
Population	75,000[a]	225,000	15,000	10,000	150
Households	13,000[a]	37,000	2,450	1,700	144
Labor force	24,000[a]	67,500	4,350	3,000	145
Employment	21,000[b]	58,500	3,750	3,000	125
Housing units[c]	13,000	37,500	2,450	2,300	107
Adequate	6,500	30,000	2,350	1,300	180
Inadequate	6,500	7,500	100	1,000	10
Schools[d]					
Primary classrooms	171	596	43	21	205
Primary schools	18	53	4	2	200
Secondary classrooms	40	100	6	10	60
Secondary schools	4	8	0.4	1	40
Special classrooms	37	137	10	28	36
Special schools	3	8	0.5	2	25
Medical facilities[e] (number of beds)	142	675	53	6	[e]
Primary roads[f] (kilometers)	10	77	7	6	117
Electric service[g] (households served)	8,000	37,500	2,950	1,800	164
Water and sewage[h] (households served)	6,000	37,500	3,150	1,500	210
Commercial floor space[i] in major centers (square meters)	45,000	169,500	12,450	10,000	125
Industrial land area utilized[j] (hectares)	172	1,002	83	60	138

a. Tentative estimates prepared as part of the Staging Study in late 1965 by the CVG's Economic Planning Section.
b. Assumes about 13 per cent unemployment in 1965 and 1975, based on Banco Central survey of February 1965.
c. Estimate of total housing units in 1965 from Staging Study tentative data prepared by the Economic Planning Section. Distribution of adequate and inadequate housing based on Dr. Rafael Corrada's analysis of the 1965 Banco Central survey. Assumption that 20 per cent of housing units will be inadequate in 1975 based on discussions with CVG and Joint Center personnel.
d. Data on existing schools and preliminary standards for new schools obtained from Human Resource Development Section. Although there has been a deficit in school construction, schools scheduled for 1966–1968 should greatly reduce or eliminate this deficit.

e. The 280-bed hospital then under construction in San Félix would bring the number of beds to 422. Applying the standard of 3 beds per 1,000 population (used by the CVG), in gross terms hospital facilities should be adequate for a population of slightly more than 140,000. The CVG indicated in its submission for the *Plan de la Nación, 1965–1968* that a similar hospital should be scheduled for construction in 1967 or 1968. In addition, negotiations were under way with the Orinoco Mining Company to provide a clinic in conjunction with its hospital.

f. Data obtained from the Urban Design Section. The past performance takes into account only roads that were completely finished and officially opened. Another 30 kilometers of provisional roads had been constructed, and 22 kilometers of major roads were under construction at the end of 1965. Thus it not only may be unnecessary to increase the allocation of funds to road construction in the future but it may prove feasible to actually reduce the amount allocated.

g. Electric service has kept up satisfactorily with the demand created by new houses, but some time lags in providing this service have resulted in delays in completing some houses. It is estimated that 60 per cent of the ranchos have electric service.

h. These estimates of households served are very rough. If the proposed improvement programs are executed, within a few years the very substantial deficits in water and sewage service could be mostly overcome.

i. The 1965 estimate is based on the tax lists of the Municipal Council as compiled by W. L. Clarke. The 1975 estimate is from an Alta Vista report prepared by the CVG.

j. These estimates are based on tentative employment estimates by the Economic Planning Section, and estimates of employees per hectare are from the CVG report, *Ciudad Guayana: Elements of the Urban Form, Industry* (Caracas, 1963).

The comparison showed that, for most elements of urban development, achievements must be greatly increased in order to meet the needs of either 1975 "target city." (See Tables 19.3 and 19.4.) Most annual attainment rates must increase by 25 per cent to more than 100 per cent to meet the needs of a city of even 225,000 population.

The elements that apparently have been provided in the past at least as rapidly as they need be provided in the future include secondary and special schools and inadequate housing (mostly shacks). Although it is not apparent in our tables because only completed facilities were counted, primary roads and medical facilities have also been provided in the past as rapidly as they need be in the future. On the other hand, the standards used for secondary- and special-school facilities are quite low. (They are based on estimated employment demand rather than social demand.) If higher standards were adopted, past attainments would be relatively less satisfactory. Moreover, having built shack dwellings in the past at a higher rate than "required" in the future can hardly be considered a positive accomplishment.

It is our evalution that even the best past progress rates in urban development are inadequate to reach the "targets" for the elements in either alternative "target city." This could imply that the targets are just too high. But these targets are based on estimates of production and employment prepared by the CVG, which are substantially lower than those prepared only a few years earlier. It could also imply that the CVG

TABLE 19.4

Annual Rates of Progress Required to Provide Elements of 1975 City of 300,000 Population (Compared with Best Past Performances)

	Estimate in 1965	Target in 1975	Required Average Annual Increase to Reach Target	Estimate of Greatest Annual Increase, 1961–1965	Required Annual Rate as Per Cent of Greatest Past Annual Rate
Population	75,000[a]	300,000	22,500	10,000	225
Households	13,000[a]	50,000	3,700	1,700	218
Labor force	24,000[a]	90,000	6,600	3,000	220
Employment	21,000[b]	78,000	5,700	3,000	190
Housing units[c]	13,000	50,000	3,700	2,300	161
Adequate	6,500	40,000	3,350	1,300	258
Inadequate	6,500	10,000	350	1,000	35
Schools[d]					
Primary classrooms	171	795	62	21	295
Primary schools	18	70	5	2	250
Secondary classrooms	40	133	9	10	90
Secondary schools	4	10	0.6	1	60
Special classrooms	37	183	15	28	54
Special schools	3	11	0.8	2	40
Medical facilities[e] (number of beds)	142	900	76	6	e
Primary roads[f] (kilometers)	10	102	9	6	150
Electric service[g] (households served)	8,000	50,000	4,200	1,800	233
Water and sewage[h] (households served)	6,000	50,000	4,400	1,500	293
Commercial floor space in major centers[i] (square meters)	45,000	226,000	18,100	10,000	181
Industrial land area utilized[j] (hectares)	172	1,336	116	60	193

a.–j. See notes to Table 19.3.

or other ministries should have more resources available. The CVG's three basic sources of revenue are the national budget, proceeds from the disposition of land, and receipts from providing public services. Strategic actions by the CVG probably could result in substantial increases in each type of revenue, but such considerations were not germane to our assignment. Inadequate performance related to the "targets" could imply instead that the CVG was not using its development resources as efficiently as it should have. Resources could have been used more efficiently by (1) adopting improved procedures and (2) further shifting the emphasis from direct CVG involvement in urban development to promotion directed at getting other government agencies and private interests more involved.

Achievement of a "balanced" city. The same "target city" comparison was used to evaluate the balance being achieved among the various elements of urban development.

The Joint Center had been recommending an *unbalanced* approach to developing Ciudad Guayana, that is, *overdeveloping* the infrastructure (including housing, roads, schools, hospitals, and utilities) in relation to current population and current industrial demand. This unbalanced development was designed to attract industry to the area. Industry would find the necessary excess capacity in these facilities to immediately accommodate its needs and those of its employees. This might offset drawbacks like the 25 per cent annual turnover in employment at the steel mill, which apparently has discouraged some industries from moving to the Guayana. As a promotional measure, the overdevelopment of urban infrastructure had considerable merit. Nevertheless, considering urban development *per se*, the achievement of a balanced city was also desirable.

Strictly from the standpoint of balanced urban development, the CVG had placed too much emphasis on the construction of primary roads, high-quality private primary schools, housing for middle-income families, and the four community centers. Insufficient emphasis had been placed on reception areas and housing for low-income families, public primary schools, water and sewer services, and park and outdoor recreation facilities. These conclusions are based on our "target city" analysis.

Comprehensive program of promotion and institutional coordination. However, we believed that these somewhat inappropriate allocations of resources were of nominal significance compared to the emphasis that the CVG had placed on financing improvements itself rather than getting other government agencies and private interests involved. CVG officials had apparently recognized the high cost of direct involvement, and they had been anxious to obtain the participation of others. However, until this desire is translated into a truly effective comprehensive program of promotion and institutional coordination (including an explicit urban development program), the CVG will continue to be confronted with the fact that its resources are inadequate for the task at hand.

Recommendations for Improvement

Data for evaluation. The preceding comparisons of urban development attainments with goals and targets were largely based on our interpretations of what we believed to be the CVG goals and on our conceptual analysis of the "target city." Although these comparisons resulted in general indications of the CVG's effectiveness in urban development, such comparisons would have been much more valuable if the data inputs had been better. Therefore the CVG was urged to make periodic and systematic evaluations of its performance in urban development related to its goals, objectives, and targets. The following inputs would be required:

1. Explicitly formulated and adopted goals.

2. Translation of these goals into specific objectives that can be measured either relatively or absolutely.

3. Clearly defined and classified projects.

4. Specific targets for each project related to the goals and objectives. These targets must be measurable in terms of quantity and time.

5. Accurate records, updated periodically (say, monthly), on the progress of each project.

The desirability of translating general goals into measurable objectives and quantitative targets cannot be overemphasized. Although it may not be possible to develop measurable objectives and targets for all goals, our experience indicates that it is possible in most instances. When it is not possible, nonmeasurable objectives should be developed, and progress compared with them subjectively.

Such statements of goals, objectives, projects, and targets, together with periodic progress reports on the projects, would permit a comparison of expectations with actual attainments. For this comparison to be even more meaningful, additional factors can be introduced. Intermediate targets are needed for effective control and evaluation of urban development projects. Project progress reports are basic to project administration because they permit quick summaries of project expenditures and attainments. But the best and most practical means of comparing project results with objectives and targets on a continuing basis is the Critical Path Method (CPM).[1] Hence we and the Joint Center emphatically urged the CVG to institute both monthly progress reports and the Critical Path Method for projects.

Administrative efficiency. It is extremely difficult to make any accurate and persuasive judgments about just how much of the CVG's failure to attain its targets and goals was caused by lack of resources and how much by inefficiency. Such estimation is particularly hard to make because not much accurate information exists concerning many of the CVG's activities during the period from 1961 through 1965, as we have pointed out. Nevertheless, an important part of our assignment consisted in evaluating the CVG's administrative efficiency and making recommendations for improving it. Therefore our analysis concentrated on the procedures used to allocate resources in urban development rather than on the substantive results achieved by such allocation. We believe we were able to discover certain inefficiencies that, if removed, would result in greater effectiveness for the CVG's future urban development program for whatever amount of resources are available to the CVG.

We broke down our analysis of administrative efficiency into five basic categories:

1. organization
2. authority and responsibility
3. programming and budgeting
4. flow of information
5. external relations.

Within each category we indicated the following:

1. the major problems we found in our study of the CVG's operations
2. the basic principles of efficient operation we believed should be used to solve those problems
3. the specific recommendations embodying those principles that we believed would improve the CVG's efficiency in urban development.

We do not believe that all of our specific recommendations should be put into effect in the near future. The CVG is a large organization that has been in operation for several years; it has therefore acquired the "behavioral inertia" natural to all large organizations. This means that too rapid an introduction of change will cause failure to understand its purposes, resistance by those accustomed to established procedures, and a serious disruption in operating efficiency. To help the CVG improve its operating procedures without creating such undesirable outcomes, we arranged our specific recommendations into a gradual and evolutionary series of steps. Thus we grouped our recommendations into the following categories:

Immediate: those that should be adopted as soon as possible.

Short-run: those that should be adopted only after most of the immediate recommendations have been carried out and "digested" by the CVG.

Long-run: those that should be adopted at some point in the future only after most of the immediate and short-run recommendations have been carried out and "digested" by the CVG.

TABLE 19.5
Summary of Recommendations, with Suggested Staging for Implementation

Recommendations	Staging of Implementation		
	Immediate	Short Run	Long Run
Organization			
Consider creation of separate organization for urban development	×		
Create operating committee of CVG staff-unit directors	×		
Authority and responsibility			
Prepare and adopt statements of goals and objectives	×		
Prepare specific definitions of functions of each staff unit	×		
Programming and budgeting			
Establish capital improvements committee		×	
Expand budget-office staff and clearly define functions		×	
Adopt project-oriented approach	×		
Initiate capital improvements program		×	
Prepare informal staff-wor programs	×		
Initiate program budgeting		×	
Establish detailed cost-accounting system			×
Prepare systematic and comprehensive cost-benefit analyses			×
Use Critical Path Method for projects		×	

TABLE 19.5—*continued*
Summary of Recommendations, with Suggested Staging for Implementation

Recommendations	Staging of Implementation		
	Immediate	Short Run	Long Run
Flow of information			
Establish monthly project progress reports	×		
Designate budget office as central programming and information systems office of CVG	×		
Establish a joint information center and data exchange program			×
External relations			
Delegate responsibility for secondary interagency contacts to intermediate-level staff			×
Create urban promotion section within urban development division		×	
Encourage informal discussions and acquaintances with officials in other agencies		×	
Increase industrial promotion staff		×	
Increase staff and financial allocations for specific industry studies		×	
Improve promotional procedures		×	
Shift emphasis from direct involvement of CVG in urban development to promotion		×	

In our summary of the recommendations made under each of the five categories just described (organization, authority and responsibility, programming and budgeting, flow of information, and external relations), we listed our recommendations and noted after each whether we considered it immediate, short run, or long run in nature. We also presented detailed analyses of each problem and of each recommendation in our original report, but these are too long to include here. Instead, a summary of our major recommendations is presented in Table 19.5.

The Significance of This Study and Its Findings to Urban Development in Underdeveloped Countries

The experience gained in conducting this complex analysis of resource allocation is richly suggestive of hypotheses and conclusions concerning urban development in general, and in underdeveloped nations in particular. Space limitations preclude anything like an adequate discussion of these findings. Therefore, we will present a summary list of the most significant ones, provocatively omitting any justification for them. The findings are divided into two major groups: procedural and substantive. Many are not new, but perhaps their repetition here will reinforce their general acceptance.

Procedural findings.

1. Urban development "according to plan" is greatly hindered by the tendency to develop long-range plans that are essentially descriptions of desired end states, without any specific translation into short-run and inter-mediate-run programs for action. Concentration upon the aspiration role of plans is perhaps appropriate in the early stages of creating a new city, but it is far too vague for the execution stages. Hence there is a crucial need for developing specific short-run programs explicitly stated in terms of particular projects, budgets, and schedules.

2. Government agencies tend to resist developing explicit action sched-ules because they imply fixed commitments. The latter in turn restrict the political maneuverability of top-level officials, who must continually negotiate to obtain financial support for urban development. Overt commitments also expose top officials to the risk of publicly recognizable failure. Furthermore, explicit schedules reduce their ability to maintain centralized control over their subordinates by generating uncertainty about who will be given what resources. Thus one of the biggest obstacles to achieving administrative efficiency in development programs is top-level bureaucratic reluctance to use methods that are fully within the technical abilities of existing personnel. The result is a lack of clarity concerning top-downward information flows (including orders and directives).

3. Equally significant are inadequate bottom-upward information flows. Two kinds of vital internal information seem particularly scarce: day-to-day reports concerning actual peformance in the field, and accurate records concerning the allocation of internal resources (especially personnel time) to particular projects or activities. These deficiencies are encouraged by the failure to develop short-run programs that clearly define individual projects to which time and money can be charged and about which progress reports can be made.

4. Effective program evaluation thus must wait upon adequate program definition and the creation of relevant information flows both downward and upward within the development agency or agencies. However, once top officials become persuaded of the need for a systematic evaluation of progress, this desire can be made into a powerful lever for creating

more effective management procedures in all parts of the agency concerned.

5. Unless top officials in fact place high priority on accurate evaluation, it will not be carried out for two reasons. First, their subordinates are not anxious to report on their own shortcomings. Second, the few people sufficiently skillful and well trained to conduct accurate evaluations are usually in great demand for other high-priority functions.

6. Thus it is unlikely that underdeveloped nations will place much emphasis on systematic evaluation in the early stages of any major development project or program. The people talented enough for evaluation will be considered far more valuable in implementation roles, since it appears that getting at least something done is more important than evaluating progress. This implies that the early stages of development projects will be marked by considerable "muddling through"—more than is technically required by the difficulty or novelty of the situation involved.

Substantive findings.

1. It is impossible for an underdeveloped country to build a new city in which all residents occupy "standard quality" dwellings. The capital expense required is too great for such a country—and perhaps for *any* country, including the United States. Moreover, the inflow of extremely poor migrants to any area of economic expansion cannot be stopped except by harshly repressive measures that no government is likely to adopt. Hence it is certain that a large number of shantytowns will appear whenever a new city is created or an existing one grows rapidly. Planners should recognize this fact by setting aside definite areas for such low-income settlements, providing minimal services there to give people an incentive to use those areas, and creating inmigration guidance centers to help people get settled there.

2. A national government agency charged with developing a certain geographic area finds itself in a dilemma regarding the relationship of its own role to the roles of established functional departments of the national government (such as the education or health departments). This is especially true if the national government dominates local and state governments, as in most underdeveloped nations. The functional departments are reluctant to expand their activities into new areas because of the enormous demands upon them from existing areas that are poorly served now. Therefore, if the area development agency attempts to get these departments to create and operate new facilities from the start, it may find itself frustrated by slow reactions and endless delays. This is

particularly likely if the development agency tries to get several different functional departments to coordinate their activities closely so as to attain "balanced" development.

The alternative strategy is to attempt rapid but "unbalanced" development by creating those facilities most likely to attract population in a hurry. Once a sizable population exists the development agency can argue that its citizens deserve as much attention from functional departments as the residents of older areas.

This strategy has several major drawbacks. First, it means that the development agency must initially "get into everybody's business." It has to build at least some schools, roads, utilities, and housing, as well as start the basic economic activities around which the city will be created. This tends to spread out and exhaust its resources, create conflicts with established functional departments, and involve its personnel in jobs for which they have no specialized training. Second, this strategy attracts population first and only persuades functional departments to serve them later. Hence it creates a time lag between population growth and even minimal public services, thereby imposing heavy costs on the current population. Nevertheless, the experience of the CVG suggests that the "unbalanced" strategy may in the long run be the best way to bring new cities into existence rapidly. It also has the advantage of providing at least an early period of relatively good coordination among diverse elements of urban development (such as housing, schools, and roads), since they are all under one authority.

3. The process of developing a major new city is inevitably saturated with political considerations right from the start. At every moment, choices must be made involving basic value judgments about the proper use of national resources. It is natural for the leaders of an area development agency to become advocates of using resources to assist their area. But they must contend in the political arena with others equally dedicated to advocating competitive areas, both old and new. Thus purely technical and managerial considerations must often be subordinated to political ones if the area development agency is to flourish—or even survive—in the rough struggle over the allocation of the limited resources available for development. This situation is not only inescapable, it is proper, since politics is the legitimate way to settle basic value conflicts.

This conclusion has two crucial implications. First, area development agencies must be run by leaders who have a significant political following and are extremely skilled in political negotiations. The need for this talent is illustrated by the delicate dealings with national functional departments described earlier. This talent is just as important as technical competence in administration or full understanding of the complex issues involved in economic development. The CVG was indeed fortunate to have a man with both these types of skills leading it. Second, management experts and other technicians advising such agencies must both take political factors into account in formulating recommendations and expect their findings to be attenuated in practice by political factors they cannot easily perceive.

Chapter 20

Employment Effects of the Urban-Rural Investment Choice

Edward Moscovitch

To many people the process of economic development conjures up images of shiny new factories and a rising gross national product. I am interested in development not because national income is low but because people are poor. The groups that most need help in an underdeveloped economy are the small subsistence farmers and the rural people who have moved to the cities in a futile search for work and now live at very low levels of income in the huge slums that surround these cities. Eliminating this sort of poverty means creating more jobs, either on farms using modern techniques or in factories or other forms of full-time urban employment.[1] Development should seek to spread the modern economy to encompass the whole population—to raise as many people as possible out of the subsistence sector into the modern sector by providing them with training and with modern tools of production.

A country's progress toward achieving this development goal can be measured in part by its unemployment rate. By this standard, many countries are doing very poorly. Venezuela is no exception: according to the national planning agency (Oficina Central de Coordinación y Planificación—Cordiplan), 13 per cent of the labor force was unemployed in 1962, and another 37 per cent was in the "gray zone" of underemployment.[2] The latter are the people occupied at make-work: peddling on street corners, swelling government payrolls, or doing odd jobs on farms or in small towns. The agency estimated that the work they do could be done just as well by half the number of people.

Thus the equivalent of 32 per cent of the labor force was unemployed in

1962. In terms of individuals, however, the total was far grimmer, for fully 50 per cent of the labor force was either out of work altogether or working at very unproductive tasks. This half of the labor force is outside the modern economy and lives in grinding poverty.

Many observers have suggested that more attention be paid to the unemployment problem in Venezuela. In its evaluation of the 1963–1966 plan the Alliance for Progress stated that Venezuela must still be considered "underdeveloped," despite its high per capita income, because of its high birth rate, high illiteracy, and high unemployment and because primitive methods of production still coexist with the more modern methods.[3] Dudley Seers argues that in economies like that of Venezuela the unemployment problem is more serious than inadequate national income.[4]

This leads us to the question dealt with in this chapter: Can Venezuela reduce its unemployment rate by modifying its planning targets to have a slightly faster rate of growth of agricultural production, at the expense of a slightly slower growth of industry? Is it preferable to speed up investment in agriculture, and help people while they are still on the land, or to expand industry more rapidly, thus employing people after they have moved to the cities?

We are interested in comparing more than just the employment consequences of a change in the mix of new investment projects. Thus an agricultural project might generate more employment than an equivalent industrial project, but only at the expense of greatly reducing over-all output and the sums available for reinvestment. Therefore, the income, savings, and foreign exchange consequences of alternative investments are also explored.

Although the comparison made in this chapter is for the investment mix of Venezuela as a whole, it has great relevance for the Guayana project for two reasons. The first involves the rate of expansion of the Guayana program: Should Venezuela push ahead rapidly with the heavy industry envisioned for the Guayana, or should it slow down this project somewhat and use the funds thus released to create additional employment in agriculture and thereby reduce unemployment? By so doing, it might be possible to reduce the flow of inmigrants to Ciudad Guayana. This new city has attracted poor inmigrants at a rate much greater than it can employ them, and it may be that it would be easier to employ them back on the farm rather than wait for them to create slums in Ciudad Guayana.

The second reason involves priorities within the Guayana program. Should industrialization be given priority or should more attention be paid to developing agriculture in the Guayana highlands or the Orinoco Delta? If a firm decision is made to create a large agricultural development in the delta, should it be composed of small, labor-intensive farms or of large, capital-intensive units?

Autonomous versus Induced Activities

A useful way of making our comparison is to imagine that an economic plan for the period to 1975 is being prepared for Venezuela. Most of the production targets have been set and include substantial growth in both the industrial and agricultural sectors. Nonetheless, a large block of investment capital remains. Our question is how to use that capital. Should it be put into a few extra industrial projects and thus speed up the growth of industry? Or should we give up that potential extra growth in industry and instead use the extra money to achieve a faster growth in agriculture? In allocating this block of capital, then, we are not deciding whether to have an exclusively agricultural or industrial development. But we are deciding whether to speed up one sector slightly at the expense of the other.

In the preparation of our hypothetical plan we have made projections of likely demand (including the demand generated by the value added that our as yet unallocated capital will create), and we can assume for the time being that the over-all pattern of demand will be the same regardless of our choice. (Later this assumption is modified.) Before we can compare possible projects we must have some way of knowing which few products could be produced in greater amounts if investment funds were made available. To do this we turn to an analysis of autonomous and induced economic activities.

As the economy grows, the demand for various products grows with it. Those with high income elasticities of demand, such as appliances, grow rapidly, while products with lower income elasticities, such as most foods, grow more slowly. If the government wishes to expand production of a particular product more rapidly, it may do so in either of two ways. The first is to lower its price, so that consumption of the product increases more rapidly than it otherwise would. Whether this can be done depends on how responsive the quantity demanded is to a change in price—on the price elasticity of demand.

In countries like Venezuela, where the bulk of the population is poor, these elasticities are low (quantity demanded will change very little when prices change). The reason for this is that when people are very poor they spend most of their money on the necessities of life, and the way they divide their expenditures among broad classes of goods, such as food, shoes, and housing, is not likely to change significantly when prices change.[5] For example, if the government should wish to increase the production of grain (and reduce the consumption of clothing so that people could buy this increased grain output), it would take very large decreases in grain prices and very large increases in clothing prices to adjust demand to the new production patterns. These changes would be so large as to make the grain production very unprofitable. Thus this method of changing production patterns is not likely to be used.

The second approach is to change the country's balance of trade. If foreign markets are available, more of various products can be exported. A rapid growth of industry could be achieved by exporting steel. Or, if a large proportion of a country's consumption of a particular product comes from imports, rapid growth of production can be supported by replacing these imports by domestic output. Venezuela's production of milk could rise much more rapidly than consumption if the large quantities of imported powdered milk could be replaced by the output of new dairy farms.

Because increases in the output of export- or import-substituting industries are not tied directly to increases in consumer demand, these industries may be called "autonomous industries." Those industries that do not export and fill domestic needs without substantial imports may be called "induced industries." Industries in this category (such as housing construction) can increase output only if income increases or if relative prices change. As indicated earlier, only increases in income are likely to be important in countries like Venezuela.

This distinction is useful in explaining the growth of many countries.[6] In Venezuela, oil exports were an autonomous industry that grew rapidly and created a growing market for a wide range of induced industries. In addition, these exports financed a variety of imports. As the growth of oil exports slowed down, Venezuela turned to import substitution (to domestic production of many items) to maintain its rate of growth.

Thus the choice open to Venezuela is to spend that sum of additional investment capital on autonomous projects in either the agricultural or the industrial sector. The government does have this kind of influence over the Venezuelan economy, since it finances about 40 per cent of the country's investment. Moreover, the government has concentrated its investments on precisely those autonomous activities between which we must choose.

It is a safe guess that our hypothetical new investment will be made in an export- or import-substituting industry. But which industries in particular?

Venezuela is already very close to self-sufficiency in a wide range of consumer goods, and, for those few products still supplied by substantial imports, current plans call for their replacement within the next few years. Thus there is little room for additional investment in these industries. Imports of machinery and other capital equipment are fairly large, but many of these items are used in such small quantities as to make domestic production impossible. A modest program of heavy machinery manufacture in the Guayana is included in the current plans, and, given the complicated nature of such products, it is hard to see how a more rapid advance could be achieved.

In the industrial area, then, more rapid growth can be achieved only by an increase in exports. The most promising areas here are steel, prereduced iron ore, and petrochemicals. Venezuela's endowments of iron ore, natural gas, petroleum, hydroelectric sites, and industrial sites at port locations can be expected to facilitate low-cost export production. Venezuela already exports large quantities of iron ore; the domestic value added of this ore could be increased greatly by treating it with natural gas to eliminate much of the oxygen content, leaving a product with a 90 per cent iron content. Although some steel and petrochemicals are now imported, plans are under way to expand their production, and someday expansion into export markets should be practicable. All of these industries are being established in previously unsettled areas; they are urban in the sense that they require large numbers of workers who will live in the cities now being planned and built around them.

In the agricultural sector, there are two major autonomous-demand crops: milk and fruit. Venezuela currently imports almost 40 per cent of its milk, in powdered form. With the relatively high income elasticity of demand for milk and milk products added to this deficit, there should be room for a rapid increase in milk production during the next few years. Fruit is a potential export crop. The Venezuelans have received several purchase offers from abroad—for tropical fruits in pulp or concentrates for juices and preserves, and for fruits such as melons and tomatoes that can be sold in northern markets during our winter.

In addition to these two crops, Venezuela also has significant imports of corn, oils, and animal feeds. The projected production of other foods, such as meats, appears to be too low to meet rising demand. Although the potential import substitution of these crops is not large enough to be considered a major item in itself, the inevitable meat sales of dairy farms and nonfruit sales of fruit farms will nonetheless prevent the imports of these crops that would otherwise be necessary.[7]

TABLE 20.1

Industrial Projects Accounting: Individual Plants

	Steel Mill	Prereduced Iron Ore
Annual output (thousand metric tons per year)	2,000[a]	660
Project accounting ($ millions)		
Factory investment	680	36
Housing and social investment	102	6
Total investment	782	42
Sales	225	23
Purchases	90	10
Gross value added	135	13
Depreciation	36	2
Net value added	99	11
Payroll	49	2
Profit	50	9
Value added in housing	10	0.5
Total value added[b]	109	11.5
Housing payments[c]	7	0.4
Total funds available for investment[d]	93	11.4
Imports on current account	26	0.5
Net exports[e]	199	22.5
Import content of investment	444	25.0
Employment (number of persons)	12,000	660

Source: Edward Moscovitch, "Urban-Rural Investment Allocation in Venezuela" (Ph.D. dissertation, Massachusetts Institute of Technology, Department of Economics, 1966), p. 16.
a. Ingot basis.
b. Net value added in industry is added to value added in housing to get total value added.
c. This housing figure is on a gross basis. The depreciation allowance would be small—about 22 per cent of the total for a forty-year home life.
d. This is the sum of housing payments, profits, and depreciation. Following Domar, depreciation reserves have been included in reinvestable funds. See Evsey Domar, "Depreciation, Replacement and Growth," *The Economic Journal,* Vol. LXIII, March 1953.
e. As these are export projects, gross exports equal sales, and net exports equal sales minus imports on current account.

The Industrial Projects: Steel and Iron Ore

Any substantial exports of steel from Venezuela would require the construction of a new mill in the Guayana, as expansion already planned for the existing mill will just about exhaust its capacity. The investment costs, value added, and employment of a new two-million ingot ton mill are summarized in Table 20.1. In the calculations I have assumed that the government has extra investment funds at its disposal and can put them in either industry or agriculture. As the government will organize the project, the gross returns on capital—profit, interest, and depreciation

TABLE 20.2
Dairy and Crop Farm Accounting

	Dairy Farm (15 Hectares)	Small Dry Farm (10 Hectares)	Large Dry Farm (200 Hectares)
		Dollars	
Farm investment	9,100	9,100	200,000
Housing and social investment	2,000	2,000	22,000
Total investment	11,100	11,100	222,000
Sales	4,050	4,450	89,000
Purchases	1,100	1,300	30,800
Gross value added[a]	2,950	3,150	58,200
Depreciation	225	550	19,200
Net value added[a]	2,725	2,600	39,000
Interest	75	150	4,000
Wage payments	100	250	17,000
Farmers' income	2,550	2,200	18,000
Total labor income	2,650	2,450	35,000
Value added in housing	150	150	2,000
Total value added[b]	2,875	2,750	41,000
Farm and home amortization payment	500	375	6,200
Total available for investment[c]	725	925	18,400
Imports of machinery (tractors)[d]	445	1,550	58,000
		Number of Persons	
Employment	1.05	1.10	8

Source: Edward Moscovitch, "Urban-Rural Investment Allocation in Venezuela" (Ph.D. dissertation, Massachusetts Institute of Technology, Department of Economics, 1966), p. 20.
a. These are for value added in farming.
b. This is net farming value added plus housing value added. The housing figure is gross, but the depreciation adjustment would be small—about $35 per year.
c. Total available for investment is the sum of interest payments, amortization payments, and depreciation, excluding $75, $150, and $11,000 of tractor depreciation for dairy, dry, and large farms, respectively.
d. On capital account.

payments—will accrue to the government. It can use them for reinvestment in other projects, so they may be considered as the savings generated by the project, or funds available for reinvestment.[8] By comparing the gross return on capital for all projects, regardless of how it is distributed between interest or rent or profit, we can abstract from different financial mechanisms to examine the underlying capital-output relationships. After these are made clear, modifications could be made for other cases, such as government loans to private entrepreneurs to have them build a plant.

The plant for prereducing iron ore would, like the steel mill, be built in the Guayana. A small plant is planned; exports could rise to much higher levels than the 660,000 tons shown in the table. Although no data are shown explicitly for the petrochemical complex, the capital-employment and capital-output ratios for such a project would closely approximate those shown for the ore-reduction plant. The Instituto Venezolano Petroquímica is currently operating an ammonia and soda-chloride plant at Morón; a large expansion to serve export markets would include facilities for explosives, polyethylene, and synthetic rubber.

The Agricultural Projects: Dairy and Fruit Farms

The investment, output, and employment estimates for potential farm projects, given in Table 20.2, are based on farm plans prepared by a group of Israeli agricultural planners and their Venezuelan students. These planners are working on a joint venture of several government agencies to raise the levels of production and standards of living of campesinos on land-reform settlements in Venezuela. Their methods are being applied to a rapidly expanding number of such settlements. The farm sizes—10 to 15 hectares (25 to 37 acres)—are small, but, given the chance for two growing seasons and the fact that in many Asian countries the average size is close to one hectare, these farms are large enough to produce a standard of living quite high for the underdeveloped world. By teaching the farmers to use modern farming techniques, such as proper water management and the use of improved seeds, fertilizers, and insect and weed sprays, the planners hope to achieve a target income of $2,200 per farm family. Thus this is definitely modern, if small-scale, farming.

Since detailed estimates for the economics of small-scale fruit farming had not been prepared at the time I left Venezuela in 1965, the estimates for a 10-hectare dry farm, which include some land devoted to fruit growing, are used as a proxy. The accounting for a 200-hectare farm is my own estimate, made by combining twenty of the smaller farms and assuming that much of the campesino labor would be replaced by tractors.

Industrial and Agricultural Projects Compared

Before we turn to the actual comparison of industrial and agricultural projects, two possibly confusing points should be made clear. The sales and value added data in Tables 20.1 and 20.2 were derived by valuing milk, steel, and other products at world (import) prices, not at the artificially high domestic prices made possible by tariff and other protection. If Venezuela should produce more milk and reduce its imports, the value to Venezuela of that additional output is the value of the imports it replaces. Similarly the value of increased steel output is the value of the extra export revenue gained. If planned production should go to increased milk output rather then to increased steel production, foreign exchange will be saved by not importing milk, but at the expense of not earning foreign exchange by the export of steel. By measuring these goods at their world market prices we are measuring their opportunity cost to Venezuela.

Some people might be tempted to argue that additional investment in agriculture will increase productivity in agriculture and therefore reduce employment there. If output were not increased at the same time that additional investment was made, this would be correct. But we have limited our choice to autonomous industries precisely because we wish to avoid this problem. In both industry and agriculture we are discussing investment in *new projects* that will increase over-all output in the sector. Production methods on existing units will be unaffected by our decision. Thus the agricultural investment under consideration will clear new lands and build up new dairy herds, not buy tractors to replace hired hands on existing large plantations.

We are now ready to discuss the comparison that lies at the heart of this chapter. Suppose Venezuela had enough money to build another new steel mill and the necessary worker housing and training facilities—$782 million. This money could be invested in 1 steel mill or almost 19 ore-reduction plants, or in 70,500 small farms or 3,525 larger farms. Table 20.3 shows the employment, value added, and potential savings that would be generated by this sum in each of the various projects in which it could be invested. The comparison laid out here is neutral in the sense that it spells out only the consequences of different choices; the reader is free to choose between them on whatever grounds seem appropriate. (The next section discusses various criteria for choosing between projects.)

Contrary to the expectation of those who equate development with industrialization, the value added yielded by the agricultural projects is the same as or greater than that yielded by the industrial projects. While yielding a value added similar to that of the industrial projects, the small farms generate six times as much direct employment and four times as much labor income for the same investment. If agriculture is increased at the expense of industry, then, six jobs will be created in agriculture for each job lost in industry.

If demand for other products remained the same regardless of how our investment were used, we could say that our hypothetical investment would give us 60,000 more jobs if used in agriculture rather than in industry. But it is unlikely that this would be true. Instead of accruing to relatively high-paid workers and to the government (or private owners), who would

TABLE 20.3
Industrial and Agricultural Projects Compared

	Steel Mill	Ore-Reduction Plants	Dairy Farms	Small Dry Farms	Large Dry Farms
Number of factories and farms	1	19	70,500	70,500	3,525
Project account		Million Dollars			
Investment	782	798[a]	782	782	782
Sales	225	437	285	314	314
Gross value added	145	256	218	234	213
Net value added	109	218	202	194	145
Labor income	49	38	187	173	123
Savings					
profit and interest	50	171	5	11	14
depreciation	36	38	11[b]	29[b]	29[b]
home payments	7	8	35	26	22
total savings	93	217	51	66	65[c]
Current imports	26	9	—	—	—
Exports[d]	225	437	285	314	314
Net annual exports	199	428	285	314	314
Capital imports[n]	444	475	31	110	204
		Number of Persons			
Employment	12,000	12,500	74,000	77,500	28,000
		Dollars			
Investment per worker	65,000	64,000	10,600	10,100	28,000
Net value added per worker	9,100	17,500	2,700	2,500	5,200
Investment/sales	3.5	1.9	2.7	2.5	2.5
Investment/net value added	7.8	3.7	3.9	4.0	5.4
Investment/gross value added	5.4	3.1	3.6	3.3	3.7
		Dollars			
Labor income per worker	4,100	3,000	2,500	2,200	4,400

Source: Calculated from Tables 20.1 and 20.2.
a. 19 ore plants at $42 million each. This is more meaningful than using 18 + plants to keep capital exactly equal.
b. Since tractors wear out quickly, these figures are net of tractor depreciation of $5, $11, and $39 million, respectively.
c. This figure is misleadingly low. If the owners save 20 per cent of their $18,000 incomes in addition to house payments, this would make available an additional $13 million.
d. Exports or import substitutes.
e. These capital imports are not annual requirements but represent the imported machinery or tractors.

use it for investment (or luxury consumption), the value added of farm projects goes to a large number of relatively lower-paid workers and to many more workers. Thus the demand would be greater for basic consumer goods such as clothing, small appliances, and housing, which are themselves made by labor-intensive processes. The value added of agricultural projects, then, would be spent on items that generate far more employment than the value added of industrial projects. I have estimated that this indirect effect might mean an additional 60,000 jobs.[9] Thus the overall net employment advantage of the agricultural projects could be as high as 120,000 jobs.

Because such a high share of the value added goes to labor, less is available for possible reinvestment. Estimates of the amount of reinvestable funds—profits and interest, home and farm purchase payments, and depreciation—are given in Table 20.3. For the same investment the steel mill generates half again as much for this purpose as do the small farms, while the ore plant generates four times as much. Nonetheless, the farm savings are still sizable—30 per cent of gross value added. In both cases, possible savings out of personal income by farmers or workers are not included in the estimates. The figures represent those funds that the government in its role as project developer could be sure of receiving —funds such as the home purchase payments it charged to farmers or workers.

The usefulness of the comparison made here depends on the reliability of the estimates. Although it would be impossible to describe their derivation and indicate all the elements of reliability and doubt in this brief chapter, the reader might be interested in knowing in a general way the sources of my information. Estimates on the costs of possible new steel mills were based on discussions with American advisers to the Orinoco Steel Mill, and the ore plant figures were taken from a feasibility study prepared for the Corporación Venezolana de Guayana (CVG). The farm plans were derived from estimates made by the Israeli advisers in the Centro de Capicitación e Investigación Aplicada de Reforma Agraria. An important question with these farm estimates is whether the favorable early results that had been obtained at the time of my visit could be duplicated on a large scale. This question could not be easily answered at that time; today, with the Israeli methods being used on several additional projects, it should be possible to shed additional light on it.

Generally the ratios between investment and employment, and between investment and total product, are likely to be quite reliable. For industry these were based on my contacts' knowledge of industrial processes; for agriculture they were based on the current settlement practices of the Centro's projects and on output targets that seem conservative in relation to the yields actually realized in the early years of the projects. In both areas the value added estimates are likely to be much less reliable, since costs may always be higher than expected. This source of error is probably more serious in the industrial projects, since one of their most attractive aspects—the high potential savings—is probably overstated by the estimates in Table 20.3. One reason for this is that the profits component of industrial savings is a residual, estimated by subtracting estimated costs from expected sales. Relatively small drops in price may mean fairly large drops in profits. Similarly, if the plants are too inefficient to operate at a profit, this source of savings would not exist.

Another problem results from our convention that the government owns and operates the industrial projects. Because of this, value added goes to only two sources—wages and possible savings. This leads us to a dilemma. Neither the government-owned petrochemical plant nor the government-owned steel mill in the Guayana had been able to operate at a profit at the time of my stay in Venezuela. Private management might be more efficient, and thus return a profit. But some of this profit would then go to stockholders, who would consume some of it. If the government used its money to make loans to private entrepreneurs to build new facilities, it might receive interest on these funds, and the private entrepreneur might voluntarily reinvest some of his profits. Also, the government might tax some of the profits. In any case, the amount of funds available for reinvestment would surely be much less than the totals shown here. As long as government ownership is less efficient than private management, then, these savings figures are something of a mirage.

One possible solution to this problem is better training and more experience for government entrepreneurs. Another is to have the government enter into joint ventures with private business, and also to lay a tax on the private share of profits. Still, private business will not be interested unless its after-tax return on its own investment is sufficiently lucrative. And even if these estimated profits are eventually realized, there will be a considerable delay between the time a plant is begun and the time when output is brought up to full-capacity, profit-yielding levels.

If we examine the effect on the balance of payments of each project, we see that the farm projects make a smaller contribution to net exports on current account than does the ore plant, but a larger contribution than the steel mill. In addition, the farms need to buy much less imported capital equipment when they are started up.

Merely to state our comparison is not to say that all of the various projects could actually be completed, in the sizes metioned here, if the government should choose to carry them out. Really large exports of fruit, chemicals, and iron products might be possible only if Venezuela accepted greatly reduced prices. Also, trained personnel, such as engineers, workers, agronomists, and extension agents, might be a more serious limitation than the supply of capital. Certainly any new investment of these magnitudes would need to be accompanied by large training programs. Despite these limitations, however, the comparison is useful because it gives the trade-off between the two types of investment. Except for the steel mill, it tells us how employment changes as we make relatively small decreases in investment in one sector and corresponding increases in the other. As industrial investment is slowed down and agricultural investment increased, industrial jobs are lost and agricultural jobs created in the ratio of six jobs gained to each one lost.

Although this ratio is more important than the absolute amounts, it is still important to know how large $782 million is in the context of the Venezuelan economy. Some very rough figures on this can be derived from the 1975 forecasts contained in the 1963–1966 national plan. A $782 million investment represents 5 per cent of the $16 billion investment requirements for the period 1966–1975. The $200 million of value added generated by these projects would represent just over 1 per cent of the projected 1975 national output ($15 billion). The extra employment from the agricultural alternative—60,000 direct jobs—represents just under 2 per cent of the expected employment of 3.5 million persons, or 3.5 per cent including the extra 60,000 jobs created indirectly. Given a family size of five, this would mean helping 600,000 people in all, which is 5 per cent of the expected 1975 population. The two million ingot tons of steel generated by our hypothetical investment compare with the 1965 production of 550,000 tons and the planned 1975 production of 2.1 million tons. This same investment would create enough dairy farms to provide 1.75 billion liters of milk annually—approximately the 1975 consumption, if historical income elasticities are maintained. This compares with the 1965 milk production of 500 million liters and consumption of 840 million liters. Thus an investment of the size we have been discussing bulks very large in the Venezuelan economy.

Investment Criteria

How shall we choose between the possible alternatives, now that we have estimated the consequences of each choice? The standard procedure is to judge a project by its contribution to over-all output.[10] Traditionally projects that yield the highest rate of profit are chosen, on the grounds that profits reflect the net contribution of the investment to the economy as a whole. This traditional argument rests on the assumption of a full-employment economy in which the prices for necessary inputs reflect what they would contribute to the economy if employed elsewhere. Under these circumstances the labor and raw materials used on a new project have to be taken away from other activities, thereby reducing output in the other activities by the value of these factors. Thus the net contribution of the new investment is the sales of the output made possible by the investment, less the labor and raw materials necessary to those sales—precisely the profit generated by the enterprise. Under these circumstances, then, the project with the highest profit does indeed contribute the most to over-all output.

The basic assumption of the traditional argument—that the labor hired by one firm must be taken away from other firms and thus reduce output elsewhere in the economy—does not fit the Venezuelan situation. With Venezuela's high unemployment and underemployment, there is little reason to believe that an increase in employment by one sector will lead to a very significant reduction in output elsewhere. Since the value of extra labor to the economy therefore approaches zero, the appropriate measure of the contribution of capital would use a zero wage.[11] Such a measure subtracts from sales purchases and depreciation, but not payroll, and therefore relates capital invested to value added rather than to profit. In a high-unemployment country like Venezuela, then, the capital–value added ratio is a more useful measure of a project's contribution to over-all output than the profit-capital ratio.

Using this criterion, there is little difference between the small-farm projects and the more profitable of the industrial projects. If Venezuela should achieve full employment, however, on the basis of output criteria the industrial projects would then be clearly preferable to the farm projects.

This point is illustrated numerically in Table 20.4 by the use of benefit-cost ratios. If a benefit-cost ratio equals one, the benefits the project contributes to the economy exactly equal the costs of the materials it uses. If this ratio exceeds one, the benefits exceed the costs. As the price at which any input, such as labor, is valued begins to rise, the ratios fall. If labor is valued at zero wage, as is appropriate now, the projects are about the same. But at full employment, when labor should be valued at a money wage, the ore plant is preferable to the farm projects.

Both the profits and the value added criteria are output criteria and are

TABLE 20.4
Benefit-Cost Ratios[a]

	Steel Mill	Ore Plant	Dairy Farm	Small Dry Farm	Large Dry Farm
Alternative 1, money value	0.93	1.29	0.80	0.78	1.05
Alternative 2, Bs. 2,000	1.12	1.42	1.23	1.16	1.20
Alternative 3, zero wage	1.15	1.45	1.43	1.33	1.26

Source : Computed from Tables 20.1 and 20.2 according to the formula given here.
a. The formula for benefit-cost ratios relates what is contributed to the economy with what is taken out, both generally measured at market prices. It is set up in such a way that a value of 1.0 means that net contributions just equal net costs, and so the project is just feasible. The formula is

Benefits = Sales of enterprise plus value added in housing
Cost = 10 per cent of total investment plus purchases plus depreciation plus labor (however valued).

Following the discussion in the text, several different values can be assigned to labor—its money wage, an opportunity cost of Bs. 2,000 ($440), representing a generous estimate of present earnings in subsistence farming, or zero. I present benefit-cost ratios for each of our projects calculated with each of these wage alternatives. In Alternative 1, a money value of Bs. 25,000 ($5,500) has been assigned as the value for the large-farm owner and Bs. 10,000 ($2,200) as the earnings for the small farmer. Other workers are charged at their money wages. Bs. 500 per family administration cost is charged for the small farms in all cases. Under Alternatives 2 and 3, all workers are charged at the reduced wage. This leads to misleadingly low figures for the industrial projects and the large farm, since factory and farm managers are always in scarce supply and always have a value greater than Bs. 2,000, regardless of how many unemployed or unskilled workers there may be. (The ratio for the large farm under Alternative 2, for instance, falls to 1.12 if the farmer is still counted at Bs. 25,000.)

not affected by the project's impact on the distribution of income. To measure the number of people brought into the modern economy by a project, we use a capital-employment criterion. On this basis the small-farm projects are clearly preferable, since a given investment in them generates six times as many jobs as the same investment in the industrial projects. In addition to this direct effect, there will be additional employment gains in other industries due to the redistribution of income involved in agricultural projects.

In the projects we are comparing here, there is no conflict between the employment and output criteria, since the agricultural projects yield higher employment while giving the same value added. But what if this were not the case, and higher employment could be achieved only by reducing value added (and therefore reducing national product)? Gains in employment represent increases in the incomes of the very poor, so that maximizing employment is roughly equivalent to maximizing only the increases in income accruing to the very poor. Whether or not this is desirable depends on the relative values assigned to the income of poor people and rich people. (My own feeling, as stated earlier, is that we are interested in the developing countries precisely because they have so many poor people.)

But what if the increased income to the poor can be achieved only at the expense of savings and future growth? This brings us to the third basis for judging these projects—the savings criterion. Galenson and Leibenstein argue that projects that maximize profits should be chosen, since profit receivers have high rates of savings.[12] These high savings mean high investment rates and rapid growth. As they point out, the profit receiver could be the government as well as a private entrepreneur. Also, higher incomes are desirable only for those wealthy people with high savings rates: rent receivers, such as landowners, are notorious for high consumption, whereas urban entrepreneurs have a high tendency toward reinvestment of income.

This argument assumes that the only way to increase the savings rate is to pick projects that generate high savings. This contention is open to question, as we shall see in a moment. If it is correct, however, we may have to choose between high employment in the short run and higher rates of growth. On the basis of the growth criterion, the industrial alternative, particularly the ore plant, is preferable.

Our interest in employment is not limited to short-run employment. Thus an industrial project might give us smaller immediate employment, but within a few years it might lead to higher employment because of the rapid rate of growth it makes possible. A rough attempt to estimate the long-term employment effects of our different projects is made in Table 20.5. Assume that the output and employment figures of Table 20.3 are attained by 1975, that it takes five years to bring a project to full employment and output, and that the necessary investment for a project can be spread evenly over a five-year period and thus financed directly from the profits earned by other plants during the investment period. The potential 1975–1980 profits can then be reinvested in a new plant, which will begin output in 1980 and can itself begin to generate output, employment, and new savings during the 1980–1985 period. If total capital in 1980 is divided by total capital in 1975, a five-year growth rate is obtained, and this rate can then be applied to future periods as well. Since value added and employment depend directly on capital, they will grow at this same rate.

Although the steel mill grows somewhat faster than the agricultural projects, its employment lags far behind theirs, even in 1990. The faster-growing ore plant, however, catches up with the dairy farm in employment by 1990 and would catch up with the small dry (fruit) farm in 1995. The 1990 value added of the ore plant far surpasses that of the other projects.

The optimistic results for the ore plant are misleading, for they depend upon the realization of a number of quite implausible assumptions. Anticipated profits must be realized, and new plants must be brought to

TABLE 20.5
Comparison of Long-Run Employment and Output

	Steel Mill	Ore Plant	Dairy Farm	Small Dry Farm	Large Dry Farm
			Million Dollars		
1975 capital	782	798	782	782	782
Five-year reinvestment	468	1,085	255	336	390[a]
1980 capital	1,250	1,883	1,037	1,134	1,172
Five-year growth rate	1.60	2.40	1.33	1.45	1.50
Capital					
1985	2,000	4,520	1,375	1,640	1,760
1990	3,200	10,800	1,820	2,380	2,640
Value added					
1975	109	218	202	194	145
1980	174	515	268	282	218
1985	278	1,240	356	410	327
1990	445	2,960	470	595	490
Employment			Thousands		
1975	12.0	12.5	74.0	77.5	28.0
1980	19.2	30.0	98.0	112.0	42.0
1985	30.7	72.0	130.0	162.0	63.0
1990	49.2	173.0	172.0	235.0	95.5

Source: Table 20.3. The five-year reinvestment figures are the total annual savings figures multiplied by 5. The figures are based on the assumption that it takes five years to build a plant and bring it to the point where the savings it generates can be used in building still another plant. Because value added and employment depend on capital, they grow at the same rate as capital.
a. This includes the $13 million farmers' savings. (See note c in Table 20.3.)

high levels of efficiency in relatively short periods of time. If private ownership is used, as mentioned earlier, savings would be less. Finally, decision makers (government or private) must be quick enough to plan projects far enough in advance so that profits can be reinvested as soon as they are earned. In practice, uncertainties as to amounts of profits and delays in selecting new projects are almost certain to mean lower growth rates for all projects than the theoretically possible ones shown in Table 20.5. Also, there is no guarantee that demand (foreign or domestic) will grow as fast as the theoretically possible production increases projected here. Although these cautionary notes apply to all projects, they suggest that the advantage of the ore plant over agriculture—faster growth—may not be as great as shown.

As mentioned earlier, there may be ways to increase the savings rate other than choosing capital-intensive projects. In particular the choice between employment and savings criteria depends in a critical way on the capacity (and the will) of the government to redistribute income and generate savings. If government fiscal policies are incapable of increasing the national savings rate, but government programs can effectively re-distribute income in such a way that all groups in the population can share in the rising national income, then we are more likely to choose savings-creating projects. If, on the other hand, the government cannot (or will not) redistribute income, but is capable of achieving high national savings by running surpluses on current account or by inducing additional foreign or private investment, then employment-generating projects become more attractive. (Employment generation as opposed to fiscal subsidies is always a more attractive way of raising the incomes of the poor, given the independence, dignity, and political power that they can have only if they earn their increased incomes.) The capacities of various governments for redistributing incomes or raising savings will be judged differently by different individuals. It is my view, however, that large-scale redistribution, especially in poor countries, is most unlikely. (The difficulties in getting adequate funds to eliminate poverty in the world's richest nation only underline these doubts. Moderately higher taxes on the wealthy and on corporate profits, on the other hand, are probably possible, particularly if they are used for development projects.)

In making our comparison we first assumed that the pattern of demand for consumer and other products would be unaffected by our choice of projects. In discussing employment effects, we observed that in practice a redistribution of income would create additional demand for labor-intensive commodities and thus create additional, or indirect, employ-ment effects above and beyond the employment actually generated by our projects. In addition to creating additional employment opportunities, the redistributed patterns of income associated with the farm projects would mean fewer imports and larger over-all domestic demand. To the extent that textile mills have lower capital-output ratios than the luxury item factories they would be replacing, this additional demand might be satis-fied with the same capital requirements as the demand it would replace. But to the extent that this demand might require more capital, and to the extent that it might open up new opportunities by widening the domestic market for several products, it is possible that the agricultural choice would induce foreign or domestic entrepreneurs voluntarily to increase their investment in Venezuela. Dudley Seers argues that in a country like Venezuela the level of investment is determined more by investment opportunities than by the supply of capital.[13] If this should occur, the over-all savings resulting from the agricultural choice could compare quite favorably with those associated with the other choice. (If new savings were not forthcoming, it is possible that some of our $782 million would have to be diverted from farm projects to satisfy rising demands for clothing and other consumer goods.)

Large versus Small Farms

Before concluding this chapter, let us digress briefly to discuss the choice between the use of large or small farms for raising food production. This choice must be made by the Corporación Venezolana de Guayana when it opens up the delta of the Orinoco to farm settlement.

Table 20.3 compares an investment in 10-hectare farms with a similar investment in 200-hectare farms. The large-farm estimates are my own, derived from the small-farm figures of the Israeli planners by means of two basic assumptions. First, twenty small farms have the same land area as one large farm, and I assumed that the same area could produce the same output, regardless of farm size. The reason for this is that the Israeli-planned projects use modern agricultural techniques—improved seeds, fertilizers, weed and insect sprays, careful timing of farm operations, careful water management, and tractors for such tasks as planting, plowing, and some types of harvesting that cannot be done as well by hand. Both large and small farms would use identical technology, except that the small farms would replace machine labor with hand labor whenever this was possible. Thus some planting, most harvesting, and all weeding and spraying operations are done by hand. The second assumption was that ten man-days equal one tractor day. From these two assumptions the capital, manpower, and tractor-time requirements of the larger farms were estimated. As Table 20.3 shows, the larger farms produce the same output with roughly the same value added but use only one third as much labor as the small farms that could be created with the same investment.

The traditional arguments in favor of large-scale agriculture are that it gives higher yields, gives a higher income to the farmer and thus makes possible higher savings, and offers the amenities of urban life and thereby keeps people on the land. As indicated earlier, the modern methods used by the Israeli-planned projects should make high yields possible. Although these projects had been operating only a year or two when I visited them, they had exceeded their long-run target yields for corn and rice even in these early years. Thus the high-yield targets do not seem unrealistic. Because of these yields, and because the farmers must pay for the investment in land preparation and farm facilities, the projects expect to generate savings almost as large as those of the large farms. The Israeli planners prefer small farms because they allow a greater population density on the land, which makes it possible for medical, entertainment, educational, and shopping facilities to be located in relatively large towns that are within easy reach of large numbers of farmers. The lower population densities associated with large farms would make it more difficult to have these amenities accessible to the rural population.

The most important argument in favor of large farms, in the Guayana and elsewhere, is that teaching new technology to subsistence farmers is a difficult, perhaps impossible, task. But if the purpose of promoting development is to give employment in the modern sector to the largest number of people, then the opportunity to train farmers to improve their methods should be looked upon as a direct fulfillment of the development goal rather than as a nuisance to be avoided. This task may not be as difficult as many might think: one of the Israelis told me that Venezuelan campesinos were easier to train than Jews from Yemen and other Middle Eastern countries, and that the latter had been successfully trained in Israel.

In addition to the arguments already presented, large-farm advocates for the Guayana make another point particular to that situation: there is no large indigenous labor force in the Orinoco Delta area because of the annual floods that now make settlement of the land impossible. To manage the new large farms they envision in the delta, the planners would bring in trained people from outside the Guayana area, possibly from outside Venezuela. But their planning horizon is limited, in the literal sense of the term. For not far from the Guayana lies the overpopulated, poverty-stricken coastal mountain region around Cumaná. Small-scale development of the Orinoco Delta would offer farms and training to thousands of people now living in the coastal region. Indeed, since the soils in the delta area have not turned out to be exceptionally good (a layer of impermeable clay near the surface makes it quite expensive to get good drainage), it might be best to feed the new city from land-reform projects located on the southern slope of the overpopulated coastal mountains rather than from the delta.

Suppose the delta is exploited with a great many large-scale farms and, as would be most likely, those farms practically eliminate Venezuelan food imports. Then, if a later administration seeks to help the farmers near the coast by creating new land-reform projects, there will be no markets for the increased output of new projects. In this way, investment in large farms in the delta might doom these people to a long period of continued unemployment.

Concluding Comments

It would be inappropriate in an essay that argues for agricultural projects on employment grounds to ignore the common feeling in Latin

America that industrialization and development are equivalent, while agricultural development is tantamount to reaction. To a large extent this feeling is a result of the view that for a country to send primary goods to the developed nations and receive in return manufactured goods is to condemn it to a position of economic subservience. It may also stem from the view that the income elasticities of demand for primary products in the developed countries are quite low, so that exporters of these products are faced with continually deteriorating terms of trade, and the view that the low income elasticities of demand for food in all countries relative to demand for urban goods mean an inevitable urbanization.

However, the choice discussed here is between potential *autonomous* projects. Regardless of the project chosen, the pattern of induced demand will indeed become progressively more urban. The question here is how the autonomous growth that powers this expansion in induced industries should be distributed between agricultural and industrial projects. By placing subsistence farmers into the money economy for the first time, agricultural development should widen the domestic market and thus facilitate the development of domestic production of a wide range of goods. For most consumer durables, such as toasters, refrigerators, and automobiles, a minimum-sized plant is necessary for efficient production. Even if they generate the same amount of consumer demand, the agricultural projects would generate it among more people, and lower-income people. Spread in this way the income would lead to a wider market for these goods within the country than if it were concentrated in the hands of a few wealthy people who would tend to spend much more of it on imports or luxury goods. By facilitating low-cost production of these consumer durable goods within Venezuela, agricultural development could serve in the long run to lessen rather than increase dependence on foreign suppliers.

Unlike traditional agricultural exports, exports of fruit for juices and off-season sales to northern countries would be satisfying markets of relatively high income and price elasticity, and thus would be unlikely to experience a secular trend toward lower prices. On the other hand, overcapacity in steel in Europe has meant low world steel prices in recent years.

Many of the estimates in this chapter are only approximate, and a more detailed study would undoubtedly come up with better estimates for many of the capital-employment and capital-output ratios on which this study was based. Leading others to think seriously about the possible reward from changing the rural-urban mix is one of the purposes of this chapter.

Despite the approximate nature of the estimates, however, an employment disparity as great as six to one suggests that it would be desirable to move rapidly to eliminate milk imports and to find new export markets for fruit and other crops, and to obtain this new production from land-reform farms. This does not mean that industrial development would halt but, rather, that there would be significant employment benefits (and no value added costs) in slowing down projected industrial growth slightly in order to exploit the employment-generating possibilities of a slightly faster growth in agriculture.

For the Guayana, this means that a slowdown in the large industrial projects, together with the rapid development of small-scale agriculture in all of eastern Venezuela, might be the most effective way of eliminating slums in the new city, both by helping potential migrants on the farm and by creating markets for clothing and other labor-intensive products that could be made in the new city. Increased production of these products would give employment to the many jobless already in the Guayana.

Chapter 21

Social Mobility
and Economic
Development

Lisa Peattie

There is no defined pattern for what an anthropologist should do in an enterprise like the Guayana project. There are a number of anthropologists—the segment of the profession that travels under the flag of "applied anthropology"—who in recent years have been turning their attention to policy-focused studies of modern institutions, like schools and hospitals, and of government programs, especially those serving clients (for example, American Indians and Eskimos) whose culture is different from that of the program staff. At the same time, and somewhat independently, interest has been growing among anthropologists in the social and cultural changes connected with economic development. But anthropologists still operate from a conceptual base initially shaped in work on small, isolated, and relatively slow-changing societies and with a style of research that focuses on the observation of social processes at the small scale of the individual, the family, and the local community. Their conceptual and research styles are very different from those of the urban designers and economic programmers.

I began as an old-fashioned anthropologist—a "participant observer" fieldworker. I felt sure of only one thing, that I had to begin by looking and listening. So with my family I bought a wattle-and-daub house—a rancho —in a working-class neighborhood of the developing city and commenced to play it by ear. As I tried to summarize my observations in memoranda and papers relevant to the policy questions being discussed in Caracas, I gradually evolved my frame of reference.

It thus came about that I found myself looking at the social processes within my own little urban neighborhood, or barrio, first in a context of the planning of the new city and then in terms of the processes of economic development in Venezuela as a whole. I was simultaneously learning about Venezuela and about my barrio, and it was only toward the end of my two-and-a-half years of study that I began to integrate these two scales. The following pages summarize the two separately and then attempt to describe the way in which I came to conceive of the relationship between them.

The Context of Barrio Life

In all discussions of the opportunities for and obstacles to economic development, one basic principle is implicit: money is a tremendous solvent of established ways and institutions and a highly effective catalyst for the formation of new ones. Venezuela is an outstanding instance of this generalization. It has within the last forty years been transformed by the riches derived from petroleum. The oil industry was and is a classic example of foreign-run, limited-sector economic development, but it remade Venezuela.

In the new oil camp towns rural Venezuelans learned all sorts of new skills, from auto mechanics and masonry to union organizing. Oil money coming into the established cities drew additional people off the land as if by some sort of basic tropism. Venezuela, a nation two thirds rural in 1936, was two thirds urban by 1960. The capital trebled its population in a single decade. The oil boom also drew to Venezuela over half a million immigrants from Europe, mainly Spaniards, Italians, and Portuguese, who formed a large part of the new technical and entrepreneurial middle class. A new elite of commercial and industrial wealth rose to power beside a traditional upper class. There was a spread of roads, of mass communications, and of literacy. These social changes were the basis of new styles of politics. The very demographic structure of the nation was remade by oil prosperity and the medical advances that went with it; the death rate was nearly halved between 1940 and 1960, and Venezuela became one of the fastest growing nations in the world, with one of the highest proportions of young people.

There are underdeveloped countries on which tradition seems to lie like a weight. Venezuela is not one of these. The transformation of the national life, in every area, has been so rapid and so radical as to make history perceptible to its participants, in somewhat the way that the cinematic technique of speeding up changes over time can make visible the growth of a plant. History as presently going on is visible not only to the national leaders who talk about "planning" and "economic development"; there are illiterate and semiliterate people who refer to the "future of the nation" and to "making a people." Ideas of progress and of national identification are part of the common rhetoric.

But the outlook of Venezuelans at every social level seems to combine, curiously, a kind of dynamic optimism about the extent to which things are moving and a pervasive dissatisfaction or disquiet about the manner in which Venezuelans are conducting their national destiny. Some articulations of dissatisfaction refer to easily designated conditions. There is, first, the continuing dependence of the whole national economy on petroleum, an exhaustible resource and one vulnerable to unpredictable world markets. There is the grossly unbalanced distribution of the national wealth. High wages in the highly mechanized petroleum and iron-mining industries—maintained by strongly established union organizations—contrast sharply with very low earnings not only in rural areas but also in much of the urban economy. Migration into the cities continues in force, while urban unemployment remains high. There are also common articulations of dissatisfaction that are less easily related to specific objective conditions. Members of the national elite speak of "lack of consensus"; working-class Venezuelans complain about "lack of order" and excessive "personalism" in their society. Other Venezuelans speak of a "lack of education" or "lack of [character] formation" that allegedly makes them ineffective in building necessary economic institutions, and they often relate this "lack of formation" to weaknesses in the structure of the Venezuelan family. Venezuela thus seems to appear to Venezuelans as a society in rapid transformation and full of potentialities but characterized by social problems, imbalances, and incapacities.

The development effort the Venezuelan government is making in Ciudad Guayana is part of the general national strategy of "sowing the petroleum," of using the oil wealth to build a more durable and stable economic base in industry. But the growing city carries within itself the growing pains of Venezuela as a whole. The city's rapid growth reflects the national flight from rural poverty into an urban economy still short of jobs for those without technical skills. While the steel mill management tried to attract technicians, more than a fifth of the labor force in the city as a whole were out of work in 1962. The contrast between the company housing surrounded by green lawns and the sheet-metal shacks of the new barrios reflects the gap between the relatively high wage structure of the mining companies and steel mill and the rest of the local economy. Many problems of the planning and development operation itself reflected the weakness of local government and the institutions of "grass-roots politics," and the great centralism of national government.

This city and this country were the context within which I came to see my little neighborhood beside the Orinoco.

The Life of the Barrio

In 1965 my barrio celebrated—with a barbecue and community dance —its twenty-fifth anniversary. It had begun as a settlement of laborers at the Iron Mines Company, a Bethlehem Steel subsidiary, which in the forties began mining iron ore in the Guayana and shipping it down the river. There were jobs with the mining and shipping operations; there were jobs in construction; there were jobs selling to other workers; and a little settlement grew up just outside the fence around the company property. When I arrived in 1962, the barrio had just under 500 inhabitants in 80 household groups.

By 1962 only a minority of the barrio residents worked for Iron Mines. Of the 81 persons in the barrio who had regular employment, 21 worked for the steel mill, 11 worked for the U.S. Steel mining company that came in the fifties, 7 worked for Iron Mines, and 11 were in commerce. The other 31 had occupations ranging from schoolteacher to cab driver. A fifth of the barrio households had female heads, and jobs for women were scarce; working women were mainly in domestic service.

When I censused my barrio in 1962, over a third of the men of working age were out of work. Being unemployed was such a normal state in the barrio that little stigma was attached to being out of work and being supported by relatives, often female relatives with limited resources. An unemployed man could spend his afternoon drinking beer in the bar without being gossiped about or criticized, provided that his behavior was generally orderly.

The 81 men and women with regular incomes represented only about one sixth of the barrio's total population of 490. There were no government relief or welfare programs and very little organized private charity. But people did not starve. The people without steady jobs worked occasionally, for example, as construction laborers. They also tended to attach themselves to related households with some source of income. A great deal of petty borrowing went on. In effect, the other five sixths of the population (many of them young children) were able to make some claim, generally through kinship, to the earnings of the employed sixth.

No one in my barrio had finished secondary school. But illiteracy was generally confined to the older people. Newspapers were read; radios were common; national political events and international events affecting Venezuela were generally discussed. When the members of the barrio had a communal grievance, they knew how to get it publicized through the local newspaper and radio station. There was a good deal of participation in political party activity at the local level. Although in many ways the barrio was not a tightly knit community (a fifth of the people had lived there less than a year, everyone did not know everyone else, and no local issue drew participation from more than a minority of the residents), it was able to muster active leadership that could relate to the local power structure of the city.

Moreover, although my barrio's consumption patterns were not the same as those of the upper classes, the difference was that of the poor imitation rather than of the affirmative difference in style. The urbanized dress and teased hairdos of the women, the plastic-upholstered living room "set" that every family buys as soon as it can afford it, the rebuilding of the rural-style wattle-and-daub houses into cement-block imitations of the middle-class residence—all attested to their being tuned in to national models.

So the people in my neighborhood were in many ways very much a part of the greater world. They thought of themselves as "the poor" in contrast to "the rich" rather than as "Indians" or "peasants."

At the same time, the gulf between my neighbors and the established middle class was very great. My little neighborhood was socially defined as a *barrio bajo*, a distinctively lower-class neighborhood. Members of the local elite—professionals, business people, and the staff of the development agency—were either dismayed at our residence there ("Suppose something happens to your daughter? Wouldn't it be better to be where your children would have friends?") or romanticized it as penetration of an exotic world. They thought of my neighbors as members of a single generalized working class. Indeed, I was struck by a similarity in the way the upper classes of nineteenth-century London saw the people below them, according to an informant of 1834:

We shall find them all jumbled together as the "lower orders," the most skilled and the most prudent workmen, with the most ignorant and imprudent labourers and paupers, though the difference is great indeed, and indeed in many cases will scarce admit of comparison.[1]

My *barrio bajo*, like the British "lower orders" of 1834, seemed, in fact, to include quite a range.

There was an English-speaking bookkeeper at the new dam site who drove a new automobile to work every day. There was a nurse at the new hospital with a host of friends in town at the schoolteacher–beauty shop operator–medical technician level. There was the foreman at the steel mill dock who was sending his daughter to a private Catholic school in town and his son to technical school. There was an electrician who used his savings from a good salary at the Orinoco Mining Company to build up a local business. There was the family consisting of a mother and three sons, one of whom was a skilled baker, one of whom had an office job at the Orinoco Mining Company and was planning to study in Canada with the assistance of one of his American supervisors, and the youngest of whom was studying engineering in the state capital.

But besides these "skilled and prudent" people, there were also the "ignorant and imprudent." Across the street from me lived a woman, her married son, and his wife and five small children; the son worked intermittently as an unskilled laborer, and the young children ran around out of school and begged snacks. Next door two sisters lived together with an unemployed nephew and several children of each by various fathers; from time to time one or the other would have a job in domestic service, but otherwise they managed to scrape by on "help" from a married daughter who had a job housecleaning and a third sister whose husband worked for the Iron Mines Company. In the next street an earth-walled house painted in melting pinks and blues housed another large family group of two sisters and their children, with no reliable source of income and the children only intermittently in school.

It would seem that in the course of becoming urbanized the old Venezuelan lower class has been becoming differentiated. My barrio contained not a single class but the beginnings of at least two levels—a stable working class or lower middle class, and an unskilled and "imprudent" lower class. The layering of these two levels was incomplete; in my barrio they were next-door neighbors and even members of the same extended family groups, for the transformation was still very recent. But the difference in style of life was already clear.

One group of people in the barrio had been able to get a toehold in the new system, and then to consolidate their footing in it. One means of consolidation was through acquiring skills; my neighbor across the street, for example, learned enough through on-the-job training with the company to qualify as a skilled electrician. A second way was through the accumulation of capital. A very common pattern was for employees of "the companies" to use their income, especially lump sums given as annual bonus or severance pay, to start a small business. Even more general was the accumulation of capital in the form of houses, the "property mobility" that seems to have been so important in stabilizing the American working class in its formative period.[2] Many people in the barrio owned one or several houses besides their own residence; at the time of my census three families were building houses specifically for rental. A third way of consolidating was through formal education, for one's children if not for oneself. Very striking to me was the way in which the process of social consolidation was expressed in styles of child rearing. In my barrio the families that had established themselves economically quite characteristically exercised much more control over their children—keeping them cleaned up, supervising school attendance, and enforcing orderliness in their behavior.

It would be possible to think of the contrast between the "skilled and prudent" and the "ignorant and imprudent" in my barrio as two stages in a single process, and to suppose that those at the bottom will, with time, follow their successful neighbors' example and consolidate their positions, in turn, in the new economic order. To some extent this will occur. But there are also forces tending to push the two farther apart.

Economic development is coming to Venezuela in a rather different form from that in which it came to England. It is arriving in the form of the most advanced, capital-intensive technology, requiring a relatively small number of workers with relatively high levels of skill. The Venezuelan workers are many and relatively unskilled. The high wages in the major industries, firmly supported by the national political and labor union institutions, coupled with the relative availability of capital resources, tend to strengthen this economic focus. The result is rapid growth in the "developed sector" along with a high level of unemployment and underemployment.

When the oil boom came to Venezuela it was possible to get a foothold in the developed sector with almost no formal education or technical skills. Skilled workers were not to be had, so the companies did their own technical training. "It was like a school," said one of my neighbors. Now the formal educational institutions are being developed, and it will be harder to get started without those credentials. As formal education becomes more established as part of the entry requirements for many jobs, it is likely to become more important to have the kind of parents who get you through school.

The families who have already achieved established positions in "the companies" have a tremendous advantage in giving their children the right start. Because of the extensive fringe benefits provided to them under Venezuelan law and collective bargaining practices, they have not only more adequate incomes than those outside the system but also medical care, schools, school buses, and even books and pencils. The public schools are free, but books and transportation are a considerable expense for families at the economic margins.

Moreover, in looking at my neighbors I came to believe that the economic situation is itself an educational force of tremendous power. People who live in but at the margins of the urban economy seem, in widely different parts of the world, to develop variants of the life-style that Oscar Lewis has identified as the "culture of poverty." Participating in the life of my barrio, I could understand why. In that life situation, long-term planning and the husbanding of resources become not only difficult but nonadaptive. People who live in the cash economy but have no skills or social position with which to derive security in it, in effect find their only possible security in social relations with others. In the short run, at least, it may be more useful for the unemployed laborer to spend the afternoon drinking beer and keeping up his contacts than it would be for him to spend the time looking for a job he is quite unlikely to find.

In the United States a striking correlation has been noted among Negroes between the rate of male unemployment and the proportion of women separated from their husbands.[3] The hypothesis is that marriages of people at the economic margins are vulnerable to the loss of jobs, which undercuts the role of the male in the family. A similar explanation seemed to me to fit the high rate of separations in my barrio. In effect, a marriage maintained neither by pressure from interested kinship groups on both sides (for marriage in my barrio, as in the United States, is primarily a matter of individual agreement), nor by the need to maintain property in common, nor by a system of social statuses and roles requiring husband-wife teams for full participation has very little to hold it together. When the male has no economic role, the marriage has nothing to maintain it but personal affection, and that is not enough in many families. The consequence is that families at the economic margins are more likely than the better-established ones to be headed by women, and a female-headed family in an economy with few and poorly paid jobs for women is on an even shakier economic footing than the average worker's family, and even less well adapted for giving children the right start.

Inferences for Development Strategy

So, starting as an anthropologist "participant observer" at the small scale, I arrived at questions of national and regional economic development strategy. Venezuela had been transformed by the oil boom into a relatively rich and economically dynamic nation, but Venezuelans were still left with a sense of pervading unease as to the shape of that development. I began to believe that Venezuela might translate its oil money into heavy industry and be left, still, with something of the same disquiet—and a disquiet that might, with time, be harder to bear and to deal with politically.

The attraction of heavy industry is basic to the development of Ciudad Guayana. But it may be that it should be thought of as only the beginning of a development strategy, and that the development strategy should be centered not so much on aggregate growth as on the form of development. The conception of the problem to be solved would be focused not so much on generating economic activity and urban development as on deconcentrating economic activity and developing a city that will contribute maximally to this deconcentration and to the social mobility that would have to be one of its aspects.

"Economists in the twentieth century usually call upon governments to redress the imperfections of the market, just as their forebears in the nineteenth century looked to the market to replace the imperfections of the government," says W. Arthur Lewis in an article calling on developing countries to "give the highest priority to providing employment now rather than to maximizing consumption or income or employment in ten years time."[4] Unfortunately, I suspect that the specification of strategies to carry out this mandate requires a good deal of rethinking of traditional policy tools, and that its enactment involves any nation, including Venezuela, and any agency, including the Corporación Venezolana de Guayana (CVG), in the manipulation of political and social forces that are by no means easy to command.

We seem to know a good deal more about how to develop basic industry than about how to bring about rapidly a broad spectrum of job-generating economic activities, especially in a society whose existing economic institutions make it hard to substitute labor for capital. We have a fairly clear idea of what sorts of educational institutions contribute to the acquisition by a mass of unskilled persons of the competences demanded by a new economic order, but the specific policies for building such institutions in Ciudad Guayana are yet to be developed. We know that job training without jobs and the raising of social aspirations without the broadening of social possibilities can be disastrous. Urban design, starting from a base in architecture and working from a body of experience derived mainly in the developed cities of Europe and North America, is only beginning to develop the intellectual tools for shaping cities by criteria not of aesthetic excellence or adequate "standards" but of the adequacy of the urban framework for rapid social and economic change.

A new city in a developing region has certain advantages in the generation of jobs. Construction work, particularly housing construction, is an extraordinarily effective source not only of incomes but also of on-the-job training, and it provides a convenient point of entry into the skilled labor market for people with minimal urban skills. Also, given a sturdy base of capital-intensive industry, to some extent the other jobs will come with time. But the Venezuelan situation seems to call for a special effort to promote in Ciudad Guayana not only basic industry but also a variety of other economic activities. The CVG has done some exploration of the possibilities in agriculture in the region, but it is still too early to tell whether labor-intensive agriculture would be economically feasible. If holding people on the land means a rather heavy subsidy—for it is clear that Venezuelans will not stay on the land unless they can have schools, clinics, and other urban amenities—then farming in the Guayana may have to be another capital-intensive industry. It might be possible to promote the development, at an early date, of such job-generating manufactures as clothing factories. A focus on jobs also suggests that in planning for commercial facilities an emphasis on concentration and efficiency may be less appropriate than one on maximizing activities.

Such an approach to the development problem in the Guayana suggests further a massive and broad-scale effort in the field of basic and technical education. It suggests an effort to provide the books, buses, school lunches, and scholarships to support primary- and secondary-school attendance. It suggests support of in-service training and special programs to improve the quality of public education, especially in relation to the skills and understandings particularly relevant to economic change and development. It suggests tutorial and guidance services to help children and young people find their way effectively into a world in which their parents' experience can hardly serve them as a model.

Institutions for specialized technical education are already developing in the Guayana. They will need to be extended as time goes on. There are remedial classes to give basic primary education to adults who missed out earlier. However, if the aim of development in the Guayana is to bring about a general social transformation as rapidly as possible, adult education might be expanded to include using radio, newspapers, and such other means as local libraries to help people understand the nature of the new economy and society. People need to learn how to organize their lives and their children's in order to become something new. They need to be informed about job opportunities—not only those available now but those that will be available in a few years—about opportunities for education, and about successful examples of social mobility and self-transformation.

In physical planning for the new city, the promotion of growth and development must be the primary goal. This means not only creating the urban amenities to attract the skilled technicians and managers who are needed to run the new industries but also building a physical structure that can accommodate a rapid rate of economic growth and change. It means urban design policies aimed not only at the maximization of present efficiency but also, and perhaps even more important, at adaptability to future change. It means, for example, developing residential areas with a certain flexibility about densities, types of structures, and who occupies them to allow for rapid transformation and to permit the socially mobile and change adapted to remain as models for their less mobile and adapted neighbors. It means patterns of land-use regulation that will maximize economic activity even if at a certain cost in visual order.

Chapter 22

Social Attitudes
and Planning
in the Guayana

Arthur L. Stinchcombe

What concrete uses can attitude studies have for a planner? In order to answer this question, we must distinguish three major types of planning programs to which attitudes are relevant.

Some programs, to achieve their objectives, need complementary activity by a large number of people. A housing program to provide "decent" housing for some population group needs people who want to live there and who are willing to live in such a way that the planned characteristics of the area (for example, sanitation and green areas) are not destroyed. People's attitudes about what kinds of houses are attractive, how one ought to live, and public responsibility to the neighborhood, all help to determine whether the necessary complementary activities of a mass of people occur.

Some programs can be executed purely with activities by men paid to do them and officials paid to administer them. In this situation the crucial attitudes are those that determine whether the men will indeed do the jobs they are supposed to do. Such attitudes as a sense of responsibility, a willingness to leave the capital and work in the interior, lack of partisan political attitudes that might cause deviation from the plan for party advantage, career aspirations inside or outside the organization, and intolerance of corruption become critical for the success of the program. It is the attitudes of the staff toward their work that are important in supplying electricity or creating a system of roads or sewers.

Finally, there are programs that can be ruined by a political explosion. Technical-aid programs can blow up because of an anti-American (or antiforeign) movement, or a group of advisers may be ejected for having been too friendly with the previous government. Plants can fail or close because of strikes or class conflict. All plans go awry in times of civil war. In short, explosive attitudes of national, ethnic, class, or political hostility can create difficulties or destroy plans.

Attitudes Affecting Mass Cooperation

The achievement of planned objectives in the Guayana depended on mass cooperation in four principal areas: migration and population growth, career commitment to work in the industries of the area, housing and neighborhood maintenance, and the proportion of students who stay in school.

The fundamental attitude affecting migration was that almost everyone in the middle classes, and many in the lower classes, would have preferred to live elsewhere if the income were the same. This was particularly true of the North Americans, but the attitude was general. In a study of white-collar steelworkers and other middle-class people in steel-producing cities in three countries, we asked whether people would move to another city for a much better job there.[1] We found that 76 per cent of Ciudad Guayana's middle class would move, compared with 61 per cent of the middle class in an Argentine steel city and 68 per cent of the middle class in a Chilean steel city. That is, people in the Guayana are more inclined to move than people in other steel areas.

The primary reason for this attitude was the much higher cost of living in the Guayana. The inefficiency of commerce and the necessity of persuading people to migrate there forced wages and salaries up to a considerably higher level than elsewhere. North American personnel cost at least twice as much in the Guayana as in the United States, primarily because North Americans would rather not live there. The cost includes travel and moving households and would not be as burdensome if those who came would stay. I cannot estimate the premium paid for the higher preference of other groups for living elsewhere, aside from the cost-of-living difference. I doubt, however, that the total cost of this preference for living elsewhere is less than about a fifth of the total wage bill.

As efficient wholesaling and more competitive retailing come to the area, the cost of living should decrease. As North Americans become less important in the executive labor force, the premium paid for living in the Guayana will decrease. And as people acquire personal investments—in property, children in school, and community ties—more of them should come to prefer the Guayana as a place to live. In the meantime, it is important to find out whether there are any urban amenities or planning policies, cheaper than the wage differential, that could decrease this motivation to migrate.

My observations on this question were casual and mostly confined to the middle class. Many middle-class Venezuelans owned homes elsewhere, but few owned houses in the Guayana, which had a great effect on their tendency to leave. Many complained vaguely of promises not kept, especially promises of housing, by the steel company. Those who were settling complained of great difficulty in finding a place in which to build their own house and considered the housing developments overpriced. A few spoke of a deep investment in some community enterprise: political parties, trade unions, or charities. Conversely, the North Americans were quite different from their homeland counterparts, not interested in building churches or hospitals or in buying a home. There was an extremely close two-way relation between investment in the community (property owned or effort expended) and preference for staying. Programs to encourage property ownership and to create community enterprises with local power and local support would decrease the burden of having to pay higher wages.

A similar problem is that of career commitment to the industrial enterprises planned for the area. These enterprises have a high turnover, though not very much higher than such enterprises have in other countries. One cause of this turnover is the fact that inmigrants from rural areas do not understand and are not motivated by those pictures of future welfare through career advancement that keep most people at their jobs. Another factor is that the career development policy of the plants might have been developed by David Ricardo: fire whenever convenient and make no promises you might want to break. In the steel plants of the three countries, 72 per cent in Ciudad Guayana knew of a man in a position of responsibility having been let go, compared with 69 per cent in the Argentine plant and 59 per cent in the Chilean plant. To find out whether this tough-minded policy had more advantages (in getting rid of incompetents) than costs (in not motivating people to stay until they became competent) would require a detailed study. Of those who knew of firings, 37 per cent of the Venezuelan white-collar steelworkers considered at least one of them unfair, as against 18 per cent in Argentina and 17 per cent in Chile. The perception of irrational career development can hardly encourage career commitment. Due process in firing, clear criteria for promotion, and higher wages would probably decrease the burden of industrial turnover.

A housing program's success depends on people wanting to live in the fashion for which the housing is designed. And over-all planning of a city's residential development depends on people's individual actions not departing too radically from the projected land-use plans. It would be exaggerating somewhat to say that everybody who wanted to stay permanently in the Guayana, and could do so (building contractors, local businessmen, local professionals), built his own house in the slums near the main business district. But there was a definite tendency, among those who could choose, not to buy officially developed housing that was designed differently from housing they would buy for themselves. Comparing spontaneous housing with planned housing for the middle classes, the spontaneous housing (a) was nearer the central business district, (b) had less lawn space, (c) had better fences, more solid steel grating at the windows, and provision for a large, vicious dog, (d) paid less attention to the social status of neighbors, (e) was much more often part of a business property, and (f) was somewhat more subject to flooding.

The spontaneous lower-class housing differed from the project housing for workers by being (a) farther from communal centers but closer to small stores that sell on credit, (b) of much less permanent construction, (c) much more subject to flooding and other natural disasters, (d) much less protected against insects and breezes, (e) much less isolated from smells, bars, houses of prostitution, and other "nuisances," and (f) much more convenient for raising chickens.

All this suggests that in housing construction the values for which the planner was willing to pay were not the same as those for which the people were willing to pay in the free market. People whose pattern of life is governed by the criteria just cited may make bad human material for a well-planned housing project because the plan generally involves their paying for what the housing planner has bought for them. Surely some of the things a planner wants for them should be forced on them for reasons of public health and morals, such as sanitation and isolation of children from prostitution. Other impositions are, in my opinion, more doubtful.

Attitudes Affecting Discipline in Administration

The average North American resident of Venezuela is inclined to berate Venezuelan executives for laziness, corruption, indifference to the goals of the enterprise, and general inefficiency. He usually does not comment on his own appearance at first-class bars, with a company car, promptly at quitting time plus fifteen minutes. (We need not explore how I know exactly when they get to the bar.) The blunt fact of the matter is that top Venezuelan industrial executives work longer hours than top North American industrial executives in the Guayana.

But this pattern of nonperformance by North Americans and, in their opinion, by Venezuelans means only that the question of whether an administrator will do his job in a responsible fashion is problematical for all programs that depend on administrative vigor. It is not for idle reasons that the responsibility of powerful people has been at the center of political philosophy since early Greek times. The responsibility of program administrators is also no idle matter.

There are three critical questions concerning the attitudes that affect administrative discipline in the Guayana project: (1) Does work in the Guayana represent a stage in a logical career plan, or is it only a lucrative interlude? (2) If the work is part of a career plan, does "success" mean achievement of the Guayana program objectives, or does it mean achieving political favor, international scholarly renown, or advancement in some other system whose interest in the Guayana is secondary? (3) Do the administrators prefer to live and work in the Guayana or in Caracas?

Roughly speaking, and with great variations within groups, the crucial administrative groups are ranked about as follows in these aspects.

The North American technical experts in the steel mill and the mining company regarded their stay in Venezuela as a lucrative interlude, were completely uninterested in political favor and mostly uninterested in international professional recognition, and had no strong preference for living in Caracas rather than in the Guayana. Thus their career motivation was relatively low and was devoted exclusively to local technical problems.

The North American Joint Center personnel were heavily oriented toward a career in an international professional system. They had high motivation for success, but it was primarily oriented toward those aspects of the planning process that could be published or communicated at professional meetings. They showed some preference for Caracas as a place to live and had an acute sense of their dependence on official approval from the Caracas office of the Corporación Venezolana de Guayana (CVG). As a result they were much less knowledgeable about detailed local technical and administrative problems than the North American engineers in the plants.

The Venezuelan industrial administrators had a heavy career commitment to advancement within their companies and had very little concern with political favor. Their preference for Caracas could not be reflected in administrative patterns because they were required to work in the Guayana. These men were highly motivated, worked long hours and then went home and studied, and were well acquainted with the local details of the systems they administered.

The Venezuelan administrative personnel of the CVG responsible for city planning seemed to have considerable commitment to professional careers in the civil service. But neither their work nor the centers of power and advancement necessitated their staying in the Guayana. They had to consult the North American personnel about *local* details remarkably often.

The Venezuelan administrators of other governmental agencies involved in planning but not controlled by the CVG were not convinced that merit and responsible performance were the criteria by which they would be promoted. Friendship with powerful people, "keeping your nose clean," and political services to governing parties were the critical considerations in their minds. For instance, they much more often "kept their noses clean" by refusing to be interviewed than the personnel of the CVG. A very large percentage of these non-CVG bureaucrats were policemen or military men, which may partly explain their conceptions of their careers and their jobs.

The other principal planning group found in most American planning situations—the local political, business, and professional elite—was very poorly organized. Probably this was largely because of the frontier character of the city and the general centralized character of Venezuelan government. This meant that the building of community sentiments and powerful local interests into the plans did not take place. This would tend to produce detachment or alienation from planning in the population. My only check on this is that taxi drivers in Caracas seemed to tolerate inconveniences in the traffic system better than in the Guayana, perhaps indicating that the political system in Caracas involves the affected people better.

In summary, the administrative efficiency of the plan was decreased by (1) the lack of career commitment by the crucial group of North American engineers, (2) the heavy preference of CVG planning personnel for functioning out of Caracas, presumably because the centers of power and the control of resources are concentrated there, (3) the perception by other government bureaucrats that their futures did not depend on merit, and (4) the lack of local organized interests to relate the population to the plan. Where none of these difficulties was operative, as among the Venezuelan industrial administrators, the plans were reflected well in the actual activity of people in the area. Where crucial administrative groups failed to have "appropriate" career attitudes and commitment to the Guayana rather than Caracas, the plan tended to be more a paper plan with little relation to reality.

Potentially Explosive Attitudes

Certain kinds of planning may be more or less permanently crippled by touching on conflicting passions. National planning of the North American educational system has only lately and precariously slipped around the church-state issue. People will not usually sacrifice matters of principle for the material advantages of a plan, especially when the material advantages go to someone else. Consequently a principal question in planning is the state of attitudes on potentially explosive matters: class conflicts, conflicts over the status and privileges of immigrants and foreign investors, party conflicts, and secular-religious conflicts, especially over education. At the national level, social planning in Latin America has been crippled by conflicts over constitutional principles, especially democracy versus military rule and federalism versus centralization.

None of these conflicts is based only on principles, of course. Concrete interests are involved: the determination of workers' wages, the number of immigrants in certain skill groups, which party distributes patronage, whether the church spends the education budget, and the salaries of military officers. But attitudes are intertwined with interests as causes of explosive conflicts that can disturb plans.

In Ciudad Guayana the potential for class conflicts is relatively high, for a number of reasons. First, heavy industry and mining create a working class concentrated in a few factories, without daily contact with many middle-class people. The social isolation of workers from middle-class people is increased by planner tendencies to build blocks of lower-income housing separate from middle-class housing. The planned parts of Ciudad Guayana are much more segregated by social class than the parts that have grown up spontaneously.

This socially isolated proletarian group is, in addition, very much subject to business cycle fluctuations and to any decline in economic growth; their incomes tend to be more unstable than those of people in commerce, government services, or consumer goods industries. It is thus virtually inevitable that strong unions will play a major role in the community power system, and especially in the "government" of the heavy industries themselves. For insecurity guarantees that workers will have grievances, social isolation guarantees that they will organize, and their numbers guarantee that they will have power.

In the future, therefore, the middle classes of Ciudad Guayana will have to allow workers much greater political power, or intense class conflict will erupt. We asked our middle-class sample in the three steel cities whether they would prefer that the workers have more, the same, or less political power than they now have. The proportion saying "more" was: the Guayana, 29 per cent; Argentina, 36 per cent; Chile, 55 per cent. This indicates that Ciudad Guayana may face the possibility of explosive disruptions in which all elements of the plans become issues in class struggles. As yet the power of the workers has not been an issue, perhaps because most of the unions are controlled by the government political party, Acción Democrática. Recently, however, there has been a trend toward opposition slates, especially Christian Democrats, winning trade union posts. If class conflicts and political conflicts were to coincide, this situation could heat up a great deal; but perhaps the demands of the poor can continue to be met by taxing the politically vulnerable North American oil interests rather than the Venezuelan middle class.

At the present time political loyalties do not sharply divide the population in the Guayana. Most of my respondents did not give a party identification, often adding that "I don't get myself into such things." The percentage of people who talked little or not at all about politics with their friends was higher in the Guayana (84 per cent) than in either Argentina (70 per cent) or Chile (65 per cent). Presumably this reflects the short history of mass party organizations in the country as a whole, and the especially weak party organizations of the Guayana. Provided constitutional questions are resolved at the national level, I see no prospect of civil commotion over local party questions.

If most people in Ciudad Guayana do not have strong political opinions, almost all have strong ethnic opinions. The heavy dependence of the development effort on foreign experts (especially Italians and North Americans), the overrepresentation of certain ethnic groups in local commerce (especially Italians and Middle Easterners), the general domination of Venezuela's development effort by North American capital, and the competition from bilingual Trinidadians for manual work in heavy industry form an economic basis for ethnic conflict. Many foreigners reported feeling unwelcome in varying degrees. The Italian engineering firm that built the steel plant was booted out, to be replaced mainly by North American advisers. The Venezuelan government recently passed more restrictive immigration laws, and we were repeatedly told of the law forbidding foreigners to comment on Venezuelan government or politics. Thus immigrant groups, especially the North Americans, face considerable ethnic hostility.

Among the immigrants the feeling of "political rightlessness" is very strong. Most of them did not have, as far as I could tell by interviewing them, any attitudes on Venezuelan political questions. But their attitude was not that of colons—I cannot imagine any of the ethnic groups tearing down a Venezuelan flag, as the North American colons did in Panama. The immigrants' feelings of rightlessness will probably prevent the underlying ethnic tensions from becoming explosive in the near future. But if a general movement against North American capital should take place in Venezuela, it would activate the underlying definition of North Americans in the Guayana as unreasonably overpaid and disrespectful in small ways (for example, not learning the language, not respecting Venezuelan competence). This, combined with the focus of North American capitalism in the Orinoco Mining Company, might make it impossible for North Americans to work in the Guayana.

In the long run, the high proportion of foreign immigrants (in my middle-class sample, 43 per cent of the respondents were from abroad), if they became citizens and committed themselves permanently to the area, might form a base for ethnic politics. Most of this 43 per cent were already citizens. Ethnic politics will probably not develop during the planning period, however.

Two national constitutional issues could have a local effect. The first is military versus democratic rule. At the present time the civilian agencies are primary in planning, but the military and the police are in the Guayana in force. A shift at the national level in the direction of military rule would very probably change the present structure of planning. While I have no way of judging what the likelihood or effects of an explosive conflict over "democracy" would be, my guess is that next to explosive class conflict this is the most likely of all to destroy or disrupt the planning process. This is not because democracy seems unstable; rather, it is because military rule, if it were instituted, would have large (and unpredictable) effects.

The second constitutional question is federalism, or local autonomy, versus centralization. The planning is now definitely done from Caracas, and localism would inevitably challenge the authority of the planners. Such questions usually stir only a politically active local elite. Such an elite is developing in the Guayana, in spite of general political apathy, the recency of migration of most of its potential members and the noncitizenship of many others, and the small number of people with local property interests. When it develops, planning will increasingly devolve upon it. It is very unlikely that regionalism will be a principal explosive issue interrupting the planning process.

The secular-religious conflict over educational policy does not appear to me to be a probable source of major tensions. Most Venezuelans seem to be lukewarm Catholics. There is very little evidence of the religious devotion that is characteristic, for instance, of Catholics in Spain, Central Mexico, and North America; neither does there seem to be a substantial secularist movement comparable to that in France, Chile, and Argentina. The proportion of my sample who said they had no religious preference was 10 per cent in Venezuela, 17 per cent in Argentina, and 32 per cent in Chile. The Catholicism or secularism of the schools seems to concern very few ordinary people. The major leftist opposition party at the present time is a Catholic party, and Catholicism does not seem to be so very conservative in Venezuela as in many countries. Secularism therefore does not derive much energy from the class conflict.

Thus the potentially explosive problems that might disrupt planning seem to me to be class relations and the North American presence in Venezuela. In addition, planning might be disrupted by national constitutional questions, such as military versus democratic rule.

Planning in the Light of Attitudes

What might have alleviated some of the problems of the attitudes we have located? Which of the attitudinal variables are manipulable by planning policy, and how?

In the programs involving mass cooperation, the location of manipulable variables is very difficult. The preference for living elsewhere seems to be manipulable mainly by two factors. First, the high cost of living could have been reduced by early planning for and investment in efficient, competitive wholesaling. Given cheap wholesale goods, retail competition is fairly easy to get. Especially important at the outset would be the efficient importation and distribution of new and used furniture, which ought to be planned for.

The second holding force is a property interest, especially in a house. A program to distribute housing as individual property with a guaranteed title, perhaps at some loss, and to facilitate the spontaneous construction of private homes in areas outside the planned housing developments would decrease the preference for living elsewhere. Middle-class apartment developments, unless they are to be sold in condominium, should be kept to a minimum.

Career commitment to the industrial enterprises could be encouraged by ceding more rights in the job to workers and protecting them against arbitrary firing.

Closer study of what characteristics people are willing to pay for in a house when they build it themselves might improve the acceptability of the housing program.

Turning to the problem of discipline in administration, I have two main suggestions. If the powers controlling career advancement, that is, the central offices of the development corporation, had been in the Guayana, both the North American and the Venezuelan CVG personnel would have had less "Caracas orientation." They would have seen for themselves more often where their statistics and projections were wrong. This move would of course involve isolation from other centers of power. And if other government agencies had promoted employees on the basis of job performance, their cooperation with the CVG might have been more effective. I believe nothing can be done to give North Americans a career commitment to the Guayana, both because of their strong preference for living in the United States and because Venezuelans do not want to (and should not) promise the highest positions to them.

The probability of explosive class conflict might be somewhat reduced if there were less social-class segregation in housing. But the main goal in the long run is to educate middle-class Venezuelans to accept the idea of workers having more power, to which contact with working-class neighbors contributes very little. There are two main ways in which middle-class people might become more sympathetic to workers' aims and problems. The less effective is engaging in local charitable efforts, though surveys by local committees of the problems of the poor, to develop proposals to the CVG for alleviating their lot, might have some effect. But the middle-class people who learn best to understand workers' problems are those who want their candidates to be elected; in the Guayana no one can be elected without workers' votes. If the CVG were to give equal support and encouragement to all local party organizations, this would be very effective in educating middle-class people to workers' problems. In addition, it would provide a hedge against whatever the political chances of the future might bring.

Such programs may, for various reasons, be politically impossible in the Guayana. Further, other values—efficiency, health, beauty, and the capacity to attract resources from the outside—may be sacrificed if one guides planning solely by the criterion of public attitudes.

Manipulating attitudes by means of planning is obviously a political process, and other political interests besides the planners have a stake in how it comes out. If there were an easy, sure way to manipulate attitudes with government programs, incumbents would never get voted out. They do get voted out, in Latin America as well as in the United States. A sane planner must expect to lose sometimes because of people's attitudes: presidents do.

Chapter 23

City Designers
and the
Pluralistic City

Donald Appleyard[1]

The designers of Ciudad Guayana—planners, architects, engineers, and others—found it difficult to establish contact with the city's population. The planning office was half a day's air travel from the new city, and many of the designers were foreign by nationality as well as class to the local culture. But the problems encountered were common to most planning operations. Urban populations are difficult to understand, inarticulate, and anonymous, so designers in a decision situation tend to fall back on their own perceptions and values, supported by their professional stock of rules and models, and "objective" data, often unaware of their dissociation from the other reality.

In the first three years of the Guayana planning operation, when evidence from the site was scant and poorly understood, decisions concerning the city's development were made on assumptions about how the population perceived, felt, would, and should react to such decisions.[2] Members of the planning team, through either personal bent or their particular role, began to emphasize the objectives most meaningful to them. The transportation planners considered the long-term point of view; those resident at the site emphasized immediate needs; some designers argued for efficiency, others for urbanity. The decision-making process, complex as it was, was unrepresentative of population groups and easily unbalanced by the arrival or departure of visiting consultants.

But these attitudes were more or less consciously held. Less evidently, the planners' view of the city was also culture bound. Their working environment—the symbolic world of maps, models, and data—created unknowingly a conception of the city quite distinct from the reality of those who lived there. Not that the population's view was monolithic. They, too, saw the same city in different ways.

Uneasiness about the adequacy of communication between the site and Caracas led, in 1964, to three sets of large-scale interviews relating to housing problems, political attitudes, and environmental perceptions. The latter, reported here, were probably the first such surveys to be conducted on this scale as part of the design of a new city.[3]

Their purpose was twofold: to test the effectiveness of different environments and measure the role of various environmental factors— physical, social, and functional—in the inhabitants' urban perception; and to learn if there were significant group differences in environmental attitudes and knowledge. This was an effort to give the designer a clearer picture of life in the city and to allow him to develop a more meaningful vocabulary of forms, functions, and social groups to use in designing the future development. It was also an opportunity to extend basic knowledge in the developing field of environmental psychology.

At the time of the interviews, preliminary plans had been formulated, but few had been executed. The existing city, already occupied by 60,000 migrants, consisted mainly of indigenous development, with some planned residential fragments, the new Caroní Bridge, roads, schools, hospitals, and community facilities inserted into or added to older settlements. (See Figure 23.1 and Map 23.1.)

Seventy-five persons were randomly selected from each of four districts representing four different types of environment: the "model" middle-income community of Puerto Ordaz, the spontaneous rancho settlement of Castillito, the self-help rancho areas of El Roble, and the expanded colonial-style village of San Félix. Twenty more were interviewed in two elite residential areas, the Country Club and the CVG Site Engineers' Camp. The total sample (about three hundred and twenty subjects), was large enough to permit comparisons among various population groups. The surveys were based on the not unreasonable premise that the reactions of the future population to future environments could be partly predicted from the present perceptions.

The interviews were carried out by twelve interviewers under the supervision of a sociologist and were paralleled with systematic environmental surveys by trained observers. The subjects were asked a range of questions designed to assess the nature of their urban knowledge, starting with open-ended tasks like drawing their map of the city and recalling well-remembered features, followed by descriptions of a journey through the

FIGURE 23.1   Views from the main road. This series of 360° photographs was taken along the main east-west road as part of the photographic record of the city in 1964. The selected photographs convey some idea of the character of the city at that time. The line of the route can also be followed on Maps 23.1 and 23.4.

Entering the city from the west the traveler passed the steel mill, almost invisible on the left (1). (The right-hand side of the photograph faces east, the left-hand side looks to the west, hence the steel mill is in the center.) The road continued across featureless terrain, with no views of the rivers on either side, for about five miles before the airport (2) was reached. Soon after this the road suddenly turned and descended toward the Caroní River, opening up a dramatic view of the valley filled with scattered development (3). Very little of Puerto Ordaz was seen, since the civic center was located off the road, but the General Electric warehouse (4) (right center) and the Mobil gas station (far right) at the main intersection were among the best recalled buildings in the city. From Puerto Ordaz the road, deteriorating in quality, turned right into the rancho settlement of Castillito (5), usually crowded with people and traffic, to arrive finally at the ferry (6), which crossed the Caroní (7) to the other ferry landing at Dalla Costa (8). From Dalla Costa the road traversed another shallow ridge and descended into El Roble, past scattered ranchos lining the road (9). At the El Roble intersection (10) stood the Phillips gas station (center), a building that received more attention than any one of the three new community schools, placed off the road, in El Roble. Continuing its devious path through El Roble, the road approached the entrance to San Félix, marked by the well-known Firestone billboard (11), and the only close view of the Orinoco River (12) (center); and carried on through the market area (13) to the Plaza Bolívar (14) (center). At this stage in the city's development, in 1964, practically no planned part of the city could be seen from this road. However, the new Caroní Bridge, shown under construction (15), was about to transform this view of the city, bringing some new residential areas into view.

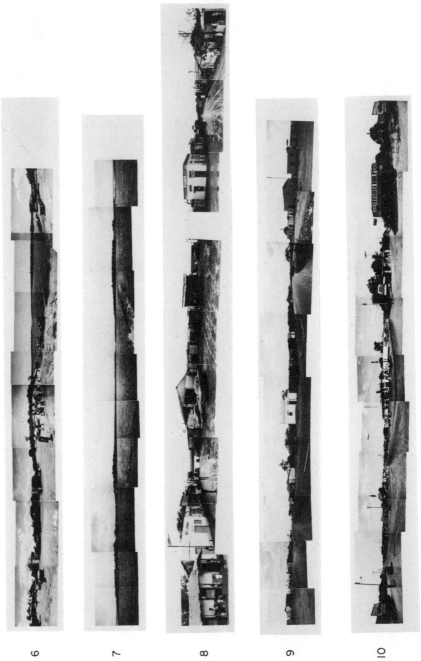

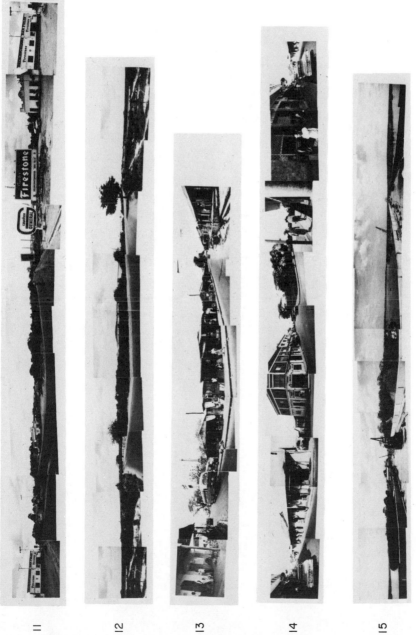

11   12   13   14   15

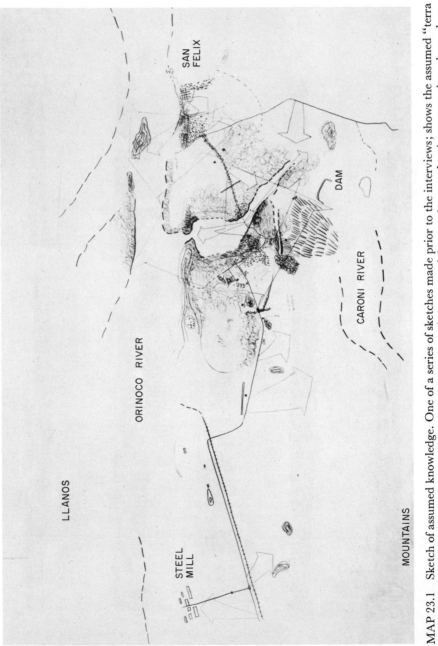

MAP 23.1 Sketch of assumed knowledge. One of a series of sketches made prior to the interviews; shows the assumed "terra cognita" of most inhabitants. The resulting interviews showed the natural form to be even less important than shown here.

city, of particular buildings and districts, of social, functional, and natural patterns, of recent and predicted changes, and opinions about their current needs and preferences. Finally, they were asked to describe their ideal and worst city, to compare Ciudad Guayana with other cities, and to assess their degree of satisfaction with Ciudad Guayana.

We decided to examine independently several aspects of environmental perception, although they are in fact merged in any one person's knowledge of a city. From a broad consideration of the scope and complexity of people's knowledge, we proceeded to investigate how they selected elements and structured them; then to look at expressed values and preferences to see how these were being communicated through the urban form; and finally, to study some effects of environmental change on conceptions of the city. Here are some of the findings and implications.

Scope and Complexity of Knowledge

In Ciudad Guayana the planners and designers belonged to a privileged group able to visit places that were out of bounds to most inhabitants, like the steel mill, the hydroelectric dam, and the waterfalls. Such knowledge was extended by arduous field surveys of the land available for future development and amplified by aerial photographs, photogrammatic maps, and social and economic data.

The inhabitants' perceptions, on the other hand, turned out to be very parochial. Half of them, when asked the name of the city, gave the name of their own district rather than Ciudad Guayana. Indeed, some thought Ciudad Guayana was a new and separate part of the city yet to be constructed around the foundation stone laid in 1961. Their knowledge, therefore, was home based, with occasional islands around shopping centers, work places, or previous places of residence. It was shaped either like a star or like a constellation of stars with tentacles of knowledge along the transportation system.

Whereas the planning team's habitual diagram of the city drew in the two major rivers, the Orinoco and the Caroní, followed by the location of the major settlements, most of the inhabitants concentrated on the urban environment, drawing little outside of it except for the parts of the waterfalls and the rivers adjacent to or crossed by the urban area. Their view was closely correlated with their use of the city, seldom extending beyond this experience, while, to the designers, many features of the city, such as the names and boundaries of barrios and many locally known buildings, were mostly unknown until our interviews were made. The inhabitant's world was a familiar territory unclear at the fringes of knowledge; the designer's world was thin in the center but bounded by the distinct outlines of rivers and urban development as etched out on his maps. In psychological language, the inhabitants saw the "figure," the designers saw the "ground." Without this detailed knowledge of local conditions it was only too easy, even for designers with the best of intentions, unwittingly to cut a community in two or block off access to commercial or recreational areas like the waterfalls.

One index of the complexity of the inhabitants' knowledge measured simply the average number of buildings and establishments drawn per interview map. It showed up some unexpected differences.

Surprisingly, the well educated drew simpler maps than those with only primary education, due partly, no doubt, to their superior ability to abstract the environment into larger units, but also quite clearly due to the restricted nature of knowledge. Here was a strange phenomenon. The lower-income groups mentioned more of the city than the educated elite, who mentioned little beyond their own residential "ghetto." (See Maps 23.2 and 23.3.) Whether the middle-income groups ignored the territories of groups below them from fear, lack of interest, or for reasons of social status, we do not know, but such ignorance was surprising and seemed to encourage social misperceptions like those described later in this chapter.

Knowledge did not fade uniformly with distance from home. Those living in the rancho settlement of Castillito, for example, despite the barrier of the Caroní River and ten kilometers of winding road, drew the center of San Félix as complexly as those who lived there, showing how strong a center San Félix had become for the lower-income groups.[4]

Neither did complexity increase with temporal familiarity. For the new migrants, complexity seemed to be more a measure of interest than of use, since newcomers in their first year drew more complex maps than older hands who had been in the city for five or ten years. The first encounter with a new city is apparently a time of intensive though not very efficient search, which subsequently becomes more routine and simple.

This information can have several implications for policy. Besides improving the knowledge of city designers, we could consider extending and coordinating knowledge among different population groups in order to reduce future conflicts, misperceptions, and errors. It may also be important to monitor the complexity of group knowledge in relation to the needs and capacities of different groups in any particular time, raising it for some, reducing strain for others. Diversity, clearer structuring, and the location of facilities to draw groups across the city are some variables that could be manipulated.

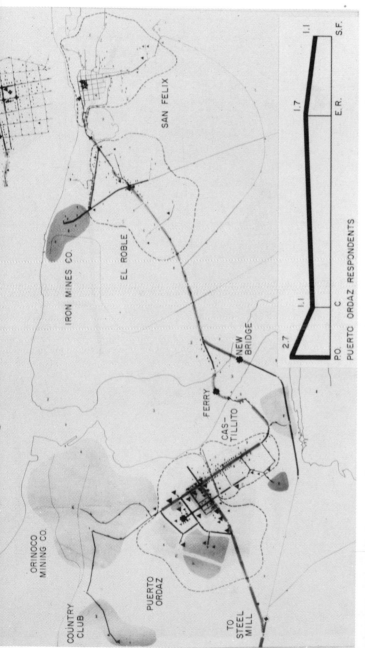
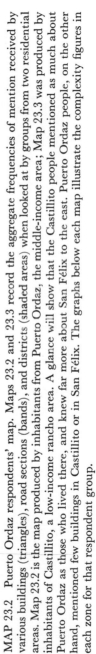

MAP 23.2   Puerto Ordaz respondents' map. Maps 23.2 and 23.3 record the aggregate frequencies of mention received by various buildings (triangles), road sections (bands), and districts (shaded areas) when looked at by groups from two residential areas. Map 23.2 is the map produced by inhabitants from Puerto Ordaz, the middle-income area; Map 23.3 was produced by inhabitants of Castillito, a low-income rancho area. A glance will show that the Castillito people mentioned as much about Puerto Ordaz as those who lived there, and knew far more about San Félix to the east. Puerto Ordaz people, on the other hand, mentioned few buildings in Castillito or in San Félix. The graphs below each map illustrate the complexity figures in each zone for that respondent group.

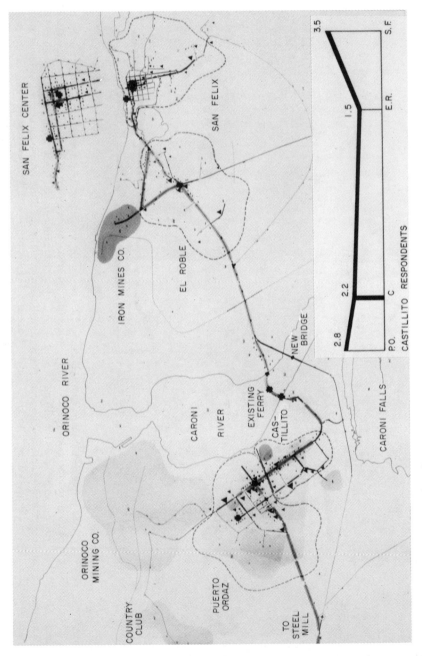

MAP 23.3 Castillito respondents' map.

Components and Attributes

The units of the inhabitants' knowledge, from such small-scale focal elements as bends, intersections, activity centers, and landmarks, to the linear roads, barriers, and edges, to the areal districts and settlements, were similar to those found in previous surveys.[5] In this study an attempt was made to discover the causes of their recall. Landmarks were taken for the subject of investigation, and over two hundred of these, mostly buildings, all of which had been mentioned in the inhabitants' maps, were rated for the presence of several attributes that might contribute to their conspicuousness.

Each landmark was rated for the intensity and singularity of its form, whether, for instance, it was large, isolated, moving, bright, complex, signposted, or of high quality; for its levels of visibility, the numbers of people likely to see it, and its location in their path of vision; and for its significance, the intensity and singularity of its use, and its historical, economic, political, and social importance.

The ratings of each component of these three main attributes were then correlated with the frequencies of response to each building on the interview maps, and regression analyses were carried out to gauge the multiple correlation coefficients for *form*, *visibility*, and *significance*, with the intention of developing a predictive formula for calculating the conspicuousness of future buildings. The buildings of this city were known, then, for some combination of their distinctness of form (their imageability), their visible exposure to the population, and their functional or symbolic significance.[6]

Of the form components, the presence of activity and movement ($r = 0.34$), the building's isolation and clear outline ($r = 0.30$), and the brightness of its surface ($r = 0.30$) were usually found to be more critical than size, quality of materials, landscaping, or signs. But the visibility of buildings, particularly at intersections ($r = 0.39$), was found to be more important than any other form component. Hence gas stations, small hotels, and, in one case, a billboard placed at a major intersection figured prominently among the known buildings of the city. (See Figure 23.1.) The multiple correlation coefficients for form, visibility, and significance turned out to be comparable, $r = 0.50$, 0.47, and 0.44, respectively, which, given the range of buildings studied, are very significant.

The role of imageability is confirmed. The role of personal action in the perception of buildings, either through their direct use or through their visible position on the paths of movement, becomes very clear. The importance of visibility, in fact, emphasizes the roles of both action and location in the recall of urban elements. Finally, the part played by significance suggests the importance of prior experience to urban perception.

Of course, these correlations do not tell us exactly how any element was recalled. A person may notice a building of high significance because he has used it, but he may have heard about it from others or through the mass media, or he may see it simply because its form looks important, conforming to some stereotype of an important building. Although it would be difficult to distinguish among these sources without a more careful analysis of use patterns and information diffusion, we can say that each of the three main attributes has an effect.

Other elements mentioned on the subject maps—landmarks, nodes, paths, barriers, edges, and districts—also appeared to be recalled in varying degrees for their imageability, exposure, use, or significance. Billboards, the Plaza Bolívar, the defined channel of the autopista, or the mosaic pattern of the Camps in Puerto Ordaz were distinct in form, and visible. A small local store, a decision point, the journey to work, a checkpoint on the road, or a person's home territory were primarily action settings, while the Macagua Dam, the railroad track to the iron mines, the fence keeping the squatters out of Puerto Ordaz, or a prestigious district like the Country Club were probably known more for their economic or social significance.

Interesting shifts in attention to these characteristics occurred between different population groups. The local inhabitants of an area usually demonstrated higher interest in form and use than strangers, who noticed more the visible buildings. In his local area the inhabitant has several means of getting to know the environment, while in remoter parts of the city he apparently depends on what is visible from the main transportation system to learn about what is going on. Only where the significant places were also imposing and visible did the perceptions of locals and strangers tend to coincide. In Ciudad Guayana this seldom happened.

New arrivals focused on economically significant elements, but subsequently their interests shifted and broadened to more highly used places. Many newcomers' descriptions focused on environmental qualities. The preconceptions about employment and industry they had developed before arriving in the city were confronted with the impact of first visual impressions—the rivers, the bridge, and new construction—before they gained a deeper knowledge of the way the city really worked. Difficulties in the coordination of attributes were encountered in the first year. The image of one building would be linked to the name of another; different approaches to an intersection could not be combined into one concept.

Other group differences were also evident. The educated, for instance, concentrated more on the skeletal—size, shape, and contour—rather than the surface characteristics of form, and more on significance, using a narrower range of attributes in their selection of elements than the less educated. Perhaps greater cognitive skill causes this higher degree of abstraction and conceptual economy.

The current tools of city design, the land-use map and the site plan, are poor descriptors of the city experience. The land-use diagram usually concentrates on functional type and residential density; the site plan on the layout and height of physical structures, the placement of trees, and the texture of ground surfaces. They are mostly guides for building location and road construction. The designers therefore do not know the effects of their plans on experience, for their design language deals with only a few of the relevant attributes. The critical variables in designing a city should relate to the actions and movements of the inhabitants, to the visible form of the environment, and to the patterns that are significant to various population groups.

The evidence from these interviews could be useful in several ways. Predictions could be made about the impact of a building or other element on the population so that its form, visibility, and function could be adjusted in response to their attention and use needs. For instance, a control strategy proposed in Ciudad Guayana imposed stricter controls on the significance and form of buildings in zones of high visibility along the main road system and in the vicinity of the major intersections. Form controls could stipulate desirable levels of isolation, brightness, and other attributes, or they could set a desirable level of recognition to be achieved by any combination of elements the individual architect or developer wished to select. Such controls would be much less restrictive than envelope or façade controls, yet would stipulate some hierarchy of importance in the form of the city. Individual architects and developers should also be interested in learning about the relative impact of various building attributes, so that they can begin more consciously to address their buildings to their critical population groups.

Structure

Designers' methods of structuring cities are at a very primitive stage. From the beginning of the Guayana project, there was a general desire to unite the diverse settlements into one city for the economy of compactness, for social and political coherence, and for a sense of urbanity. It is also a common tendency of designers to emphasize the unity of their given problem. Two methods were first attempted: the imposition of a large-scale geometrical order on the circulation system and the filling in of spaces between settlements to form a continuous urban fabric. Both turned out to be essentially "plan" techniques of dubious value in the real environment. Vestiges of one geometrical scheme are to be seen in the form of a large semicircular road to the south of San Félix (see aerial photograph of city, Figure 1.3), the geometry of which went unnoticed by our subjects, and the present interstitial development has had no apparent effect on the dissolution of barriers or the separate identity of settlements.

The inhabitants structured their maps either sequentially, using roads and river barriers, or spatially, using buildings and districts. The majority of the maps—three quarters—were dominantly sequential, a testament to the importance of the road system in city structuring. More interestingly, the maps ranged from the primitive and *topological*, relating parts through continuity, connections, proximity, and differentiation, to the more *positional*, locating elements according to direction, position, and distance.[7] (See Figures 23.2 and 23.3.)

Many of the most primitive sequential maps were no more than lists of names and fragmented sequences. Others were drastically schematic, simplifying the major east-west road to a straight line with places marked along it. The more developed sequential maps introduced bends, intersections, and districts around the line; the next level extended branches and loops from the basic linear structure; and the best maps developed complete path systems of considerable accuracy. The more primitive spatial maps were merely clustered or scattered points, often placed directionally from the locale of the interview; others linked places or districts in molecular-type diagrams, and still others consisted of joined mosaics. The most accurate maps often integrated spatial and sequential methods, achieving both continuity and positional accuracy. They were usually more schematic. Remarkably, these structuring styles were similar to various planners' stereotypes for ideal cities—the linear city, the mosaic of neighborhoods, the polycentric pattern—yet they were all discerned in the same city.

Some mix of methods was evident. Local areas were more spatially developed and accurate than the dominantly sequential distant areas. But there were marked differences among various groups, too. Very few bus riders, for instance, were able to draw a connected path system; most of them drew fragmented maps and located elements positionally in space. Car riders expectedly drew dominantly sequential maps and committed a lower percentage of directional errors.

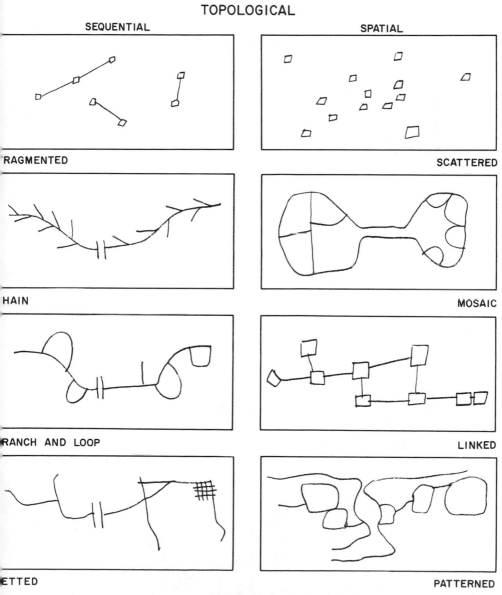

FIGURE 23.2   Structural styles.

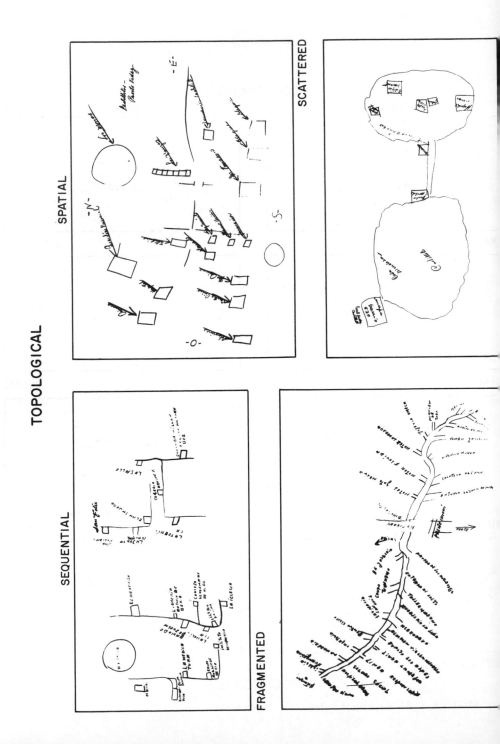

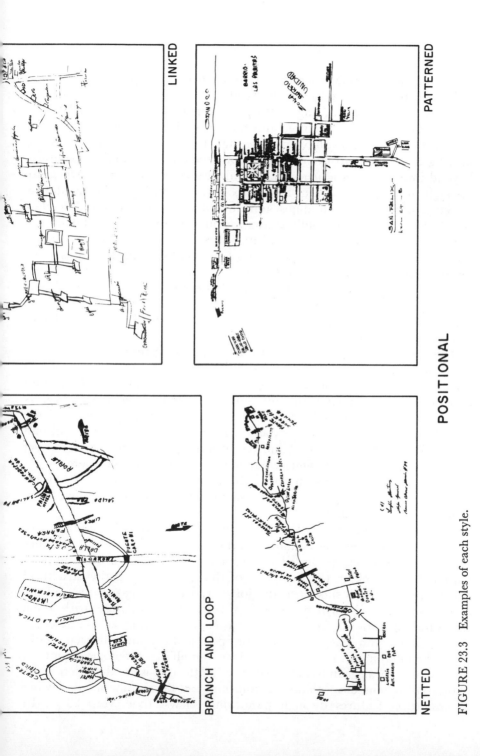

FIGURE 23.3 Examples of each style.

But the most striking differences stemmed from variations in intellectual skill. The less educated generally produced more subjective maps, distorted, reversed in parts, fragmented, and generally noninferential. Their maps appeared to be structured around personal actions and drawn along imagined journeys, magnifying and often hesitating at decision points, moving from event to event, without a developed schema or extension beyond immediate experience. Some subjects even drew their own route through the gridiron plan of San Félix without outlining the rectilinear structure of the area—an almost unthinkable operation to a middle-class North American, who usually draws a grid pattern and then fills in the parts he knows.[8] Many, too, found it difficult to integrate and coordinate information from different sources. Complex structuring tasks, like nesting one district within another or integrating two views of the same intersection, were frequently too difficult for them to undertake. Their maps were incremental rather than schematic, inferring little. The few schematic examples were reduced to simply a straight line or a few shapes representing the main settlements.

The more educated were able to avoid many of these pitfalls despite their limited knowledge of the city. They seemed better able to incorporate their experience into a more complex schema. They could predict beyond experience, even though the inference was sometimes inaccurate. A European arrival, for instance, drew three railroad lines instead of the actual two because his past experience told him to expect a railroad linkage between the steel mill and the iron-ore port, a connection not yet built. He was in effect drawing what should be, but was not, there.

In sum, the inhabitants appeared to structure the city in the same ways that they selected elements: through relationships created by action, form, visibility, or significance.

Regular journeys to work, school, shops, recreational facilities, and other destinations became action continuities, structuring the city whether or not the sequences possessed coherent form. In these terms, the new Caroní Bridge linking the two sides of the river was a major structural act simply because it shortened the journey between the two parts of the city. The physical form could either support or interfere with these structural operations. Channels of reasonably continuous character or differentiated and patterned decision points, foci, and districts could allow the inhabitant to develop and place himself in a topological context. Positional accuracy can be achieved through the consistent direction of the main road system, clear rectilinear jointing, and the simultaneous viewing of important features through panoramic views. (See Map 23.4.) In

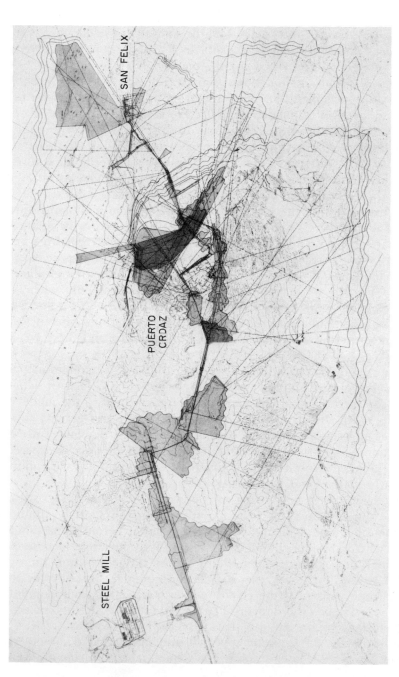
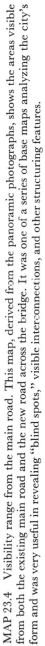

MAP 23.4   Visibility range from the main road. This map, derived from the panoramic photographs, shows the areas visible from both the existing main road and the new road across the bridge. It was one of a series of base maps analyzing the city's form and was very useful in revealing "blind spots," visible interconnections, and other structuring features.

Ciudad Guayana the intricacies of hills and rivers make this type of structuring difficult to achieve, a problem that will grow more severe as the views are closed up by new development.

Patterns of social and functional significance also played a structural role. Territory occupied by similar social groups was looked upon as an entity, and for some respondents the need to identify with areas occupied by higher social groups distorted actual distances and intervening groups to gain desired relationships. One social worker living in apartments adjacent to the squatter area of Castillito insisted that her home was really part of the Puerto Ordaz model community some distance away.

Two other systems useful for orientation, the natural context (the sun, regular breezes, and the compass) and the symbolic systems (maps, names, and numbers), did not seem to be used extensively. Only one fifth of our subjects could tell correctly where the breeze came from or the direction of the north point, a lack of contextual awareness in keeping with the incremental nature of their structuring. The names of places in Ciudad Guayana were useful in the structural sense only when they designated geographic locations like Alta Vista, Punta Vista, and Dalla Costa. Confusion only was created when districts were numbered (UV3, UV4), since the numbers had no spatial significance and there were no public maps.

Finally, the degree to which the structure of a city matches a typical urban system of probabilities can also determine the ease with which it can be organized. Ciudad Guayana neither conformed to the model of a radial city, with rising intensities of building, space, and activity toward one center, nor could it be easily seen as a string of settlements, since new construction was scattered throughout the city. Prediction was therefore difficult—another reason for the diversity of structural styles and the dominantly incremental structuring.

Given this array of structuring methods and the variety of structuring styles, the designer must face the task of structuring the city to be minimally comprehensible and coherent for all population groups, particularly for those who find it more difficult: those with less education, bus travelers, new inmigrants, housewives, and others. At the same time there are powerful reasons for developing a rich and complex structure for those who can cope with it. If the city is not organized for each population group, then it stands the danger of being either overstructured or understructured for certain groups. It might be monotonous, repetitious, and authoritarian for some or confused and disintegrated for others.

The design group's later emphasis on sequential structuring of Avenida

Guayana was more realistic than earlier attempts at unifying the city, but structural redundancy will be necessary for those of the population who structure by other methods. The pattern of physical character should be designed around the settings and patterns of habitual journeys in different travel modes. Prominent and visible sites, skylines, hilltops, and spurs should be selected now to give future landmarks a high range of visibility. The pattern of social significance and the naming of related elements should be part of the design.

Needs, Values, and Objectives

The planners' interpretation of the national and local needs and values were formulated into economic and psychosocial objectives that influenced the development of programs, the construction of facilities, and the pattern and quality of proposed urban development. While there was general agreement on the importance of developing industry, housing, educational and medical services, commerce, and recreational facilities, there were disagreements about their relative significance. The differences of opinion were even greater about the quality, pattern, and types of amenities that might be desired, particularly by the professional population that had to be attracted to settle in the city. Did these groups want urbanity, culture, and high densities or outdoor recreation, privacy, and low densities; and how important did they consider these qualities?

Our interviews probed the inhabitants' needs and values from several viewpoints. One of the more interesting sets of questions asked them to describe both the ideal and the worst city they could imagine. The responses showed strong concern for immediate needs, especially for good utility services—running water, electricity, and sanitation—and for employment, education, transportation, and medical services. Housing, cultural (often movie houses), and religious facilities were lower on the list. However, this order was caused by the predominance of lower-income groups in the sample. While the higher-income groups generally maintained the same set of priorities, they gave more weight to education and recreational facilities. Satisfaction with the city was shown by 80 per cent of our respondents, but a dissatisfied 10 per cent came largely from the highly educated groups, on whom the operation of industry depends. This could become a serious problem.

When asked to compare Ciudad Guayana with the neighboring older city of Ciudad Bolívar and with Caracas, our subjects' responses, except for employment opportunities, showed more concern for environmental and social qualities. Ciudad Guayana was said to have a climate superior to Ciudad Bolívar but inferior to Caracas. The majority preferred Caracas for its more urban character, climate, beauty, social environment, educational opportunities, living costs, recreation, and housing, while the minority (30 per cent) voting for Ciudad Guayana commented favorably on its tranquillity and economic opportunities.

Within the city, preferences were expressed for environmental values like interest, organization and beauty, recreation, and entertainment. These results give no clear support to the advocates of either high- or low-density development. It seems that the inhabitants liked both, although the elite groups appeared to be more in favor of parks, outdoor recreation, and peace—compensations for having to live out on the frontier.

Doubts have been expressed whether Ciudad Guayana, with its minimal controls, self-help housing, and indigenous development, can also be a well-designed, beautiful city. Environmental values polarize around two sets of opposite qualities: concepts like unity, order, simplicity, dominance, symmetry, articulation, boundary, and control; and notions like diversity, richness, interest, choice, meaning, ambiguity, flexibility, and independence. Historically, city design has been more under the influence of the former set of concepts than the latter, and during the design of Ciudad Guayana there was a perceptible shift in the design group's attitudes from the first to the second set as their understanding of the problem grew. We have seen that the inhabitants, too, visualized the city in a variety of ways. If the first set of qualities are to be the only criteria for success, then Ciudad Guayana will have difficulty in succeeding, for its design will be based on a narrow set of values and will require an unrealistic degree of control. If both sets are accepted as desirable, then it stands more chance of success by satisfying more of its population.

Communication of Significance

We expected the inhabitants to know the more valued and significant places in the city. To some extent this was found to be true, but for many of them the environment thwarted this effort by rendering valued places perceptually invisible and insignificant. Places of high use (an approximate index of high value) achieved reasonable but not very high correlations with map frequencies. The steel mill, hydroelectric dam, industrial ports, hospitals, and most of the schools suffered from relative invisibility or formlessness, while the main streets of the city in 1964, as in most U.S. cities, were lined with the inflated forms of gas stations, billboards, hotels, stores, and bars. (See Map 23.5.)

Ciudad Guayana also suffers from the confusion in urban probabilities wrought by the automobile. In the habitual pattern of pedestrian cities

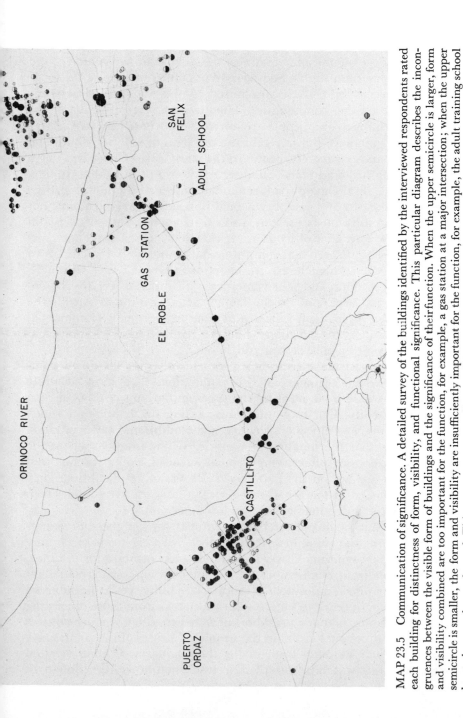

MAP 23.5 Communication of significance. A detailed survey of the buildings identified by the interviewed respondents rated each building for distinctness of form, visibility, and functional significance. This particular diagram describes the incongruences between the visible form of buildings and the significance of their function. When the upper semicircle is larger, form and visibility combined are too important for the function, for example, a gas station at a major intersection; when the upper semicircle is smaller, the form and visibility are insufficiently important for the function, for example, the adult training school located on an obscure byroad. This was one measure of how well functions were being communicated.

like San Félix, the significant buildings are located in the center of the community at the most visible and accessible points, but today the locations of high accessibility have gravitated to the major road systems, usually outside existing communities. The customary set of probabilities has been undermined, and people are not yet sure where they can expect to find certain functions. But to retain the old pattern will not work. The church, plaza, and commercial center in the new Centro Cívico in Puerto Ordaz re-established traditional building relationships but, because they were not located on the main road, remained unseen and undeveloped.

The level of access and visibility a facility needs to have depends not only on the intensity of its use but also on its spatial and social realm and on the characteristics of its users. If a facility, for example, receives only regular users, its need for communicability is less than that of an establishment whose clientele are strangers or irregular users. Hospitals, police and fire stations, and other emergency facilities especially require this kind of visual access, as do the facilities that are important for the newcomer—the employment offices and housing agencies. Commercial establishments with an irregular clientele require more communicability than the convenience stores, and so on.

The designer must make realistic assessments of what should be communicated to which segments of the population. The most accurate way to do this would be to measure the types and origins of users of each major urban facility. Our own interviews, asking the population which elements were more significant, provided some additional types of clues. Many facilities that the inhabitants considered important—such as the utility systems, housing offices, employment agencies, police stations, and movie houses—are not on the planners' stock list of key facilities. They are usually grouped in the broad categories of land-use types and left to be located by the individual agency or developer.

Once significant facilities have been identified, the designer can manipulate both form and visibility, as described earlier, to achieve any desired level of recognition. City-wide schools and hospitals, for instance, might be visible from intersections on the major road system; while gas stations, though allowed positions of high accessibility, could be subdued in form. This might result in patterns very different from those of existing cities or of orthodox planned neighborhoods, where the few more obvious community facilities are located in the geometric center of the community regardless of their visibility from major thoroughfares. Communication through visibility was later adopted as a technique in the design of Ciudad Guayana.

The perception of social characteristics was briefly studied. Among the middle classes in Puerto Ordaz, and to some extent even among the lower-income groups, we found strong distaste for ranchos (shacks), mud streets, dirt, "vice," and immorality. The middle-class respondents' distaste was often accompanied by ignorance. Several misinterpreted the meaning of the environment. Comments such as "these people have no sense of community because they scrawl signs on their walls" or "the people of . . . are nice, they keep their barrio tidy" are stereotyped misinterpretations of social character made through physical form. Yet the distaste for ranchos was so strong that there was pressure on the design group to exclude all ranchos, visible or invisible, from the western side of the Caroní, with all the dangers of a future political split along the line of the river. This is an issue still to be settled.

One way to lessen middle-class distaste and fear of ranchos would be to diversify the social cues and therefore blur social differences. Some housing types might be common for all classes; major streets in rancho areas could be well paved, homogeneous districts kept small, and well-maintained and landscaped transitional areas might be constructed. While not disguising their presence such ideas would alleviate the monotony of the low-income areas and at the same time provide them with a stimulus for future improvement.

Change

The qualities that most characterize Ciudad Guayana are change and uncertainty. As one guiding force for change, the planners lived much of their time in the future, but their image of the future fluctuated in and out of focus throughout the course of the project. From the vague figure of about 250,000 that was talked of at the beginning, the economists began to project a population of 600,000 by 1980, which, despite efforts to create alternative projections, became the principal basis for cost-of-living, land-use, and transportation projections. It was not until the later stages of planning, when the uncertainties of the future and the inertia of existing development began to reassert themselves, that attention focused again on short-term plans and the means of achieving some of the desired future states.

The effect of this future-oriented schema on locational decisions was striking. Take the location of the city center as an example. Before the CVG took over the planning of Ciudad Guayana, another agency had located the center on a ridge east of the Caroní River. As future population estimates increased and transportation factors began to be felt, the projected center was moved westward to the Punta Vista peninsula on the western bank of the Caroní. Then, as transportation simulations began to show the points of highest future accessibility moving steadily westward toward the steel mill, the center, with much anguish, was again picked up—symbolically—and moved to the Alta Vista site, a ridge to the west of the Caroní River. With the transportation planners showing the best 1980 locations as far west as the airport, the Alta Vista site looked like a good compromise; but, as we shall see, to the present-oriented inhabitant this was completely outside his realm of consideration for a future center.

Direct questions about past and present change brought forth rather general responses about progress, growth in size, numbers of people, new construction, and so on. Awareness of change was unanimous, but new buildings of themselves were not especially remarked upon—perhaps not surprising in a city where the majority of buildings were new and where new buildings and districts were frequently hidden from view.

The most influential aspects of change in Ciudad Guayana were the structural transformations in the circulation system. When the new bridge was opened, Castillito and Puerto Ordaz were bypassed, and a view of the Caroní Falls was opened up. Comparing interview maps made before and after the bridge was opened to traffic, we could see how quickly new elements entered and old ones dropped out, and the confusion caused by approaching old intersections from new viewpoints. Interviews with newcomers a year later found them placing a much greater emphasis on grosser-scale elements and on traffic circles and intersections. This may indicate the influence of faster road travel, but it may also be a sign that the inhabitants were coping with the city's increasing complexity by conceptualizing at a grosser level.

Predictions of future change depend on extrapolation from existing perceptions. Since the CVG plans were not well known, the inhabitants predicted growth in all directions, locating the future center in one or another of the existing centers, usually the one nearest to their own residence, but never in the planned future location. When asked to give reasons for their predictions, the majority pointed to the presence of current construction and housing rather than to the determinants of the growth pattern. Here again, incremental structuring, dependent on immediate sensory cues rather than conceptual thinking about cause and effect, dominated perception. Since the planned direction of growth depends also on the actions and interests of private firms and families, to whom the present plan appears improbable, an effort to inform them will have to be made.

Although the planners were initially worried that change would be unwelcome to the population, it turned out that the inhabitants were almost unanimously in favor of it. Eighty-seven per cent wanted the city to grow faster, leaving only 13 per cent (mostly from the upper-income groups) who thought it was changing too rapidly. But despite this general enthusiasm, change cannot be to everyone's benefit. The dissatisfaction of the higher-income groups, supposedly with the loss of freedom and openness, indicates that one important group is not looking forward to a larger city. The shopkeepers of Castillito, who later rose in protest when the new highway bypassed them, might then have qualified their earlier enthusiastic responses in our interviews. Notwithstanding these danger signals, the overwhelming evidence is that the population, mostly voluntary inmigrants, is resilient, expectant, and enthusiastic about change. In a sense they are participating in it by coming to the city, and many are building it with their own hands. If they lose that sense of participation and succumb to a position of powerlessness, then change imposed by others may lose its appeal.

The programming of information about change is as important as change itself. The physical construction of a new city proceeds in a manner that creates a jerky sequence in the mind of the inhabitant. New areas are opened up, or links are suddenly made that shift flow patterns and emphasis very rapidly. Ignorance or uncertainty creates surprise, anxiety, and sometimes resentment. Expectations delayed can be equally frustrating. Although ambiguity about future plans may give the planner flexibility of action, it will not help to get public support. The monitoring of change and attitudes toward change through interviews and publicity may be the most crucial aspect of future planning in Ciudad Guayana.

Conclusions

From the theoretical viewpoint we have made some steps toward an understanding of why people see the city in the way they do. Urban perception is more than imageing distinctive qualities in the environment, although these are a primary source of urban knowledge. Perception is guided also by a person's needs, purposes, and actions, by his past experience, general and particular, and by his conceptual abilities to process information. Finally, environmental information is mediated either directly through a person's mode of travel—a car and a bus mediate different information—or indirectly through the mass media, drawing attention to events and places that might otherwise pass unnoticed. These are the variables that seem to explain the differences among population groups in our surveys.

The designer differs from the inhabitant in nearly all of these variables. His motivations are general, diffuse, and future oriented, whereas the inhabitant's are usually particular, specific, and present oriented; his experience with cities is usually much greater than that of the inhabitant, which makes it difficult for him to see a city or plan with an "innocent" eye. His familiarity with the city is usually more extensive than intensive, and his information media are so abstracted and amplified with "objective" data that his world tends to become divorced from the real city. His very abilities and knowledge create the gap.

One way to bridge the gap in Ciudad Guayana was clearly to move the design operation down to the site of the city. But this would not be enough. Closer and more systematic communications needed to be set up with various representative population groups so that the designers could play advocacy roles. But even this would not be sufficient. Designers must develop a more realistic language of design. More real and manipulable simulations of the city should have been available in the planning office.

Several questions are raised by these interviews. Here we can deal only with two.

First, what are the functions of an interview that investigates urban knowledge rather than, say, urban behavior patterns or environmental values? Perhaps the influence of knowledge on urban form is not well understood. Knowledge in fact exerts a powerful influence over behavior patterns, attitudes, locational decisions, and ultimately the physical form of the city. The choice of routes to take, establishments to use, jobs to apply for, all depend on perceptions of the choices. Similarly, locational decisions for new industrial enterprises, community services, or commercial establishments are dependent on knowledge of the urban layout. There were many places in Ciudad Guayana where development took place because the location was visible. On the other hand, the projected Centro Cívico never expanded because it was hidden from view. Finally, the physical construction of the city is affected by the conceptions of the city's builders. Witness the contrast between the professionally designed parts of the city and the indigenous areas, built by nonprofessionals. The former were precisely oriented and patterned from the air but fitted uneasily on the ground; the latter looked haphazard from the air but, like medieval villages, made a better fit with the local context. Both were clear physical expressions of the mental representations of their creators. Investigations into different views of the world therefore tell us much that is useful to a planning operation. They need, however, to be problem oriented, too. Our surveys would have gained by asking more questions about the difficulties and preferences of the inhabitants; not to cater to them slavishly but to know where "felt" problems lay. Nevertheless, the interviews did uncover many latent needs and structuring difficulties that might not have emerged so clearly under direct questioning.

The value of interviews like these should be evident to those who are not satisfied with current methods of designing cities, but, at this stage of the art, the effort to translate findings into developed methods that a designer can use is a formidable one. The simplicity and quickness of continuing with known methods proved, in many instances, too powerful. But as theory and methods develop, this kind of investigation can be streamlined better to serve an ongoing operation. Until other agencies as willing to be enlightened as the CVG undertake this work, however, progress will be slow.

The second and most difficult question is how do we design for a pluralistic city? I do not mean a laissez-faire city but one in which the needs, purposes, and abilities of all population groups are considered, rather than only those of the more powerful. There is no easy answer. We can try to identify the most significant population groups: those under most stress and those who are most needed. In Ciudad Guayana the technical and professional personnel, political leaders, steelworkers, the young, and new migrants were such priority groups.

The city then could be designed to satisfy at least the minimal needs of each group. A method of selecting significant facilities according to need has already been suggested. Developing structural relationships for different cognitive skills and styles should not be difficult. A city must be complex enough to incorporate this diversity. It should be designed to facilitate easy learning by migrants while maintaining the interest and involvement of the more familiar. Simple and straightforward skeletal structures supported by more complex alternative systems could be developed. The larger structure of the city has to be designed by professionals because individuals do not have the resources, but, the tighter the designers can draw the line around the strategic variables they must manipulate, the more freedom and influence individuals and other groups can have over the form of the city. The identification of this line will no doubt be a source of continuing debate between what we may call the "pluralist" and the "total" designers within each group.

I do not suggest a purely market-oriented approach to city design, at least not one based only on extrapolations from existing perceptions and attitudes. The designer's role is similar to that of the educator. His job is to innovate, lead, and explore, but he must maintain contact with his clients. The quality of Ciudad Guayana or any city cannot depend solely on the imposition of a single conceptual or value structure. The population will rebel against it. It will be achieved, if at all, through relating the attributes and elements that are relevant to the inhabitants, through the counterpoint of planned and indigenous, through the progressive revelation of meaning and change, and perhaps through the raising of individual urban actions to a level of quality and consciousness that give it style. The raw material is there; the designer can be one catalyst.

Chapter 24

Conflicting Views of the Project: Caracas versus the Site

Lisa Peattie

The development of Ciudad Guayana provided the planners with a situation somewhere between an urban renewal rebuilding and rehabilitation project and a wholly new city. Although the planners thought of themselves as "developing a new city," they knew that they were not doing so in the same way that planners had made Brasilia or Chandigarh. Ciudad Guayana was to be planned and stimulated by the government but built primarily through private initiative; Brasilia and Chandigarh were actually built by the government. Another difference was in the situation at the site. Brasilia and Chandigarh were planned for and built in essentially unoccupied areas. The site of Ciudad Guayana was not unoccupied.

When the first members of the Joint Center planning team arrived in Caracas, some 45,000 people were already living around the site of the new city, mainly at the eastern edge. These residents had certain organized rights and interests in the area. For most individuals these were not vested in landownership. Although the two North American mining companies owned considerable amounts of land and a few individuals owned smaller tracts, most land was still publicly owned, its residents renting and owning buildings but not the land on which the buildings stood. But the site of Ciudad Guayana was the site of an existing municipality, with its government functionaries and offices. There was a lively Chamber of Commerce; there were local civic clubs, like the Rotary Club and the Masons; there was a Catholic parish headed by a Basque priest who had a strong sense of being a spokesman for the people of the town.

For the staff of the Guayana project, not unnaturally their own planning enterprise in general occupied the center of their cognitive map of the situation. They tended to see themselves as causing the city and the city as something "we are planning and developing."

The people of the developing city perceived matters rather differently. A survey in 1963 showed that half the people interviewed had never heard of the Corporación Venezolana de Guayana (CVG). Of those who had, half had a totally erroneous conception of it, and many of the rest saw it primarily as the management of the steel mill, employers or potential employers for the people of the city, the management of the dam or power complex, or in some other partial way.[1] For several years after the declared founding of Ciudad Guayana, the city planning activities of the CVG were seen predominantly as stringent restrictions on private building and as a number of relatively localized development projects. The CVG thought it better not to expose its conceptions and plans for urban development to the people of the area until those plans were complete and definite; thus only a tiny fraction of the inhabitants had any idea that the existing urbanized areas were to be integrated into the new Ciudad Guayana.

To the people on the site the city appeared, rather, as growing spontaneously around several poles. The main focus of development was "the companies"—the two North American corporation subsidiaries with their iron-mining operations in the hills farther south and their shipping and, for one company, processing operations at the Caroní-Orinoco confluence. The population and the payrolls supported by "the companies" made possible the commercial life that had formed the local elite—Spanish and Italian as well as Venezuelan—who dominated local politics. The CVG appeared on the elite's cognitive map as a latecomer and as one among several stimuli to development. The people of the site saw themselves as part of a very rapidly developing city, a commercial boomtown, a city of inmigrants and of rapid change. A claim to slow down change, to "preserve," would have appeared nearly incomprehensible to all of them. It was a city living in the future, its residents at every social level committed to economic and urban development. But they did not see the CVG as the main cause of past development and tended very much less than the development agency to focus their hopes for future development on the role of the CVG.

For the planners in Caracas it seemed not to be easy to penetrate intellectually the world "at the site." To visit it physically, although inconvenient, was not difficult; by 1964 there were four commercial flights daily from the capital, besides a large number of bus runs for those willing to undergo a fourteen-hour trip. However, "the site" was isolated from the planners in Caracas not only by the lack of telephone and even of efficient mail communication between the two but also by certain gaps less material or technical in nature. There are primitive peoples, we are told, whose words for their own tribe and for people not members of their own tribe in effect designate the two as "men" and "not men." Although civilized men make more subtle distinctions, the "we" and "they" of speech codify different ways of experiencing people. "They" seem to appear to us as essentially more opaque than those who belong to "us," and "we" tend to try to organize our experience with "them" descriptively rather than empathically.

To the visiting consultants of the Joint Center–Guayana project, most people "at the site" necessarily appeared as "others," or "them." They were different from the planners according to not just one but all the major lines of social categorizing practiced by Americans: nationality, language, race, economic status. It may be less obvious why they should also have appeared so clearly as "them" to the Venezuelan staff of the development agency. Here the barrier may be roughly identified as social class—the barrier George Orwell characterizes as being like the plate glass of an aquarium window, at once invisible and impenetrable.

The last thirty-odd years of oil prosperity in Venezuela evidently have made some considerable changes in the old social order, with its small, Europe-oriented upper class and a largely agrarian base. However, the need for middle-level people during the oil boom was so sudden and explosive that a large part of the new "middle class" positions in the society had to be filled by immigrants from Europe, who still think of themselves and are thought of by others as not really part of the national society. The discontinuity between upper and lower class still is bridged by only a very sparse native middle class. Furthermore, by greatly increasing the dominance of Caracas relative to the provincial cities, oil prosperity made the society more centralized than ever. Those 45,000 people "at the site" were not of a single class level, but they were predominantly of lower status, and were so viewed by the planners in Caracas. A member of a relatively high-status group, looking at "them" below, finds it difficult to see people below the class line with precision and clarity and even more difficult to interact with them as fellow humans with equally valid conceptions of and claims on shaping social reality. His vision is, as it were, refracted off the class barrier as off the surface of a pond.

The people below the class line, though viewed by those above as "them," can still interact with the upper groups in a common framework. One such framework, of relative impersonality, is the framework of economics. A more personal framework is that of politics. Within the structure of political institutions, various groups that are relatively opaque to each other can still make known to each other interests that will be seen to have some human validity. For the relations between "the site" and "the planners" the political structure allowed certain interactions but was relatively useless for continuing or generalized intercommunication. Local government in Venezuela, limited in powers and inadequately financed, tends to be weak and ineffective. The powers given to the development corporation overlay, rather than fit into, this structure. Democratic political institutions in Venezuela are new and still undeveloped. Political parties lack the kind of local organization that in the United States tends to aggregate local interests into the national political structure; much of Venezuelan political activity appears as one more thing that goes on in Caracas. Moreover, there is a tendency for each ministry and major agency to "belong" to one or the other of the major parties, and the party the local people saw as dominating the Guayana development corporation had almost no base in the region it was to develop.

Furthermore, ways of working strongly shape ways of thinking. Of the various types of technical experts represented among the planners, the most numerous were the urban designers and the economists. The urban designers thought of their task in an intellectual framework developed out of architecture; they thought of it as the invention and imposition, either through building or through stimulation, of urban forms. Their basic intellectual tool was the map, which represents a city as spatial relationships between locationally described entities rather than as a dynamic system of which the spatial relations are a particular expression. The economists saw their task as bringing in economic activities, especially industries. Their basic tool was the numerical statistic that describes reality as a summation of economic units and of transactions, rather than in terms of the transacting actors. Both urban designers and economists operated in a time scale in which the city of the future occupied an enlarged foreground. The 45,000 people on the site might be important to themselves, but they dwindled somewhat in importance when set next to the population of more than 600,000 that some had projected for 1980.

It thus came about that the place that was experienced by 45,000 people as their developing city was experienced by the planners of that development as "the site."

Between "the people of the site" and "the planners" there was often a lack of mutual comprehension; there were also a number of points of direct conflict. Working-class people often came into conflict with the planners over the the general freeze on building—a house that had to remain roofless, a group of families that had to move to make way for a dock, or a neighborhood that could not be allowed to build a school "until plans were completed." Leaders in the public-school system—one element of the local elite—resented the CVG's lavish support of Catholic schools. But it so happened that the major group to find itself in conflict with the Corporation was the local elite as a whole. For the planners in effect threatened them as commercial, political, and private actors. The Corporation was welcomed as a bringer of new jobs—the mill, the long-hoped-for aluminum plant. Jobs filled the cash registers in local businesses, and it was local business that supported the local elite. But in the early years of the enterprise the Corporation appeared to be reducing commercial opportunities and jobs. The local elite were affected both directly and indirectly through the freeze on building. There were the local business-men who wanted to open enterprises but could not get permission to build, pending completion of plans. There was the Pepsi-Cola bottling plant, which had to settle in a town farther south for lack of an approved site in Ciudad Guayana.

Later, as the CVG began to build, local commercial interests found themselves threatened by the new developments. For example, a new road completely bypassed an existing commercial area until political pressure from "the site" forced the CVG to build a connecting roadway. To local politicians the development corporation represented a direct attempt at conquest; most bitter was the agency's denial to the local government of rights in land, a primary and traditional source of both revenue and patronage. To an elite attacked in all these ways, and in some ways constricted personally even more than the poor by the ban on building —for it was not for them to throw up a rancho in a vacant lot overnight, and there were no places designated for them to erect the sorts of houses they saw as fit—even the amenities of the fenced CVG "camp," with its government-financed swimming pool accessible only to the Corporation's employees and their friends, was something that rankled.

Something of the quality of the confrontation, as it was experienced on the site side of it, may be given by a summary of a short speech by one of the San Félix leaders—a German-educated surgeon with professional, political, and real-estate interests in the developing city. The occasion was a meeting in May 1963 of people interested in local community development, chaired by a man from Cordiplan, the national planning agency in Caracas.

The Caraqueños who are there clinging to the air conditioning[2]—where they don't need it because they have a very nice climate—have no idea of San Félix. For instance, they will send us an electoral commission of the sort suitable for a hamlet. They do not understand that it is a little town—fifty thousand to eighty thousand people—with aspirations to be a city with urban atmosphere.

Visitors come. They stay in Ciudad Bolívar. They pass through, they have a nice drink at the Spanish Club—but they don't see the barrios like Barrio Unidad or El Roble. You have to go around in the town. For instance, Dalla Costa is not just what you see from the highway.

How did all this come about? It grew like the 23 enero—by force.[3] There are plans—marvelous plans. Since 1957 they have been making plans—where the buildings will be, where the transportation networks. But when you want to build something in a certain place the Junta Comunal [town council] can't do it—you have to ask the Corporación de Fomento, the Corporación Venezolana —which has its offices not here but in a marvelous office in the Shell Building [in Caracas]. They make plans and in a year or so they erase them to study and make another—erase them and study and make another.

The nucleus of San Félix is almost exclusively workers. It is based on the Orinoco Mining Company, the Iron Mines Company, and the steel mill. Commerce and the few industries revolve around the companies and the steel mill. When other possibilities come in sight they can't tell us where they can locate.

Now there is out for bids a beautiful aqueduct—big enough for a huge population. Meanwhile, the Junta Comunal has to keep opening wells. The Junta has to supply water to distant barrios by truck.

San Félix needs five thousand hospital beds—has about two hundred. It is the custom here to talk of the great river, of the magnificent falls, of the aluminum plant of Reynolds which will produce aluminum for all Venezuela. But I think we must talk here of the truth. We are suffering hunger, suffering thirst, suffering difficulties. . . .

In Caracas a few weeks earlier, I had a conversation, summarized below, with one of the planners, which suggests the other side of the picture. The subject was a request from the residents of an outlying barrio in the existing town that they be allowed to build a school.

That area is a natural area for development, and since this should be organized, one of the planners working on the site should make a sketch plan. Small improvements could then take place congruent with that. But where immediate changes are in prospect, no improvements may be allowed.

Look what is happening here. The planners are following the people instead of leading them. The local politicians are not only fattening on problems but creating problems, rather than trying to solve them. People are unreasonable. They would rather go off on their own and put up shacks all over the place than to go and settle in the planned building lots where they can see they will get the services.

In every enterprise that brings together groups of people with varying backgrounds to pursue goals that, even though desired in common, are desired for varying reasons, there are likely to be interesting differences in the conceptions of the various groups about the leading problems to be solved. The architects pull toward taking more time to discuss "the form of the city"; the engineers want to get on with building particular projects. For the Venezuelans the years spent in planning and developing Ciudad Guayana should help in advancing a career line shaped by personal and professional connections in Caracas; the Joint Center planner will be going back to Cambridge, and his time in Venezuela has to pay off in the speech and publication currency of academic advancement. Such differences in life situation produced interesting differences in points of view among the planners in the Guayana project. It is interesting, therefore, that the difference between the world of "the site" and that of Caracas was one that often tended to cut across others.

As I review the conversations recorded in my notes, I see that the most forceful expressions of "us" at the site in opposition to "them," "clinging to the air conditioning in Caracas," came from members of the project based at the site. These included employees of both the CVG and the Joint Center–Guayana project.

There are a number of reasons why staff members working in the Guayana should have come to feel themselves part of "us" in the Guayana as contrasted to "them" in Caracas. First, the difficulties in communication between the two cities meant that "we" at the site were always awaiting needed things from "them" in Caracas. It might be a ruling on policy, without which a number of problems had to be held pending; it might be a reimbursement for out-of-pocket expenses that was badly needed; or it might be a matter as simple as a set of forms, without which an interviewer must spend hours ruling lines with a pencil. Staff in the Guayana tended to feel that "Caracas" did not adequately understand the problems to be solved, and that their own ability to relate appropriately to these problems was impaired by the gulf between "Caracas" and "the site." Second, the staff at the site were acutely conscious of local pressures, from which distance effectively insulated the staff in Caracas. The demand for approved building lots was no abstract problem to a staff with long lines of petitioners before the door and a couple of thousand applications already on file. The staff member in charge of appraising buildings for purchase by the CVG found at one period that he could not remain in his own home evenings and weekends because he was besieged by individuals whose homes were to be bought by the CVG, but for whom payments had not yet arrived. Third, the local staff began to develop their own local interests. Holes in the streets and lack of services were not deficiencies to "a clientele"; they were personal difficulties. Finally, the local staff began to become part of the local society. They became, themselves, part of the local elite. They joined up. That Mr. Fulano who had not been able to get a permit to build a gasoline station was not just a citizen "at the site"; he was a friend and a fellow member of the Rotary Club.

The gulf between "the site" and "Caracas" was felt much more strongly at the site than among the planners in the capital. The people at the site experienced the gap as a painful inaccessibility of power—over forces affecting them, over the control of visible and desirable economic resources, and over their own ability to predict the future. It affected them in immediate and troubling ways. In Caracas it was less troubling, since much of the planners' sense of getting work done and of being able to proceed further was not closely tied to the enactment of their plans by the "local people." This was especially true in the earlier stages of the project, when planning was more generalized and "paper bound" and consisted in large part of various alternative models of the future. But it tended to be true later also, to the extent that the planners designed projects in terms of implementation by the development agency itself or by other national institutions.

To the extent that the Caracas planners were troubled by the gap, it tended to present itself to them as an exasperating (even if understandable) tendency of particular local interests, sometimes abetted by the CVG staff on the site, to press for immediate satisfaction at the expense of the long-term general welfare as represented in plans for the new city. The unsightly shacks erected, contrary to regulation, on urban land more reasonably destined for other use, the local merchants pressing for a road connection to *their* businesses, and the subdivision laid out by the local CVG staff on land intended—by the Caracas planners—for open space were examples. The "local people" thus generally tended to trouble Caracas not so much by their failure to act according to plan as by a tendency to act counter to plan. The joking comment of the head of the development agency that he wished he could put everyone in the city under anesthesia until the city was built expressed this very clearly.

In Caracas the staff members "at the site" were not perceived as having shifted to a different reference group; they were members of "the team" still, although tending with time to become somewhat peripheral to it through their prolonged absence and their development of contrasting points of view because of separation and difference of experience. It was noted in Caracas that staff members based at the site tended to identify with local interests. In some cases, this seems to have been viewed as a certain mild loss of objectivity. In other cases—notably, one of the CVG engineers from the site who returned to Caracas and went into "social planning," and the Joint Center anthropologist (this writer)—a local-interest advocacy function came to be the dominant element of their social role in Caracas. This stylizing of professional roles tended in turn to confirm the central staff's conception of responsiveness to the situation at the site as a responsiveness to particular interests.

A distinction has often been made between "comprehensive" and "incremental" planning. In thinking about the relationship between "the site" and "Caracas" in the Guayana project, I have found it helpful to make a tripartite division: comprehensive planning, an incrementalism focused on centrally generated projects, and an incrementalism that tries to stimulate an evolution from existing forces and institutions, to build up and out from what is already there. In appropriate circumstances, any one or various combinations of these kinds of planning can, I believe, be used by a central planning agency.

In the Guayana project it would appear that urban design (after some "emergency" reviewing of particular ongoing projects) for a while took a quite comprehensive form, attempted some evolutionary incrementalism, particularly with reference to low-income housing, and then moved in the direction of centralized project incrementalism, especially in the area of transportation. Economic planning maintained a fairly consistent style of project incrementalism centered around feasibility studies for various industrial packages; these projects, taken together, were fitted into the comprehensive national plan. Social planning began as projects, although these with time evolved somewhat in a generalized or comprehensive direction, and remained predominantly of a project character.

The sort of incremental planning that I have called "evolutionary" was relatively undeveloped in the Guayana project. This may be partially explained by some general characteristics of the Venezuelan situation, especially the relatively large capital resources available to the central government and the tradition of centralization of power. Also this may be generally characteristic of the early stages of planning programs, and it is possible that, as the program evolves, such comments will become inapplicable. But for the period of my observations it seems clear that serious obstacles to this kind of incremental planning arose from the gap between "Caracas" and "the people of the site." "Caracas" responded *to* "the people of the site" by yielding when they applied pressure, and

"Caracas" generated programs *for* "the people of the site," especially in the area of "social planning." But it was not characteristic for "Caracas" to work *with* "the people of the site." There were some interesting small experiments in collaboration between the development corporation and the local people in institution building at the local level—the joint municipal-CVG rebuilding of a road, the starting of a municipal library, discussions with the municipal government of plans for renovating the San Félix waterfront, a joint community center and theater, and, most interesting of all, the attempt to handle the conflict between development agency and municipality over municipal lands through a locally based housing development corporation in which both parties would collaborate. But these experiments, although connections across the gap between "the site" and "Caracas," were still not sufficient to make it easy for "the people" and "the planners" to conceive of planning and development— to which both were strongly committed—as a common effort in which they were involved together.

The evolution of programs for handling the "squatter problem" offers an interesting example of the problems in this general area. The decision to define "the city" to be designed as the whole urban complex in the area, rather than as those parts of it under the direct control of the CVG, suggested to the planners that they ought to develop programs for handling inmigration and new residential building in terms of long-term plans. The resulting program called for laying out and doing basic urbanizing of "reception areas" where inmigrants might locate and a program of "self-help housing" to assist low-income people in building their own permanent homes. That these programs had rather limited success is not the subject of discussion here: they were conceived as "pilot projects." What is relevant here is the way in which they were weakened at a number of points by the gap between "Caracas" and "the site."

The separation of "the planners" from the actual migration pressures on "the site," in conjunction with a lack of statistics on migration and population, contributed to a failure for a considerable period to plan the "reception areas" fast enough and in enough quantity to channel all or most of the flow. The drastic shortage of building lots relative to demand, combined with the general tendency of the CVG to treat the problem of dealing with people on the site in the general framework of charity, meant that the allocation of building lots became subject to investigative procedures (intended to assess "need") of such length and complexity as to ensure that the "reception areas" program could not serve newly arrived inmigrants. The difficulties of developing a decentralized program involving the spending of CVG money were so intense that they made the self-help housing program nearly unworkable. Many "social programs" were developed in the new low-income urbanizations. But the form of these programs, carried on by the social workers of the CVG and by the Catholic Church with some CVG assistance, made these urban neighborhoods responsible to a governmental structure wholly different from that in the rest of the city and, at the time of my stay, uncoordinated with it.

The distance from the site that made it hard to develop what I have called evolutionary incrementalism had some further consequences for the way in which the tasks of planning were conceived in the Guayana project. Distance from the site not only made it harder to organize and carry out certain sorts of programs; it also deprived the planners in Caracas of certain sorts of information feedback that might in other circumstances have served to integrate better the various aspects of the program.

There is always a tendency for specialists in particular areas—housing, social welfare, industrial promotion—to treat their concerns as specialities rather than as aspects of over-all development strategy. One way of integrating the particular specialities is through some sort of strong central leadership focused on a general coordinating strategy. Partly for particular historical reasons, even more because of the necessities of the consultant situation, such leadership was lacking in the Guayana project. Another way in which integration takes place is through connections made between particular policies and programs. Although a concern with operating programs in the field can easily tend to particularize and limit problem conceptions, too, it can also help to generalize and bring out connections. Experience with ongoing programs can teach, for example, that housing programs affect the patterns of economic activity and the processes of social mobility. Lacking an effective system of information feedback from the field, these kinds of connections between various aspects of the program were less readily made than they might have been, and there was, I suspect, less total focusing of the enterprise on a general development strategy.

For any given planning project, crucial questions about the technical possibilities of the particular situation will strongly affect the way planning is most appropriately conceived. How much power to initiate and control does the central planning agency have? To what extent can the planning agency in fact act comprehensively, or must it manipulate limited powers among other institutions shaping the situation? Assuming that in every situation the planning agency is not the only actor needed, where are cooperation and coordination most readily achieved: at the top, or out in the field in terms of particular programs and projects? In what sorts of areas and in relation to what sorts of changes can the planning agency initiate and control; what changes can it effect only by stimulating and directing forces and activities that are outside its range of direct influence? How are such indirect influences most effectively exercised?

Any substantial planning enterprise also raises problems of political ethics that are not easily resolved. To what extent is it right to demand that people make painful sacrifices in the alleged interest of future generations? Or, looking at it the other way, should men of today be allowed to satisfy their interests in a way that exhausts important possibilities for many men yet unborn? To what extent does superior technical knowledge justify political dominance? How much power should technical experts have, and what should validate and check their power?

The technical questions and the ethical questions are, in such problems, thoroughly interpenetrated. For example, the problem of whose interests should be compromised, and how, is thoroughly involved with questions of social and political structure. Who, in fact, is able to speak for whom?

In the Guayana project the distance between "Caracas" and "the site" was an important aspect of the technical possibilities of the planning situation. It was one factor, for example, that made it much easier to build roads than to develop a working program for low-income housing. It was also an important factor in the way the political and ethical questions presented themselves, for it made it harder for particular individual and group interests to play themselves out and be resolved, if not solved, in the framework of common discussion of a common commitment.

Part 4
Concluding
Observations

Chapter 25

Reflections on Collaborative Planning

Lloyd Rodwin

The Guayana program had an official historian, but this was one of those deceptively attractive ideas that just did not work out. About the only persons who spoke seriously to the historian were those whose observations did not matter one way or the other. The major difficulty, however, as Lisa Peattie has observed, was not "in getting people to level as informants (although that is always a problem—for anthropologists as well as historians) but in presuming to describe an institution with which one is involved, which one is still trying to promote, and with respect to which certain particular ways of viewing are operationally functional. There is not only the need for deletions; there is the fact that one's way of conceptualizing necessarily takes a form that responds to the needs of the enterprise. In short, there is a good reason why history is written about the past and why certain kinds of history have been or are virtually impossible."[1]

In lieu of the history, perhaps the reader ought to be given some inkling of the questions about which the Corporación Venezolana de Guayana (CVG) and the Joint Center disagreed as well as the questions about which some of the members of the staff of the CVG and the Joint Center disagreed with their leaders. Over a period of five years, there were differences of opinion on many matters. The issues I have selected illustrate the problems of establishing rapport with our Venezuelan colleagues plus some of the misgivings that arose concerning policies and methods. In focusing on these items I have two purposes in mind. One is to provide a glimpse of how technical problems of collaboration sometimes produced unexpected complications—often because of subtle differences in values and in judgments of the effects of proposed changes on power, status, or self-esteem. My second purpose is to relate the inferences one might draw from our experience in the Guayana to more general questions of strategy in planning urban and regional development.

The Art of Collaboration

Giving assistance or taking it is never easy. It should have been all the more difficult in Venezuela, for Venezuelans are supposed to dislike foreigners—Latin Americans generally, Italians in particular, and North Americans often, but not always, at the top of the list. We were there five years, and we parted friends—with some expectation of further association in the future. So the collaboration appears to have been somewhat successful. But was it really? Or perhaps one should ask, what were the kinds of difficulties encountered in a presumably successful relationship?

Even in a successful marriage, there are often conflicts and serious misunderstandings. These are all the more likely if one starts with significant differences in habits, values, and aims—which certainly was true for the Joint Center and its Venezuelan associates. But, however widespread hostility to foreigners may generally be in Venezuela, such attitudes did not pose serious problems for us in dealing with the principal staff of the CVG. This was partly because of a deeply shared concern about common technical problems, partly because of the friendships that grew up between the two staffs, and partly because the leaders of the CVG had studied in the United States and admired the two universities we represented and appreciated the potential contributions and prestige this collaboration would lend their efforts.

Despite these favorable circumstances, there was a gulf between the Venezuelans and the Joint Center. It manifested itself in several ways: in social relationships, in basic attitudes, in some of the problems of establishing confidence and rapport.

For example, some of our staff were disappointed at not being invited into the homes of Venezuelans. This complaint is frequently heard in developing countries. In Venezuela, there were probably many reasons: the extended family, the wives not speaking English, inadequate or noncomparable housing, and the fact that many Latin Americans do not feel comfortable with North Americans—nor the same need to be liked that Americans do.

On the job our staff got along well with the Venezuelans. True, they fought like cats and dogs on occasion, and there were strong reservations about individuals on both sides. Nonetheless, when our task ended, several members of our team decided to remain, and some of them were employed by the CVG. The Joint Center was pleased that this occurred. We knew the Venezuelans found us harder to take than we found them. Our manners occasionally irritated them, perhaps inadvertently. Our being there implied some kind of superiority. Not all of our staff earned their respect or sympathy. But what the Venezuelans—or at any rate their chiefs—most admired were our energy and devotion to the task rather than our ability to redefine problems, formulate new ways of doing things, or show how a job might get done. With the exception of the principal staff, the Venezuelans did not show the same zeal, for several reasons. Aside from individual differences, there were different rewards, career lines, and cultural and personal motivations. These factors help to explain, as one thoughtful Venezuelan put it, why a bunch of North Americans would come down to work on a Venezuelan problem and slave away night and day and battle among themselves and lose their tempers—as though it were their own people and their country's future that were at stake. He said he often talked to his men about what we were doing and how we were doing it, and he seemed to hope that some of this way of working and feeling might rub off on them.

Still another consideration may have been involved. Our staff liked Venezuelans—not just their professional associates but the people. Most of our staff were do-gooders, in the best sense of the term. They thought what they were doing was important. They were glad to be there and they wanted to do their best. The Venezuelans were do-gooders, too. Our men could not have sustained their efforts if there had not been a general conviction around the CVG that what they were doing mattered very much. But although many of our Venezuelan associates felt that they were doing something significant for Venezuela, as well as for their own careers, many (though not all) of the most important Venezuelans did not really respect or trust the local people or the inmigrants. They identified them with narrow vested interests, traditional views, and inferior social elements. These attitudes colored the CVG's approach to many matters. Almost everyone wanted to do a first-rate technical job—but to the key Venezuelan officials it often meant preventing these local elements from botching up the plans or interfering with development priorities favoring the foreign firms, the modern sectors of Venezuelan enterprise, or the skilled technicians and elite groups that could spur the economy forward, staff the economic activities, and provide social tone and quality to the community. Some of our staff shared, or at least went along with, these views; but others who were in a position of authority balked at these attitudes and stressed the need for more cooperation with local groups and for more intensive efforts to accommodate the inmigrants, serve their needs, and help them get a better foothold in the economic and social system. I am oversimplifying, of course. Certainly both points of view were found on the staffs of the CVG and the Joint Center. But the variation of emphasis in the two perspectives was enough to make the difference an important one between the two groups.

We also had the initial difficulties one might expect as an outside group coming in and trying to establish rapport. Perhaps a personal experience may help to make this clear. When I made my first trips to Venezuela in 1959 and 1960 to work out the arrangements for Joint Center participation, I took it for granted that the program would provide attractive job and training opportunities for students—Venezuelan as well as our own. I thought we ought to establish some university connections and develop close relations with our counterparts at the university. Such efforts might enable us to enlarge our contribution to the Venezuelan scene. One reason this appeared to be feasible was the formation of Cendes (Centro de Estudios del Desarrollo), an organization the Venezuelans had established to train people and promote research on a wide range of problems associated with development. Two of the founders I knew as former students. One of them, a top official in the administration of President Betancourt, arranged for a dinner meeting with the director of Cendes to explore how we might best work together and help each other. The net result was, to say the least, disconcerting. I got along well enough with the director, but when I broached the possibility of working together he smiled and shook his head. "Association with you and the Joint Center," he said, "would be the kiss of death for me—and maybe even for you." He then explained how delicate his relationships were with his associates at the Central University of Venezuela, with whom collaboration was essential.

About eight or nine months later, however, the director met with me and said, in effect, "Let's cooperate or collaborate, if you still wish to do so." I was delighted and asked whether he had solved his intra-university problems. "In a way," he said, smiling; and he explained that they then appeared so hopeless that he saw no reason to avoid association with North American universities. I promptly got in touch with two of the principal CVG staff to pass on the good news. And I got a rude surprise. "Absolutely not!" was one response. "Probably not," was another. "Why?" I asked—incredulous. "That group is infested with left-wing and irresponsible elements," I was told, "and any information passed on to their students about our activities might well be twisted and used against us." I protested, but to no avail. My efforts were considered well intentioned but naïve.

North Americans were regarded by their Venezuelan associates as political babes in the Venezuelan woods, and all the more so to think that such associations might work. I decided not to press the issue, but I did remind these officials how seriously staff was required and what a significant contribution such an organization—in principle—could make.

The recruitment problem eventually helped to thaw attitudes. For a long time some of the officials of the CVG were suspicious of the Joint Center as well as of Cendes. They not only saw the invitation to an outside group as a reflection on their capacity to handle the job; they also feared that our presence would prevent them from getting the necessary funds and staff. The need for technical assistance was not questioned; but this looked like displacement, pure and simple. They suspected that the team of the Joint Center would enable the Corporation to get the technical job done without building up its own staff and without all of the headaches of recruitment.

This state of affairs boded ill for the future. Attempts to reassure these officials were met with quizzical smiles and the skeptical rejoinder "We shall see." It was clear that the Joint Center had to support the top officials of the CVG in getting staff. There was a good basis for such a request. The agreement between the CVG and the Joint Center specifically spelled out the need to establish counterpart relationships. Also, the President of the Corporation had asked me to confer with his staff and to indicate what I considered the high-priority problems. I therefore approached two of his principal associates and expressed my misgivings about whether either of them could discharge his responsibilities unless he got more staff quickly. I told them I saw no alternative but to make this clear to the President of the Corporation. Their reactions were mixed. The first said he had always been suspicious of the Joint Center, but now he was convinced that we were really working with him. The other reply was blunt and discouraging: "Who the devil are you," I was told in effect, "to say that I don't have enough staff to do my work?" He was right, in a sense; so I quickly mumbled some soothing remarks, beat a hasty retreat, and decided to reflect a bit more carefully on the next move. That was to invite the two men (who were good friends) to join me for drinks that evening. Fortunately they *both* came. I told them frankly that I was puzzled by their radically different reactions to the same proposal. I suggested that I was quite prepared either to advance or to withdraw it if they wished me to do so, but surely it was something they had to agree on. Otherwise I was bound to make at least one enemy. The subsequent discussion cleared the atmosphere. There was no question that both wanted more staff. The hostile staff chief conceded that he might have been a little peremptory, but then he exploded: "Damn it! You know and I know you're going to get the staff, and I know that I need the staff. But this is wrong. I should get the staff because I asked for it and not because of the Joint Center." I could not help but agree, but I also said that we did him no good by remaining silent. After all, our aim was to arrive at a point where the Joint Center could retire from the scene and he and his staff would receive the respect and funds they now seemed to lack. Regrettable as such procedures might be, it often happens that the outside consultant has to serve as an amplifying device for the views and needs of the staff. The point was conceded. We then agreed to make this recommendation a joint proposal of the CVG and the Joint Center technical staff as High Priority Problem No. 1 that the CVG had to solve if it was to do the job.

I should add one qualification. The way I have told this story, the Venezuelan reaction might seem unduly temperamental. The fact is that, if I had presented the matter as a joint proposal or as a recommendation of the Venezuelan staff backed up by the Joint Center, it is possible that there might never have been such a blowup. I was so sure the reaction would be favorable that it just did not occur to me that the proposal could be construed as smug or patronizing.

We did finally get the staff we wanted, but there were still many difficulties to overcome. All of us worked hard to spell out the nature of the expanded organization and the staff responsibilities. And the President of the Corporation agreed to give the matter his attention. But his subordinates continued to smile skeptically and say "We shall see." That led me to take up the matter directly with the President of the Corporation. I knew he did not like big staffs; and he made it clear to me that he did not think his subordinates could get the technical personnel they required, and he did not want to be subject to pressure to take on or retain incompetent personnel. It was easy to share these views. But unless more staff were obtained, counterpart relationships were clearly impossible. Nor would it be feasible for the CVG to carry on the work after the Joint Center left. It was even doubtful, I thought, that the present Venezuelan staff could be retained, for they were overloaded, suspicious, and resentful, and rightly so. I went over these matters with the President. Although he still demurred on the grounds that his associates would not be able to obtain the necessary staff, we finally worked out a compromise. The President was to insist on quality, and the Joint Center would try to help his subordinates find first-rate personnel, through recruitment of Venezuelans completing their graduate studies in American universities. That broke the deadlock. It is possible I am exaggerating the significance of this incident. But in my judgment no single experience in the relations between the Joint Center and the CVG contributed as much to the improvement of rapport between the two groups.

The agreement also affected relations with Cendes, but more gradually. The possibility now of hiring staff placed heavy pressure on the subordinates to find first-rate assistants. This was more easily said than done—especially if the chief program at the Central University of Venezuela turning out specialized and able students was to be ignored. Staff in other agencies and universities could be tapped, and to a limited extent they were. But apparently it was less easy to establish contacts and to obtain candidates of comparable quality and skill. Meanwhile, CVG officials were invited to give lectures from time to time at Cendes. Members of the staff attended Cendes meetings and conferences. Eventually one or two graduates, after careful screening, were offered positions with the CVG. They performed very well. Still more were taken on. Suspicion still lingered in some quarters, but the process of recruitment continued. Today a fair proportion of the staff, including the private secretary and assistant to the President of the Corporation, are Cendes graduates.[2]

Disagreements about Policies

Anthony Downs notes (in Chapter 19) that he found it difficult to analyze the urban development aspects of the Guayana program because the goals were never clearly articulated by the CVG. To do his job he spelled out the aims he could infer from discussions and documents and then rated those goals on an intuitive basis. This tack was necessary for almost all other aspects of the program—though the appraisal of the goals was generally less systematic. Thus in the debate over the form of the city and the location of the city center, the planners found it necessary to define the objectives in order to evaluate the alternatives. The same held true for the discussions about the best means to promote the business center and about the criteria for the development of industrial activities, land policy, transportation, housing, local government, and education.

The objectives, which were often discussed with the President of the CVG and his principal associates, varied in scope and clarity. Fostering the economic growth of the region and especially encouraging enterprises that could compete in international markets were often declared to be the principal goals. But there were other aims, such as minimizing capital outlays, maximizing employment, reducing the labor turnover resulting from inadequate housing and community facilities, getting private enterprise and other government agencies to make the maximum contribution to the Guayana's development, recapturing some of the increments in land value resulting from the government's massive investment, reducing labor and social conflict, meeting the needs of the existing and the future population, and maintaining the national image of the enterprise and a high standard of design as well as an efficient, economical, imageable, and flexible physical development pattern. Still other aims were less explicit, such as enhancement of the prestige and authority of the CVG and maintenance of the loyalty of the staff, high professional standards, and the power of the President of the Corporation.

Some of these objectives could be, and were, quantified in the plans; others were more ambiguous, though, as Corrada suggests, not less influential for many decisions. But except for an "outsider" like Downs, who for the purpose of his evaluation of land-use development on the site was encouraged by the Joint Center to define and rank the goals, almost nobody thought that the management of the CVG would welcome sustained and systematic efforts to clarify and make explicit the most important goals, values, and assumptions. Exposing markedly different values— which were roughly understood—might only encourage misleading generalities, cause embarrassment, and perhaps even sharpen differences. In this environment, where overt political neutrality was the symbol of virtue, those who stressed the conflicts in values ran the risk of making themselves obnoxious. On the other hand, glossing over the ambiguity of some goals and the implicitness of others did not preclude a general appreciation of the CVG's objectives or some sharp disagreements about which aims should be served in a particular case and which means would best serve them.

What I have in mind can be made clearer by aggregating the various avowed objectives of the CVG into three general categories: economic development, welfare, and management. Economic development was the primary goal. The aims here could be and were spelled out for specific economic activities and infrastructure requirements and could be restated and quantified in terms of growth rates or stages as well as investment, output, employment, and other targets. Translated into general economic policy, development involved the encouragement of efficient, capital-intensive activities, preferably private in character, that could compete in the international market and help to promote the diversification of the Venezuelan economy.

The welfare goals were either complementary to the development goals or of secondary importance. That is to say, they were seriously taken into account only when they could be shown to affect directly and significantly the achievement of the primary goals. Some of these welfare goals were translated into policies for encouraging specific activities, quantified, and directly related to the economic development efforts. The most important examples were the housing built directly by the CVG for the steelworkers (to satisfy the requirements of the CVG contract with the union) and the education program geared to produce the trained labor force required for the expanding economic activities.

The management goals were instrumental. They were the link to carry out the development and welfare aims. They could be formulated as policies, but they could less easily be spelled out in detail and were somewhat less amenable to quantification. Enhancement of the power, prestige, and authority of the CVG, maintenance of the loyalty and quality of its staff, identification of the goals of the program with national development aims, and encouragement of high professional and development standards are some examples. Although never explicitly formulated as such, the management aims just cited, especially the first two, were considered complementary to the CVG's primary goals. Such identification is characteristic of almost all organizations; and the CVG is no exception.

The management of the CVG did not relish welfare responsibilities, nor did it feel especially competent to deal with them. In addition, staff shortages made it all the more plausible for the CVG to assume that welfare goals that did not decisively contribute to its primary objectives ought to be the responsibility of other agencies, which the CVG might assist but not supplant. They were problems about which the CVG was concerned but did not feel that it alone was obliged or able to solve. Thus the CVG reluctantly entered the field of housing. It hoped that private builders and the government housing agency (Banco Obrero) would eventually tackle this problem effectively. Nonetheless, the CVG provided sites where Banco Obrero could build housing; it helped to set up a savings and loan association; it conducted experiments in self-help housing and prefabrication; and still later, it stimulated the setting up of a local housing agency to build low-income housing or to provide sites with utilities and technical assistance for migrants and squatters who wished to build. On the other hand, the CVG adopted ambiguous positions on the integration of different income groups in Ciudad Guayana—especially in the new developments on the western side of the city. Still other welfare goals, such as maximizing employment or attracting firms that could supply jobs for women, were neglected because they affected less directly the realization of the primary goals.

As one might expect, there were differences of opinion on some of these matters. If the disagreements had become too radical the Joint Center might have found it pointless to stay, and the CVG might not have wanted us to stay. This possibility was a vague—but nonetheless very real— constraint for both groups. Since the nature of our collaborative relationships put a premium on understanding the other side's point of view, there was often a searching dialogue about matters on which we differed. Let me cite a few examples.

Welfare versus development goals. The general economic policies and program favored modern, capital-intensive, export-oriented activities (not only industrial but possibly also agricultural in the Orinoco Delta region). The CVG and the Joint Center generally took it for granted that successful promotion of these activities would ensure more rapid and sustained economic growth and was therefore the most effective way of assisting the local population as well as implementing the nation's general development goals. But though the chief of the Joint Center economics staff backed the CVG to the hilt on this issue, other Joint Center personnel voiced misgivings. They feared that the net effect of these decisions, if not offset by other actions, would be to turn a significant part of the population into a permanent lower class because not enough opportunities were being devised to help them climb the ladder. This group wanted to see more concern manifested for the needs and employment of the immediate population, even if it meant a slower rate of growth for the region's economy. This led them to favor more labor-intensive activities, more self-help housing, less stratification of housing by income level, a more favorable attitude toward family-sized farms, more emphasis on job opportunities for women, and educational and informational programs better geared to serve the needs of the relatively unskilled inmigrant and his family.

The basic rejoinder was that labor-intensive activities would not thrive in the Guayana, a high wage area, and it was therefore pointless to divert scarce resources for such poor prospects. Some comfort was also drawn from the fact that the building of the Guri Dam and the housing program, not to mention the steady growth of service activities, would alleviate the unemployment problems over the next decade at least. Changes in skills and motivation accompanying the education and free book program were also expected to play their role. The evidence for the time being tends to underscore some of these views. For example, data as of September 1968 show that unemployment is dropping, skills rising, and economic activity becoming more diversified. But this evidence has not yet stilled the sense of disquiet about these matters. For even with the significant employment effects induced by the building operations, the rate of unemployment is still in the neighborhood of 12 per cent; and the dam construction and housing activities do not suit the requirements of the households with female heads. Moreover, sooner or later the building program will dwindle, and the problems may then prove even more intractable.

Decentralization and local relations. The location of the CVG's head-quarters in Caracas was an even more sensitive issue from the CVG's point of view. The President of the CVG argued that the Guayana program was and had to be kept national in character. He felt that location in the Guayana would change the CVG's image and produce really intolerable local pressures. The Joint Center did not agree. But in all fairness it must be pointed out that some of our staff, who originally were hostile to a Caracas location, shifted their views, and not simply because Caracas was a more delightful location. Because of the poor communications and services in Ciudad Guayana, there was probably no alternative but to locate in Caracas during the early period. Afterward it was hard to get the Caracas staff to move. There was also the special position of the President of the Corporation. He was a highly able engineer and an extra-ordinarily talented and sophisticated administrator; but he was an influential military figure, too. I would guess (this is a purely personal estimate) that the President of Venezuela felt it was desirable to have him close at hand for advice and support during the touch-and-go period when plots and insurrections were being hatched.

One may ask whether the location in Caracas did any harm. We were never able to gauge fully the net effects. The Joint Center staff to a man felt that the CVG staff in Caracas did not know as much as they should about what was happening in the field—in terms of building, migration, and general economic and social activity. You do not necessarily acquire this knowledge if you are in the field; but you are more tempted to acquire it, and you doubtless can absorb it more easily. In addition, all the experi-ences we were familiar with suggested that there would be problems between the big, relatively powerful development corporation and the local population. Our visceral reaction was to want such a corporation in the field, identifying more with the local population and attempting to minimize the frictions. No agency can play this development role—own most of the land, be the biggest employer, be responsible for most of the decisions affecting the community—and not become the butt for resent-ment. For these reasons we urged the CVG to make more of an effort locally to explain some of the critical alternatives, and we hoped the CVG would provide more local options. But this was our style—based on our traditions. In Venezuela the fear of corruption, local interests, and private interests; the long tradition of the central government exercising its power with limited consultation; and the differences in class status, education, and relative responsibility of central government officials led to different—and perhaps not necessarily less perceptive—visceral reactions. It is possible that effects just the opposite of what we anticipated might have been produced, but we thought, nonetheless, this risk should be run.

We argued our views at great length and in different ways, but generally to no avail. Some of the Venezuelans felt that working out of Ciudad Guayana was an excellent idea—perhaps—but that it was wrong to do it at the risk of losing a large part of the staff or turning their backs on a powerful national image. Others felt we were merely sowing Anglo-Saxon ideals on a rather inhospitable Latin reality. I do not believe this is correct, nor do some of my Venezuelan friends outside the CVG. But we may have been wrong. We suggested that at the very least a significant regional office be established. (There were such offices for the steel operations and for the public works program.) But for a long time even this proposal was resisted. CVG officials did say in 1966 that the time was getting ripe to get the design staff and maybe some of the planning staff into the field. But the resistance was still so strong in some quarters that many of us are skeptical about the ultimate outcome.

We also urged the CVG to set up an urban development corporation. (Corrada describes this proposal in detail in Chapter 18.) Several of our experts independently recommended the creation of this subsidiary to permit decentralization of the public works and infrastructure activities and the closer coupling of this program with project planning and design and with the complementary activities of other ministries. We do not think that this work will ever be conducted as efficiently as it should be unless it is conducted semiautonomously in the field. But we failed to persuade the CVG that such action is essential. The officials expressed genuine concern about spinning off a subsidiary that would be less subject to control. Another objection was that more of these infrastructure developments ought to be and will be handled in the future by other ministries. The CVG wants to reduce its responsibilities in these matters. We doubt that the CVG's commitments would be reduced significantly; but even if we are wrong, the responsibility for guidance of project development depends on the planning and design staff, and the more detailed this work becomes, the more essential it is, in our judgment, to do this work in the Guayana.

Despite these general differences of opinion, the CVG on occasion accepted specific proposals designed to minimize frictions with the local authorities. One interesting example involved the ticklish issue of *ejido* rights, that is, the granting of public land to the community for distribution to citizens (see Chapter 15). Our specialists thought it might be wise to give the new local officials this responsibility, especially since it was a traditional local privilege in Venezuela. We felt that land could be provided in areas that were not critical in terms of the land-use plans, where various types of development might be permitted. Because of the limited administrative capacity available in underdeveloped countries, it seemed to be a serious mistake to try to exercise full control everywhere. We wanted to define a few key zones where regulation might serve a special purpose and be effective, and we wanted to allow more freedom and initiative elsewhere. But at first some CVG officials thought we were mad. They had gone to great lengths to get that land in order to control development and recover some of the rise in value that would occur largely because of the CVG's investments. The fact that they owned the land was supposed to be the answer to the planner's dream. And now we were advising them to give some of the land away, land that belonged to the nation, to a group they hardly considered responsible.

After much discussion we reluctantly gave up hope of changing the CVG's views on the issue. And then, to our great astonishment, the policy was abruptly reversed. Pressure and persuasion played a role, but I am not sure of the relative weights to be ascribed to these factors. In addition to the local opposition, there was a strike at the steel mill and there were differences of opinion within the government. Meanwhile, the arguments in favor of providing *ejido* rights were not forgotten. A moment came when the opposition appeared to be formidable; and at the same time there was a possibility of mollifying some of the opposition with a plan fully worked out and supported by some of the CVG President's advisers, a plan that probably had more merit than was officially acknowledged. The episode provides a good example of one aspect of the CVG's administrative style. On occasion, proposals were questioned—sometimes very firmly. But they were never rejected out of hand. Sometimes an idea would lie dormant, and positive action seemed to be out of the question; but an incident or an issue might spark the whole question anew, and then action came swiftly. Everybody behaved as though this was what had been intended all along; and—who knows—perhaps it was?

Promotion of economic activities. The disagreements about how the promotion effort was to be handled were all the more puzzling because initially there was agreement on the goals and even agreement on the means—in principle. Indeed, the idea of the Joint Center's participation in the promotion phase of the operation came from the President of the CVG. At first we hesitated; it was a far cry from research. But he argued that we did not want paper plans and therefore ought to help in the promotional aspects as well. We went along, reluctantly at first, and later with the strong conviction that it certainly would be dangerous to separate plans for development from the means of fulfillment.

Nonetheless, efforts along these lines lagged. The Joint Center hired promotion staff, but the CVG did not provide equivalent counterparts. They went through the motions of recruitment, but they did not find qualified specialists. It is not easy to explain why. I would have guessed that the CVG would have pushed this phase of the program more vigorously than any other. And it would be wrong to say they were not promoting many things in their own way; but we thought what was being done was not at all adequate, measured against what needed to be done. For example, the Joint Center favored a separate promotion office and a massive campaign to interest appropriate types of firms in Venezuela and in other parts of the world, especially North America. But to date the bulk of the promotional efforts has been handled by the President of the Corporation, assisted by two or three overburdened members of the economics staff. Members of the CVG staff from other departments pitch in from time to time. The work is mainly following up inquiries and leads that have cropped up with relatively negligible effort. These possibilities have emerged, so to speak, out of the existing complex of economic activities or because of relatively profitable prospects that private investors have spotted, for example, the sponge-iron operations, the aluminum program, and the activities in the field of forestry and pulp and paper. However, a good deal more might be done in other areas, such as light industry, construction materials, and housing.

These problems may be solved slowly in the course of time. But such growth ought to be accelerated by sustained, vigorous promotional efforts comparable to those made initially to promote the business center. It is hard for someone not familiar with these operations to grasp how much thought and energy it takes to link physical and economic plans, work out practicable fiscal arrangements, and answer the thousand and one technical questions and problems that crop up during inquiries or negotiations. One must usually count on servicing a half dozen to a dozen prospects before the nibble turns into a serious bite. The President of the CVG is accustomed to running this aspect of the operation on a personal basis because of its importance and because he does it so well. For that matter, it will have to continue on this basis for the largest firms under any circumstances. But the program is close to a new threshold where small and intermediate-sized firms must be attracted; and we do not see how this can be done without creating a special service to handle the job.

In one sense there is little cause for worry, for, sooner or later, action will have to be taken because of the sheer workload—if not because of the pressure to generate more jobs. But we would prefer to see the CVG on top of this problem rather than have them wait until a crisis impels action.

Joint Center field management. When we set up our team in Venezuela we took it for granted that the Joint Center Resident Director would have a Venezuelan equivalent, but there was no such equivalent. Therefore, when our Resident Director resigned after a year and a half, we were somewhat loath to replace him until the Venezuelans had appointed a director for their planning and development staff. Under any circumstances, it would not have been easy for us to find someone with just the right qualifications. Even with the right person we anticipated problems because the Venezuelans disliked our having staff meetings from which they were absent, and they did not want to attend meetings run by the Joint Center. For many reasons they could not accept the Joint Center Resident Director as their director; nor would we have permitted it, even if they had been so tempted. The CVG President promised to appoint a Venezuelan to direct their staff, since he was aware of the problem. Meanwhile, I assumed even more responsibility for the program for the Joint Center. I spent two summers there and made more frequent visits during the year. This was not altogether satisfactory, but the Venezuelans preferred this alternative until they hit on a man that the President would trust.

Eventually it became clear that one of our men, a Puerto Rican with considerable experience in Puerto Rico and Africa, had our confidence and theirs as well—and so, nine months after the resignation of the Director he was appointed Resident Coordinator. That was a very popular move since the Venezuelans were persuaded, we think, that they could more easily influence him and he could influence us. We thought just the opposite. In any case, he did a fine job, and we eventually appointed him Resident Director. He met frequently with the CVG high command (including the CVG President)—it took a long time to get this group to confer regularly—and he met privately with our own division chiefs. It was an improvised solution but it worked. In this instance both the CVG and the Joint Center were content to satisfice, since we could not do otherwise.

Planning Style

The approach to planning also provoked some differences of opinion—not with the leadership of the CVG but among the members of the staff of the CVG and the Joint Center. The dissenters cited Lindblom, Hirschman, and other writers on the merits of "incremental," adaptive problem-solving strategies. These writers emphasize the advantages of adjusting ends to means, selecting ends and means simultaneously, moving away from ills rather than toward known objectives, and tackling sequences and limited segments of a problem rather than all relevant aspects or consequences more or less simultaneously. They argue that most decision making occurs in this fashion, that we really do not know enough to do more, and that when we try to be comprehensive we usually fail.

Other writers disagree. More comprehensive approaches are indispensable and come into being, they say, because minimum adaptive responses to the most urgent problems prove inadequate. Their position, in substance, is that if you want to solve complex problems, and to avoid inconsistencies and undesirable side effects, you cannot do it by influencing a very restricted set of variables; you have to take into account all or as many of the important interlocking systems and relationships as possible. Sooner or later this leads to planning methods and decision making based on clear specification of aims and priorities and to more systematic evaluations of alternative ways of achieving these aims. This presupposes analyses (quantitative wherever feasible) of the effects of all relevant changes on the achievement of these objectives—at least to the extent of your ability to do so.

The real objection to both positions, however, is their vagueness and inadequacy in actual practice. Since one can never be completely comprehensive, it is essential to identify the critical problems, the important systems and relationships, and the most significant methods and alternatives. These decisions are the most vulnerable to error because they require imagination, knowledge, and judgment. On the other hand, though we gain in realism and stimulus by working closer to felt needs and actual problems in the field, we can also get too close for comfort or for real insight. The pressures are more intense, and the inclination to adopt promptly remedial measures encourages limited and relatively superficial solutions rather than the more significant and powerful ones. Neither approach, in short, provides much guidance on how the right problems, goals, resources, and means are to be identified or agreed upon or on what is and what is not relevant, significant, or feasible.

Dissatisfaction with both strategies besets one all the more in a developing country, especially in a resource development region. In these circumstances the planners often must engage in a wide range of actions in many sectors to produce a pattern of growth that will be self-sustained and self-reinforcing. But difficulties multiply when you try to do too much. On paper, or for expository purposes, comprehensive or systems planning appears reasonable enough, perhaps even indispensable. It provides a set of directions for all the things you are supposed to do and when you should be doing them. Such efforts, however, presuppose the staff, the knowledge, and the judgment, not to mention the willingness and the capacity, of many public and private organizations to handle the necessary tasks. These assumptions are often the ones that turn out to be wrong in whole or in part. That is why, when one looks at what actually happens, the results seem far less attractive than those envisioned—though not necessarily less attractive than the results produced by more modest, adaptive measures.

For pedagogical purposes, it is stimulating to define sharply contrasting alternatives, but a little knowledge of the history of similar controversies ought to inoculate one against taking such alternatives too seriously. There is hardly much difference between the older ideological conflicts—the concept versus the percept, the general versus the particular, rules versus a particular case, theory versus empiricism—and the current conflict, comprehensive versus incremental planning. In such disputes the great danger is the tendency to overemphasize the one and exclude the other. What is essential is a readiness to apply both strategies, according to the circumstances.

Our experience in the Guayana region may serve as an illustration. At the outset, members of the urban design staff objected that the efforts were too pragmatic. When the first Joint Center staff members arrived on the scene in the summer of 1961, the city's population was soaring, there was clamorous agitation for action, and the hard-pressed staff of the CVG and other agencies were doing their best to provide a variety of key facilities—a bridge, sewage facilities, water, roads, and schools. These, in essence, were adaptive solutions. Ideally, however, the Joint Center staff and some of the top Venezuelan officials would have liked to stop almost everything until they had a better idea of the probable rate of growth and future size of the city, the kinds of activities it was to have, and where some of these activities might best be located. This would have involved a general review of the economy and of the social patterns and trends as well as an evaluation of the basic goals and policies of the government and the most feasible development strategies. Other Venezuelans, troubled by the acute shortage of facilities of every kind, wanted to build and build, and "to hell with plans or any other activities that might slow up the provision of essential facilities." Both points of view had strong proponents, and we therefore moved warily. Our staff had no desire to gum up the works; neither did we intend to serve as an auxiliary fire brigade or to make long-range plans for urban renewal.

We compromised. Our staff pitched in to help improve the arrangements and decisions for immediate facilities. Only in very special situations were delays allowed. One was to improve the design of the bridge; another was to shift the location of the ring road, which was considered a desirable site for housing. The main emphasis was on firefighting and the preparation of short-term physical development plans. Some basic studies were also initiated. But it was not until some sixteen months after arriving on the scene, and after some strenuous insistence on the part of the Joint Center and the CVG management, that the staff managed to focus a reasonable proportion of its energies on the long-term urban and socio-economic perspective studies essential for the preparation of staged, comprehensive plans.

In retrospect, the decision to pay the most attention at the outset to immediate needs seems to have been wise as well as almost inescapable. Because of recruitment difficulties, some of the economic and social specialists arrived many months later than planned; and even if they had arrived on schedule, no adequate general land-use plans could have been prepared until some of the basic economic, social, and land-use studies had been made. During this period, however, the work on immediate projects helped to familiarize the physical planners and designers with the situation in the field and with their Venezuelan counterparts.

Eventually, however, there was a shifting of gears. The bulk of the staff had arrived and had become acclimated to their new environment. Many of the basic data had been obtained. It then became feasible to explore systematically the implications for the Guayana of the national goals for development and to draw inferences from the studies of the resource endowment, the physical conditions of the site, the economic development potentials, and some of the social characteristics and requirements of the population. These efforts enabled us to gauge the dimensions and critical elements of the program, to rough out some basic projections and targets, and to hazard some preliminary economic, social, and land-use plans.

Since we were understaffed,[3] many other things were neglected. Before long some of our staff associates—especially those who had not been around during the earlier period—began to complain about the need to get close to the problems of the local population and to the realities of what was happening at the site. They were right. Nonetheless, the perspective studies produced some tangible effects. For example, the location and kinds of facilities depended on the probable future population of the town. There were wide differences in the initial estimates. Those on the scene guessed it would ultimately reach 250,000. A distinguished economist in Cambridge, Massachusetts, who had had some experience in Venezuela warned the planners that at best the population was unlikely to exceed 100,000. However, the studies by the economics staff, based on regional implications of national investment goals, confounded everyone with a figure closer to 500,000 by the year 2000. Even though this figure subsequently appeared to be too high, it compelled us to rethink a lot of the specific plans for housing, utilities, roads, location of the business center, and other facilities.

The economic projections and the comprehensive investment plans also influenced other national and international agencies. For Cordiplan (the national planning agency of Venezuela), they provided a basis for linking the Guayana program with the national planning program and for determining the funds required for the major investments in this region. The studies also played a role in reversing a previous judgment of the technical staff of the World Bank, thus paving the way for a loan of 85 million dollars for the expansion of the Guri Dam. In addition, the evaluation of the feasible economic activities for the region made it possible to orient the efforts of the Corporation on the industrial promotion program as well as on the staging of the various infrastructure investments. On the physical planning side, the new population projections definitely eliminated Punta Vista as the location of the proposed center as well as the idea of building a town south of the steel mill, which some of the steel mill officials had pushed again and again. Also, the analysis of the physical development alternatives persuaded almost everyone that a linear development pattern would provide a relatively inexpensive framework for physical development, involving the least risk and the maximum flexibility, and yet ensure a consistent and firm basis for decisions about the location of infrastructure and private investment.

One ought to compare this approach with an incremental stategy. But it is not possible to spell out the alternative in any detail. One member of our staff urged more emphasis on "means available, wants felt, and programs already under way." An incremental program doubtless would be less ambitious (or less "unrealistic") and more responsive to immediate needs, the handling of specific problems, and some of their sequential relationships. It might emphasize more coordination and adjustment of interests among the various local, provincial, and federal agencies working on different programs in the region. We slighted such suggestions for several reasons. To begin with, they were often too vague to be operational. Even more important, we thought the evaluation of needs and timing—in employment, housing, education, and other sectors—would quantify the dimensions of the problems and play a significant role in spurring the necessary response. We were persuaded, too, that this approach would give us a clearer basis for coordinating the work of existing agencies, for providing a lead for changes of priority and emphasis, and for pursuing and encouraging within this framework a wide range of adaptive and sequential strategies. Many national agencies, such as the Ministry of Education and the Ministry of Public Works, not to mention the local authorities, had no clear sense of the scale and kinds of programs required to serve the region until we had prepared and discussed with them our regional studies, plans, and proposals. Moreover, if we had failed to make this assessment we would not have been able to provide a lead to key decision makers—the President, the head of the national planning agency, the international loan and technical assistance agencies, and various private interests—on the role they might choose or be induced to play in assisting this development process.

The comprehensive plans did not exclude pragmatic responses. Quite the contrary. They provided an interrelated set of targets and stages for investment and production for particular industries; similar targets and stages for providing the required housing, education, and other facilities; and a general land-use plan indicating where the economic activities, roads, housing, schools, and other facilities would be located at various stages of development. But these were guides for action, not straightjackets. Carrying out this program presupposed many significant adjustments and innovations. The program did not require the CVG to confront all relevant problems simultaneously. Considerable attention was paid to priorities and key sequential relationships, and some elements of the physical development strategy commanded far more attention than others. For the industries that would enjoy comparative advantage in the Guayana region, the plans did anticipate that detailed feasibility studies and lengthy negotiations would be needed to provide a basis for agreements that would prove attractive to both the firms and the CVG. The discussion of industrial promotion in Chapter 8 shows how the level and timing of investment, the size of plant, and the type of output were often quite different from the original estimates. Similarly, Chapter 11 indicates how the policies, the financial plans, and even the physical plans for the commercial center changed substantially in the course of the negotiations with prospective investors. Somewhat similar processes of promotion, bargaining, and compromise proved essential to spur on the housing and education programs. These improvisations were essential to produce an operational program that took realistic account of the specific requirements or capacities of the private or public organizations that would make the investments, do the building, and serve particular markets or clients.

Sometimes, institutional innovations were necessary. For example, a building and loan association was established to serve one segment of the housing market. A local housing authority was created to produce housing for low-income families. It also took charge of the self-help housing programs and attempted to remedy some of the defects disclosed by the study made of the pilot program. Some members of the design staff were also put to work on model plans for the remodeling of existing squatter housing. To guide the general educational development strategy, a special research, planning, and service center was established under the joint auspices of the CVG and the Ministry of Education, with technical advisers provided by the Center for Studies in Education and Development of Harvard University. In addition to the systematic analysis of educational requirements and the general plans to build schools and reorganize the educational system, specific remedial measures were proposed and acted upon. Thus the CVG provided a special grant to the Venezuelan Book Bank to provide textbooks for students and to help establish school libraries. To improve the land-use plans, the CVG financed a special study of the way local residents used the city, valued the facilities, and viewed their environment. There was also a systems analysis of the allocation of resources for urban development to determine the relative adequacy and efficiency of building activities on the site. These activities and studies, described in more detail in earlier chapters, indicate some of the many efforts made to guide decision making, spur private development, create new institutional arrangements, adapt the program to felt needs, get the information needed to help reformulate policies and programs, and spot and correct errors before they became too serious.

Many of these efforts encountered resistance. Aims were not always shared. Nor was it easy to obtain scarce funds and staff for research and experiments. The feedback of information and recommendations from the Guayana to Caracas often produced no changes in standard operating procedures. Staff shortages often stymied actions on which there was agreement in principle. Perhaps the least controversial example was the trouble we had getting the economists and physical planners to work out alternative phasing and stages in case the targets or projections proved unrealistic. There simply were not enough men to do the job. The chief economists (both CVG and Joint Center) also felt that working out such alternatives might discourage achievement of the targets. But eventually, when the use of the computer made the task more feasible, we did modify the methods, since we needed clearer ideas about those aspects of the program that were inconsistent and how the investment and other policies might and ought to change if the actual trends varied significantly from the projections.

In retrospect, if one were to ask which approach was followed in Venezuela, the most accurate answer would be a combination of comprehensive and adaptive styles. The role of the comprehensive plans was to provide a relatively consistent framework and guide for a whole range of subsequent measures to carry out the purposes of the CVG. However, the planners were forced to resort to adaptive, pragmatic measures, not only at the stage of implementation—which was when we took such efforts for granted— but also in the early stages of planning, because intense pressures for remedial actions had to be satisfied. The choice and timing of the adaptive measures were influenced by many things: public preferences and pressures, complementary requirements, constraints limiting action to the tasks that were feasible or that some organization was ready and able to handle, the steps already taken, new information and insights gleaned from experience, and not least the internal logic and sequences suggested by the plan.

At the time the planner comes to the scene, too little is known about the character of the problems to be able to articulate clear goals or to appreciate fully the important constraints or the most effective means in the given circumstances. Some of the problems and the appropriate solutions often appear simpler, or more formidable, than they actually are, and more often than not the most critical questions turn out to be quite different from those originally envisaged. Meanwhile, some immediate steps must be taken to deal with the most urgent matters while efforts are made to obtain a better grasp of what generally ought to be done. One is obliged, among other things, to make quick diagnoses of immediate issues and of the available repertory of tools to get some remedial action under way.

In the course of plan making, one aim of the planner—although not always an explicit one—must be to produce ideas and feedback mechanisms that take reasonable account of these uncertainties so that the planners can redefine the problems and tackle them more effectively as they go along. The issue is not whether comprehensive and adaptive methods are essential. Both are, but they have to be tailored to the different stages and requirements of the planning program.

A great danger is that the daily pressures and skimpy resources may hobble the more searching examination required, and the ad hoc measures may become institutionalized and difficult to change. Sooner or later, however, limited or improvised measures prove inadequate, and more data and more intimate knowledge of the environment, the needs, and the alternative ways of coping with them generate pressures for more effective efforts. From this point of view, adaptive solutions—*faute de mieux*—often receive the principal emphasis in the initial stages as well as in the stage of plan implementation; but—standing alone—they are unlikely to survive very long if they are (or appear to be) inadequate or inconsistent and if more systematic and comprehensive measures appear feasible and likely to ensure more satisfactory results.

Summary Observations

If collaboration involves close, long-term relationships between professional specialists from different cultures, it requires sensitive adaptations in social behavior, in professional methods, and in the basic aims and values of the two groups. Such adaptations are not easy to make or to maintain, at either the leadership or the staff level; and the collaboration may prove quite unsuccessful if some of these adaptations break down. One of the most unusual aspects of the Guayana project is the fact that the CVG and the Joint Center managed to maintain successful collaborative relationships over a five-year period despite numerous differences between the participants in behavior, working styles, and values.

Although the Joint Center was invited to Venezuela by the CVG to provide technical assistance, many of its activities appeared at the outset to threaten key members of the CVG staff. Cultural differences sharpened the threat, but sincerity and devotion to the job, coupled with frank and good-natured give and take on both sides, managed to dispel many of the early suspicions and difficulties.

The more nearly intractable differences of opinion arose on matters of policy. In substance the CVG stressed the primacy of the economic development goals, centralized administration, and the maintenance of the national image of the agency; and disagreement occurred when the Joint Center sought to upgrade the importance of the welfare goals, decentralize the administration, and provide more options for local choice. Behind these disagreements lay a basic difference in attitudes toward the people of the region and the extent to which their needs should affect or be the direct concern of the CVG. On some items, however, such as the promotion of economic activities and the appointment of a Venezuelan director of planning, the disagreements were not about goals or means but over the CVG's willingness to satisfice rather than optimize for the sake of ensuring trustworthy staff and perhaps more effective centralized direction and control.

Our opportunistic style of planning also aroused controversy during different stages of the program. When at the outset the Joint Center applied adaptive, remedial measures to serve the immediate needs of the CVG, there were some objections to the pragmatic efforts at the expense of more comprehensive plans. Later, when the emphasis shifted to more systematic planning methods, there were criticisms of the neglect of many of the immediate requirements of the local population. But a review of the reasons for varying the methods with the circumstances helps to explain the superficiality of the current distinction between adaptive and comprehensive planning and why planning styles must vary with available resources, immediate problems, and different stages of the planning effort.

The differences of opinion—sometimes quite strong—were overshadowed by the mutual benefits. Collaboration offered an opportunity for a trade-off of prestige, professional skills, and relative objectivity and political neutrality for a remarkable professional experience. The Joint Center served several other functions. It could help to recruit staff and, on occasion, mediate informally with groups hostile to the CVG. The participation of the Joint Center also reinforced the CVG's image as an agency devoted to the development of the Guayana region by using modern technical methods and highly qualified specialists to carry out its responsibilities. The policies of the development agency, however, involved views that were not always shared by the Joint Center. It was the responsibility of the CVG to set the goals, but the Joint Center also had the responsibility of indicating in its technical documents and reports that it did not necessarily agree with some of the values, policies, and methods of the CVG.

Despite the differences of opinion, however, the mutual respect and friendship, the conviction that a major contribution was being made to a significant enterprise, and the opportunity to disagree and to get a serious hearing made the Joint Center value this association. Collaboration also provided an exceptional opportunity for the CVG leadership to be exposed to sharply different views on some basic issues. If the two groups had had a larger consensus, collaboration might have been easier, perhaps even more efficient; but it would also have been far less stimulating. Certainly none of the major participants—CVG or Joint Center—will ever forget some of the moving discussions and subsequent crises of conscience that these conflicts generated.

Notes

Introduction

1. The reader needs to be cautioned, however, that the issues and the differences of opinion as well as the accomplishments are being recorded by the Joint Center staff—with the natural bias this may imply. Some Venezuelan contributions were sought but were not obtained. This is a pity because they would have provided other revealing perspectives. One reason those contributions were not obtained was that the Venezuelan staff—as civil servants—are less prone to write up their individual views. Another was that the Joint Center staff had more time and a greater academic interest in articulating their ideas and experiences.

Chapter 2

1. Based on Chapters 6 and 10 of my *Regional Development Policy: A Case Study of Venezuela* (Cambridge, Mass.: The M.I.T. Press, 1966).
2. The term "space economy" means the economy in its spatial dimension, described in terms of either (1) point location and interacting flows of goods, capital, labor, and information or (2) regional constructs.
3. See *Regional Development Policy*, Tables A.1 to A.10 (pp. 235–242), for the detailed calculations from which this summary was derived.

Chapter 3

1. Oficina Central de Coordinación y Planificación (Cordiplan), *Plan de la Nación, 1963–1966* (Caracas, 1963), and *Plan de la Nación, 1965–1968* (Caracas, 1965).
2. Alliance for Progress, Ad Hoc Committee of the Committee of Nine, *Evaluation of the Venezuelan Plan de la Nación, 1963–1966* (Washington, D.C., September 1963).
3. See Chapter 8, "The Promotion of Economic Activity."
4. See Corporación Venezolana de Guayana (CVG), *The Guayana Economic Program, Key to the Development of Venezuela* (Caracas, July 1966).
5. See J. R. Miller, "The International Market for Iron Ore: 1975," paper presented at the American Iron Ore Association Meeting, Cleveland, Ohio, June 29, 1966 (Columbus, Ohio: Battelle Memorial Institute).

492

6. See Alexander Ganz, "Economic Growth and the Demand for Steel," report presented to the Third Latin American Steel Congress, Caracas, Venezuela, July 1963.

7. See United Nations, Economic and Social Council, *World Economic Trends: Study of Prospective Production of and Demand for Primary Commodities* (New York, May 1962).

8. See Naciones Unidas, Comisión Económica para América Latina, *Los Principales Sectores de la Industria Latinoamericana: Problemas y Perspectivas* (Mexico City, April 1965), Table I–9, and David A. Kendrick, "Programming Investment in the Steel Industry" (Ph.D. dissertation, Massachusetts Institute of Technology, Department of Economics, 1965), Appendix G.

9. The development area is made up of Ciudad Guayana and its industrial complex, the nearby iron-mining operations, electric power dams, forest reserves programmed for exploitation, and agricultural projects, including the reclamation program for the Amacuro Delta—roughly a radius of 100 miles.

10. Banco Central de Venezuela, *Survey of Family Living Conditions in Santo Tomé de Guayana* (Ciudad Guayana) (Caracas, September 1962), and *Survey of Demographic Characteristics and Family Income in Santo Tomé de Guayana* (Caracas, February 1965).

11. This problem is discussed in more detail in Chapter 8 of this volume.

12. Cordiplan, *Plan de la Nación, 1965–1968,* Table V–2, p. 40.

13. See Tables 3.4, 3.6, and 3.12 in this chapter.

14. See George Kalmanoff, "Financing Strategy for the Guayana Region Development Program, 1965–1975" (unpublished working paper, Corporación Venezolana de Guayana, Departamento de Estudios, Planificación e Investigación, Sector Económico, Caracas, June 1965), and CVG, *The Guayana Economic Program, Key,* Charts VI–2, VI–4, and VI–5, pp. 28 and 29.

15. *Ibid.,* Chart VI–5, p. 29.

16. *The Corporación Venezolana de Guayana and the Development of the Southeastern Region of Venezeula,* report presented by President Betancourt to President Kennedy on his visit to Venezuela in December 1961.

17. Corporación Venezolana de Guayana, *The Guayana Region: A Portfolio of Investment Opportunities* (Caracas, July 1963), pp. 42 and 43.

18. In April 1964 an independent review group, made up of Max F. Millikan and Paul N. Rosenstein-Rodan of M.I.T., Edward Mason of Harvard, and Jorge Ahumada of Venezeula's Central University, recommended the need to study a range of alternatives.

19. The computer model is discussed in more detail in Chapter 17 of this volume.

Chapter 4

1. For a detailed analysis see Richard M. Soberman, *Transport Technology for Developing Regions: A Study of Road Transportation in Venezuela* (Cambridge, Mass.: The M.I.T. Press, 1967).

2. Details of the procedures are covered in the following mimeographed working papers (unpublished) of the Corporación Venezolana de Guayana, Caracas, Joint Center–Guayana Project: Alexander Ganz, "Preliminary Perspectives on the Role of the Guayana Region in the Economic Development of Venezuela," File No. B–6, March 26, 1962, and "World Demand for Present and Potential Guayana Region Minerals, Metals, Machinery and Chemical Fertilizer Products; and Rest-of-Venezuela Demand for Guayana Region Metals and Machinery Products 1950–61, 1961–65–70–80–2000," File No. B–14, May 7, 1962; and Leonard Fischman, "Notes on the Domestic and Export Markets for Certain Selected Materials," File No. D–14, June 16, 1962.

3. This old and very picturesque railroad carries Venezuelan and Colombian coffee (which arrives by way of a rail connection from Cucuta) to Encontrados, where it is transshipped to river barges and then carried to Maracaibo for export. The new highway will thus eliminate at least two transshipments and provide much faster service.

4. International Bank for Reconstruction and Development, *The Economic Development of Venezuela* (Baltimore, Md.: The Johns Hopkins Press, 1961), pp. 452–456.

5. Cost estimates for highway transportation are treated in detail in my report, "Economic Analysis of Highway Design in Developing Countries," *Record 115* (Washington, D.C.: Highway Research Board, 1966). For shipping and railroad cost calculations see Soberman, *Transport Technology*, Chapter 4.

6. In other words, customers for steel pipe will usually know their requirements far enough in advance to permit shipments to be made by boat. Anticipating the delays of ship transportation, however, such customers will maintain larger supplies on hand, thereby incurring higher inventory costs.

7. For example, the cost per ton to Maracaibo estimated in Table 4.2 is about Bs. 70, whereas rates of Bs. 194 have been quoted for this trip. The World Bank mission calculated costs for the same trip at Bs. 67 per ton and suggested that this might be reduced to Bs. 40 per ton (International Bank, *Economic Development of Venezuela*, pp. 457–458).

8. Soberman, *Transport Technology*, Chapter 4.

9. In fact, estimates made by the World Bank indicate shipping costs to be cheaper even when the channel toll for the Orinoco River is included. See International Bank, *Economic Development of Venezuela*, pp. 454–456.

10. Another example of poor transport administration is that of the boats that carry iron ore from the Guayana region to the United States. They may not carry return loads to Venezuela or engage in domestic coastal transportation. If these ships were used to transport coal and limestone from Guanta on the northern coast to the steel mill, transport costs for iron ore as well as for coal and limestone could be lowered.

11. By contrast, Louis Lefeber has estimated that the transport sector generally requires from 20 to 50 per cent of the total capital needed for development programs. See his *Economic Development and Regional Growth* (New York: National Bureau of Economic Research, Inc., 1963; mimeographed), Section III, p. 10.

Chapter 5

1. Compared to eastern Venezuela, Ciudad Guayana has a "normally" high proportion of children under fifteen (half the population). The excess of males in some adult age brackets is considerably modified by slight deficits in other mature brackets. The sex ratio is normal.

2. Strictly speaking, much of the city is neither urban nor rural as these terms are usually understood.

3. The considerable percentage of migration for family motives is largely derived from, and secondary to, migration for employment. Health reasons do not apply in the case of Ciudad Guayana. Its health facilities are about average for Venezuela's small cities. The site is not unhealthy, but the extreme heat is repellent to people from the highlands. Movements to the city are not often inspired by religion or by ideologies because the people are not inclined toward them. Not being endowed with above-average secondary schools and lacking tertiary education entirely, the city is not a destination of the migration for education that is so conspicuous in the other expanding urban centers of Venezuela.

4. Chain migration is that movement in which migrants learn of opportunities, are provided with transportation, or have initial accommodation or employment arranged by means of personal ties with previous migrants. See John S. and Leatrice D. MacDonald, "Chain Migration, Ethnic Neighborhood Formation, and Social Networks," *Milbank Memorial Fund Quarterly*, Vol. XLII, No. 1 (January 1964), pp. 82–97.

5. However, even before the CVG, the distinctions between foreigners and Venezuelans were less sharp than in the oil towns. The Orinoco Mining Company built a large part of its company town with vacant lots alternating between its employees' dwellings. These building lots were sold to noncompany buyers, most of them Venezuelans, in accordance with the company's policy of encouraging an "open town" instead of a "closed camp."

6. Scarcely any of the public and semipublic housing in the city is for rent. Most is on time payments, giving the occupant eventual equity.

7. Number of persons in each household, number of children under five, ratio of houses to shanties in the barrios, proportion of migrants from the eastern states, proportion unemployed, proportion in each income bracket, and proportion of skilled and unskilled.

Chapter 7

1. For a general review of the TVA experience see Roscoe C. Martin, ed., *TVA: The First Twenty Years* (Knoxville, Tenn.: The University of Tennessee Press, 1956). Also relevant in this context is John Friedmann, *The Spatial Structure of Economic Development in the Tennessee Valley* (Chicago, Ill.: The University of Chicago, Department of Geography, March 1955; Research Paper No. 39).

2. For further discussion of the differences between regional planning in transitional and in industrialized economies see John Friedmann, "Poor Regions and Poor Nations: Perspectives on the Problem of Appalachia," *Southern Economics Journal*, Vol. XXXII, No. 4 (April 1966), pp. 465–473.

3. For more details on the characteristics of resource frontiers and regional development strategy see John Friedmann, *Regional Development Policy: A Case Study of Venezuela* (Cambridge, Mass.: The M.I.T. Press, 1966), Chapter 5.

4. On the role of Cordiplan in national planning and Cordiplan's response to the challenge of regional planning see John Friedmann, *Venezuela: From Doctrine to Dialogue* (Syracuse, N.Y.: Syracuse University Press, 1965).

5. Albert O. Hirschman, *The Strategy of Economic Development* (New Haven, Conn.: Yale University Press, 1958), and Paul Rosenstein-Rodan, "Notes on the Theory of the 'Big Push,'" in Howard S. Ellis and Henry C. Wallich, eds., *Economic Development for Latin America* (New York: St. Martin's Press, 1961), pp. 57–81.

Chapter 8

1. See International Bank for Reconstruction and Development, *The Economic Development of Venezuela* (Baltimore, Md.: The Johns Hopkins Press, 1961), pp. 51–52. The report stated: "In the judgment of the mission, the amount of power that is implied in the first stage of this project is so great that even if power intensive industries like aluminum were established on a large scale, a considerable part of the power would still have to be absorbed in the central area of Venezuela. . . . A decision . . . must await more precise estimates of costs, *a clearer appraisal of—if not actual experience with— industrial possibilities in eastern Venezuela,* and a closer examination of the comparative costs of thermal power generation."

2. World Bank, Department of Technical Operations, "Venezuela, Guri Power Project" (Washington, D.C., October 1962), confidential report.

3. See United Nations, Economic Commission for Latin America, *Principal Sectors of Latin American Industry: Problems and Perspectives* (Mexico City, April 1965), Tables 1–9, and David A. Kendrick, "Programming Investment in the Steel Industry" (Ph.D. dissertation, Massachusetts Institute of Technology, Department of Economics, 1965), Appendix G.

4. For a description of the "firm" and "potential" targets of the development program, see Chapter 3 of this volume.

5. Corporación Venezolana de Guayana, *Guayana: Cornerstone of the Development of Venezuela* (Caracas, July 1963), and *The Guayana Region: A Portfolio of Investment Opportunities* (Caracas, July 1963). (Both were also published in Spanish editions.)

6. This problem is discussed in more detail in Chapter 12 of this volume.

Chapter 9

1. The first attempt in practice to estimate a new town's future transportation demands was made by the planning team of Cumbernault in Scotland toward the end of the 1950's. This was followed by a similar study by the designers of Hook new town in England, a settlement that was never built but whose plan was published in full in 1961 (see London County Council, *The Planning of a New Town* [London, 1961]). Both studies were, of necessity, simple. They demonstrated the value of making estimates of future traffic demands for new towns and the ease with which these estimates can be successfully introduced into the planning process.

The stimulus that concentrated attention on this facet of traffic planning in practice was provided in 1956 by the United States Federal-Aid Highway Act. This act granted liberal funds for the building of a national network of arterial highways, and cities were able to obtain grants to study their transportation requirements. A significant landmark was the Detroit Metropolitan Area Traffic Study 1953, followed by those of Chicago 1956 and Pittsburgh 1958.

Simply stated, a study of this type includes an inventory of existing metropolitan conditions, such as land use, population, economic activity, and vehicular and person travel. Present trip generation characteristics are established, and a mathematical model is constructed to simulate the area's actual travel patterns. This is checked against field counts. Once the model has been calibrated—that is, once there is a good "fit" between theoretical and actual trips—it can make an approximate prediction of future travel patterns based on projected urban area growth. The results are then assigned to networks to test alternative transportation plans.

A transportation model for a new city cannot, of course, be calibrated in this way since the city does not yet exist; nor can the results of past transportation studies of existing cities be applied directly to new cities as a substitute. They will rarely agree. However, past studies can help if the differences between the known city and the new city, and the effects of these differences, are understood.

But it is only in the United States that a wide range of cities has been subjected to transportation studies. The fact that other countries have very few, or none at all, of their own is a handicap, but not a crippling one. Some national data can usually be obtained, and these, in combination with the cautious use of studies made in other countries, can guide hypotheses. The demand studies of both Cumbernault and Hook new towns were made at a time when not one such transportation study of any British urban area was available. A similar dearth of local data faced the planners of Ciudad Guayana. Such limitations mean lower levels of confidence in results but do not render them worthless. They are still more useful than conjecture, if only because assumptions are explicit and the area of speculation is curtailed.

2. The *por puesto* is equivalent to the "jitney" that was popular in the United States in the 1930's. It is a chauffeur-driven automobile that is licensed to pick up passengers at any point along a fixed route.

3. The firm appointed was Urbanismo y Vialidad, S.A. This firm is still retained by the CVG. Antonio Boccalandro was consultant during the phase of model development and application. Antonio Vincentelli and Eudaldo Vila continue to advise on the functional planning of the road network of the city.

4. For a statement of the law see Article 23 of the *Ley del Trabajo* (Labor Law), 1961. Regulations under the law that further relate to the transportation of employees are set forth in Articles 18–22 in the *Reglamento de la Ley del Trabajo*, 1961.

5. Walter G. Hansen, "How Accessibility Shapes Land Use," *Journal of the American Institute of Planners,* Vol. XXV, No. 22 (May 1959), pp. 73–76.

6. William Alonso, a visiting consultant during mid-1962, was the first to raise the importance of accessibility in connection with a potential model he proposed for studying the development alternatives of Ciudad Guayana with particular reference to the location of its center. (See William Alonso, "Development Alternatives for the Urban Mass and the Centro of Santo Tomé [de Guayana]" [Cambridge, Mass.: Joint Center for Urban Studies, 1962; mimeographed].) The model called for the hand computation of a set of potentials of "fixed" employment (see note 8), excluding city center employment, for thirty-three zones of the study area for the years 1970, 1975, and 1980. It further required other sets of potentials based on alternative hypotheses of city center employment location for the same time increments. Each of the latter potentials was then summed with the former, and the results were traced in the form of isopotential surfaces of total "fixed" employment. "Distributed" employment (see note 8) was ignored. Subjective scoring of the zones as to their suitability for residential development from the point of view of natural characteristics assisted the interpretation of the results.

   The model failed to play an effective role in the planning process of the city partly because members of the staff— both among the consultants and within the CVG—could not readily understand the results in their somewhat abstract form of relative potential scores. The population distribution models run subsequently, in 1963, attempted to correct for this lack of communication by assigning absolute populations to zones. Perhaps the main reason for its weak participation was that no resident member of the planning team was sufficiently committed to the model to promote its use.

7. See, for instance, Alan Voorhees, "A General Theory of Traffic Movement," *Proceedings of the Institute of Traffic Engineers,* 1955, pp. 45–56. Continuing the earlier work of others, such as William Rielly and Harry Casey, Jr., Alan Voorhees is frequently recognized as the person most responsible for the rapid development of the traffic model field with particular reference to the gravity model.

8. "Fixed" employment refers to existing or projected centers of employment that tend to determine a residential population's physical location, for example, heavy industry and ports. "Distributed" employment tends to follow residential population, for example, schools, commerce, and artisanal industry.

9. The gravity model was not used to simulate present travel patterns for calibration purposes. The reader is referred to note 1 for a brief explanation of the reason for the omission of a phase of the work that is essential in transportation studies of existing cities. Since it was not practical to calibrate the model, the exponential value of spatial separation for work trips had to be arbitrarily assumed. Using the results of studies abroad as a guide, the value 2 was selected. Given the hypothesis that the future city would spread out over some fifteen miles, with the major industries at one extreme, and making some allowance for terminal times, it is possible that the

selected value may be fairly representative over the planning period for work trips as a whole, assuming no radical change in transportation technology.

10. Regional traffic was not accounted for, as it was judged to be insignificant during peak-hour traffic periods on a normal workday.

11. The five income groups employed, in bolivares per month, were as follows: 0–500; 501–1,000; 1,001–1,500; 1,501–2,500; and 2,501 or more. The economists were not prepared to provide income distributions by zone of employment. Rather than forgo this variable, the transportation team made its own rough distribution estimates based on the general character of the employment zones. Other physical planners hypothesized family income distributions by residential zone. Both distributions were consistent with the control distributions of employee and family incomes for the city as a whole over time provided by the economists.

Chapter 10

1. Albert O. Hirschman, *The Strategy of Economic Development* (New Haven, Conn.: Yale University Press, 1958).

Chapter 11

1. For a discussion of the decision to locate the business center at Alta Vista, see Chapter 6 of this volume.—Editor.

2. CADA is a successful, high-quality supermarket chain controlled by the International Basic Economy Corporation (IBEC).

3. In Peru the IBEC supermarket subsidiary is called "Todos."

4. In Venezeula there are three stages in the design of a building: (1) the sketch plan consists of conceptual drawings and general ideas, (2) the preliminary plans define the size, layout, and general structure, and (3) the final plans are the definitive construction drawings and specifications for plumbing, structure, electricity, and the like.

5. Nathan C. Fitts and Philip E. Beach, Jr., "The Economic Situation of the Centro Comercial Alta Vista and Recommendations for CVG Action," Joint Center–Guayana Project, File No. B–77, December 1964 (unpublished CVG working paper; mimeographed).

6. The promotional brochure (52 pages) included

   1. statements about Ciudad Guayana and the planning of Alta Vista
   2. projections of the demand for commercial space in Alta Vista
   3. selected drawings from the preliminary plans
   4. analyses of space usage, rental income, and financing requirements
   5. conditions that proposals must meet
   6. the basis for judging the proposals.

7. William A. Doebele, Jr., "Recommended Policies for Land Tenure in the City of Santo Tomé de Guayana," Joint Center–Guayana Project, File No. A–15, September 1963 (unpublished CVG working paper; mimeographed).

8. To assure their continued existence as such, the numbered parking areas, the pedestrian ways, and the bus terminals (P–1 and P–2 on Figure 11.1) will remain the property of the CVG.

9. This means that if the CVG wishes to sell or rent these areas to any third party, the developer first must be offered the land on the same terms.

10. In the British new towns, for example, conditions of low-risk, long-term lease arrangements and a tradition of stable, reasonable government have enabled similar policies to be implemented successfully.

11. A condominium is a form of cooperative ownership under which each store or apartment in a building may be owned separately. The common areas and the administration of the building are operated by the owners, usually through a managing agent. In Venezuela, as in other Latin American countries, the condominium form is widely preferred by developers, because it permits a quick disposition of the building and facilitates a rapid turnover of capital.

12. The race against time was accentuated by the condition in the CADA contract that the supermarket space in Alta Vista be ready by the end of 1966, or early 1967 at the latest. CADA has been approached by Puerto Ordaz developers and has indicated a willingness to accept their offer if the developer does not move quickly. As of September 1968 the fate of the Centro still hung in the balance.

Chapter 12

1. Corporación Venezolana de Guayana (CVG), División de Estudios, Planificación e Investigación, "The Staging of Guayana Economic Development Program" (unpublished CVG document, 1965).

2. Luis Ayesta and Rafael Corrada, "Oportunidades de Inversión en Industrias de Materiales de Construcción y en Financiamiento y Construcción de Viviendas" (unpublished CVG document, 1964).

3. Based on national averages. See Banco Central de Venezuela, Caracas, *Memoria y Cuenta* for 1962.

4. CVG, División de Estudios, Planificación e Investigación, "Financing Strategy for the Guayana Development Program" (unpublished CVG document, 1965).

5. The steel mill's management and labor union agreed on a contract clause that substituted for the existing housing subsidy a financial contribution by the company of 20 per cent of the selling price of a house purchased by a worker. The selling price may not exceed 800 times the worker's daily wage. Five per cent is contributed in cash at the time of purchase and the remaining 15 per cent in monthly payments equivalent to the existing housing subsidy, $20 per month. See Luis Ayesta and Rafael Corrada, "La Implementación de las Cláusulas sobre Vivienda del Contrato Colectivo de Sidor," Joint Center–Guayana Project, File No. B–81, 1965 (unpublished CVG working paper; mimeographed).

6. Rafael Corrada, "Financiamiento Hipotecario Asegurado" (unpublished CVG document, 1963).

7. For a broader statement on land policies see Real Estate Research Corporation, "Summary of Conclusions, Land Development Strategy Analysis, Ciudad Guayana, Venezuela" (unpublished CVG document, 1964).

8. Richard Durstine, "Toward a New Housing Program," Joint Center–Guayana Project, File No. B–87, 1965 (unpublished CVG working paper; mimeographed).

9. Rafael Corrada, "'El Roble' Pilot Project," Joint Center–Guayana Project, File No. B–43a, November 1962 (unpublished CVG working paper; mimeographed).

10. Julio Silva, "Plan Piloto 'El Roble': Evaluación," Joint Center–Guayana Project, File No. B–75, November 1964 (unpublished CVG working paper; mimeographed).

11. Rafael Corrada, "Un Contrato de Autoconstrucción" (unpublished CVG document, 1964).

12. Richard Durstine, "El Faseamiento de Proyectos de Vivienda," Joint Center–Guayana Project, File No. B–78, December 1964 (unpublished CVG working paper; mimeographed).

13. Rafael Corrada, "An Urban Development Corporation," Joint Center–Guayana Project, File No. F–55, 1965 (unpublished CVG working paper; mimeographed).

14. Eduardo Niera, "Evaluación de Cinco Prototipos de Vivienda para Guayana" (unpublished CVG document, 1965).

Chapter 13

1. The UD's were not different from the UV's except for their designation: both were generally the superblocks left over between the major roads. Design contracts were normally awarded to architectural firms by UD. When the design was complete, the contracts were awarded for construction, again by UD. This meant that blocks of 150 acres or more were coming onto the market in a fairly homogeneous style of design, with a fairly narrow price range of houses, all at the same time.

2. Census data of 1960 became available; there was some feedback from the experience of the El Roble pilot project; some of MacDonald's analyses of migration and of Russell Davis' and Noel McGinn's analyses of the education and training problem became available; and Lisa Peattie's observations of barrio life in Ciudad Guayana became better known to the staff.

3. Donald Appleyard was in the process of carrying out a survey of how people perceived the city and what some of their attitudes were toward it.

4. Evidence for some of the foregoing observations can be found in W. L. Clarke, "Analysis of Social Characteristics of Ciudad Guayana for Physical Planning" (paper prepared for the Joint Center, August 1967). In this report factor and discriminant analyses were used to determine which social characteristics related highly to spatial characteristics of the city. The data were from surveys by John MacDonald (see Chapter 5) and by Noel McGinn (see Chapter 14).

5. The approach outlined here had been abandoned for Dalla Costa in late 1966 in favor of a more conventional approach in which a single architect was hired to design the entire project.

Chapter 14

1. It has not been possible to determine whether current migration flows into the city will continue through 1975 or whether future migrants will be like those now arriving. If current trends continue, it cannot be expected that the educational deficit at the middle level described in Table 14.1 will be completely met by the influx of trained and educated workers. On the contrary, unless there is an active recruitment policy to attract skilled manpower to Ciudad Guayana, industries will not find the human resources necessary to meet production targets.

2. A detailed description of steps to implement these strategy recommendations is contained in the forthcoming volume, *Human Resources Development in Ciudad Guayana, Venezuela,* to be published by the CVG. "Expand to the maximum" should be read in terms of the largest possible increase in productivity of the various school programs, that is, in terms of students graduated rather than enrolled. Increased enrollments beyond the level projected would not necessarily lead to more students *graduated* and would represent a waste of vital resources.

Chapter 15

1. One of the most urgent—and perhaps least appreciated—examples of this need is the failure in almost all developing countries to define the real property rights of squatters. This failure appears to be based on three common misconceptions: that squatters on the outskirts of cities are "the lowest of the low," impoverished, and irresponsible; that the legal status of their land and improvised dwelling is of little consequence to them; and that recognition of rights acquired by squatting or other self-help means would undermine a respect for law in general. As we learn more

about the nature of peripheral squatting around the great cities in developing countries it is becoming increasingly clear that (1) far from being the lowest economic group, squatters represent a class that has made considerable economic progress (against enormous odds) in the new urban society; (2) lack of clear title in the investment that represents their greatest material achievement in life can be a profound source of anxiety and discontent; and (3) aside from the original act of invasion or squatting, squatters (as is generally true of upwardly mobile groups) have a strong sense of legality and rapidly create a real-estate market that in its own terms is often highly formal and organized.

2. In Portuguese, the *"Nucleo Bandeirante."* A *bandeirante* in Brazil refers to the rough-and-ready armed men who in the old days accompanied expeditions or were hired to pursue Indians.

3. "Ciudad Kennedy" outside Bogotá is a development that seems to have had at least moderate success in this respect, even though it is far from the city and has tended to benefit a higher-income group than most squatters.

4. This situation is not unique to Venezuela. The relationship between tenant and public housing authority in U.S. projects has been a source of continual controversy since the beginning of the program.

5. "Police power" devices as used here refer to zoning, building codes, subdivision regulations, and the like. These exist in Venezuelan law, having often been taken from North American models.

6. Since investment in Venezuela customarily operates on something like a 10 per cent interest rate, the amortization period for investments of all types is much more rapid than in the United States. However, even in this context a five-year leasing limit imposes a threshold that makes it inapplicable to most commercial transactions, where the length of the lease is related to questions of finance and amortization. Leases on commercial and industrial property in the United States commonly run for 10, 25, or even 99 years, and valid leases in England have been established for 999 years.

7. The position of the CVG with respect to these exorbitant land claims has always been that they have no legal validity whatever, a position that, to the author's knowledge, has never been contested by the parties concerned.

8. For an interesting paper on this subject, comparing the British new towns, Brasilia, and Ciudad Guayana and proposing a model enabling act for new towns in Latin America, see G. Oliver Koppell, "New Towns for Latin America," third-year paper, on file at the Harvard Law School, dated March 15, 1965. See also United Nations, *Joint Report on the Public Administration Problems of New and Rapidly Growing Towns in Asia and the Moscow Symposium on the Planning and Development of New Towns* (New York, 1967; Sales No. 67.IV.5); Jean Viet, *New Towns: A Selected Annotated Bibliography* (Paris: UNESCO, 1960; Doc. SS. 60. XV. 12 AF); Housing and Home Finance Agency, *New Communities: A Selected, Annotated Reading List* (Washington, D.C., January 1965); and Oliver Oldman, Henry Aaron, Richard M. Bird, and Stephen L. Kass, *Financing Urban Development in Mexico City: A Case Study of Property Tax, Land Use, Housing, and Urban Planning* (Cambridge, Mass.: Harvard University Press, 1967); and Daniel R. Mandelker, "Some Policy Considerations in the Drafting of New Towns Legislation," *Washington University Law Quarterly*, February 1965, pp. 71–87.

Chapter 16

1. Material for this chapter was gathered in Venezuela between June and December 1964 under a grant from the Latin American Studies Committee of Harvard University. I would like to thank Earl Latham for his very helpful advice on this

manuscript. A considerably fuller account is contained in John R. Dinkelspiel, "Administrative Style and Economic Development" (Ph.D. dissertation, Harvard University, Department of Government, 1967).

2. Accounts of the political history of modern Venezuela, particularly since 1945, may be found in Edwin Lieuwen, *Venezuela* (London: Oxford University Press, 1961); Robert J. Alexander, *The Venezuelan Democratic Revolution* (New Brunswick, N.J.: Rutgers University Press, 1964); and John T. Martz, *Acción Democrática* (Princeton, N.J.: Princeton University Press, 1965).

3. Although the Corporación Venezolana de Guayana (CVG) has been in existence only since December 1960, its top leadership is essentially the same as that of the Comisión de Estudios para la Electrificación del Caroní (CEEC) between 1953 and December 1960. There is, therefore, a real and tangible continuity in the administration of the Guayana development program from 1953 to the present.

4. This concept of administrative style is derived from Philip Selznick, *Leadership in Administration: A Sociological Interpretation* (Evanston, Ill.: Row, Peterson and Co., 1957), although Selznick does not use the term "administrative style." See Earl Latham, *The Politics of Railroad Coordination, 1933–36* (Cambridge, Mass.: Harvard University Press, 1959), Chapter 12, for a discussion of the term "administrative style," and Albert O. Hirschman, *Journeys Towards Progress* (New York: Twentieth Century Fund, 1963), for a consideration of some broader aspects of decision-making styles.

5. The CVF's relations to the Guayana have undergone several basic changes since it was established in 1945. From 1945 to 1948 the CVF was at the center of the government's economic development programs and, as is discussed in the following paragraphs, took the first steps in the development of the Guayana. Between 1948 and 1958 it was downgraded to a minor regulatory agency, and the Guayana's development was taken up mainly by the CEEC. In 1958 the CVF was again put in the fore of the government's economic development efforts and was placed under the direction of the erstwhile head of the CEEC, who took the CEEC with him to his new job. From 1958 to the end of 1960 the CEEC was nominally a part of the CVF, which therefore had formal responsibility for the Guayana's development. In practice, however, the CEEC worked more like a staff group attached to the President of the CVF. In 1960 the CEEC was transformed into an autonomous agency, the Corporación Venezolana de Guayana, and the CVF thereby lost all direct responsibility for the Guayana.

6. The new oil company regulations included the first fifty-fifty formula for the sharing of oil profits in the world.

7. It had been known since at least the eighteenth century that there was iron ore in the Guayana. In the 1930's Bethlehem Steel had begun a modest mining operation on the east side of the Caroní, but this did not approach in scope the U.S. Steel discovery on the west side a decade later. John C. Rayburn, "Development of Venezuelan Iron Ore Deposits," *Inter-American Economic Affairs*, Vol. VI, No. 1 (Summer 1952).

8. Burns and Roe, Inc., New York, "Informe y ante-proyecto: desarrollo hidroeléctrico salto mas bajo del Rio Caroní, Estado Bolívar, Venezuela" (unpublished report, 1949).

9. V. Martín Elvira, "La electrificación del Caroní," *Revista de Fomento* (Caracas), No. 75 (January–March 1952) and No. 76 (April–June 1952). Elvira's plans included a four-stage development of the whole Caroní, which is essentially the same as that currently being implemented. These articles also hint at the possibility of an associated heavy industry development based on the processing of local minerals by

electrochemical processes. An outline of such a development was prepared by M. E. H. Rotival for Elvira's office; it too bears a striking resemblance in its fundamentals to current plans, but its contents were unknown to the planners of the Joint Center and the Guayana Corporation. See Corporación Venezolana de Fomento, Departamento de Electricidad, "Aprovechamiento hidroeléctrico del Caroní inferior" (unpublished report by V. Martín Elvira, March 20, 1951).

10. This conclusion is supported by investigations carried out by several government agencies between 1958 and 1960. No accounts of the investigations have been published, but much of the evidence is presented in a report of the Instituto Venezolano del Hierro y Acero, "Informe de la junta directiva," May 31, 1958 (commonly referred to in Venezuela as "The White Book").

11. *Ibid.*

12. Alfonzo was evidently able to insist on this condition because of his personal influence with Pérez Jiménez. It appears that despite fundamental differences over their conceptions of Venezuelan politics, Alfonzo Ravard and Pérez Jiménez were on friendly terms.

13. See Corporación Venezolana de Fomento, *Memoria y Cuenta* for 1955 and 1956, for the suggestions about this industrial development, and Oficina de Estudios Especiales de la Presidencia de la República, "Normas que regiran el proyecto en la comunidad para la planta siderúrgica" (unpublished report, August 1956), for planning on the community needed for the steel mill workers. Most of the work on the latter report was done by the Ministry of Development, not the Office of Special Studies.

14. Alfonzo had also been offered the governorship of the Federal District (that is, Caracas), now one of the more important cabinet positions. One may surmise that he turned down the governorship because it would probably have destroyed his political neutrality and because he would have had to abandon direction of the Guayana development.

15. Rómulo Betancourt, *Tres años de gobierno democrático*, Vols. I–III (Caracas: Imprenta Nacional, 1962), a collection of Betancourt's speeches delivered during his first three years in office. For Betancourt's ideas on the Guayana see especially the speeches during his first six months in office.

16. The only other agency with a similar bureaucratic position is the national planning agency (Cordiplan), which in some respects has formal powers like those of the U.S. Bureau of the Budget. Cordiplan, however, is a staff agency providing advice to the President; it does not have operational (line) responsibilities as does the CVG.

17. Even more in Spanish than in English, the meaning of "coordinate" is ambiguous about whether a passive or an active function is implied.

18. The CVG's power has other limits as well. All major decisions are subject to review by the President and the Council of Ministers (cabinet), although these reviews seem to be largely *pro forma*. Budgetary restrictions are, of course, real, but neither the Treasury nor Cordiplan has had much influence on the substance of the major policy decisions of the Corporation.

19. Although the Corporation's style is a rare occurrence in Venezuelan politics, it is not unique. Cordiplan has practiced an administrative style similar to that of the Corporation. See John Friedmann, *Venezuela: From Doctrine to Dialogue* (Syracuse, N.Y.: Syracuse University Press, 1965).

Chapter 17

1. Corporación Venezolana de Guayana (CVG), *Informe Anual* for 1963 (Caracas, June 1964).

2. Banco Central de Venezuela, *Encuesta sobre condiciones de vida en Santo Tomé de Guayana* (Caracas, 1963).
3. G. A. Marker and Johanna de López, "The Staging of the Guayana Regional Development Program" (unpublished CVG document, 1965; mimeographed).
4. CVG, "A Financing Strategy for the Guayana Development Plan" (unpublished CVG document, March 1965; mimeographed).
5. We can dispose of the problem of obtaining data processing facilities in a footnote. The Venezuelan Ministry of Mines and Petroleum made its IBM 1401 available to us for "off-hours" use. This 16K character, five-tape unit proved quite adequate for our purpose. The CVG itself has a small unit-record installation that proved helpful for preparing inputs to the computer.
6. W. W. Leontief, *et al.*, *Studies in the Structure of the American Economy* (New York: Oxford University Press, 1953). In order to reflect economies of scale, we extended the concept of the simple Leontief coefficients to include a fixed component, the production function thus taking the form
$$I_{ij} = a_{ij} + b_{ij} X_j, \text{ where } I_{ij} \text{ is the total requirement for}$$
commodity i to produce X_j units of commodity j.
A similar production function applies to both the monetary and physical measures of inputs; for each input we have, separately, a pair of monetary and physical input coefficients.
7. This may, however, be a fundamental difference between regional and national planning.
8. See, for example, P. N. Mathur, "An Efficient Path for the Technological Transformation of an Economy," in T. Barna, ed., *Structural Interdependence and Economic Development* (London: St. Martin's Press, 1963).
9. It was not feasible to retain *all* the production and financing aspects of the previous plan for comparability. With the passage of nearly a year, certain changes in production levels and the rescheduling of targets were inevitable; the Economics Section decided that incorporation of these changes was preferable to an attempt to duplicate in its entirety the previous plan.

Chapter 18
1. The word *efficiency* is used to depict performance to the best of the organization's capability, and *effectiveness* to indicate its success in achieving certain goals in the field.
2. This dichotomy is only partially useful; obviously the planner can be an executive in his own operations, and the executive often plans his actions in terms of given strategies.
3. This section deals only with housing. The promotion of other private investment is dealt with in Chapters 8, 10, and 11 of this volume.
4. See Harlow Osborne, "A Financing Analysis for the Urban Development of Santo Tomé," Joint Center–Guayana Project, File No. B–96, June 1966 (unpublished CVG working paper; mimeographed).
5. Captain Rowan never delivered the message to García but wrote a best seller about his trip. In Latin America it is nonetheless common to refer to this historic episode as an example to be followed by executives who do not know how to achieve a given task but identify able people to tackle it. Needless to say, the results are often as irrelevant as those achieved by Captain Rowan.
6. Naturally, there are some exceptions to this "normal" sequence, but that does not invalidate its advantages. In fact, exceptions to this sequence in Ciudad Guayana

have resulted in serious mistakes. In some housing projects, for example, the houses were built before the site improvements were made, and in several places street levels are above floor levels.

7. This department could be subdivided into private, municipal, and interagency promotional activities.

Chapter 19

1. The planning technique known as Critical Path Method (CPM) is described in laymen's terms in the April 1963 edition of *House and Home*. CPM, the author says, is a graphical planning technique that

> is no more mysterious than the bar chart used . . . to schedule . . . work. The bar chart has a bar for every job in the operation. CPM uses an arrow on a diagram for every job. But where a bar chart calls for . . . reading between the bars to figure where each job stands in relation to the others and where it should stand at any given date, a CPM diagram shows visually the exact interrelationship of every job that has to be done to complete the operation—whether there are 10 or 10,000.
>
> The name, critical path method, grows out of a unique advantage of the . . . system. It shows graphically exactly which jobs—and they seldom total more than 10% of the total jobs in an operation—are critical; that is, will delay the whole operation if they are delayed. These are the jobs that must be tightly scheduled and controlled, that must be completed on time, that must be speeded up if the schedule must be speeded up. . . .
>
> With CPM, it is harder to overlook a small but critical operation in planning. Making the inevitable scheduling changes after the job is underway is easier. The CPM diagram gives . . . a better picture of how . . . jobs relate to others. It gives . . . an incentive to schedule . . . work . . . better.

For those interested in further explanations of CPM, two books should prove helpful: Joseph J. Moder and Cecil R. Philips, *Project Management with CPM and PERT* (New York: Reinhold Publishing Corp., 1964), and K. G. Lockyer, *An Introduction to Critical Path Analysis* (London: Pitman, 1965).

Chapter 20

1. This concept of the growth of an underdeveloped economy as the spreading of the modern sector to encompass the large numbers of unemployed and underemployed comes from W. Arthur Lewis, "Economic Development with Unlimited Supplies of Labour," *The Manchester School,* May 1954. Lewis, however, was developing a model of how such economies grow and did not deal with normative considerations.

2. Oficina Central de Coordinación y Planificación (Cordiplan), *Plan de la Nación, 1963–1966* (Caracas, 1963), p. 18.

3. Alianza para el Progreso, Comité de los Nueve, *Evaluación del Plan de la Nación de Venezuela, 1963–66* (Washington, D.C., September 1963), pp. 15–16.

4. Dudley Seers, "The Mechanism of an Open Petroleum Economy," *Social and Economic Studies,* Vol. 13, No. 2 (June 1964).

5. P. N. Rosenstein-Rodan, "Problems of Industrialisation of Eastern and South-Eastern Europe," *The Economic Journal,* Vol. LIII, June–September 1943. R. Nurkse, "Some International Aspects of the Problem of Economic Development," *The American Economic Review,* Vol. XLII, No. 2 (May 1952).

6. This process is described by North, who maintains that the nature of the autonomous industries has a strong influence on the pattern of growth. He explains the growth of different regions of the United States according to this pattern. See D. C. North,

The Economic Growth of the United States, 1790–1860 (Englewood Cliffs, N.J.: Prentice-Hall, 1961), Chapter 1.

7. For a complete description of how these crops were selected see Edward Moscovitch, "Urban-Rural Investment Allocation in Venezuela" (Ph.D. dissertation, Massachusetts Institute of Technology, Department of Economics, 1966), Chapter 2.

8. The use of gross rather than net savings is explained in Evsey Domar, "Depreciation, Replacement and Growth," *The Economic Journal*, Vol. LXIII, March 1953.

9. Moscovitch, "Urban-Rural Investment Allocation," p. 39.

10. A review of this subject is found in Otto Eckstein, "Investment Criteria for Economic Development and the Theory of Intertemporal Welfare Economics," *Quarterly Journal of Economics*, Vol. LXXI, No. 1 (February 1957).

11. The zero wage concept is discussed in Lewis, "Economic Development."

12. Walter Galenson and Harvey Leibenstein, "Investment Criteria, Productivity, and Economic Development," *Quarterly Journal of Economics* Vol. LXIX, No. 3 (August 1955).

13. Seers, "The Mechanism." A similar argument is made by Hirschman, who argues that investments are made in response to obvious imbalances. See Albert O. Hirschman, *The Strategy of Economic Development* (New Haven, Conn.: Yale University Press, 1958).

Chapter 21

1. Quoted in M. Dorothy George, *London Life in the Eighteenth Century* (New York: Harper & Row, 1965), p. 210.

2. Stephan Thernstrom, *Poverty and Progress: Social Mobility in a Nineteenth Century City* (Cambridge, Mass.: Harvard University Press, 1964).

3. U.S. Department of Labor, Office of Policy Planning and Research, *The Negro Family* (Washington, D.C., March 1965).

4. W. Arthur Lewis, "A Review of Economic Development," *American Economic Review*, Vol. LV, No. 2 (May 1965), pp. 15 and 14, respectively.

Chapter 22

1. This study involved interviews with 124 middle-class people in the Guayana, 142 in San Nicolás in Argentina, and 136 in the Concepción metropolitan region in Chile. The samples in each case were about equally divided between a sample of steel mill white-collar workers and a random sample of middle-class male heads of households. Thus the figures given do not "represent" the population of the area. But the figures are based on asking the same questions of as nearly identical a sample of people as we could get in three steel centers. The study was financed by a grant from the Olivetti Foundation to the Joint Center for Urban Studies to support comparative urban studies. I lived in the Guayana for seven months in 1965 and talked to many people about many things in a quite unsystematic way. Except where data are given, the assertions here are based on my impressions and judgment. My impressions and judgment have been wrong before, and may be wrong here.

Chapter 23

1. I would like to acknowledge the assistance of Anamaria Sant'Anna and Carl Steinitz in the research on which this chapter is based.

2. A familiar procedure for designers, which is well described in Gilbert White's "Formation and Role of Public Attitudes," in Henry Jarrett, ed., *Environmental Quality in a Growing Economy* (Baltimore, Md.: The Johns Hopkins Press, 1967).

3. Kevin Lynch conducted his pioneer interviews on small samples in three U.S. cities. See his *The Image of the City* (Cambridge, Mass.: The M.I.T. Press, 1961).

4. Robert Sommer, in "Space-Time on Prairie Highways," *Journal of the American Institute of Planners,* July 1967, notes that distance, size, and emotional involvement affected recall of small rural towns. For recall of segments of the city, social similarity, upward visibility, and actual use would be among the variables.

5. Lynch, *Image of the City.*

6. John Gulick suggested the importance of social significance in the city image in "Images of an Arab City," *Journal of the American Institute of Planners,* Vol. XXIX, No. 3 (August 1963).

7. Anyone familiar with Piaget's work on the child's conception of space may be surprised to notice similarities between these styles and the topological, projective, and euclidean phases of space conception that children go through. But his children were dealing with small-scale tasks. To structure a nongrid city in euclidean terms would be quite a feat. See Jean Piaget and Bärbel Inhelder, *The Child's Conception of Space* (first published in France in 1948), trans. F. J. Langdon and J. L. Lunzer (New York: W. W. Norton & Co., Inc., 1967).

8. More recent interviews that I have made in Boston indicate that working-class North Americans structure the city in a similar way.

Chapter 24

1. Cendes (Centro de Estudios del Desarrollo) study of "Conflict and Consensus" (unpublished document, n.d.).

2. A cliché accusation in the site-Caracas confrontation.

3. The speaker is referring to an aspect of local history strongly present in the memories of his local hearers: the building boom that saw—it is said—a thousand homes built east of the town plaza in one year, when the fall of the dictatorship brought about a temporary failure to enforce the freeze on building. He is comparing it to a well-known aspect of Caracas history: a stream of people poured into the blocks of public housing so rapidly that the government had little control and was unable even to collect rents in a systematic way.

Chapter 25

1. The citation is from a memorandum from Mrs. Lisa Peattie addressed to the author.

2. Subsequent to the preparation of this concluding chapter, Dr. Clemente Chirinos Carnevali, the very able private secretary and assistant to the President of the CVG, was killed in an automobile accident.

3. The CVG and the Joint Center combined did not as a rule have more than 30–35 full-time professionals—and often fewer—for the economic and social studies, the physical planning, the urban design, and the promotion efforts. The Joint Center full-time resident staff generally ranged from 10 to 15 persons after the first year of the program. From time to time the CVG and the Joint Center resident staff was backed up by part-time consultant assistance drawn from the faculties of M.I.T. and Harvard University and, when necessary, from other universities and private organizations.

Acknowledgments

Evaluative studies require the help of many people. This book is no exception. We are especially indebted to our Venezuelan associates—to General Rafael Alfonzo Ravard, President of the Corporación Venezolana de Guayana (CVG), and to his colleagues, Dr. Gustavo Ferrero Tamayo, member of the Corporación; Dr. Juan Andrés Vegas, Chief, Urban Design Section, and his assistant, Victor Artis; Dr. Roberto Alamo Blanco, now Director of the Planning Division, and his former assistant, Pedro Maal; Dr. Héctor Font, Chief, Human Resources Section of the Planning Division, and his former assistant, Mario Testa; and Dr. Luis Pietri, Chief, Urban Development Division. Needless to say, much of what we did would not have been possible without the aid of many other Venezuelans on the staff of the Corporación and in many other walks of life.

The vertical photograph of Ciudad Guayana, by C. A. Tranarg (Avenida Blandin, Chaca Caracas), was made available for this volume by the CVG. Most of the other photographs were obtained from the Public Relations Office of the CVG.

This effort at self-appraisal and self-criticism is not always flattering. It was supported, nonetheless, by the Corporación Venezolana de Guayana. My colleagues join me in expressing our appreciation for this opportunity to describe as honestly as we could what happened in Guayana—as we saw it.

Mrs. Janet Eckstein merits a special accolade. This volume is much more readable and accurate because of her assiduous editorial efforts.

I owe a special debt to Martin Meyerson, who shared with me during the early years the responsibilities for the direction of the Guayana project.

James Q. Wilson persuaded me to take charge of the editing of this volume. To that extent, alas, he may be blamed for failings for which I alone should be held responsible.

LLOYD RODWIN

Cambridge, Massachusetts
May 1968

Notes on Contributors

ROBERTO ALAMO BLANCO, a leading Venezuelan economist, is Director of the Economic Division of the Planning and Research Department of the Corporación Venezolana de Guayana. He is also a Professor of Economics at the Catholic University and at the Central University of Venezuela. Earlier, he was an economist with the Corporación Venezolana de Fomento (Venezuelan Development Corporation) and economic adviser to the Venezuelan Embassy in Washington.

DONALD APPLEYARD is Associate Professor of Urban Design at the University of California at Berkeley. An architect and planner, he has practiced urban design in Great Britain, Italy, and the United States. From 1961 to 1967 he taught urban design at M.I.T. and was a member of the Joint Center for Urban Studies. He is co-author of *The View from the Road* (with Kevin Lynch and John Myer) and of various journal articles.

PHILIP E. BEACH, JR. is with the International Basic Economy Corporation in Venezuela. He spent two years in the promotion office of the Corporación Venezolana de Guayana. He also spent two years as Assistant Secretary of the Ministry of Trade and Industry in Sierra Leone, specializing in industrial development and the operation of a small industries loan bank. His publications include "Industrial Development Banks, Operating Practices" in *Managing Economic Development in Africa* (edited by W. H. Hausman).

RAFAEL CORRADA is at present Under Secretary of Education of the Commonwealth of Puerto Rico and Professor of Social Planning in the Graduate Planning Program of the University of Puerto Rico. He has directed the housing research activities of the Puerto Rican Urban Renewal Administration and has participated in technical assistance missions in Peru with the Pan American Union and in Somaliland with the United Nations. He served first as housing adviser and later as Resident Director of the Joint Center–Guayana Project.

RUSSELL G. DAVIS is on the staff of the Center for Studies in Education and Development and Professor of Education and Development at Harvard University. He has had extensive experience in educational planning in the developing countries of Africa, Asia, and Latin America. Latin America is his principal area of interest. He is the author of children's books, novels, and short stories and has recently published a book on mathematical models for educational planning.

JOHN R. DINKELSPIEL is an Assistant Professor of Political Science at Amherst College. He has recently completed a doctoral dissertation on some political aspects of the Guayana development and the Corporación Venezolana de Guayana.

WILLIAM A. DOEBELE, JR. is Professor of City and Regional Planning and Associate Dean for Development of the Graduate School of Design at Harvard. He has studied problems of land-use controls in many parts of the United States and has worked with various international agencies in Indonesia, Chile, and Venezuela. He served as a specialist on land tenure with the Guayana project during the summer of 1963 and as assistant coordinator of the project for four months in 1964.

ANTHONY DOWNS is Senior Vice President and Treasurer of Real Estate Research Corporation, the nation's largest consulting firm specializing in urban problems, real estate economics, location studies, and economic planning. He works mainly in the areas of urban and regional economic analysis and planning. He is also a member of the National Commission on Urban Problems and a consultant to The RAND Corporation, and has taught in the Department of Economics and Political Science at the University of Chicago. His publications include *An Economic Theory of Democracy*, *Inside Bureaucracy*, and a number of journal articles.

JOHN FRIEDMANN is Director of the Ford Foundation Advisory Program in Urban and Regional Development in Chile and a visiting professor at the Interdisciplinary Urban Development Center of the Catholic University of Chile. Formerly an associate professor in the Department of City and Regional Planning at M.I.T. and a member of the Joint Center for Urban Studies, he has been an adviser to governments in Brazil, Korea, and Venezuela. He is the coeditor of *Regional Development and Planning: A Reader* (with William Alonso) and the author of *Venezuela: From Doctrine to Dialogue* and *Regional Development Policy*. He has also written numerous articles on planning, urbanization, and regional development.

ALEXANDER GANZ is a lecturer in the Department of City and Regional Planning at the Massachusetts Institute of Technology. He is also conducting research on regional economic programming and emerging patterns of urban growth and economic development. He was Chief Economist of the Joint Center–Guayana Project team in Venezuela. His earlier work with the United Nations Economic Commission for Latin America involved studies of the economic growth of the region as a whole and analyses of the development problems and potential of Argentina and Colombia. He is the author of many journal articles on economic development.

JOHN STUART MacDONALD is Chairman of the Division of Social Sciences at the University of the West Indies in Trinidad. He has written several articles dealing with social change, migration, and urbanization in Latin America and sub-Saharan Africa. He has been an Associate of the United Nations Population Branch and Bureau of Social Affairs and a Visiting Associate Professor at the Graduate Faculty, New School for Social Research. He was Demographer with the Joint Center–Guayana Project from 1964 to 1966.

NOEL F. McGINN is a Research Associate in the Center for Studies in Education and Development and Lecturer on Education at Harvard. His special interests are the engineering of planned change and the effects of change on individuals. He is coordinator of the CSED's Guayana Educational Planning Project. He is the author of a number of journal articles.

WILLIAM MORSCH is presently affiliated with David L. Hackett Associates of Washington, D.C. and Cambridge, Massachusetts. He was head of the Management Systems Staff of T-R-W Systems, Inc. from 1961 to 1963 and data systems analyst and management systems adviser to the Air Force while with the MITRE Corporation from 1963 to 1965. The design and implementation of the system described in this book occupied him for one year in Caracas. Consulting activities have included work for the U.S. Office of Education, the Venezuelan national steel mill, and Policy Management Systems, Inc. of Washington, D.C.

EDWARD MOSCOVITCH is Assistant Professor of Economics at Williams College. He also serves as a consultant to the Office of Research, Plans, Programs, and Evaluation in the Office of Economic Opportunity. He spent eight months in Venezuela in 1965 with the Joint Center–Guayana Project, studying the economics of agricultural and industrial enterprises.

LISA REDFIELD PEATTIE is an Associate Professor in the Department of City and Regional Planning at M.I.T. and a member of the Joint Center for Urban Studies. A social anthropologist, she has studied American Indians and city schools. She was with the Joint Center–Guayana Project from 1962 to 1964 and lived in a working-class neighborhood of Ciudad Guayana. She is the author of several journal articles and a book, *The View from the Barrio*.

ANTHONY PENFOLD is with Alan M. Voorhees & Associates in Venezuela as a consultant to the Oficina Ministerial del Transporte, which is responsible for the Caracas Area Transportation Study. In England, he has been a city planner in the London County Council and a member of the Ministry of Transport Study Group that prepared *Traffic in Towns*. During the four years he was associated with the Joint Center–Guayana Project group, which he joined in 1962, he was closely concerned with the transportation problems of the new city. At the end of 1964 he became chief consultant to the CVG on urban design. His activities in Venezuela have also included consulting work with the Caracas central area redevelopment agency, Centro Simón Bolívar.

WILLIAM PORTER, an architect and former fellow of the Joint Center for Urban Studies, is an Assistant Professor at M.I.T., holding a joint appointment in the Department of Architecture and the Department of City and Regional Planning. He was with the firm of Louis I. Kahn in Philadelphia for two years before joining the Joint Center–Guayana Project as Assistant Chief of Urban Design.

LLOYD RODWIN is Chairman of the Faculty Committee of the Joint Center for Urban Studies of the Massachusetts Institute of Technology and Harvard University and Professor in the Department of City and Regional Planning at M.I.T. He is also Director of SPURS, the Special Program for Urban and Regional Studies of Developing Areas in the School of Architecture and Planning at M.I.T., and Associate Editor of *Daedalus*, the journal of the American Academy of Arts and Sciences. He has served as Director of the Guayana project of the Joint Center and as a consultant to the United Nations, the Organization for European Economic Cooperation, the Agency for International Development, and a number of other government and private agencies. His publications include *British New Towns Policy* and *Housing and Economic Progress*, and he is the editor (together with Kevin Lynch) of *The Future Metropolis*.

RICHARD M. SOBERMAN is Associate Professor of Civil Engineering at the University of Toronto. He has worked on regional transportation studies in Venezuela, Israel, Colombia, and the Maritime provinces in Canada. He is the author of *Transport Technology for Developing Regions* and the coauthor of *Urban Rail Transit: Its Economics and Technology* (with A. Scheffer Lang).

ARTHUR L. STINCHCOMBE taught at The Johns Hopkins University from 1959 to 1967, where he served as Assistant and Associate Professor and as Chairman of the Department of Social Relations. He is currently Professor of Sociology at the University of California at Berkeley. His principal research interests are in the field of economic organizations, especially in poorer countries. He is the author of *Rebellion in a High School* and *Constructing Social Theories*.

He is currently writing a monograph dealing with Latin American steel bureaucracies.

WILLO von MOLTKE was Director of Urban Design for the Guayana project of the Joint Center for Urban Studies from 1961 through 1964. Since then he has been Professor of Urban Design and Director of the Urban Design Program, Graduate School of Design, Harvard University. He received his architectural degree from the Technische Hochschule, Berlin, and an M.A. from Harvard. He has been associated with architectural offices in England and in Stockholm, Sweden; as well as with Alvar Aalto; Hugh Stubbins; Howe, Storonov, and Kahn; Marcel Breuer; Skidmore, Owings, and Merrill; and Eero Saarinen and Associates. Among the projects on which he has worked are the campus plans for Brandeis University and the University of Michigan. From 1954–1961 he was with the Philadelphia City Planning Commission, where he held the position of Chief Designer.

Index

Aaron, Henry, 501
Acarigua, 54
Acción Democrática, 302, 303, 418
Administration, CVG, efficiency analysis of, 371–373
  in developing countries, 347
  failures of, Venezuelan, 302–303
  see also CVG, administration of
AGAP (Asociación Guayanesa de Ahorro y Préstamo—savings and loan association), 22, 237, 242, 244, 250
Agriculture, capital-intensive versus labor-intensive, 380, 409
  compared with industry, 385–390, 398–399
  employment in, 57, 63, 379, 385–398
  for exports, 382, 383, 385, 398, 399
  investment in, 79, 381, 386–388
  location of, 380
  neglect of, 89
  promotion of, 175–176
  see also Amacuro Delta and Farming
Ahumada, Jorge, 493
Alamo Blanco, Roberto, 508, 509
Alcasa (Aluminio del Caroní Sociedad Anónima), 170–171
Alexander, Robert J., 502
Alfonzo Ravard, General Rafael, vii, 1–2, 278, 306, 307–308, 310, 377, 471, 472, 474, 477, 479, 480, 481, 503, 508
Alliance for Progress, 60, 379, 492
Alonso, William, 497, 510
Altagracia de Orituco, 54
Alta Vista, 35, 127
  Avenida Guayana in, 143–144, 192
  as city center, 19, 136–139, 188–189, 213, 215, 219, 229, 448
  commercial center in, 21–22, 220, 222, 229; see also Centro Comercial
  early plan for, 142, 213
  mercado libre in, 142, 143, 144
  promotion of, 222–223, 224, 228, 234–235, 498
Aluminum industry, 80, 88, 458
  establishment of, 170–172
Amacuro Delta (Orinoco Delta), 57, 79, 123, 476
  food production in, 15, 311, 396
  labor force in, 397
  land reclamation in, 89, 152, 175–176, 311, 397, 493
Anzoátegui State, 46, 123
Appleyard, Donald, 500, 509
Artis, Víctor, 508
Asociación Guayanesa de Ahorro y Préstamo, see AGAP
Attitudes, see Social attitudes
Avenida Guayana, 20–21, 33, 34, 141, 442
  in Alta Vista center, 143–144, 192
  early plans for, 139–140, 143
  see also Highway network and Traffic planning
Ayesta, Luis, 499

Bacon, Edmund, concept of city design, 134–135
Baldios, 293
Banco Central, see Central Bank
Banco Obrero, 22, 237, 240–241, 245, 249, 250, 260, 290, 343, 344, 475
  Los Olivos project of, 260
  see also Housing, low-income
Barcelona, 55
Barinas, 54
Barna, T., 504
Barquisimeto, 46, 55
Barrios, 401–407
  family stability in, 407
  see also Shantytowns and Squatters
Battelle Memorial Institute, 173
Beach, Philip E., Jr., 498, 509
Betancourt, President Rómulo, vii, 1, 13, 302, 304, 305, 307, 308, 309, 493, 503
Bethlehem Steel, 403, 502
Bienhechurias, law of, 288–289, 290
"Big Push" theory, 155
Bird, Richard M., 501
Boccalandro, Antonio, 497
Bolívar State, 95, 123
Brasilia, 178, 238–239, 251, 290, 453, 501

Cachamay Falls, 27, 129
Cachamay Park, 39
CADA (Compañía Anónima Distribuidora de Alimentos), 220, 222, 223, 225, 228, 229, 498, 499; see also Centro Comercial
Cantaura, 46
C. A. Pulpa Guayana, 172
Caracas, city development near, 48
  comparison with Ciudad Guayana, 443–444
  as core region, 55
  employment in, 120
  as intermontane city, 49
  as national metropolis, 41, 46, 48
  planning done from (CVG), see Caracas versus the site
  population growth of, 46, 47
Caracas Basin, 54
Caracas versus the site, 145, 346, 415, 416, 419, 421, 422, 423, 450–464, 477, 478
Caroní Bridge, 15, 20, 27, 34, 97, 129, 192, 256, 423, 440, 448
Caroní Falls, 19, 28, 448
Caroní lagoon, 131
Caroní River, 11, 13, 18, 19
  as city barrier, 130
Casey, Harry, Jr., 497
Castillito, 34, 423, 430, 432, 448, 449

514

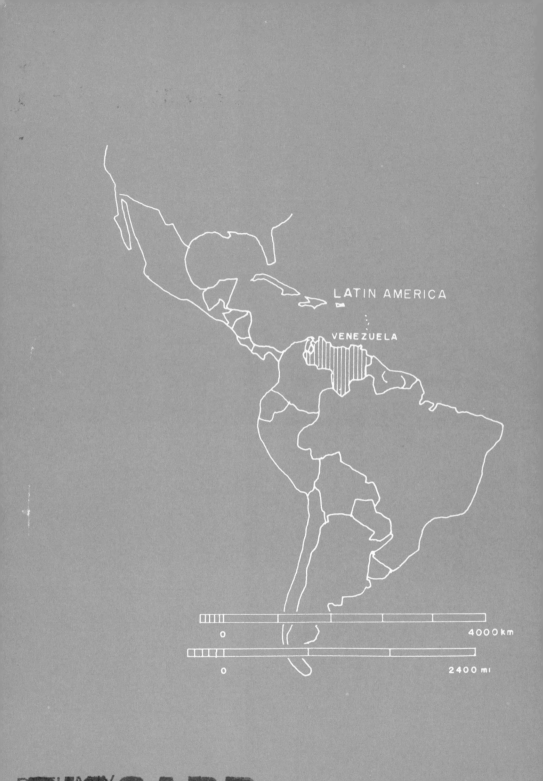

LATIN AMERICA

VENEZUELA

0   4000 km

0   2400 mi